National Th

PLAYS FOR

Wind / Rush Generation(s)

Tuesday

A series of public apologies
(in response to an unfortunate incident in the school lavatories)

The IT

The Marxist in Heaven

Look Up

Crusaders

Witches Can't Be Burned

Dungeness

With introductions by
KIRSTEN ADAM and OLA ANIMASHAWUN

methuen | drama
LONDON • NEW YORK • OXFORD • NEW DELHI • SYDNEY

METHUEN DRAMA
Bloomsbury Publishing Plc
50 Bedford Square, London, WC1B 3DP, UK
1385 Broadway, New York, NY 10018, USA

BLOOMSBURY, METHUEN DRAMA and the Methuen Drama logo are
trademarks of Bloomsbury Publishing Plc

First published in Great Britain 2020

For details of copyright of individual plays, see page 518
Introduction copyright © National Theatre, 2020
Resource material copyright © National Theatre, 2020

The authors have asserted their rights under the Copyright,
Designs and Patents Act, 1988, to be identified as authors of this work.

NATIONAL THEATRE and CONNECTIONS typographical font style are used
with the permission of the Royal National Theatre.

Cover design by National Theatre Graphic Design Studio
Photography © Ekua King

A catalogue record for this book is available from the British Library.

A catalog record for this book is available from the Library of Congress.

ISBN: PB: 978-1-3501-6100-9
        ePDF: 978-1-3501-6102-3
        ePub: 978-1-3501-6101-6

Series: Modern Plays

Typeset by RefineCatch Limited, Bungay, Suffolk

To find out more about our authors and books visit www.bloomsbury.com
and sign up for our newsletters.

Contents

National Theatre Connections

Connections is the National Theatre's annual, nationwide youth theatre festival. It's a celebration of youth theatre, new writing, creativity and partnership, and most importantly it is an opportunity for young people to access the arts.

Every year Connections offers a unique opportunity for youth theatres and school theatre groups to stage new plays written specifically for young people, by some of today's most exciting playwrights, and then to perform them in leading theatres across the UK.

In 2020, nearly 300 companies from across the UK took up the challenge of staging a brand-new Connections play. Over 7,000 young people aged 13–19 took part, supported by thirty-one brilliant and innovative partner theatres from across our nation. By mid-March 2020, 218 companies had rehearsed and presented their productions to audiences in their school halls, youth centres and community hubs.

By mid-March it also became clear, in response to the outbreak of the Covid-19 pandemic, that theatres across the UK would have to temporarily close their doors. Sadly, as a result, none of the thirty-one Partner Theatre Connections Festivals or the National Theatre's own Connections Festival, due to take place in June, could happen. This was a difficult and incredibly disappointing situation for the young companies; the results of so much creativity, imagination and hard work would not be seen by a wider audience, and the companies would not yet get the experience of performing in a professional theatre.

However, the resolve, tenacity and inventiveness of the Connections companies in response to not being able to perform has been inspirational to all of us working on the programme. Without a physical stage these young companies have instead celebrated the work they and their peers created through digital festivals and sharing work online. And supported by our wonderful partner theatres they have connected with each other and shared their love of this collection of plays.

These challenging and distinctive plays are for and about young people, and across this year we have seen how deeply young people have connected with them. We hope this anthology serves as a record and a celebration of all their hard work.

We also hope that, for everyone who took part in Connections 2020, despite the unprecedented challenges of living through a pandemic, it remained a positive and confidence-building experience in teamwork and creative self-expression that will enrich the rest of their lives.

We look to the future with hope and excitement and to the return of Connections next year and for many years to come.

Kirsten Adam, Connections Producer
National Theatre 2020

For more information and to get involved visit:
nationaltheatre.org.uk/learning/connections

Introduction

As we enter the third decade of the twenty-first century, it begs the question: is this the moment this century comes of age? If it is, then what exactly will that mean for the people who still have most of their lives to live in a world where the pace of change is now so fast the adage 'blink and you'll miss it' has never felt so true?

When commissioning this year's Connections plays, I asked the writers to apply their vision and though none of them had the foresight to predict a pandemic, these plays all possess a laser-like clarity. Through their scripts the writer's provide the young people with a vehicle that enables them to interrogate, embrace, explore and even make sense of the coming world; to bring the near future squarely into focus. These new plays don't pull their punches. They are rich, playful and provocative, as well as hopeful, heartfelt and truthful.

From the direct command to *Look Up* and truly see the world, to the gentle search for identity and meaning in *Tuesday* and *The Changing Room* or the wiliness of *A series of public apologies . . .*, the rallying calls to action in *Crusaders*, *The IT*, *The Marxist in Heaven*, *Wind / Rush Generation(s)* and *Witches Can't Be Burned* all the way through to the celebratory anthem of *Dungeness*: these are plays for a generation of theatre-makers who want to ask questions, challenge assertions and test the boundaries. But they are also plays for those who love to invent and imagine a world of possibilities.

Ola Animashawun, Connections Dramaturg

The Plays

Wind / Rush Generation(s) *by Mojisola Adebayo*

This is a play about the British Isles, its past and its present. Set in a senior common room in a prominent university, a group of first-year undergraduates are troubled, not by the weight of their workload, but by a 'noisy' ghost. So they do what any group of self-respecting and intelligent university students would do in such a situation – they get out the Ouija board to confront their spiritual irritant and lay them to rest, only to be confronted by the full weight of Britain's colonial past in all its gory glory.

However, if you think you know about British history, empire, slavery, economics, racism and humanity, then this play might get you to think again. As the planchette on the Ouija board skates from letter to letter at an ever-increasing breakneck speed, the students are catapulted through space and time, witnessing the injustices, incongruities and inhumanity of the past. This is a smorgasbord of genres and styles. Fusing naturalism with physical theatre, spoken word, absurdism, poetry and direct address, this is event theatre that whips along with the grace, pace and hypnotic magnetism of a hurricane.

Tuesday *by Alison Carr*

Tuesday is light, playful and nuanced in tone. And a little bit sci-fi. The play centres on an ordinary Tuesday that suddenly turns very weird indeed when a tear rips across the sky over the school yard. Not only that, but it starts sucking up pupils and staff while at the same time raining down a whole new set of people. But, then, that's what happens when parallel worlds collide!

Confusion reigns as the 'Us' and 'Them' try to work out what is going on. How are Ash and Magpie identical? Can Billy cope with having his sister back? Who is Franky? Eventually, though, cracks appear between the two groups. As the air here starts to disagree with the 'Them', the race is on to try to get things back to how they were and safely return everyone to the universe they came from.

The play touches on themes of friendship, sibling love, family, identity, grief, bullying, loneliness and responsibility. And in the process we might just learn something about ourselves as well as some astronomical theories of the multiverse!

A series of public apologies (in response to an unfortunate incident in the school lavatories) *by John Donnelly*

This satirical play is heightened in its naturalism, in its seriousness, in its parody and piercing in its interrogation of how our attempts to define ourselves in public are shaped by the fear of saying the wrong thing. Presented quite literally as a series of public apologies this play is spacious, flexible and welcoming of inventive and imaginative interpretation as each iteration spirals inevitably to its absurdist core. This is a play on words, on convention, on manners, on institutions, on order, online and on point.

The IT *by Vivienne Franzmann*

The IT is a play about a teenage girl who has something growing inside her. She doesn't know what it is, but she knows it's not a baby. It expands in her body. It starts in her stomach, but quickly outgrows that, until eventually it takes over the entirety of her insides. It has claws. She feels them. Does it have teeth, skin and hair as well, or is that feathers or spikes she can feel, butting up against her organs? What is it? It makes a noise, like a lizard or a snake. No one must know about it. She has to keep its presence, its possession of her, concealed. She pulls away from her friends. She refuses to speak in case the It is heard. Then the It tries to escape from her body. She can't let that happen. She cuts an isolated weird figure at school, trying to live her life normally, but battling to keep the It inside of her. But she can't contain it for ever – sooner or later something's got to give . . .

Presented in the style of a direct-to-camera documentary, this is a darkly comic state-of-the-nation play exploring adolescent mental health and the rage within, written very specifically for today.

The Marxist in Heaven *by Hattie Naylor*

The Marxist in Heaven is a play that does exactly what its title page says it's going to do. The eponymous protagonist 'wakes up' in paradise and, once they get over the shock of this fundamental contradiction of everything they believe in, they get straight back to work, and continue their lifelong struggle for equality and fairness for all – even in death. Funny, playful, provocative, pertinent and jam-packed with discourse, disputes, deities and disco-dancing by the bucketful, this upbeat buoyant allegory shines its holy light on globalisation and asks the salient questions: who are we and what are we doing to ourselves, and what conditioner do you use on your hair?

Look Up *by Andrew Muir*

Look Up plunges us into a world free from adult intervention, supervision and protection. It's about seeking the truth for yourself and finding the space to find and be yourself. Nine young people are creating new rules for what they hope will be a new and brighter future full of hope in a world in which they can trust again. Each one of them is unique, original and defiantly individual, break into an abandoned building and set about claiming the space, because that is what they do. They have rituals, they have rules; together they are a tribe, they have faith in themselves – and nothing and no one else. They are the future, unless the real world catches up with them and then all they can hope for is that they don't crash and burn like the adults they ran away from in the first place.

Crusaders *by Frances Poet*

A group of teens gather to take their French exam but none of them will step into the exam hall. Because Kyle has had a vision and he'll use anything, even miracles, to ensure his classmates accompany him. Together they have just seven days to save themselves, save the world and be the future.

And Kyle is not the only one who has had the dream. All across the globe, from Azerbaijan to Zambia, children are dreaming and urging their peers to follow them to the promised land. Who will follow? Who will lead? Who will make it?

Witches Can't Be Burned *by Silva Semerciyan*

If you keep on doing the same thing, over and over again, you'll keep on getting the same results, time and time again. St Paul's have won the schools Playfest competition three years in a row, by selecting recognised classics from the canon and producing them at an exceptionally high level; it's a tried and trusted formula. With straight 'A's student and drama freak Anuka cast as Abigail Williams in *The Crucible* by Arthur Miller, the school seem to be well on course for another triumph, which would be a record. What could possibly go wrong?

However, as rehearsals gain momentum, Anuka has an epiphany – an experience resulting in her asking searching questions surrounding the text, the depiction and perception of female characters, the meaning of loyalty, and the values and traditions underpinning the very foundations of the school. Thus, the scene is set for a confrontation of epic proportions as Anuka seeks to break with tradition, before tradition breaks her and all young women like her, and reality begins to take on the ominous hue of Miller's fictionalised Salem.

Dungeness *by Chris Thompson*

In a remote part of the UK, where nothing ever happens, a group of teenagers share a safe house for LGBT+ young people.

While their shared home welcomes difference, it can be tricky for self-appointed group leader Birdie to keep the peace. The group must decide how they want to commemorate an attack that happened to LGBT+ people, in a country far away. How do you take to the streets and protest if you're not ready to tell the world who you are? If you're invisible, does your voice still count? A play about love, commemoration and protest.

The Changing Room *by Chris Bush*

A lyrical piece about existing on the cusp of growing up. Are we teenagers? Are we children? What are we? It's about bodies in flux and perspectives shifting; knowing change is coming but not what that change will look like.

Set in and around a swimming pool, *The Changing Room* follows a group of teens full of excitement, impatience and uncertainty, each with their own secret worries and desires for what comes next.

The Changing Room was previously published by Methuen Drama in the *National Theatre Connections 2019* anthology.

Wind / Rush Generation(s)

by Mojisola Adebayo

This is a play about the British Isles, its past and its present. Set in a senior common room in a prominent university, a group of first-year undergraduates are troubled, not by the weight of their workload, but by a 'noisy' ghost. So they do what any group of self-respecting and intelligent university students would do in such a situation – they get out the Ouija board to confront their spiritual irritant and lay them to rest, only to be confronted by the full weight of Britain's colonial past in all its gory glory.

However, if you think you know about British history, empire, slavery, economics, racism and humanity, then this play might get you to think again. As the planchette on the Ouija board skates from letter to letter at an ever-increasing breakneck speed, the students are catapulted through space and time, witnessing the injustices, incongruities and inhumanity of the past. This is a smorgasbord of genres and styles. Fusing naturalism with physical theatre, spoken word, absurdism, poetry and direct address, this is event theatre that whips along with the grace, pace and hypnotic magnetism of a hurricane.

Cast size

Minimum ensemble of 8 (with a core group of 6) or up to 30,
ideally with a mixture of genders

Most suitable for ages 15+

Mojisola Adebayo BA (Hons), MA, PhD, FRSL has worked in theatre, radio and television over the past two decades, performing in over fifty productions, writing, devising and directing over thirty plays, and leading countless workshops worldwide, from Antarctica to Zimbabwe. Her publications include: *Plays One: Moj of the Antarctic: An African Odyssey, Muhammad Ali and Me* and *Matt Henson: North Star* (Oberon); *Plays Two: STARS, I Stand Corrected, Oranges and Stones* and *The Interrogation of Sandra Bland* (Oberon); the play *48 Minutes for Palestine* in *Theatre in Pieces* (Methuen Drama); *The Theatre for Development Handbook* (with John Martin and Manisha Mehta, available through www.pan-arts.net); and several academic chapters. Mojisola is an Associate Artist with Pan Arts, Black Lives, Black Words and Building the Anti-Racist Classroom, a Visiting Artist at Rose Bruford College and Goldsmiths, and a Lecturer at Queen Mary, University of London. Her next play *STARS* will be staged in 2020/1. See www.mojisolaadebayo.co.uk for more.

With thanks to Ola Animashawun – dramaturg

Author's Note

This is a play about the British Isles, its past and its present. It is written for all young people and youth theatres to perform, regardless of their cultural background, skin colour or gender.

Characters

There is potential for doubling of roles, as necessary. The names of the characters below are in some cases historic, in other cases symbolic, playful and/or deliberately ambiguous in terms of gender and culture. The play is partly an exploration of names, naming and calling things as they are.

David Lammy MP – a living figure, played by the entire cast, at least *ten actors*, preferably more, but not less than seven. The role needs a powerful collective voice.

Students

Six first-year university students doing a History degree. They are close-knit team of outsiders, aged around eighteen, but they can be played by younger actors, of any culture or gender. Names are androgynous. Some character traits are indicated below but don't get too hung up on these. The play is driven by the story and by storytelling.

Ola, *intelligent, very anxious but brave – their name means 'wealth'*
Zhe (*pronounced Zee*), *dynamic, driven by curiosity, extrovert*
Ali, *a playful, loveable, joker*
Xia (*pronounced Shia*), *cool, understated, sharp*
Kit, *rational, focused, caring – closest to Ola*
Jay, *gentle, sensitive, spiritual*

NB: For reasons that will become clear, it makes some sense if Ola is played by a young person of African/Caribbean descent. However, this is not absolutely necessary if there are no black members of your youth group. Equally, if there is only one black member of your youth group they do not necessarily have to play Ola.

Monte Rosa – an elderly German female of around 100 years old. Each time Monte Rosa speaks she is played by a new female actor. She may alternatively be played by one female actor throughout, or any actor playing female. She is a romantic, poetic, vain, egocentric, sweet old lady with an unpleasant streak. Again, as with all acting in this play, let the storytelling drive the performance choices.

Seven Villagers

A group of middle-aged, middle/upper-class residents of a small wealthy rural community, somewhere remote in England. Suggested names:

Theresa
Nigel
Caroline
Sajid
Boris
Diane
Jacob

Zong Characters

Captain of *Zong*, Luke Collingwood *(English, historical figure)*
First Mate of *Zong*, James Kelsall *(English, historical figure)*
Judge Mansfield *(historical figure in the* Zong *case of 1781)*
Sailors on *Zong* *(working men from all over Britain and Ireland, with fictional names, they can be played by actors of any gender, double roles if you need to)*:

Matthew
Mark
Luke
John
Simon
Peter
James
Thomas
Andrew
Nathan
Jude
Paul

British Citizens

The words spoken by British Citizens are all inspired by real lives. However, their names have been made anonymous. They have been re-named in memory of various black British/African-Caribbean heroes. Some died at the hands of racists or in police custody and some were allowed to live great lives:

Nanny (in memory of Nanny of the Maroons)
Bernie (in memory of Bernie Grant)
Joy (in memory of Joy Gardner)
Smiley (in memory of Smiley Culture)
Stuart (in memory of Stuart Hall)
Cherry (in memory of Cherry Croce)
Kelso (in memory of Kelso Cochrane)
Stephen (in memory of Stephen Lawrence)
David (in memory of David Oluwale)
Mary (in memory Mary Seacole)
Marcus (in memory of Marcus Mosiah Garvey)

Olive (in memory of Olive Morris)
In memory of too many to mention. Rest in peace, ancestors.

Sam and **Sim** – *two computer gamers:* teenage friends, they speak in a stilted rhythm, mechanically, without much emotion, like figures from a video game.

Wind – the embodiment of Wind, male, Jamaican, dub poet, inspired by Linton Kwesi Johnson, played by the entire cast in chorus. The role could alternatively be played by one actor who is particularly skilled at/enjoys spoken word/rap/poetry.

Notes on Playing

- Yes poetry
- Yes rhythm
- Yes to pace, pace, pace!
- Super-fast scene changes – oh yes!
- Yes musicality
- Yes theatricality
- Yes ensemble, chorus, team, collectivity, togetherness
- Yes movement
- Yes to creative accessibility for D/deaf, blind and disabled performers and audience members – e.g. BSL interpretation, audio-description, surtitles
- Yes to flexibility, experimentation, inventiveness, playfulness
- Yes to small cuts but the scissors are mine – thanks! Requests to the author
- Yes it's a challenge and yes it's challenging
- Yes to taking pleasure in playing with it and seeing what can be created

Technical Notes

There are a few sound effects but nothing hard to source. Projection of certain words is very important for the storytelling and the audience understanding. If a projector is not available, you could use an old-style overhead projector, placards or sound. Experiment. As long as the meaning is clear, you can do this play simply or high tech, raw or cooked.

Notes on the Text

- A slash like this / indicates that the following person's line crosses over the person speaking at that point, i.e. two people talk over each other.
- These brackets [. . .] indicate the sense of the line but are not heard out loud.
- Please read the stage directions carefully: they will help you as each scene/ setting is very different and necessitates its own distinct style.

Scene – House of Commons

The whole cast stand and play **David Lammy MP**, *speaking the verbatim text below, powerfully and passionately together. The actors embody and magnify* **Lammy**'s *physicality on the day he gave the speech/posed the questions in the House of Commons. If you have a large cast, some actors could play opposition MPs nodding their heads and calling 'hear, hear' beside him. With a very large cast you could also show the then Home Secretary Amber Rudd and the government front bench, fidgeting nervously. See this link for guidance on movement and theatricality in staging:* https:// www.youtube.com/watch?v=Y2q2dQlsywY

Sound recording from the real debate where several MPs stand to speak and then the Speaker of the House selects David Lammy MP:

Speaker of the House (*voiceover*)   Mr David Lammy!

Opposition MP (*voiceover*)   Hear, hear . . .

Lammy, *played by multiple actors, speaks exquisitely clearly and is unashamedly bold, building in vocal, emotional and physical intensity and volume.*

Lammy   Can I say to the Home Secretary, that the relationship between this country and the West Indies and the Caribbean is inextricable. The first British ships arrived in the Caribbean in 1623, and despite slavery, despite colonisation, 25,000 Caribbeans served in the First World War and Second World War alongside British troops.

When my parents and their generation arrived in this country under the Nationality Act of 1948, they arrived here as British citizens. It is inhumane and cruel for so many of that Windrush generation to have suffered so long in this condition and for the Secretary of State only to have made a statement today, on this issue.

Can she explain how many have been deported? She suggested earlier that she would ask the high commissioners – it is *her department* that has deported them! She should know the number! Can she tell the House how many have been detained as prisoners in their own country? Can she tell the House how many have been denied health under the National Health Service, how many have denied pensions, how many have lost their job?

This is a day of national shame, and it has come about because of a 'hostile environment' policy that was begun under her prime minister! Let us call it as it is: if you lay down with dogs you get fleas! (*He continues speaking as some of the cast gradually, and in low volume at first, start growling and then barking and finally howling like dogs/bitches.*) And that is what has happened with this far-right rhetoric in this country.

Can she apologise properly? Can she explain how quickly this team will act to ensure that the thousands of British men and women denied their rights in the country, under her watch, in the Home Office, are satisfied?

The dogs continue in blackout. The sound culminates in wild howling with a few whimpering in pain until the start of the next scene. The effect should be chilling.

Scene – Senior Common Room

Lights dimly up on the old Senior Common Room (like a communal living room) of a prestigious university. Old chairs, coffee table(s), books, a rocking chair downstage right (which remains on stage throughout the play from here on), plus pictures of old – now long dead – white male academics hang on the walls. The set, however, does not need to be naturalistic. The Senior Common Room setting could be suggested with a few well-chosen items or conveyed through projection. However, the one item that needs to be physically present is a rocking chair, downstage right.

Sound of a big old wooden door creaking open. The **Students** *are revealed in the doorway, some wearing pyjamas, dressing gowns, slippers, holding mobile phones as torches. They speak in hushed tones, secretly seeking out a ghost, in a space they are not allowed in . . . They are all scared, but some more so than others.*

Ola   This is a bad idea.

Zhe   Are we going in or not?

Ola   Not!

Ali   But we said:

Xia   Truth or dare?

All (*except* **Ola** *and* **Kit**)   DARE!

Ola   But I'm scared.

Kit *comforts* **Ola** *as* **Jay** *continues.*

Jay   You've got more to fear from the living than the dead.

Ali   It's true. Think of Trump. (*Approaching* **Ola** *with a zombie-Trump impression.*) Aaaaamericafiiiiiiirst. . . .

Zhe   Climate catastrophe, ISIS,

Xia (*continuing* **Zhe**'s *list)*   white supremacists . . .

Zhe   Much more scarey.

Ola   Why is this not helping me?

Jay   Let's just put this thing to bed so we can all sleep at night.

Ali   Nice.

Kit (*to* **Ola**)   And there'll be a perfectly rational explanation.

Zhe   Let's see shall we? . . .

Jay   So, we just go in and calmy *talk* –

Xia   to a freaking ghost.

Jay   And ask it –

Zhe   *politely* –

Ali (*putting on a posh voice*)   to go a-way . . .

Ola   You lot don't even know what you're messing with – I'm telling you!

Ola *goes to leave.* **Ali** *is disappointed.* **Kit** *pulls them back.*

Ali   Arrhh . . . we said we'd stick together . . .

Zhe   You won't be able to sleep anyway!

Kit   [Let's just give it] two minutes (*Setting phone timer.*)

Ali   Then we order delivery! I'm hungry.

Xia   Me too.

Ola   Can we *please* just go back down to halls? We're not even allowed in the Senior Common Room. Let's just do a different dare!

Zhe (*to* **Jay**)   You got this, babe.

Kit *starts timer. They all step cautiously into the room.* **Jay** *in the lead, others following.* **Jay** *begins to talk, louder now, into the space, slowly, gently, addressing the ghostly presence.*

Jay   Hello . . .?

Ali (*comic ghost voice*)   HELLOOOOOOOOOOOOHHHH . . .

Ola   Stop it!

Xia   Hey there . . . spirit thing . . .

Kit   Spirit thing?

Ola (*whispering a line from the Lord's Prayer*)   'Forgive us our trespasses as we forgive / those who trespass against us . . .'

Jay (*speaking over* **Ola**)   We mean you no harm . . .

Zhe (*to* **Jay**)   That's good, keep going.

Ali   We beg you – don't hurt us!

Ola (*snapping out of the prayer*)   What you giving them ideas for?

Kit (*to* **Ola**)   Breathe.

Jay   Thank you for . . . reaching out . . .

Ola   *Please.* (*Begging to leave, but feeling compelled to stay.*)

Jay   But the truth is . . . we are all really . . .

Kit   Tired, stressed

Xia   – shitting ourselves.

Jay   And we are only freshers.

Zhe   And we've got history assessments coming up.

Xia   And we are paying nine grand a year.

Ali   And I just wanna get my two-one and done.

Zhe   So . . .

Jay   We respectfully ask you, spirit –

Kit   – if you even exist –

Jay   that you please –

Ali   LEAVE US THE FREAK ALONE!

Everyone is startled by **Ali's** *volume. They all shush* **Ali***.*

Kit (*reprimanding*)   You'll wake security.

Zhe (*reminding*)   *Politely.*

Ola (*praying quietly but even more urgently*)   'Lead us not into temptation, but deliver us from evil . . .'

Jay (*to the ghost*)   We are very sorry if we've offended you in anyway.

Ali   Sorryyyyyyy . . .

Jay   You can talk to us anytime . . .

Xia (*not sure if what* **Jay** *has just said is a good idea*)   Errrrmm . . .

Jay   And if there's something you want from us . . . just give us a sign.

Ola   What did you say that for?

Kit   Rewind.

Zhe (*to the ghost*)   What *do* you want?. . .

They all pause silently, for quite a while, trying to sense the ghost, waiting for an answer, breathing deeply, alert. **Ali** *breaks the silence*

Ali   Wiiiiiings . . . chicken wiiiiings . . .

Xia   Fufuuu, nooodles . . .

Ali   Baba ganoooooooooush! . . . (*They all laugh except* **Ola***.*)

Ola   [We are leaving] NOW!

Ola *drags* **Kit** *away. They all start turning and leave with the lines below, saying goodbye to the ghost: 'job done'.*

Ali   Salaam.

Xia   Shalom.

Zhe   Salmon.

Ola   What?

Ali   Nah, don't fancy that.

Zhe   Can't you smell it?

Ali   It wasn't me.

Ola   Yeah . . . (*Repulsed.*)

Jay   Fish? . . .

A sudden cold breeze sweeps in. **Kit** *is startled by feeling something brush past.*

Kit   Don't touch me!

Ali   I didn't do nothing!

Xia   It's freezing.

Ola   My phone's died!

Jay   Everyone keep calm.

Zhe   Can you taste salt?

Ola (*in fear*)   Please Lord . . .

Xia (*confused by the taste of salt on their lips*)   Urgh . . .

Zhe   Oh my days – the chair! It's moving!

The rocking chair is moving of its own accord. This could be conveyed by a transparent wire on the base of the rocking chair being pulled by a stage manager in the wings, or wind machine. Sudden backout. They all scream in fear.

All   AAAAAAAAAHHHHHHHHH!

Scene – Monte Rosa 1

Lights up. The **Students***.* **Monte Rosa** *rocks very gently in her rocking chair in the Senior Common Room. She wears a blue shawl. There is a faint memory of the German language in her speech (e.g. she says 'Ja' – pronounced 'ya' meaning yes) but don't push the accent, just focus on telling the story to the audience.*

Monte Rosa

    Ja, I don't look bad
    Considering
    I am one hundred years old!
    I still feel so young . . .
    I was born in Germany, 1920
    They cracked champagne when they got me!
    And named me after the second highest mountain in the Alps.
    Rosa.
    Blanc is the highest so I'm lucky I wasn't the first!
    Blanc is no name.

    I travelled the whole world
    But I've never seen the Alps.
    I have always preferred the sea
    Or perhaps the sea preferred me.
    Not surprising really
    I come from Hamburg
    Eine schöne Stadt
    Such a pretty city
    My heart is always in a harbour
    Every port an opportunity
    And the best playground
    To come of age
    Every day a new ship
    A new face
    A new suitcase
    Filled with music . . .
    Ja, es war ziemlich toll
    Quite quite exciting
    Hamburg.

    Und no need for school
    When there was plenty of work
    Tourism was new in the 1930s
    My job was to take people away
    On holidays.
    German folk wanted to see the world
    We crossed the North Sea and the Mediterranean
    Mexico, Madeira, Spain . . .
    Ja, sailing wasn't for everybody
    Most got sick
    But I was born for it!
    Rocked by the vind
    Kissed by the sun

With moon and stars and tides for guides
One moment, you feel the ease of a breeze
Then bluster, gale and gust the next!
Such a sense of adventure,
The weather.

Scene – Ouija Board and Pizza 1

Monte Rosa *has gone and her rocking chair is perfectly still. The* **Students** *are back in the Senior Common Room. There is considerable tension amongst The* **Students**, *except for* **Ali** *who is focused on enjoying the pizza. A large pizza box with one slice left is on the table, plus a candle, matches, pen, paper and an unopened Ouija board, wrapped in a piece of cloth. Nothing need be naturalistic.*

Kit   It was just a gust of wind.

Xia   And the lights?

Kit   Momentary power cut.

Zhe   What, *only* in here? Affecting *nowhere* else on campus?

Kit   I'm just saying there's probably a scientific explanation.

Zhe (*sarcastic dig*)   Sorry, Professor . . .

Jay (*peacemaking*)   We need to bring our energies together.

Kit   What's all this 'energy' shit?

Ola   Stop fighting! Let's just get it over with.

Jay *smiles a 'thank you' at* **Ola** *then slowly reveals the Ouija board from the cloth.*

Jay   So, a Ouija board is just like a phone, to communicate with . . . the other side. We call and . . . if there is a spirit trying to reach us, they send us little . . . text messages.

Kit   This is ridiculous.

Kit *folds their arms.* **Ola** *moves back. Deep breaths as they all stare at the box.*

Ali   Ommmmmmm . . .

Ola   Stop it!

Ali (*laughing*)   I'm just trying to get everyone relaxed!

Jay   That's not a bad idea actually. What if we do some kind of ritual before we start?

Ola   Ritual?

Ali   What, like, slaughter a chicken?

Xia   Yummm . . . (*Laughing with* **Ali**.)

Ola   That's it! (*Gets up to leave.*)

Kit   Don't go without me.

Ola *reluctantly sits down beside* **Kit**.

Jay   It's important that we 'act collectively'. (*Recalling the instructions.*)

Zhe   How about a song?

Ali (*singing the Liverpool anthem*)   'You'll never walk alone / you'll never walk alone . . .'

Xia (*talks over*)   I'm not singing that. I'm Man United.

Ola   I shouldn't even be here. I'm Christian.

Jay   Then you've got nothing to be afraid of.

Zhe   We could do that game from drama society where we close our eyes and say our names, one at a time, randomly. If we talk over each other we go back to the start but we keep going until we get it right.

Ali   If I win can I eat the last slice of pizza?

Zhe   It's not about winning. It's about collective action. Hold hands. (*They do.*) Close your eyes. (*They all do except Ali who keeps one eye clearly open.*) *Both* of them.

Ali *closes both eyes. The actors genuinely play the game with their characters' names, until they get it right. We never know what order the game will go in . . .*

Ali   Nice.

Zhe   That was good guys. Really focused.

Jay   Ready?

Various nods, deep breaths, swallowing in anticipation, covering faces. **Jay** *strikes a match and carefully lights the candle, then slowly and silently opens the Ouija board box. They fold out the board.* **Zhe** *picks up the instructions and reads.*

Zhe   OK. 'Two or three people gently place their index and middle fingers on the planchette.'

Kit   It's just a stupid bit of plastic.

Zhe *offers the planchette to* **Kit** *who shakes their head.* **Zhe** *puts the planchette on the board and they wait for someone to place their fingers on it.*

Ola   Count me out.

Ali (*making an excuse*)   Er, I've got pizza fingers.

Zhe   Well my fingers are far too long.

Kit (*sarcastic*)   Really?

Jay   If no one else wants to . . .

Xia   I'll do it too.

Jay *and* **Xia** *slowly place their fingers on the planchette, on the board.*

Zhe (*reading the instructions*)   'Choose one person to scribe the messages.'

Kit   OK.

Kit *takes the paper and pen. Ready waiting for letters to come through.*

Zhe   'Do not force anything to happen. Simply stay open.'

Long pause. Nothing. Then after some time the planchette starts slowly moving around the board, randomly. It would be great if the audience could see the board.

Ali   Shiiiiiiit . . .

Ola   Are you lot pushing it?

Xia and Jay (*really focused*)   No.

Kit   It can't just –

Xia   – I swear.

Jay   It's weird.

Xia   It's got a life of its own.

Ola (*fearfully*)   Ohhhh . . .

Jay (*to the ghost*)   Are you here? . . .

The planchette rests on the word **'Yes'.** *This is projected.*

Zhe   Yes! It said YES!

Ola   Mummy . . .

Ali *hugs* **Ola.**

Jay   Have you got something you want to tell us?

The planchette stays on **'Yes'.**

Xia   Do you want us to leave you alone?

Ali   We really don't mind going.

Kit   It's got to be a trick [i.e. it's just getting interesting].

Ali *covers* **Ola's** *eyes and their own. The planch moves to 'No'.*

Jay   NO! – It wants us to stay!

Zhe (*following the instructions*)   Ask their name!

Jay   What . . . is . . . your . . . name?

The planchette slowly moves to the following letters, speeding up gradually. The text here and throughout is projected/shown somehow for the audience. It is important that the audience see the letters as they come through. The **Students** *repeat the letters out loud and* **Kit** *writes them down.* **Ali** *and* **Ola** *can't resist looking.*

All
   P
   R
   O
   B
   L
   E
   M

All   Problem?

Ola   I told you! We don't know what we're getting into!

Jay (*to the ghost*)   What is the problem?

All (*except* **Ola**)
   N
   A
   M
   E

All   Name?

Kit (*reading what they have scribed*)   It doesn't make any sense.

Ali   We said WHAT IS YOUR NAME?!

Zhe   No need to shout.

Xia   They are all the way over on the 'other side'.

Ola   I feel sick.

Jay   It's moving!

All (*except* **Ola**)
   G
   U
   E
   S
   S

Ali   Funny name. Maybe it's French?

Zhe   Guess! They want us to play a game!

Xia   This is too weird, even for me.

The planchette moves again.

Jay It's moving again.

Kit Are you pushing it?

Jay I promise [I'm not].

All
  N
  O
  T
  I
  N
  O
  T
  I

Kit (*writing*) Noti-Noti?

Ali Definitely foreign.

Zhe Not I? *NOT I*!

Jay It's moving again!

All (*except* **Ola**)
  C
  L
  U
  E

Zhe It's giving us a clue.

Jay Keep breathing.

All (*except* **Ola**)
  F
  A
  R
  M

Ola (*confused*) Farm? . . .

Ali Moooooooooooooo . . . (*Then all the others join in with the mooooooing sound, while the rest of the cast mix in other farmyard sounds. The final sounds are dogs barking and howling again as the scene transitions.* **Ola** *remains on stage, watching the next scene and all of the scenes inspired by the word clues coming from the Ouija board.*)

Scene – Wind Farm

The Ouija setting quickly becomes the setting of a very heated debate at a local parish meeting in the church hall of a small village somewhere in rural England. The characters sit around the table. New actors play the roles below. If need be, roles (except **Ola***) can be doubled, to accommodate cast size. The characters are posh. A* *forward slash (/) indicates that the following line comes in at that juncture, causing an overlap of speech – this is important. The scene is naturalistic but slightly absurd with a quick pace. Be very tight on cues. **Ola** is visible, observing the scene and all the scenes arising from the words/clues.*

Theresa   And what about house prices? If we let them take over the land / the value of our houses will inevitably fall.

Nigel   Colonise more like.

Caroline   No one is talking about the impact on migrating birds.

Sajid   They'll put tourists off.

Nigel   We don't want tourists either.

Sajid   But if we did, one day, want to attract tourism / they would definitely be put off . . .

Caroline   What about the birds?

Boris   They kill bats!

Nigel   They're bloody ugly.

Diane   You can't say that.

Nigel   I can say what I like, it's a free country.

Jacob   And we want to keep it that way!

Diane   What I mean is / beauty is in the eye of the beholder.

Nigel   I am saying it like it is. They stick out, they don't fit in and we don't want them here!

Diane   Oh, I thought you were talking about bats.

Jacob   Keep up, love.

Caroline   Well, I find them quite beautiful / in their own way.

Boris   You should have your eyes tested.

Caroline   I'm just saying it's not the way that they look that bothers me. I think there's something quite elegant about them, the way they all move / together.

Jacob   That's when they work. Most of the time they don't even work. Waste of space!

Nigel   And they're bloody loud!

Diane   You're quite loud.

Sajid   Well, I've never been up close to one.

Jacob   Keep away from them I say, you never know what they might / do to you.

Caroline   I'm not saying I want them in my field –

Nigel   Well, there you are then!

Boris   Apparently each one does barely enough to power a hairdryer.

Diane   We could do with a hairdresser around / here.

Boris   *Hairdryer* I said!

Diane   A hairdryer is quite powerful actually. Mine keeps fusing.

Sajid   / Does it?

Nigel   They can't even boil a kettle for a decent cup of tea!

Theresa   That's decided then. We move to a vote . . .

Boris   We vote NO.

Caroline   We haven't discussed their benefits.

Jacob   What benefits?

Nigel   They'll be cutting disability benefits to pay for them / mark my word!

Jacob   A lot of them are bogus too.

Diane   You just can't say that.

Nigel   FREE COUNTRY.

Caroline   I mean what the countryside can gain from having them here.

Theresa   Whose side are you on?

Caroline   I just think we should have a balanced / debate. We are still a *civilised* country.

Nigel   Who's going to pay for all this? Taxes will go up, you mark my words.

Sajid   Let her have her say.

Caroline   Thank you. Well. They are quite . . . natural.

Nigel   Primitive!

Caroline   They harness a *natural* power. Lest we forget we are an island.

Boris   They'll build a bloody bridge to France next.

Caroline   How are we going to survive / without their energy to re-build the country?

Boris   That's just scaremongering.

Nigel   Stick them in the sea! If the council are so in love with them, stick them in the sea!

Sajid   Or find another island.

Nigel   Just not in my field!

Diane   But they are modern.

Theresa   They've ruined Denmark. And it was such a pretty little country. You can't get more modern than Denmark.

Jacob   The whole landscape is riddled with them. Riddled! / Everywhere you look.

Sajid   It's true. My cousin married a Danish man. Such a lovely family. So much style.

Jacob   They'll be next to leave the EU I bet. Dexshit.

Diane   What?

Jacob   Danish Brexit.

Boris (*quoting Hamlet*)   'Something is rotten in the state of Denmark.'

Theresa   To leave, or not to leave, that was the question . . . (*They laugh.*)

Boris   Long live Shakespeare! (*Singing started by Boris.*) 'Rule Britannia! Britannia rules the waves!' (*Then they all join in . . .*)

All   'Britons never, never, never shall be slaves!'

Theresa   All those against having a wind farm erected in our parish say neigh.

Ola (*observing, trying to figure it out*)   Wind farm?

All   Neighhhhhhhhhh! (*They continue with horsey farmyard sounds and dogs again during their exit and transition into the next* **Monte Rosa** *monologue.* **Ola** *leaves.*)

Scene – Monte Rosa 2

Another actor can play **Monte Rosa**. *We know it is her because she always sits in the rocking chair, swaying gently back and forth in the same light, telling her story to the audience, alone. She wears the same clothing, e.g. a blue shawl. Eerily quiet.*

Monte Rosa
    And then the Nazis came to power
    And we had to fly the Swastika
    I'm not going to lie, why should I,
    I wore it proudly.
    Ja, you're looking at me like that
    But you don't understand
    It made us feel good about ourselves
    We were besser than anyone else
    No more hunger, no more shame
    Could you blame us after the first war?
    Only *pure* Germans were allowed on our holidays
    No Roma, or Poles or Slavs, or blacks or Jews
    No handicapped, no homos,
    No '*unter-mensch*' allowed
    We were the captains now!
    We ruled the waves!

From Hansa Stadt Hamburg to Windhoek Namibia
The world was ours
And it was love!
Ja, that was our only song.

You got given a medal if you had four children for the Reich
No medal for me.
I was selected for a more important job
Because of my experience at sea
I was ordered to transport passengers
From Norway
To Germany.
Jews.
All ages.
From Oslo . . .
The songs they sang were different from those
We heard before the war
Their hums hung in the air
Like the thick clouds of smoke . . .
In Auschwitz.
(*With remorse.*) The children . . .
I had no choice!
I was doing my job.

Ach, but you know the history
And because of the work I had done
I was captured by the Royal Navy as a 'prize of war'
The Britishers were not so different from us
Cousins really: same Royal Family
And their language is easy
Land, land
Buch, book
Vind, wind . . .

Scene – Ouija Board 2

The next letters from the Ouija board are projected. **Ola** *reads them out loud, slowly.*

Ola
F
A
L
L
Faaaaaaaaall . . .

Ola *starts falling slowly to the floor. They sit and watch the next scene.*

Scene – Windfall

Deck of a slave ship, Zong. *Year 1781. The upper-class* **Captain Luke Collingwood** *and the working-class* **First Mate James Kelsall***, both looking rough, look out. The ship rocks. Heightened playing. High stakes. Pace!*

First Mate   We're fearfully low on water, Captain.

Captain   How are we doing for rum?

First Mate   Just one bottle left, sir.

Captain   How far away from drinking our own piss?

First Mate   About as far as we are from Jamaica, sir.

Captain   How could we miss it?

First Mate   These islands all look the same, sir.

Captain   300 miles you say?

First Mate   300 miles out of the way.

Captain   How many blacks below deck?

First Mate   379, sir.

Captain   And how many did we have in Accra?

First Mate   442, sir.

Captain   How many was our legal capacity?

First Mate   193, sir.

Captain   And how many look like they'll live?

First Mate   Less than half, sir.

Captain   I'm a surgeon not a mathematician but that doesn't sound good.

First Mate   It don't bode well for profits, sir. And the men, sir –

Captain   Our men . . .

First Mate   are somewhat disgruntled, sir. We should have arrived two weeks ago and . . . all this thieving, rape and torture is thirsty work.

Captain   Hmm . . .

First Mate   I have a thought, sir.

Captain   Just one?

First Mate   Just one, sir.

Captain   Go on, man.

First Mate   We are, of course, insured.

Captain   Indeed, we have to be.

First Mate   We can, alas, make no claim for goods damaged during the course of the voyage . . .

Captain   Go on.

First Mate   But if we throw the blacks overboard, sir, to save on water for us hard-working men, the insurance company will see that we dispensed with the cargo to save our pale skins and our Christian souls.

Captain   Dispense with the cargo . . . I have an idea, First Mate.

First Mate   You have so many, Captain.

Captain   I say we begin with the children, then the women, then the men, sickest first.

First Mate   It'll be heavy work, sir.

Captain   Well keep them in chains, and throw them in batches. It'll be as if we were to throw cattle into the sea. Not a pleasant sight but a hearty breakfast for sharks!

First Mate   And not a scrap of evidence.

Captain   Not an eyeball. Get to it, man!

First Mate   But, Captain, who shall we say is to blame for all we are about to do . . .

The **Sailors** *creep onto the now more gently swaying deck, one by one. Cast size can be reduced if necessary. They hatch out the murder plot. Feel the rhythm. Pace!*

Matthew   Let's blame this old Dutch ship – *Zong*!

Mark   Her name means 'care'. Ha! She cares for none.

Luke   She's a monster made by Nether men.

John   Full to bursting, feeding on flesh, so much more than she can digest.

Simon   The greedy Dutch bitch swallows dish upon dish of –

Peter   Ashantes, Mandinkas, Igbos, Yorubas . . .

James   Women, men, boys, girls, babies . . .

Thomas   Stuffed to the sin brim with human suffering.

Andrew   She stinks of fish, piss, shit and vomit!

Nathan   So much that when we dock at Liverpool –

Jude   Cardiff, London, Glasgow, Bristol –

Paul   – the ladies and gents have to cover their noses, hold their breaths.

Matthew   She drags us down to her depths.

Mark   She gets so drunk on flesh she makes us forget our Christian selves.

Luke   She got so pissed she got lost! 300 miles off the coast of Jamaica.

John   Sailed right past the dock at Black River.

Scene transforms from a ship to a courtroom. The **Sailors** *give evidence in court, swearing on the Bible, passing it one-by-one, rapid, testifying, feigning regret.*

Simon   And so many of the poor Africans died . . .

Peter   But we were running out of water . . .

James   And we pleaded with her! 'Carry us to safer shores!'

Thomas   But instead she said –

Andrew   You'll have to lighten my load.

Nathan   I am too full I cannot go on.

Jude   And *Zong* she spat 131 blacks into the sea.

Paul   A shark's breakfast!

Captain   So we have no choice. We *must* make this insurance claim.
To recompense, to compensate.

First Mate   And the judge will say . . .

Judge Mansfield (*formal, slower, concluding the case*)
'These slaves were no more human than horses.'
And it must have been a sorry sight
But the men tried with all their might

First Mate   but it was the ship, it was *Zong*, that made us do this wrong . . .

Captain (*back in the present, slower, satisfied with the plan*)
And when we get back to Tilbury Dock,
We'll open that sweet bottle of Jamaican rum
And count our little . . .

Ola (*figuring it out*)   Windfall . . .

Optional visual or movement sequence here, e.g. pound notes start falling from above. Cast members enter with scissors, snipping the notes, like the mouths of little fish. They cut out little human figures from the notes and hang them up, like bunting on a ship. Or this could be a movement sequence with music. **Ola** *watches, pained.*

Scene – Monte Rosa 3

Monte Rosa *rocks in her chair. Alone again. A new actor. Same light. Blue shawl.*

Monte Rosa
The only thing I really *didn't* like is they made me change my name
They have a habit of doing that, the British
And I adore my name,
Monte Rosa
But I had no choice again
So yes I worked for them
All over their huge empire!

Life on ship could be animated physically here by the cast.

My favourite job was Kingston, Jamaica, to London, Tilbury Dock
Transporting the great-grandchildren of those slaves
Now sailing the other way
The West Indies fought against the Nazis
And since Elizabeth was their Queen
They were invited to come for a new life in England
'Come and re-build the country!'
Quite a story really . . .

Ja, that was one of my favourite passages
So much hope and dancing and stories

*Singing the Lord Kitchener song 'London Is the Place for Me', the cast involved in
the next scene join in, singing the song in full, quietly underneath* **Monte Rosa**'s
*speech. They continue singing gently and acting out playing dominoes, cards,
chatting, relaxing on the* Windrush *ship, approaching England.*

What a lot people don't know
Is that I also carried Poles
Sixty-six women stranded in Mexico
Ja, Polish refugees
And when they got to England
They got passports and set up Polski shops
A new life made possible.

They said the other day that
The British were trying to send them away (**Monte Rosa** *watches the cast*)
Not the Polish of course
The *blacks*
Even though some are as old as me
And worked all these years for the Mother Country
Saying 'they had no place in Britain',
'The Windrush generation'.
A scandal!
If they ordered me to transport them back to Kingston today I would have said
Nein! No! I'm too old
And they were nice folk.

Take the blacks back under your own steam
You're on your own now, Queenie!
I've had enough of governments
Making me move people around like cargo
There were times when I should have said no . . .
(*Pause for thought about the Norwegian Jewish children.*)   I
should have said no . . .

Scene – Ouija Board 3

Ola *reads the Ouija board letters projected again. They are still afraid but moved.*

Ola
 C
 H
 I
 L
 L
 CHILL . . .

Scene – Wind Chill

The people below all speak in one rhythm. Almost like a song. The second line has more space than the first and third line of each stanza. Keep in time. The word 'wind' comes right on cue. Feel it. The feel is influenced by hip hop and also the dub poetry of Linton Kwesi Johnson (LKJ). Watch him performing 'Inglan Is a Bitch' online:
https://www.youtube.com/watch?v=Zq9OpJYck7Y

The tempo of the speeches below is faster than this LKJ poem but the idea is the same: telling true stories to the audience, in rhythm. No breaks between voices/ characters. Keep pulsing forward. It can be spoken with a beat/music underscored if this helps timing. You can use a little movement/gestures to animate the text. If possible, project the years (below) to punctuate each stanza, locating us in time.

NB: A note on use of the 'N' word. The word is a weapon with a painful and violent 500-year history. It is still used to assault black people today. It is harmful and should only ever be used in the context of the scene, where it is actually a direct factual quotation. Treat the word in rehearsals as you might treat a gun. It is never to be played with casually. Handle with care and caution. Discuss its use with your groups – have a 'health and safety' briefing, as it were. Only ever use the 'N' word where it is in the script. Lock it away, like a gun, when it is not being used directly in a scene. Directors, actors and the creative team are advised to refer to the word simply as 'the N word'. The use of the 'N' word by rappers and writers of African descent (who use a different spelling of the word) is a different subject, and for a different play, entirely.

Projection: 1948.

Nanny   Ivor Cummings walks up the gang-plank
Civil servant, gay and black
'Things will not be easy for you here'

All (*punctuating in rhythm, in time*)   Wind
Chill
Fact.

Projection: 1948.

Bernie   Tilbury dock was a bit of a shock
Dirt, smog and faces flat
'Welcome party? What did you expect?'

All   Wind
Chill
Fact.

Projection: 1948.

Joy   'No dogs, no blacks, no Irish'
'I'm not renting your kind this flat'
'But I've got no-where, to sleep tonight'

All   Wind
Chill
Fact.

Projection: 1959.

Smiley   They murder Kelso Cochrane
And yes we must fight back
They say 'riot', we say 'uprising'

All   Wind
Chill
Fact.

Projection: 1964 and 1968.

Stuart   'If-you-want-a-nigger-for-a-neighbour-vote-Labour'
The Tory election tract
Enoch comes with 'Rivers of Blood'

All   Wind
Chill
Fact.

Projection: 1981.

Cherry   Child-ren of the New Cross fire
They were treated like suspects
'13 dead and nothing said'

All Wind
Chill
Facts.

Projection: 1993.

Kelso They called out 'what, what, nigger'
It was *us* who was under attack
Cops screwed the names of Stephen's killers

All Wind
Chill
Fact.

Projection: 2017.

Stephen Served in the British army
Paid every penny of tax
Said I had no right to draw my pension

All Wind
Chill
Fact.

Projection: 2018.

David I've been here all my life!
Work still give me the sack
'No passport? You can sleep on the street!'

All Wind
Chill
Fact.

Projection: 2019.

Mary 'You got ten days to leave the country
It's time to go home and pack'
I was an NHS nurse for seventeen years

All Wind
Chill
Fact.

Projection: 2020.

Marcus They keep me in detention
Cos I'm African. Cos I'm black. [Alternatively: 'Cos she's African. Cos she's black.']
If I was Irish or a dog they wouldn't lock me up [Or: 'If she was Irish . . . lock her up.']

All Wind
Chill
Fact.

Ola (*joining in*)   Wind
Chill
Factor

We go into a call and response section. Divide **All** *cast onstage into Half Calling and Half Responding.* **Ola** *joins in everything.*

All (*calling*)   Spring or winter
(*responding*)   Wind-chill factor
(*calling*)   Fall or summer
(*responding*)   Wind-chill factor
(*calling*)   Do you feel it?

Ola (*responding alone*)   Yes you feel it!
And you deal with it

All (*calling*)   You wrap up
(*responding*)   You rise up
(*calling*)   You step out
(*responding*)   Face the cold
(*calling*)   Fire inside
(*responding*)   Walking tall
(*calling*)   Give a hand from a fall

All (*everyone together*)   And carnival
(*calling*)   you play on
(*responding*)   you pray on
(*calling*)   you march on
(*responding*)   you work on
(*calling*)   you fight on

All (*everyone together*)   and never give up
Never give up
Never give up
Never give up
Cos come what may . . .

Pause. **All** *look at* **Ola**

Ola   We're here to stay.

Blackout, exit. **Monte Rosa** *gets in position.*

Scene – Monte Rosa 4

In her rocking chair. Stage directions as above.

Monte Rosa
> My last trip was transporting soldiers and their families from
> Korea and Japan back to England

But there was a terrible fire below
And one by one
The sailors who all said they loved me
Even my beloved captain
Abandoned me
Jumping into the sea
Left me to sink into the bed
Alone.
It's pretty cold
Down here
Even in the Med
When you're dead
It's pretty cold . . .

So many
Skulls
Skeletons
Children
Left to drown . . .
I could have carried them back to shore
Yesterday: 500 or more
So many lost souls
Calling for a home
While you sit on food mountains
Refusing to see what lies beneath
Ja, the sea is history,
It repeats . . .

Scene – Ouija Board 4

The students take a break. It's been intense. They are all more at ease now. The pizza box is empty.

Kit   I don't get it.

Ali   They went to the farm, they had a fall and then: chill.
FarmfallchillFarmfallchill!

Xia   Maybe it makes sense if you say it slow. Farrrrrm. Faaaaall. Chiiiiiillllllll . . .

Kit   You lot are bonkers.

Jay   What do they *want*?

Zhe   Do you think they understood the question?

Kit *and* **Ali** *take over the planchette.* **Xia** *scribes.*

Zhe   Who are you?

The planch moves to N-O-T.

All   NOT.

Kit   Here we go again . . .

Jay   Who are you, *not*? . . .

The planchette is still. They wait. They get tired. **Xia** *takes their fingers off the planchette. Pause.* **Xia** *breaks the silence.*

Xia   Have you lot all finished your essays?

All (*not in chorus, just naturally*)   No . . .

A beat.

Jay   Shall we try again tomorrow? (*They casually respond 'yeah / yep / thank God', etc. by getting up and starting to pack away.*)

Ali   Who ate the last piece of pizza?

Ola (*ignoring* **Ali**, *packing away*)   Maybe we're not supposed to know . . .

Ola *goes to pick up the planchette and it suddenly starts moving wildly seemingly on its own, flinging* **Ola** *around who is trying to hold on. This effect could be created physically by the actor. They all try to help* **Ola** *who is screaming.*

Ola   NO!

The planchette whirls around and lands at 'No'.

Ola (*out of breath*)   They don't want us to go!

Jay   Someone write it down!

Zhe *grabs the pen and scribes frantically. Letters are projected.*

All (*not in unison – sense of chaos*)
G
O
L
D
S
U
G
A
R
G
U
N

Ola   GOLD? SUGAR? GUN?

Sudden loud sound of rapid gunfire.

Xia   GET DOWN!

Ola   WHAT THE HELL?!

Scene – Gold-Sugar-Gun Gamers

*Sound of gunfire continues. The rest of the cast run on with lolly pops, firing them like weapons, laughing. They sit on the floor downstage and suck lolly pops throughout the scene. The two computer gamers, **Sam** and **Sim** also run on, they don't suck lolly pops, but they sit down on the 'sofa' (or any seating indicating a sofa), also facing the audience. **Sam** and **Sim** speak in a very rhythmical and electronic/mechanical way, with minimal emotion, like the figures in the video game, with an urgent pulsating beat beneath it all. The scene might be animated physically but let the words do most of the work. It must have pace, rapid fire but crystal clear; nothing can be lost in delivery, just like the game. It will need a lot of rehearsal. The scene is a response to the popular video game* Resident Evil 5. *Here is a trailer (trigger warning – it is violent):* https://www.youtube.com/watch?v=xxJbz_3PKQo

Sim   What's this?

Sam   Wait.

Sim   Is it Hostile Environment 6?

Sam   No.

Sim   Hostile Environment 9?

Sam   No.

Sim   Looks like Hostile Environment 3.

Sam   Wait.

Sim   Or Hostile Environment 4. (*Beat.*) Is this the one with the swamp?

Sam   Wait.

Sim   The one that starts with the boat? Speedboat through the swamp to the mud huts. And its Sheva and Chris.

Sam   Wait.

Sim   Chris Redland and Sheva who sounds like a cat but she's not.

Sam   Wait.

Sim   Sounds like a Hindu Goddess but she's not.

Sam   Wait.

Sim   Sheva.

Sam   Wait.

Sim Spelt like in Hebrew but not a Jew, Hindu or cat.

Sam OK.

Sim She's a girl.

Sam OK.

Sim She's more like some kind of mixed race.

Sam OK.

Sim 'cept her hair's really straight.

Sam OK.

Sim She's got this really small waist.

Sam OK.

Sim Nice tits.

Sam OK!

Sim Walks like this.

Sam OK!

Sim But Chris is the boss. Cos he is. He's the protagonist. Is that what this is?

Sam No.

Sim The one with the African villages? And they've all got some kind of mad virus.

Sam Wait.
  Wait.
  Wait.
  Wait.

Sim OK.

Sam Thanks!

Silence. **Sam** *plays on.*

Sim Sure it's not Hostile Environment 3?

Sam No.

Sim More like Hostile Environment 4.

Sam No.

Sim Where you blow off the Africans' heads. They jump out and scream and go ARGH!

Sam Huh?

Sim They don't even know how to speak.

Sam Huh?

Sim   They jump out and scream and go ARGH!

Sam   OK.

Sim   Black men they scream and go ARGH!

Sam   OK.

Sim   Black men, no t-shirts, just trousers, bare feet and viruses jump out and scream and go ARGH!

Sam   OK.

Sim   And then you blow off their heads.

Sam   Wait.

Sim   Destroy as many as poss.

Sam   Got it.

Sim   And you're Sheva or Chris with big guns but Chris's are bigger cos he's the boss.

Sam   Yes.

Sim   And he smashes the masks and smashes the pots and takes all the gold so it's his.

Sam   Yes.

Sim   And Sheva's got really nice tits, small waist, mixed race or something like that but straight hair like a Hindu a cat or a Jew but she's not.

Sam   Yes.

Sim   Says 'OK, thank you, watch out, help me up, over here Chris!'

Sam   OK.

Sim   'Thank you, watch out, help me up, over here, Chris!'

Sam   Yes.

Sim   She's just like this stupid sidekick but it's Chris who's the man.

Sam   Yep.

Sim   Blonde hair and American.

Sam   Yep.

Sim   Chris's got one black friend but he doesn't blow off *his* head. Cos he's an American. Like Kanye West.

Sam   OK.

Sim   Not like the African blacks in the villages swamps to the mud huts and viruses wearing no t-shirts just trousers, muscles and bare chests and jumping with ARGGGGGHHHH! Not real words but ARRRRGGGGGGHHHHH!

Sam   WAIT! Wait. Wait. Wait.

Beat

Sim   Is that what this is?

Sam   No.

Sim   OK.

Sam   This game is much more advanced.

Sim   Slow down.

Sam   This game is way more advanced.

Sim   Slow down.

Sam   Makes Hostile Environment 3 –

Sim   OK –

Sam   – look like a walk in the park with a pond and ducks that go quack as you feed them white bread from a baker that isn't Greggs. A baker that still exists. This game makes Hostile Environment look like a walk in a park in a town with a clock in a tower still ticking still tocking, somewhere in England or Scotland or Ireland or Wales – but with jobs.

Sim   Can I have a go?

Sim *plays the game.*

Sam   OK. Just shoot.

Sim   OK.

Sam   The blacks. Just shoot.

Sim   OK.

Sam   Muslims just shoot.

Sim   Got it. Anything darker than shit just shoot.

Sam   Just shoot and collect.

Sim   Where? What?

Sam   Gold.

Sim   Pause. Where?

Pause game but keep the pace, urgency and internal rhythm. However, **Sam** *is more human now the game is on pause.*

Sam   There's gold in the camel sacks. The camels belonging to Musa the King. One hundred camels and one thousand Africans, Timbuktu, Mali – ready to go. Not a fictional kingdom, not Black Panther Wakanda. No. 500 years ago. King Mansa Musa the richest man ever is going on Hajj: its a pilgrimage. To Mecca, Medina and maybe Jerusalem. To say 'thank you' to God. He gives alms. Not arms. Alms. He gives out his gold on the way and prays five times a day. And he's really really famous. More than Martin Luther King or Muhammad Ali. The Egyptian economy crashed cos of all the gold he gives away from his camel sacks. And that's how they hear about Africa. The white people hear about Africa's gold and then the Portuguese come. Then the French, the Spanish, the Germans, Italians, the Belgians, the Dutch, the Danish, the Brits, they don't give a shit, take gold from your hand and the land. But it's not enough. They want more: black gold, black old, black young, black men, black women, black children, take them to America, to the soil of Chris Redland and Sheva. And they've killed the first people who lived there. Strike African names and make them cut sugar cane. Sugar to make us fat addicts who sit on sofas like this playing video games to kill blacks.

Sim   Rules?

Sam   Shoot. Kill Mansa Musa the black Muslim king who makes Bill Gates and the Queen look like Barbie and Ken. He's way richer than them. But if white people hear of his gold, black people get sold or die trying for Europe in boats. So shoot. Before anyone hears of the gold. Before anyone comes for the land. Before they get carried away. Before we all get carried away.

Sim   OK.

Sam   It's not Hostile Environment 3. Or Hostile Environment 4. Or Hostile Environment 6. Or Hostile Environment 9. This is Hostile Environment zero. The Indians invented the zero. Or Arabs invented the zero. Someone invented the zero. Let us go back to the zero.

The game resumes. **Sim** *shoots while* **Sam** *continues speaking.*

Sam   Maybe then they will never be slaves. Maybe then they will never lose names. Maybe then there will never be race. The colour of our skins will be no more significant than the colour of their eyes,* my eyes, your eyes, our eyes watching the killing of blacks from the sofa suck sucking on lolly pops –

Sim   (*rapid rhythm*)   pop pop pop pop pop pop pop!

Sam   Too fat in the head to get up and say STOP!

The gamers freeze in their scene as the next scene immediately starts.

Scene – Last Ouija Word/Voice of the Wind

Ola *immediately comes in: 'STOP! MAKE IT STOP!' as the students are blown back into the Common Room.* **Ola**, *struggling with the planchette, is held by the group.*

Ola   STOP! MAKE IT STOP!

---

*   Paraphrasing a speech by the Ethiopian Emperor Ras Tafari Haile Selassie I to the United Nations, quoted by Bob Marley and the Wailers in the song 'War'.

The letters are spelt out boldly through projection. They don't have to just be on the Ouija board; this could be in movement in the space, for example.

All
W
I
N
D

A huge gust of wind and the rest of the cast is scattered on stage. **All** *play the voice of the wind. Some can take a solo stanza – whatever is clearest and most powerful. The whole speech could also be taken by one person. Experiment. The style is inspired by Linton Kwesi-Johnson performing the dub poem 'Inglan is a Bitch'. However this speech is much faster in rhythm. See Caliban's speeches in Shakespeare's* The Tempest, *for reference. This speech has its own defiant pace, as unpredictable as the wind itself. A kind of hip hop, but not. Make it your own. Some stanzas are a slow breeze but the end is a wild and fast hurricane! You could choreograph it. Whatever you do, hold nothing back. The wind knows no borders.*

Wind   English is a bitch
Been no escaping it
English is a bitch
I want a word with it

You named oceans 'oceans'
And earth you gave 'quake'
But what a careless noun
For me
You did make
You called forest 'forest'
'Desert', 'fire' and 'sky'
But if you did not feel me
You'd say what am I
From this name?

Ind
W-ind
A fart of a word
A foul letter word
A trump up word
Hot air
A tight little title
A mean little rival
For *vento, viento, upepo*!
Could have named me something
Arabic, Gaelic, Bantu, Asiatic
You could have had Latin but you chose Germanic: Vind.
Wind.

Only a *liar's* rhyme you can make with it.
Even Shakespeare couldn't much play with it.
Sinned, pinned,
Mind, kind
Kindred spirits
My name has not
Elemental insult
My name is wind up.
English is a bitch
Been no escaping it
English is a bitch
And I want a word with it

Anglo I am angry!
Long neglected by language
What kind of mother tongue
Is so lazy, limp and languid
That she can't even credit her subject
With a password he can be proud of.

My moniker makes a mockery
Of all I've done for this country
My label should be libellous
Would it really have been so onorous
To make me a lickle more sonorous
Add a lickle consonant, a lickle vowel . . .
So yes I'll howl through your doors
In a rush!
In a wind rush!
I DESERVED MORE!

This linguistic disrespect
Needs a diction fixing
Some lexiconisation
Some thesaurisation
A new appellation
For this misrepresentation
Proper noun reparation!
With certification.

I demand new nomenclature
Powerful elegant mature
Sounding
Reflecting the true status
Of my intrinsic Englishness
For an island is not an island

Without the weather you see
You should show me some respect
I've been here for centuries.

English is a bitch
Been no escaping it
English is a bitch
And I want a word with it

Didn't I give birth to breeze
On this land?
I delivered you the tempest
Right here where I stand.
Bluster, gale, gust – I raised a hurricane!
Yet you classify me with a mere
One syllable name.

Didn't I turn your mills
To grind your grain?
To make your bread
So you would never feel the pain
Of hunger like your empire inflicted upon
Thirty million Indians
One million in Ireland!

English is a BITCH!
Been no escaping it
English is a bitch
And I want a word with it

Building to a hurricane.

So don't blame me
When you chop too many trees
And I race across your fields
And reap devastation
Don't blame me
When you turn up the heat
And it makes me swell
And arrive unexpected
Don't blame me
If I bring the desert to your door
The waters to your window
If I bring war
If I rise up
From 'rivers of blood'
Don't blame me!

For this hostility
For this, Britannia, is your legacy
And this you must know
You reap what you sow
And despite this pitiful one-syllable name
A mere footprint on a missing document that's still a source of shame
The nature of wind
The nature of wind rush
The nature of this generation
Has changed!

Howling dogs/howling wind into the next scene.

Scene – Senior Common Room

Quiet after the storm. Just before sunrise. They look at the rocking chair.

Jay   Wind farm.

Zhe   Windfall.

Ali   Wind chill.

Xia   Gold rush.

Kit   Sugar rush.

Jay   Gun rush.

All   'Windrush'.

Ola   The. Empire. *Windrush.*

A beat.

Zhe   She's a she.

Xia   She's a ship.

Jay   Rest in peace.

Kit   Why us?

Ola   Why *here*?

They look around the room at the pictures of old dead white male professors. Pause for thought. **Ola** *tries to figure out the mystery, through their lines below; it is not all worked out yet, use the lines to process.*

Ola   An empire's gotta have either an emperor . . . or an *empress*. Right?

All   Right.

Ola   Our uni's named after the same empress from when the *Windrush* set sail from Jamaica. This queen's grandma. Mary of Teck. Some German countess. Wrote an essay about her. Empress of India, all her colonies . . . The West Indies . . .

Jay   . . . Head of the Commonwealth . . .

Ola   *Common* wealth? They should call it like it is. Universities, cities, all over, Glasgow to Greenwich, Belfast to Bristol, Cardiff to Carlisle, made *untold money* off of slavery. They even got compensation when they set the slaves free. And a lot of *these people* (*referring to the portraits*) invested their dirty money in our universities.

Ali   It's true. The SU's running a campaign about it, but our uni's staying silent.

Kit   Rewind. They paid the slave *owners*?

Ola   Yep. And black people are still paying for it.

Zhe   Cleaning their offices, doing security, paying the fees . . .

Ali   And more time, it's the black and brown students getting two-twos.

Xia   Really?

Jay   They call it the 'BME attainment gap'.

Kit   They should call it the 'white privilege gap'. Maybe then someone would sit up and take notice.

Ali   I better leave here with a two-one or I'm gonna take them to court. 50k debt for a Desmond Tutu – no thank you.

Ali *and* **Ola** *punch fists, etc. in agreement.*

Ola   And uni managers are all white guys paying themselves, like, half a million a year.

Xia   Half a million?!

Ali   Minimum. Plus a free car, a flat –

Kit   – and a bodyguard!

Zhe   Principals with no principles.

Jay   But why does Empire *Windrush* want to talk to us?

Ola   Cos of the Windrush scandal?

Xia   Cos we're all doing History?

Zhe   She could have just sent us to the library.

Jay   I get the feeling she's still trying to tell us something.

Kit   Why?

Ola (*fearfully, though much less so than earlier*)   Look . . .

Ali   Oh shit . . .

The chair is rocking vigorously as if it is nodding 'yes'. The group brace themselves. **Ola** *bravely gets the Ouija board and offers it to* **Jay**. *They are all surprised but go with it, silently.* **Jay** *sets out the Ouija board and places their fingers on the planchette.*

Ali *places their fingers on it too.* **Xia** *picks up the pen and paper.* **Kit** *watches* **Ola**.
Ola *is totally focused on the letters. Deep breaths, they summon all their courage.*

Ola   Empire *Windrush*. JUST TELL US WHAT YOU WANT!

*The planchette starts to move to the letters below. More quickly than at first. The
group are well practiced now so they pronounce the letters, making out the words.*

All   T-R-U-T-H OR D-A-R-E

Silence. They look at each other. They look at the rocking chair.

Ola   TRUTH.

All *look at* **Ola**.

Scene – Monte Rosa 5

In her rocking chair again.

Monte Rosa
    Rest in peace?
    They won't let me!
    In the newspapers, on the TV
    They keep calling me, calling me
    Windrush Windrush
    Empire *Windrush*
    Naming streets after me, writing books about me
    And now they want to name this room in the university after me
    So the 'Windrush' name game got your attention
    But now my children, I want you to tell them
    THAT IS NOT MY NAME!
    Mine is so much more beautiful!
    Monte Rosa!
    Birthed in Hamburg, 1920
    I worked for the Nazis
    The British captured me
    And painted over my name
    It is a bad habit
    Not calling things as they are
    The English would rather talk about the weather
    They didn't have Auschwitz but, *ach*,
    They weren't much better
    It was the *British* who invented concentration camps – in Africa!
    We Germans were just more efficient in murder
    And if they cared so much about the Jews
    Why did they wave that letter, appeasing Hitler?
    And let so many migrants burn and drown
    Just like they are doing now

From Grenfell Tower to the bottom of the ocean
They don't like you saying it
But they were not so different
Re-named me after 500 years of crime
Rape and murder, kidnap and torture
500 years of empire
And a dirty little river running away from the Thames:
'Windrush'
Best remembered for 800 West Indians
Most forgotten for sixty-six Poles
Invited to come and make a home.
And what names did they call *them* when they arrived?
Tell the truth! Tell them from me:
If you want to keep dragging me up from the depths of the sea
If you want to name this place after me
Call me by my name!

Scene – Morning in the Common Room

The students lift their fingers off the planchette at the same time. Stillness. Sun rising.

Jay   'Monte Rosa' . . .

Kit   It's over.

Zhe   Holocaust to Windrush.

Ola   Same damn ship. Diff'rent racist shit.

Pause.

Kit   So all she *actually* wants is for the university to re-name this stuffy old place the: 'Monte Rosa Room', instead of the 'Windrush Room'. That's it?

Ali   She kept us up all night, man.

Zhe   She's just vain.

Xia   Sea dog.

Jay   We musn't speak ill of the dead.

Xia   She wasn't even a person. She was a boat!

Ali   A Nazi one!

Kit   And now she's just a heap of rusty metal at the bottom of the sea.

Zhe   We should care more about the people she carried inside her.

Ola   The uni are no better. They think calling this the 'Windrush Room' will make us all feel better about how racist it is. Why don't they ask *us* what we wanna call it?

Xia   Just some bullshit tick-box exercise. I can't stand it.

Pause.

Ali   At least now maybe we'll get some sleep.

Ola (*turning very serious, bold and focused, slowly*)   We will not sleep until we expel this evil spirit.

*They all look at **Ola**, perplexed by the transformation.*

Kit   Ola?. . .

Jay   Are you ok?. . .

Ola *has a look of determination about them, trance like. The scene immediately transitions into the next with no pause. It is an extension of this scene.*

Scene – Exorcism/Protest/Student Occupation

*Bright light. **Ola** gets on a table. **Ola's Friends** (**Kit**, **Ali**, **Zhe**, **Xia** and **Jay**) gather round-what is happening? All **Monte Rosas** enter, underscoring **Ola's** text with fragments from **Monte Rosa's** earlier speeches. The first **Monte Rosa** sits in the rocking chair, the others form a ship on a stormy sea. **Monte Rosa** resists the exorcism through movement and text fragments building under **Ola**'s lines. There is a battle of wills. No guarantee who will win. High stakes! Important: **Ola** does not know what they are going to say. There is fear but they grow in courage. See the occupation of Goldsmiths University for inspiration!* https://secure.avaaz.org/en/ community_petitions/Goldsmiths_University__AntiRacist_Action_for_Hamna/?fCK Bfob&fbogname=kitty+M.&utm_source=sharetools&utm_medium=facebook&utm_ campaign=petition-703176-AntiRacist_Action_for_Hamna&utm_ term=CKBfob%2Ben

Ola   Vessel of racism
    Ship of hate
    Leave this space!
    Go tell your sob story to the salt-water fish cos –
    WE AIN'T INTERESTED!
    We speak! (**Ola** *gestures for the* **Friends** *to repeat.*)

Ola's Friends   We speak!

Ola   In solidarity!

Ola's Friends   In solidarity!

Ola   With Windrush generations

Ola's Friends   With Windrush generations

Ola   Old and living

Ola's Friends   Old and living

Ola   Dead and young.

Ola's Friends   Dead and young.

Ola   So Nazi Monte Rosa and the British Empire of hate!
Go back to hell!
We exorcise you!
We cast you away!
Set sail!

Ola's Friends   GET OUT!

All of the **Monte Rosa***s suddenly exit, dispersing as fast as possible. They are exorcised! The rocking chair is left gently rocking, now empty*

Ali   Wooooooooow . . .

Brief excited chatter as **Ola's Friends** *take in all that has happened, e.g. 'that was crazy', 'what just happened?', 'was that real?' etc. During this all of the rest of the cast gradually enter the Senior Common Room, playing* **Students***, also in their pyjamas, awoken by the commotion, confused, improvising, e.g. 'what's all the noise?' 'why is* **Ola** *on the table?' etc.* **Ola** *calls them to attention with their line!*

Ola   Shut up! I'm just getting started (fam)!
Now,
We who stand on land
Are seizing this room
We are occupying this space!

All Students *improvise cheering and text here and throughout this section. Not just generic sounds but individual lines as well.* **All** *back* **Ola***'s lines up, responding, but don't let the cheering slow things down. Power through with pace* **Ola***!*

Ola   And we won't go away
Until all the money
Made from slavery
In this university
Is paid back to the descendants of African slaves! (*Cheering here and throughout.*)
We want scholarships!
Reparations!
No tuition fees!
Free education!
For EVERYBODY!
We demand that all the pictures and symbols
Of slave owners are taken down! NOW!
We demand that our lecturers
And our books
Start to LOOK like ALL of the people
And ALL of the histories
Of these islands!
We demand that you DE COLONISE THIS SHIT!

All   TODAY!

Ola   WE DEMAND EQUALITY!
WE WANT FAIR GRADES!

Ali   AND FREE PIZZAS!

Laughter.

Ola   Yeah! Bring us some food!
Cos we are not going away
Like the Windrush generations –
All Students WE ARE HERE TO STAY!

Ola *remains centre stage with the five* **Friends** *and* **All Students** *around them.* **Ola** *smiles. They are not scared anymore. Blackout then projection:*

> *Dedicated to the survivors of the Windrush generation scandal of 2018 and the victims of the Grenfell Tower catastrophe of 2017.*

End.

Wind / Rush Generation(s)

BY MOJISOLA ADEBAYO

*Notes on rehearsal and staging, drawn from a workshop with the writer,
held at the National Theatre, October 2019*

How Mojisola came to write the play

Mojisola opened with a note to the group about her role as a writer: 'I think of myself as a maker even more than a writer. I think of the play as an offer. I think of myself as someone who creates events (through the page, here). It's a piece of work for you to get messy with, to bring to life.

Themes: the title as a way into the play

Lead director Matthew Xia asked Mojisola about the play's title (where it came from, what it signified).

Mojisola said: 'The title was informed by the Windrush generation scandal and the *Empire Windrush* ship. A desire to respond to the scandal. I was appalled, shocked and upset at some of what happened to elders from that generation. When I saw David Lammy's speech, it seemed to capture my own feelings of rage and sadness. That was what needed to be spoken about at that time. With the knowledge that the play would go on a couple of years after that incident, I wanted to write something that would still be relevant. Not just speak of that generation but generations and generations beyond it.

'The title also sets up the play's playfulness with words. I see the English language as a colonial language. Colonialism didn't just come about through actions but also language. The delivery of colonialism is tied up with the English language.'

The *Empire Windrush*

Mojisola then shared some of her own historical research into the *Empire Windrush*: 'I was curious about the name of the *Empire Windrush*. Why it is such an evocative name? Why have we heard of this ship and not the other two before it? Partly it's because of the name: a grandiose title that suggests expanse in the empire and brings a sense of history, power, the globe. Wind/rush: it's a poetic name that evokes environment, landscape and weather (Brits and the weather!). The title is also the play in that it's about digging into that name.'

Mojisola outlined the history of the *Empire Windrush* ship, which was initially birthed as the *Monte Rosa* and used, amongst other things, to transport Holocaust victims to concentration camps in the Second World War. This play was about unpacking and talking about some of those stories, which are often not disclosed, hidden or pushed to the sidelines.

Empire

Mojisola discussed how, whereas in British society the word 'empire' is still embraced, for her it evokes a history of colonialism, slavery, genocide and famine. It's associated with a horrendous violent past with a legacy for the present day unacknowledged in British society. She further offered: 'If we scratch under the surface there's still a sense of pride attached to our history of empire, embodied in ideas or phrases such as "Britannia rules the waves".'

Windrush

Mojisola shared that her interest in 'the wind and the rush' of the title came from a sustained creative engagement in making work about climate change. A task for an artist is 'to try to get climate change in the body and to encourage an emotional response to it'. Mojisola pointed towards the connections between climate change, race, racism, the industrial revolution and the slave trade. The writer opened up further on framing racism 'as a kind of climate that you live in, as a kind of weather', talking through the idea that 'when adequately dressed we might not notice it, whereas sometimes it feels like walking about naked in the rain'.

Mojisola closed this introduction to the play with the provocation that in Britain, 'We find it easier to talk about the weather and hate talking about racism. Racism is pervasive and it's better to talk about it, as scary as it is. To engage with it. Together.'

Approaching the play

Matthew facilitated a discussion in which each director introduced themselves, the group they were working with, what drew them to the play and any concerns they had at this point in the process.

Some common things that drew directors to choose this play were:

- Telling the story of British history from a different perspective; telling a story that needs to be told.
- The play as a learning tool with mostly white groups.
- Being both scared and excited by the play.
- The scope for telling the story in many different ways.
- The offers the play presented to specific students or young people directors worked with, whether trans learners (the play treating gender openly and inclusively) or young people interested in rapping and drill music.
- Unlocking something in themselves as artists, addressing the gaps in their own knowledge.

- Creating an opportunity for students with African-Caribbean heritage to have a conversation about the issues in the play with their own families.

Some common things that directors felt concerned about, having chosen the play, were:

- Making sure that it's done right.
- For white directors, feeling concerned about whether it was their story to tell.
- Managing the structure and various narrative strands, bringing them together as a whole.
- Representing a Ouija board in a Christian school or working with students who have for religious reasons expressed discomfort with representing a Ouija board dramatically.

Mojisola and Matthew then addressed two key anxieties:

Structure

Key points Mojisola talked through were:

- That the Lammy speech should be a catalyst for the performers. That fire in the belly never dies down.
- That the common room can be seen as a base camp, a holding ground we repeatedly return to, from which the other scenes spin off.
- That the various kinds of scenes offer particular kinds of young performers particular opportunities and directors should go with the strengths of the group in their casting choices. For example: the Windrush monologue could be taken on by a young person who prefers working by themselves.

Ownership of the story

Matthew opened up the question of how groups could own the story, particularly relating to majority- or all-white groups representing this particular history.

The writer shared with the group that *Wind / Rush Generation(s)* is a: 'British story. I wrote it knowing there would be a range of groups performing it. Feel that you have permission. Thank you for doing it. It's your play now. It's all of our history. I don't own any of these stories, they are our stories. We are all implicated in racism, we are all part of this.'

Mojisola noted that with the character of Ola it does make sense for a black young person or person of colour to play the role, but if they didn't want to play the role (they have first dibs!) that was totally fine or if there are no black people or people of colour in the room that was okay, too.

Approaching the language in the play

Matthew offered advice on approaching the directing with regards to the two quoted uses of the word 'nigger' in the script, especially in a room with white people.

Matthew began this discussion by saying to the group that there is something in the sanctity of the theatrical space and what can happen in there that can't necessarily happen in other spaces.

Mojisola offered the group a metaphor to contextualise this directing work: 'The n word is a weapon. I treat it like a gun in the space that should never be played around with. [In the scenes in which the word 'nigger' is used] we are doing a scene where there is a gun. Talk about it, recognise it. If it were a gun – before working with it in rehearsals you would unload it and take it apart. It's not just a word, it's an emblem of a weapon as well. You don't just take it out anytime, you prepare people for it. If someone took the gun outside the rehearsal room and walked down the street with it that would be a bad idea. Emphasise that it's never to be played with. It's used in quotation in the script (from both a Conservative Party slogan and Stephen Lawrence's murder) and in each instance it's white people saying the words.'

Matthew offered the technique of running the scene without using the word, then putting it back in again at the end of the rehearsal. Mojisola added that in the context of discussing it you should use the phrase 'the n word' where in the scene you are using the quoted use of 'nigger' by white people.

Mojisola clarified: 'to not use it (i.e. to edit it out) is to not deal with the reality. The quotation marks are really important.'

Another technique Mojisola offered was for the actor to play the words with real clarity, to be really clear that these are quoted uses of 'the n word'. This could be achieved through splitting the lines in the two sections referring to the Conservative Party election slogan and the words of Stephen Lawrence's murderers so that the quotation is read out by one actor and the commentary is read out by another actor.

Dedications

Mojisola shared a final note on her own practice of using dedications (which can be found in the script): 'You can hold hands together before the show and dedicate the performance to someone. This can be done anonymously; they could be a figure from history or someone linked to you personally, they don't have to have died.' Mojisola reminded the group that through this work 'we're trying to change the world, change the country. We're trying to do something really positive.'

Exploring key scenes

Prologue: David Lammy Speech

Mojisola remarked that 'the physicality grabbed me more than the words. Watch the scene with the volume down. In the context of images and fears around black masculinity you can see he is really containing himself.'

Matthew referenced the approach to verbatim speech in the National Theatre's show *London Road* in which the text was treated as notation. He noted that the challenge for this scene is capturing that kind of quality in a chorus, in which the chorus don't blend into a drone, sounding like Gregorian chanters, but follow the nuanced vocal delivery and pitch of the original recording.

Matthew suggested researching the Recorded Delivery Technique, created by Anna Deavere Smith and pioneered by Alecky Blyth (who co-authored *London Road*). This technique, as applied to rehearsing this scene, would involve the director playing the original David Lammy speech (via YouTube), one line at a time. After each line the director pauses the recording and the actors repeat what they have heard, copying the exact intonation with which Lammy delivered the words, including any hesitations or coughs he made, too. The director then presses play for the next line or manageable chunk of text, repeating the process for the full speech.

Mojisola suggested that with a smaller group, you could potentially play the speech under the performance to support the work.

To research this scene groups could visit Parliament (it's free!) but shouldn't get too focused on in-depth research into the House of Commons rules and systems.

Discoveries made through the group's exploration of this scene:

- Creating a simple physical motif (one group rocking forward and backwards as David Lammy does in the YouTube clip).
- Adding in voices (and people) one by one, building up the dynamic.
- Creating clear visual structures: whether two lines facing one another from stage left and stage right or a triangle pointed towards the audience (suggesting the bow of a ship).
- Layering a bed of sounds (whether dog calls or brays from MPs) underneath the speech speaker(s). The fact that the brays can blend/bleed into the dog barks too.
- Togetherness and separateness – a mix of singular voices and collective voices. For example: coming into unison in a clear moment (such as a point towards the audience).

Monte Rosa scenes

Mojisola noted that there is a musicality/poetry to these monologues. As the character is reminiscing there is air in there – she has time and space.

We discussed the balance between playing/suggesting the boat and playing the person, letting her simply be a lady in a rocking chair. The shawl and the rocking motion of the chair are devices at your disposal to suggest the boat.

The group's research suggestions for approaching this scene included:

- The Polish people who also travelled on the *Empire Windrush*.
- 1920s–30s Germany.
- Music of 1920s–30s Weimar Germany, a symbol of liberty when Germany was becoming oppressed.
- The history of the ship, including the ship's log.
- The Calypso artist Lord Kitchener.

Common room scenes: Ouija board exploration

You could support the rehearsal of this scene through researching the history and psychological and physiological phenomena of Ouija boards, particularly to contextualise the scene for young people from religious backgrounds with concerns about representing or acting in a scene or play involving Ouija boards.

Mojisola noted that she has deliberately written a character (Ola) who is Christian and opposed to what they are doing, so there is space for a religious young person, who wouldn't be sinning by representing that which they are critical of.

The group also talked through the mechanics of the Ouija board: someone puts their finger on the planchette, and the group push towards certain letters (which can be explained as something they self-direct without a conscious awareness but is understood in the context of the play as communication from Monte Rosa).

The creative challenge posed by the scene is: how do you spell out the words (such as P-R-O-B-L-E-M) in a way that is theatrically interesting, as well as being clear?

Mojisola asked: 'How does the fact that it's Monte Rosa who is sending the messages inform the stylistic choices? How might she send the messages? Remember, Monte Rosa likes to have fun (she tells us of music, champagne and good times as part of her story). Is she writing, speaking, texting or shouting? The audience won't know this, but it's good for you the company to know.'

Some discoveries the group made in workshopping this scene were:

- Adding sound effects helped to emphasise and clarify.
- To reflect the actual workings of Ouija boards, you would come back to centre after each letter is discovered.
- You could approach physically: group members standing in a circle place their hands in the centre. They then hurtle about the stage to different imagined letters, their hands remaining connected, spelling out P-R-O-B-L-E-M.
- You could create a naturalistic version in which the group huddled around a small table. The characters whose fingers are connected with the table begin to slowly move (or be moved) around the table, and as they *land* on each letter the actors speak out the letters, ultimately spelling out P-R-O-B-L-E-M.
- You could choose to combine the two modes with naturalistic performances around the Ouija board, through which a bigger style evolves.

Wind-farm scene

Matthew and Mojisola's key provocations for this scene were that it needs to be played at a fast pace, with characters interjecting over one another's lines. The challenge for this scene is to not let the audience get ahead of you (in realising the punchline that the parish council group are talking about wind farms rather than 'undesirable' people).

As with other scenes in the play, the naming of these characters (such as Theresa, Boris, Nigel, representing Theresa May, Boris Johnson and Nigel Farage) could be something to play with in terms of the mannerisms of each character. Rather than having to delve too deep into an exact character study or in-depth impression, this could simply involve playing off their key characteristics.

Some discoveries the group made in workshopping this scene were:

- Working with a variety of vocal qualities created a range of characters, rather than all characters sitting within the same vocal tone or rhythm.
- Committing to the shift into the cacophony of animalistic neighing, braying and barking was really dramatically effective.
- To capture the fast pace of the scene, the actors should follow the stage directions closely, coming in with their own line right on the forward slash.

Windfall scene

This scene presents the 1781 *Zong* massacre.

Mojisola on the historical event: 'It is one of the most shocking stories that comes out of the history of the slave trade. It's something that British people did off the coast of Jamaica and it's shocking that people don't know about it. It's a really important part of our history and an important part of insurance law. The facts in the scene are correct, though not everything is exactly as they said it. In understanding racism we need to understand an idea at the heart of imperial racism in the slave trade: the idea that humans are not humans. The Captain and First Mate don't care about the people they talk about and in fact don't see them as people.'

Mojisola acknowledged that this kind of scene work is painful and traumatic work to do, especially for those for whom this directly affects their ancestry. It's a scene that needs to be held by the director, who is positioned to look after everyone in the company in rehearsing and presenting this scene.

Taking this into consideration, the other key note for approaching this scene, as Matthew pointed out, is not to play this challenge. The work is to put aside the sensitivity of the scene and look at the robustness of the arguments, the characters' statuses and the mechanics of the scene. Matthew observed that the Captain and the First Mate aren't thinking about the humanity of the people they are talking about. In their mindset, they effectively are trying to decide 'how many cows to take off the field'. This kind of thinking was supported broadly by Enlightenment thinking and what we would now call eugenics.

Again, the naming for this scene (with its biblical suggestion) points towards the fact that the characters in the scene were Christians, using religion as a reason and an excuse for their actions.

Mojisola added that the horror for the audience is in the words themselves and so you don't necessarily have to play that horror in the performance. Pace enables the actors to dissociate a little: powering through the scene, working through the pace of it, could offer the actor a way to cope emotionally with it.

Another choice would be to double the casting of Sim and Sam with Captain and First Mate. Both sets of characters are linked thematically, but also in performance technique through a rapid, functional vocal delivery.

Another key consideration in rehearsing this scene is the deliberate choice the writer has made about not repeating imagery which shows black people in pain. Mojisola was clear in writing this scene not to repeat those images or create a context within which black actors would have to experience playing people who have been enslaved.

Matthew pointed out that this was part of a wider conversation about depicting things on stage (such as domestic violence and rape) with regards to perpetuating a set of imagery.

The writer noted that what we do see is images of white people doing terrible things. Key takeaways in approaching this scene:

- Explore working with the given circumstance of urgency, playing the scene with pace.

- Consider using music and soundscapes in suggesting the events through symbolism.

- Find a visual symbolism to represent the event, whether creating your own symbolism or using the writer's offer in the stage directions of the pound notes that fall and are cut into shapes as a symbolic way of representing the atrocity. This is a visual symbolism which conveys the relationship between the greed for money and the murdering of people, in ways that aren't literal.

- Look after your company and be prepared to have some really complex conversations about race.

Wind-chill factor scene

In exploring this scene in the workshop, the writer performed the 'wind-chill' poem on a mic with the company coming in on 'wind-chill factor' off mic. The performer on the mic controls the pace of the flow and when the refrain of 'wind-chill factor' should land.

In rehearsing this scene it would be useful to do a little bit of research into the activists and historical figures honoured within it through character naming (such as Stuart in memory of Stuart Hall and Stephen in memory of Stephen Lawrence).

Naming, throughout the play, is about how the company connects with the script, enters into the work and understands the background of the piece. It's not for the audience to know or for actors to actually play the exact people named, but rather a dedication to them. In a spiritual gesture, those named are there present with the company but not present on the stage.

As suggested in the stage directions, projection is a really effective device through which to historically contextualise the events described by the characters. If you don't have access to a projector this could be pointed up through voice; e.g. one actor says '1948', followed by another who says, 'No dogs, no blacks, no Irish'.

Gold sugar gun scene

Matthew's provocation for this scene was about how you can make it feel pixelated and not as fully rendered as other scenes; how it can feel like a new performance language.

A key note from the writer on this scene was that, though on the surface the game looks like *Resident Evil*, they are in fact playing a radicalised version of *Resident Evil*: 'Hostile Environment'. The scene is about playing a game that means the slave trade and colonialism never happens. Sam is on a mission from the beginning of the scene, whereas Sim thinks it's a regular *Resident Evil*-style computer game. There is a pause in the game where the two talk about the background to Mansa Musa. They want to kill him so that no one hears about the continent of Africa. Sim and Sam are radicals.

Mojisola noted that the scene embodies a sugar rush (linking our contemporary dependence on sugar with the role sugar played in the slave trade). There might be pleasurable ensemble moments in this scene in which the ensemble all lick lollies, for example.

Useful research in approaching this scene is into Mansa Musa (the richest person who lived). This is an opportunity for black young people and white young people to unpack the stereotype of Africans before Europeans came.

The group's discoveries in creating several versions of this scene were:

- Working with a limited sequence of movements that repeat; finding a mechanical physical language.
- Layering as sound design a repetitive beat under the scene, which the characters' physical movements and lines sat in sync with.
- Really investing in playing on the video controller pads.
- Creating emoji-like gestures in the repeated refrain of 'OK' and 'wait'.

Characterisation and casting

Character lists

Matthew outlined Stanislavksi lists as useful character exploration exercises:

- Each actor reads through the play just for their own character.
- They find and note any line of text that their character speaks describing themselves.
- They find and note any line of text in which other characters describe them.
- They find and note any line of text in which their character describes another character.

In addition to this, when actors are working with naturalistic scenarios that are close to themselves they can create two lists:

- One list of things they have in common with their character.
- One list of things they don't have in common with their character.

Matthew said that it's in the space between these two lists that the acting happens.

Monte Rosa

A note on accent from the writer was that it should ideally 'have the memory of German but don't push it. The accent is the least important thing here. Go for sense over accent. You could take liberties with the German if you're having trouble.'

Unless you have a very small cast, Monte Rosa could be cast through a multi-roling approach. Any woman/girl or person playing a woman/girl can step into the role. A black or white person can play her – she's a spirit.

Mojisola noted that Monte Rosa is written deliberately as a sweet, grandma-figure, a maternal old lady, but that there is no such thing as a sweet old lady. An inspiration for this character was one of Hitler's servants in one of his country homes who, in an interview which took place after the Second World War, still retained a pleasure, joy and pride in her role. In the same archival footage is a shot of her experiencing the shame of the Holocaust, too. Monte Rosa is complex like we are.

Structure

Acknowledging that the play is 'massive' in terms of its elements, Matthew and Mojisola led the group through three ways in which they could approach the play from the point of view of structure:

1 Sticking the play script up on the wall and annotating

Cut out and stick up the actual script pages (cutting into half or quarter pages where a scene ends before the end of a page) and stick them to the wall. If a scene is three pages long, this is represented by a column of three pages, one below the other. There are as many rows as scenes in the play.

Once the play is stuck up on the wall you can then begin to annotate it visually using colour lighters or marker pens.

Examples of annotations:

- Red underlines detonating all common room scenes.
- Green boxes squaring all Monte Rosa scenes.
- Unique sections or transitions highlighted in yellow.

Matthew outlined that this exercise can be used as a tool to offer you a sense of how much time you might want to spend on each scene by noting how long the scenes are in relation to one another (as written on the page). A discovery for the group was that the gold sugar gun gamers scene was particularly long, for example, and so would need a good amount of time allotted to rehearsing it.

The exercise was also helpful to get a sense of the rhythm of the scenes; for example, noting how often the Monte Rosa scenes reoccurred.

2 The scene chart

Matthew then drew up an example of a chart (see below) in which you list the play's page numbers in one column on the left and fill in the following information in the columns to the right: scene, characters, location and miscellaneous information (such as special theatrical moments or things to watch out for).

The scene chart

Page	Scene	Characters	Location	Misc.
1				
2				
3				
4	1	Full company as Davids	House of Commons	Dogs
5				
6	2	Ola, Xia, Ali, Kit, Zhe	Common Room	
7				
8				Blackout
9	3	Monte Rosa	Common Room	

3 The storyboard

Mojisola often draws a storyboard of the scene as she's writing it. She offered that, as a director, you might storyboard a scene before you work on it.

Production, staging and design

Matthew offered a set of provocations that the director Sacha Wares asks of a production, using parameters to encourage lateral thinking:

- What are you told that the environment should look like and what is necessary?
- Push the play through a set of slightly different filters, reading the play for different qualities, including: colour, light, time, weather, objects, smells, imagery, nature, animals, liquids, boundaries.
- Look for written words (or signage) that appear in the play (as performed).
- How would you tell the story if you could only use light? Or if you could only use the furniture you have in the room you rehearse in?

- Imagine a brilliant theatre-maker who has a really clear style, someone whose work you know (e.g. Katie Mitchell, Rupert Goold, Ivo van Hove). What aesthetic qualities would their production have, how would it feel, sound or look, how would they have it staged or designed?
- What's the £500,000 version of this show and what's the £5 version?

Use the above provocations as obstacles to limit and liberate yourself and to trigger the imagination in different directions.

Exercises for use in rehearsals

Exercise: call and response

A fun, easy, choral call and response exercise.

The caller begins a syncopated rhythmic phrase with the words (with a short pause represented by a *): 'Shake * ba-na-na, shake shake * banana.'

The group then calls back: 'Shake * banana, shake shake * banana.'

You then pass this rhythmic phrase around the circle, with each group member supplementing 'shake' with their own original verb, e.g. 'eat' or 'paint', with its relevant fun gesture phrase, which is also echoed by the group.

Exercise: conductor's circle

A group music-making exercise. The group stand together in a circle. Led by the conductor in the centre, the group make a choral soundscape of character lines and key words/phrases/sound effects from the play. The conductor's role is to orchestrate this soundscape, bringing combinations of voices in and out to create interesting dynamics. At times there are many voices and at times there are only a few. The conductor uses their instinct to decide what sounds and lines should be in the mix.

You can start it off as a facilitator, but then the individual group members can take it on and run it. It's a really nice one to hand over to the group, particularly if you aren't confident with the rhythm yourself.

The conductor generally works through gesture, controlling the rhythm of each phrase – when it will land and its dynamic, throwing in the odd word of explanation if needed.

The conductor's tools/gestures are: *a point* (which cues each person), *keep it going*, *louder*, *quieter*, *stretch*, *shrink*, *cut*.

In the first round, the conductor brings in the voice of each group member one at a time with a clear, bold pointing gesture. Each group member offers in a phrase from the play (that they have independently chosen), such as: 'Monte Rosa', 'free education', 'English is a bitch', 'chill', 'the children' or a rhythmic 'woof woof'. The conductor brings in all participants in the group, playing phrases off one another and playing some phrases together, but doesn't loop any phrases. Each participant keeps to the same phrase.

In the second round, the conductor now encourages each participant to add their own seasoning or flavour to their phrase (keeping the same phrase), looping some phrases (with the 'keep it going' gesture) to create a rhythmic or melodic baseline layer on top of which other phrases can layered.

As the exercise goes on the conductor might build in lots of voices (indeed, all of the group's voices) so that the group have created a cacophony/symphony of phrases/characters/sounds/rhythmic moments from the play. Matthew noted to the group that by the end of the exercise this becomes a kind of story.

The conductor might let this ride out for a little and then begin to bring out elements one by one with their 'cut' gesture. The conductor might point up certain sounds, asking many voices to take that one sound on (probably a sound that offers a clear bottom-line rhythm) to create a simpler but bolder/dynamic sound mix.

Exercise: counting with names

This is an exercise which is represented in the play when the university students enter into this game as a ritual before they begin the Ouija board.

To begin with, the group try to count from one to twenty, with each group member adding the next consecutive number. If two speakers clash vocally, the group must begin again. The aim is to get to twenty (or beyond!) without any clashes.

The next stage is to supplement numbers with participant names. The same rules apply: you are trying to say all the group's names in one flow without any clashes, if there is a vocal clash (two names called out at the same time) then you start again. Each participant needs to say their name once only. If the group find this a bit easy, you could ask them to close their eyes to increase the stakes/risk of clashing.

Exercise: resistance and the voice

Matthew referenced two Cicely Berry (an influential voice coach) resistance exercises that could be used to find a grounded vocal quality (useful for scenes such as the David Lammy Prologue):

- A group of people hold back a singular actor as they work through the speech, and try (safely) to push through the group. The group then release their hold and the actor starts again from the beginning of the speech, retaining some of the vocal quality they found in working with resistance.

- The actor works through the speech whilst pushing against a wall and potentially also intoning the words (speaking them with elongated vowels in a low, drone-like chanting quality). The actor then releases from the wall and speaks the speech back out into the room, again retaining some of the grounded vocal resonance experienced whilst pushing physically against the wall.

From a workshop led by Matthew Xia
with notes by Nathan Crossan-Smith

Tuesday

by Alison Carr

Tuesday is light, playful and nuanced in tone. And a little bit sci-fi. The play centres on an ordinary Tuesday that suddenly turns very weird indeed when a tear rips across the sky over the school yard. Not only that, but it starts sucking up pupils and staff while at the same time raining down a whole new set of people. But, then, that's what happens when parallel worlds collide!

Confusion reigns as the 'Us' and 'Them' try to work out what is going on. How are Ash and Magpie identical? Can Billy cope with having his sister back? Who is Franky? Eventually, though, cracks appear between the two groups. As the air here starts to disagree with the 'Them', the race is on to try to get things back to how they were and safely return everyone to the universe they came from.

The play touches on themes of friendship, sibling love, family, identity, grief, bullying, loneliness and responsibility. And in the process we might just learn something about ourselves as well as some astronomical theories of the multiverse!

Cast size
9–50, any gender
Suitable for all ages

Alison Carr's recent theatre credits include: *The Last Quiz Night on Earth* (Box of Tricks Theatre Company); *Caterpillar* (Theatre503/Stephen Joseph Theatre); *Hush* (Paines Plough/RWCMD/Gate Theatre); *Remains* (troublehouse theatre, Octagon Theatre); *Clothes Swap Theatre Party* (Forward Theatre Project, Derby Theatre); *Iris* (Live Theatre, Winner – Writer of the Year, Journal Culture Awards); *Fat Alice* (Traverse Theatre/Oran Mor/Aberdeen Performing Arts); *The Soaking of Vera Shrimp* (Winner, Live Theatre/The Empty Space Bursary Award); *A Wondrous Place* (Northern Spirit, tour); *Can Cause Death* starring Olivier Award-winning actor David Bradley (Forward Theatre Project, National Theatre, Northern Stage and Latitude Festival). Radio credits include *Dolly Would* (*Afternoon Play*, BBC Radio 4) and *Yackety Yak* (*The Verb*, BBC Radio 3).

Characters

Note, for the purposes of writing the script the principal characters have been allocated a sex (5F and 4M) but this can be changed as required.

'US'	'THEM'
Alex (*F*)	**Magpie** (*F*)
Ash (*F*)	**Sam** (*F*)
Mack (*F*)	**Jay** (*M*)
Franky (*M*)	**Cam** (*M*)
Billy (*M*)	

Plus an ensemble of as many performers as you wish including –

Ali	**Figure 1 and Figure 2**
Remy	
Charlie	
Lou	
Naz	

Notes

The dialogue should be performed with pace.

Direct address to the audience telling them the story of what happened is in italics.

Dialogue between characters in the moment is not.

Lines that are not allocated to named characters can be performed by individuals or multiple speakers. I'd encourage the performers to find characters in the unallocated lines too.

There are no breaks between the narration sections and the scenes, and there are no scene changes. Each section flows quickly and smoothly into the next.

There is no set and there are minimal props.

≡ *It happened on a Tuesday.*

≡ *Which is surprising, cos nothing decent ever happens on a Tuesday.*

≡ *Everyone knows that.*

≡ *Tuesdays – they're nothing.*

≡ *They're grey.*

≡ *Beige.*

≡ *Lame.*

≡ *Boring.*

≡ *But this Tuesday . . .*

It started off the same as any other.

Wake up.

≡ *Alarm.*

≡ *Snooze.*

≡ *Alarm.*

≡ *Snooze.*

≡ *Alarm.*

≡ *Snooze.*

≡ (AS A PARENT SHOUTING) *Get up!*

All   *Groan.*

≡ *Have a wash.*

≡ *Get dressed.*

≡ *Have breakfast.*

≡ *Brush teeth.*

≡ *Shoes on.*

≡ *Coat on.*

≡ *Bag on.*

All   *And go to Lane End School.*

≡ *Even the name is dull. It's not even at the end of a lane.*

≡ *Old concrete buildings and plastic annexes. A sports field. A yard. A car park.*

≡ *Just a normal school.*

≡   *We do Breakfast Club before lessons. Have some cornflakes and then do aerobics. It's fun.*

≡   *It's knackering.*

≡   *Morning registration.*

≡   *Here, miss.*

≡   *Here, sir.*

≡   *A sneaky last look at our phones before we have to put them away for the day.*

≡   (AS A TEACHER) *Is that a phone?*

All   *No.*

≡   (AS A TEACHER) *Give it to me. Now. You'll get it back at the end of the day.*

All   *Groan.*

First lesson.

≡   *Physics.*

≡   *English.*

≡   *Art.*

≡   *P.E.*

≡   *History.*

All   *Bell rings.*

Break.

≡   (AS A TEACHER) *Wait. The bell is for me, not for you. You are dismissed.*

All   *Break.*

Second lesson.

≡   *Geography.*

≡   *Chemistry.*

≡   *French.*

≡   *Business Studies.*

≡   *Maths.*

All   *Lunchtime.*

≡   *And that's when it happened.*

≡   *It started off the same as every other Tuesday lunchtime.*

I was eating a Mars Bar.

≡   *I was in detention.*

≡   *I was kicking the football with Josh and Tia.*

≡   *I was standing in the lunch queue.*

≡   *I was on the toilet.*

≡   *I was biting my nails.*

≡   *I was avoiding Mr Simmons.*

≡   *I was sneezing.*

≡   *I was crying.*

≡   *I was playing hockey.*

≡   *I was talking to Alex.*

Alex   Shhhhh. Can you hear that?

≡   What?

Alex   That.

≡   *It started off quiet. A low hum. You barely noticed it.*

Just a scratching out of sight, an irritation in your ear.

≡   *Suddenly, though, everyone was pouring into the yard from all directions. Hundreds of us. All of us. From every year. Staff too. Flocking into the yard to see what that sound was.*

≡   *The sound that was building and growing to a loud squealing.*

≡   *A high screeching.*

≡   *A cracking.*

≡   *A breaking.*

≡   What is it? Where's it coming from?

Alex   The sky.

≡   Are you sure?

Alex   Positive.

≡   *We all looked up. We squinted.*

≡   *Peered.*

≡   *Stared.*

All   *Gasped.*

≡   *The sky over the school yard started changing colour. From turquoise to sapphire to aqua to navy, and every shade in-between.*

≡   *It swirled and pulsed. It was beautiful.*

≡   *It was scary.*

≡   *Then suddenly it ripped apart. Loud scraping. Blue away from blue. Clouds torn in two. A fat, jagged tear across the sky.*

≡   *For a moment nobody moved. Nobody breathed.*

Then whoosh. We started to be pulled up towards the tear.

≡   *A force. A strength that yanked us off our feet and dragged us up towards the rip in the sky.*

≡   *Those on the outskirts found themselves being dragged along on their toes towards it, lifting and falling.*

Ali (BEING DRAGGED ALONG)   I can't stop!

≡   *But those right underneath it were whipped straight up into the air, sucked up into the gaping split.*

Remy (IS SUCKED UP)   Aaarghhhhhh!

≡   *Quick thinkers grabbed for the nearest thing to cling on to – a bollard.*

≡   *A drain cover.*

≡   *A railing.*

≡   *Some kept their grip.*

≡   *Others didn't.*

≡   *And not everyone had something nearby to grab on to.*

≡   *The sky groaned and creaked as pupils and staff disappeared up through the tear.*

≡   *The birch tree planted in memory of the old headteacher got unearthed, its roots flapping as it spun up into the sky.*

Ash   But – look – it's stuck. The trunk's gone through the tear but the leaves are blocking it.

≡   *The pull stopped. Those still in the air dropped out on to the ground. Piles of us – confused.*

≡   *Frightened.*

≡   *Relieved.*

≡ (AT THE BOTTOM OF A PILE?)   *Squashed.*

≡   *The birch tree quivered and shook, but it stayed plugging the hole.*

Alex   This is our chance. Now! Let's get inside.

≡   Come on. Don't look back.

≡   Hurry up!

≡   Come on!

Alex   Is everyone inside?

≡   I think so. Wait. Who's that?

≡   Where?

≡   Over there. It's Miss Moore. What's she doing?

≡   Making sure everyone's in, I suppose.

Alex   She needs to get inside. The tree's not going to hold.

≡   *And it didn't. It disappeared through the tear with a 'thwoop'.*

≡   *Miss Moore followed close behind, 'thwoop'. Gone.*

≡   *All of this on a Tuesday lunchtime.*

≡   *It was really, really weird.*

≡   *The teachers – those that were left – were wide-eyed and ashen as they ushered us along to the Assembly Hall. Even Mr Chandra who's always bragging about that time he dodged a stampeding cow –*

≡   *A stampeding cow?*

≡   *Yeah. He was on holiday and –*

≡   *Anyway.*

≡   *We all stood blinking and shivering in the hall as they called the registers.*

FOR THIS SECTION THE NAMES AND RESPONSES (OR NO RESPONSES FOR THE MISSING) CAN OVERLAP AND EXTRA NAMES CAN BE ADDED IF REQUIRED UNTIL WE GET TO **ASH** WHO IS CALLED LAST.

≡   Joey?

≡   Here.

≡   Evie?

≡   Here.

≡   Mack?

Mack   Here.

≡   Franky?

Franky   Here.

≡   Yasmin?

≡   Here.

≡   Leon? Leon?

≡   *Mrs Turner took our class register cos Mr Humphries was gone, last seen spinning up through the sky.*

≡   I was meant to have detention with him later.

≡   Not anymore.

≡   Chloe?

≡   Here.

≡   Billy?

Billy   Here.

≡   Ash?

Ash   Here

}   BOTH AT THE SAME TIME

Magpie   Here

ASH AND **MAGPIE** EMERGE. THEY ARE IDENTICAL. THIS COULD BE ACHIEVED BY THE TWO ACTORS WEARING THE SAME OUTFITS, HAVING THE SAME PHYSICALITY, WAY OF SPEAKING, ETC. HAVE FUN WITH IT.

THE REACTION FROM THE OTHERS WILL ALSO PLAY INTO THIS – IS THERE POINTING AND WHISPERING AT THE TWO OF THEM? DOES THE GROUP MOVE AWAY, ISOLATING THEM?

Ash   Hang on.

Magpie   Hang on.

THEY STARE AT EACH OTHER. MIGHT THEY MIRROR EACH OTHER'S MOVEMENTS?

Ash   You're –

Magpie   You're –

Ash   No.

Magpie   No.

Ash   Stop copying me.

Magpie   Stop copying me.

Ash   Why do you look the same as me?

Magpie   Erm, it's you who looks the same as me.

Ash   Freckles here, here, here.

Magpie   Wonky ears. Trying to hide them under your hair.

Ash   Can you do that thing with your little finger?

Magpie   Yeah.

Have you got that scar on your knee?

Ash   Yeah.

Magpie   From falling off your bike?

Ash   Yeah. It hurt.

Magpie   Really hurt.

Ash   What's your favourite crisps?

Magpie   Pickled Onion Monster Munch.

What's your favourite colour?

Ash   Green.

Have you got a dog?

Magpie   No. A cat.

Both   Called Errol.

Cool.

≡   *Two identical people. One who hadn't been here before the sky tore in two.*

≡   *And as the sky swirled outside and the windows shook, we actually looked around us and realised that this was only the start of it.*

≡   *As well as Ash suddenly having a double and the people who were missing, there were new people too. People we hadn't seen before.*

≡   *There was at least one teacher I didn't know and quite a few kids.*

It's a big school, we don't all know everyone, but these kids – no one knew them. No one.

≡   *And then there were the ones who we did recognise – classmates, teammates, friends – who were acting different. Dressed different. Being, just, different.*

Charlie   That was weird.

≡   Sorry?

Charlie   That, out there. One minute we're talking to Emma, the next the ground opens up.

≡   The ground?

Charlie   Yeah.

≡   Why are you talking to me, Charlie?

Charlie   We're best friends.

≡   No we're not. We haven't spoken since Juniors.

Charlie   What?

≡   *And slowly the hall split in two. Split into Us and Them.*

Ash   *Faces that were the same as ours, but not us.*

≡   *Faces we didn't know, that we'd never seen before.*

≡   *Faces that we did know but were different. We stared.*

≡   *Blinked.*

≡   *Smiled.*

≡   *Frowned at each other across the Hall.*

≡   (US) Who are you?

≡   (THEM) Who are you?

≡   (US) We asked first

≡   (THEM) What's going on?

≡   (US) You tell us.

≡   (THEM) We don't know.

One minute everything was normal and then an earthquake or, I don't know.

The ground opened up, a zig zag across the school yard. We got dragged towards it and fell through.

≡   (US) The ground didn't open, the sky opened.

≡   (THEM) The ground.

≡   (US) The sky.

≡   (THEM) The ground.

≡   (US) The sky.

≡   *And just when we thought things couldn't get any more bizarre –*

Sam   You haven't said my name, miss.

≡   Who said that?

Sam   Me. You haven't said me. I'm here.

SAM PUSHES HER WAY THROUGH FROM BEHIND A GROUP.

Billy   Sam?

Sam   Billy. I'm so glad you're okay.

Billy Sam, is that you?

Sam I'm scared, what's going on?

Billy It's you. (HE HUGS HER TIGHT.)

≡ Is that . . .?

≡ It can't be.

≡ It is.

≡ I don't believe it. It's not possible.

≡ She's right there.

≡ But how?

≡ Who is it?

≡ Billy's sister Sam.

≡ Sam who died. Last year. Run over by a driver who was texting.

Sam What? What are they saying?

≡ This can't be happening.

What . . . what if we're all dead?

≡ I don't think so.

≡ Is this heaven?

≡ I hope not.

Alex We're not all dead.

≡ Good.

Alex It's obvious really, what's happened.

≡ Is it?

Alex Parallel universes.

All What?!

Alex Parallel universes. And our world and their world have collided.

What else could it be?

EVERYONE (UMS) AND (AHS) BUT CAN OFFER NO ALTERNATIVE.

Alex I've been waiting for something like this to happen. I'm surprised it's taken so long. The signs have been building up for a while.

≡ Have they?

Alex Of course.

≡ Like what signs?

Alex   The friction from the different universes piling up and getting squashed together has obviously been causing build-ups of radiation –

≡ (SARCASTIC)   Obviously.

Alex   Which has been making people act weird. Make odd decisions.

≡   But isn't that just everyone all the time?

Alex   Okay. Making people act weirder than normal. Make odder decisions.

Get more irritated and angrier with each other.

An increase in anxiety and depression.

Jay   Headaches?

Alex   Yeah.

Jay   Being tired but not being able to sleep?

Alex   Yeah.

Jay   I knew it.

Alex   This is all a bit of a relief, really. It's good to know there's been a reason for it all.

Jay   I was worried we were all just going mad.

Alex   Me too.

I'm Alex, by the way.

Jay   Jay.

Alex   Are you from up there?

Jay   Yeah.

Alex   But you knew this was coming too?

Jay   I knew something was going on, but no one would listen.

≡   Sorry to interrupt, but there's no such thing as parallel universes.

Both   Yes there is.

≡   Says who?

Alex   Me.

Jay   Us.

Alex   Isn't the fact that all this is happening all the proof you need?

≡   I don't understand.

≡   Me neither.

≡   It's just stupid.

Alex   No it's not. There's loads of different theories about parallel universes – what they are, where they are, if they are.

Jay   Some people say that déjà vu is evidence that parallel universes are real. Or the Mandela Effect.

≡   The what effect?

Jay   People en masse remembering things differently. Google it.

≡   I'm still confused.

Alex   Okay. Clearly what's occurred is, the new people, the doubles, the different people – their universe and our universe have collided which caused a tear.

≡   As simple as that?

Alex   Why not?

Here the tear is in the sky and people got pulled up and out.

Jay   There the tear is in the ground and people got sucked down and in.

≡   But in all the chaos and everyone whizzing around in the sky, we didn't realise at first that people were falling into our Universe too?

Alex   Exactly.

≡   But how are there different universes? Where do they come from?

Alex   That's the question.

Jay   I'm sure between us . . . two heads are better than one.

Alex (UNSURE?)   Yeah. Okay.

Jay   We should start by making a list. Working out who is where.

Alex   That's exactly what I was going to suggest.

So first – who is missing from this universe?

≡   Miss Moore.

≡   Mr Humphries.

≡   Half the netball team.

≡   A whole load of Year 9s.

MACK APPEARS. SHE'S CLEARLY LOOKING FOR SOMEBODY.

Mack   Has anybody seen Ali and Remy?

≡   They're usually glued to you. Where you are, they are.

Mack   Exactly. So where are they?

≡   Where have you looked?

Mack   All over.

≡   They've gone.

Mack   I know that. Where?

≡   Where do you think? (POINTS TO THE SKY.)

Mack   No.

≡   I saw them. They spiralled up into the sky, around and around each other so fast I couldn't tell which was which anymore, higher and higher. Then gone.

Mack   But what about me?

≡   You'd rather be up there?

Mack   Dunno. It depends what it's like.

They'll wish I was there. They're going to be lost without me.

≡   They've got each other. Who have you got, Mack?

Mack   What do you mean? Loads of people. Everyone knows me.

BUT **MACK** IS STANDING NOTICEABLY ALONE. SHE SCURRIES AWAY.

Jay   And who do we have from the other universe who fell in?

≡   A few Year 7 boys. They're in a huddle in the corner.

≡   That teacher over there in the ugly cardigan.

≡   Yeah, that cardigan is definitely from another dimension.

≡   There's Ash and Other Ash –

Magpie   Can you not call me 'Other Ash'. My name's Magpie.

Ash   Why do they call you that? No one calls me Magpie.

Magpie   Cos I like shiny things.

Ash   What?

Magpie   My grandad called me it once as a joke but it stuck.

Ash   I don't get it.

Magpie   I take things. Sometimes. Things that aren't necessarily mine.

Ash   You steal things?

Magpie   Just little things. It's no big deal.

And actually it's not even accurate cos I Googled it and magpies are scared of shiny objects so, yeah.

Ash   What kind of things do you steal?

Magpie Sweets. Crisps. Jewellery. Make-up. Anything.

Nothing big.

Everyone does it.

Ash I don't.

Magpie Don't look at me like that.

Alex Is there anyone else from up there?

≡ Billy's sister, Sam.

Alex Yes. Sam who died here but didn't die up there.

Jay Is that everyone?

Alex Well, there's you.

Jay Me. Yes.

And although we're not doubles like Ash and Magpie or related like Billy and Sam, there's definitely some similarities between us.

Alex Definitely.

Jay Have you lived around here for a long time?

Alex My whole life.

You?

Jay Just moved here last year, my mam got a new job.

Alex What's your mam called?

Jay Sue.

What's your dad called?

Alex Tony.

Yours?

Jay I don't know my dad.

≡ And, you know, one of you is a girl and one of you is a boy.

Both So?

Jay It's only the chance of which sperm is the quickest that decides your sex.

Alex In this universe a sperm carrying a X chromosome got to the egg first.

Jay In my universe a Y chromosome won the race. That's all it is.

≡ *While we tried to work out what was happening, outside the sky continued to swirl and churn, changing colour like a bruise. But no one new fell in. We figured they'd probably all taken cover too.*

≡   *We could hear sirens wailing in the distance and catch the flicker of blue lights flashing, but no one came.*

Mack   Why is no one coming to help us?

≡   How can they? Anyone who comes near will get pulled up through the tear.

Mack   Urgh. My phone's totally dead. Is anyone's phone working?

≡   No.

≡   No.

≡   There's no dial tones or WiFi on anything.

Mack   This is an actual nightmare.

≡   Do you think this is just happening here or everywhere?

Mack   I don't know.

I hope my brother's ok.

≡   I hope my dad's ok.

≡   I hope my step-sister's ok.

≡   I hope my mam's ok.

≡   I hope my nan's ok.

≡   I hope my hamster's ok.

≡   *The Them seemed alright. We were all just scared.*

≡   *Confused.*

≡   *Hungry.*

≡   *The two sides merged. We chatted.*

≡   *Laughed.*

≡   *Worried.*

≡   *Hoped.*

≡   *Waited. All we could do was wait.*

CAM LOITERS. HE'S KEEPING TO HIMSELF, BUT **MACK** SEES HIM.

Mack   You. You.

Cam   Me?

Mack   Yes. I don't know you. Are you from up there?

Cam   Yes.

Mack   Why didn't you speak up when they were asking who else fell through?

CAM SHRUGS.

Mack   Did you really fall through the ground from another universe?

Cam   S'pose so.

Mack   What's your name?

Cam   Cam.

Mack   Why don't we have a Cam here?

CAM SHRUGS.

Mack   Do you have a me up there?

Cam   Dunno.

Mack   Oh you'd know. Everybody knows me.

CAM SHRUGS.

Mack   What's that?

Cam   An orange.

Mack   A what?

Cam   An orange.

Mack   What's that?

Cam   You don't have oranges?

Mack   No

Cam   It's like, a fruit.

Mack   A what?

Cam   You don't have fruit?

Mack   No.

Cam   It's good for you.

Mack   What does an orange taste like?

Cam   Like . . . sort of like . . . it tastes like . . . An orange.

Mack   Like chicken?

Cam   No.

Mack   Like liquorice?

Cam   No.

Mack   Like cabbage?

Cam   No.

Mack   That's a shame.

Cam   Sorry.

Mack   I'm joking with you, stupid. I know what an orange is.

Why are you holding it?

Cam   It's all I've got from up there.

Mack   It'll get sorted out, they'll find a way to get you back.

Cam   I don't know if I want to go back.

Mack   Why not?

Cam   Here might be better.

Mack   Why do you say that?

Cam   You know when you just want the ground to open and swallow you up?

Mack   Yeah.

Cam   It did. And it was great.

Mack   What were you doing when it happened?

Cam   Eating my lunch behind the new science block.

Mack   What new science block?

Cam   Our school has a new science block.

Mack   Ours doesn't. Mind you, I hate science.

Why were you eating your lunch there?

Cam   It's quiet. And they leave me alone.

Mack   They?

Cam   I'd been off school for ages with glandular fever. Today was my first day back.

Mr Simmons pointed me out in registration, said 'welcome back' and made everyone turn around and say it too.

All   Welcome back, Cam.

Cam   He's horrible, Mr Simmons. I hate him. Do you have him here?

Mack   Yeah.

Cam   What's he like?

Mack   Horrible.

Cam   So everyone said 'welcome back' and I said 'thank you' and smiled. Tried to.

Sometimes in photos I think I'm smiling then when I see it I look like I'm having a really difficult poo.

Mack   I look great in photos.

Cam   The morning dragged so slowly but eventually it was lunchtime.

I was just starting my sandwich when they came around the corner –

FIGURE 1 AND **FIGURE 2** EMERGE. **CAM'S** MEMORY OF THE INCIDENT PLAYS OUT –

Figure 1   What you doing?

Cam   Just having my lunch.

Figure 2   What you having it round here for?

Cam   Dunno.

Figure 1   Do you think you're too good to sit with the rest of us?

Cam   No.

Figure 2   Have you got any crisps?

Cam   I'm not allowed crisps.

Figure 1   Why not?

Cam   Mam says.

Figure 2 (MOCKING)   Mam says.

Cam   I've got an orange.

CAM HANDS THE ORANGE TO **FIGURE 2**, WHO TAKES IT AND THROWS IT.

Figure 1   Go and get it, then. Go on.

Cam   It doesn't matter.

Figure 2   Course it does, it's your lunch. Look it's rolling into the yard.

CAM GOES FOR THE ORANGE BUT THEY KICK IT OUT OF REACH. THE **TWO FIGURES** SURROUND HIM, PUSHING HIM BETWEEN THEM.

Cam   Please, just leave me alone.

Figure 1   We're not doing anything.

Figure 2   Stop running into us.

THE PUSHING CONTINUES, UNTIL **CAM** PUSHES ONE OF THEM BACK. HARD. HARD ENOUGH FOR THE **FIGURE** TO FALL OVER.

Cam   Sorry. I'm sorry.

Figure 1   You've had this coming for ages.

Figure 2   You're so stuck up.

Figure 1   Think you're better than us. You're not.

Cam   And then the ground started to shudder and shake.

Figure 2   What's happening?

Cam   I didn't even see the crack open. It must have been right underneath me.

I thought I was falling down cos they'd pushed me over, but I just kept falling and falling and falling. Straight down. Arms by my side, legs straight, like when I went down the log flume that time at Alton Towers.

It was blackness all around me, darker and darker until it spat me out and I landed in the yard.

Just me, though. Not them.

Then something bounced off my head and dropped with a thud beside me.

It was my orange.

A GROUP WALK PAST. SOMEONE GLANCES OVER.

Mack (AGGRESSIVE)   What are you looking at?

THE GROUP HURRY AWAY.

Mack   Come over here, you can sit with me.

No one's sitting with me and I don't know why.

CAM AND **MACK** MOVE AWAY.

Billy   Are you warm enough?

Sam   Yes.

Billy   Are you hungry?

Sam   No.

Billy   Thirsty?

Sam   No.

Billy   Do you need the toilet?

Sam   I'm not a baby. If I need the toilet I'll go to the toilet.

Billy   Sorry. I just want to make sure you're okay.

Sam   I'm fine.

SAM STANDS UP.

Billy   Where are you going?

Sam   Nowhere. My foot's gone to sleep.

Billy   Is it okay?

Sam   It's just from sitting down for too long.

Urgh, you know when you get pins and needles.

Billy   It's horrible.

Sam?

Sam   What?

Billy   When Mam sees you she's going to . . . I don't know. Cry probably. Loads.

Sam   Yeah.

Billy   And swear. Loads.

Sam   It's funny, I only just saw her this morning.

Billy   It's been nearly a year since we saw you.

Sam?

Sam   What?

Billy   I love you.

Sam   What?

Billy   I love you. I want you to know that.

Sam   Okay.

Billy   I always wish I'd told you I love you more often. Every day.

And . . . I left Flopsy's cage open when he escaped that time but I let Mam blame you.

Sam   I knew it.

Billy   Sorry.

Sam   You don't need to say sorry.

Billy   I do, though. I always felt bad about that. She really shouted at you.

Sam   I know but it wasn't you, was it?

Billy   It was, I just said. I was feeding him and I didn't close the lock properly.

Sam   No, I mean it was my Billy, not you.

Billy   Oh.

Sam   I'm not being nasty.

Billy   I know.

Sam   Are you crying?

Billy   No. (BUT HE IS UPSET.)

FRANKY APPEARS, ANXIOUS. HE ACCIDENTALLY BUMPS INTO SAM. BILLY OVERREACTS AND SQUARES UP TO HIM.

Billy   Oi. Be careful.

Franky   Sorry.

Billy   Watch where you're going.

Franky   I'm sorry.

Billy   What use is sorry?

Sam   Stop it. It was nothing. I'm fine.

Billy   He's barging around like an idiot. Like he owns the place.

Sam   That's enough.

(TO **FRANKY**.) Sorry about him.

Billy   Don't apologise for me.

Sam   You do it, then.

Franky   He doesn't have to.

Sam   He does.

Go on.

Billy (QUIET)   I'm sorry.

Sam   I can't hear you.

Billy   I'm sorry.

Sam   I'm sorry who?

Billy   What? I don't know. I don't know who this is. Don't you?

Sam   Oh. You're from up there too?

Franky   Erm . . .

Sam   Sorry, I didn't realise. What's your name?

Franky   Franky.

Sam   I don't recognise you, sorry. Not that I know everyone, it's a big school.

There's quite a few of us fell through, isn't there.

Do you think it smells different here?

Franky   A don't know. A bit.

Sam   I do.

Billy   A bad smell?

Sam   No, just different. Like when you go round a friend's and their house smells different. Not bad, just different to your house.

Billy   I'm sorry you don't like the way we smell.

BILLY WALKS AWAY.

Sam (CALLING AFTER HIM)   I didn't say that.

(TO **FRANKY**.) He's in a mood.

Franky   Why?

Sam   Cos I didn't say I love him back.

Franky   Why didn't you say it?

Sam   Cos I don't. I love Billy, my Billy, but he isn't him.

I'm not being horrible but I might look the same and sound the same as his sister, but I'm not her.

And I'm sorry his Sam died, but it's not my fault.

The things that have happened here, they're not my problem, you know. They're not our problem, are they?

BILLY REAPPEARS.

Billy   Mr Chandra is taking groups of us to the canteen for snacks.

I saved you a space in the first group.

Sam   Okay. Are you coming, Franky?

Billy   I only saved one space.

Franky   I can wait.

Sam   See you in a bit then.

Franky   Okay.

SAM AND **BILLY** GO.

Franky   Not my problem.

Not. My. Problem.

A GROUP NEARBY LAUGHS AMONG THEMSELVES.

FRANKY MOVES OVER TO THEM.

Franky   Hi.

≡   Hello.

Franky   I'm Franky, Other Franky, from up there. Can I sit with you?

THE GROUP HAPPILY MAKE A SPACE FOR **FRANKY**.

ELSEWHERE **MACK** AND **CAM** SIT TOGETHER.

Mack   I'm hungry.

Cam   It'll be our turn soon.

Mack   But I'm hungry now. Let's eat your orange.

Cam   I don't know.

Mack   Just holding it isn't helping anyone. Come on.

MACK PULLS SOME PEEL OFF.

Mack   Urghh. It's all rotten inside.

Your mam's giving you rotten oranges to eat?

Cam   No.

Mack   It stinks. Go and throw it away.

SHE PUSHES **CAM** AWAY, ALTHOUGH HE DOESN'T GET RID OF THE
ORANGE.

NAZ APPROACHES **MACK**.

Naz   Where's your little friends, Mack?

Mack   You know where, they got pulled up.

Naz   I don't think I've ever seen you by yourself before.

Mack   Unlike you, Naz, I have friends.

Naz   I've got friends too.

Mack   Where?

Naz   Here.

A SMALL GROUP EMERGES.

Naz   I think you know them. You've made their lives miserable for years.

Mack   No I haven't.

Naz   You've made my life miserable.

Mack   It's not my fault you're such a loser.

Yeah, can you all take a step back please.

BUT THEY DON'T AND **MACK** IS NERVOUS ALTHOUGH SHE'S
TRYING NOT TO SHOW IT.

Naz   Not so brave without Ali and Remy here, are you.

DO THEY TIGHTEN AROUND **MACK**? DO THEY START TO PUSH AND
JOSTLE HER?

Cam (QUIET)   Leave her alone.

(A BIT LOUDER.) Leave her.

Naz   Get lost.

Cam (LOUDER)   Leave her.

Naz   What do you care?

You don't know what she's like.

Cam   And this makes you just as bad.

Naz   It'll do her good to know what it's like to be on the receiving end.

It might make her think twice next time before she says or does something nasty.

Cam   How bad is she?

Naz   The worst.

Mack   Cam, I'm not. They're just soft. Can't take a joke.

Naz   This is our only chance.

Mack   Too scared to take me on normally.

Naz   No, you've always got your sidekicks with you.

Mack   They're my friends.

Naz   They're as scared of you as we are.

Mack   No they're not.

Naz   I bet they're glad to be up there, free of you.

Mack   Don't say that.

Naz   What do you say, Cam?

Cam   I don't know.

THE GROUP TIGHTEN AROUND **MACK** BUT **CAM** TRIES TO PULL **NAZ** BACK.

Cam   No.

Naz   Too late.

Cam (CALLING TO A TEACHER)   Miss! Miss!

THE GROUP SCATTER LEAVING **MACK** SHAKEN.

Cam   Are you okay?

Mack   Course I am. I could have taken them on.

Cam   It's scary, isn't it. Being one against a group, all with angry eyes and clenched fists.

Mack   I wasn't bothered.

Cam   You look bothered.

Mack   How come you'll stand up to that lot, but up there you hide behind the science block?

Cam   I don't know. It's different.

Mack   No it isn't.

Cam   You could just say thank you.

MACK DOESN'T REPLY.

MAGPIE APPEARS.

Magpie   I don't know if this is really obvious, but why don't we just go outside?

≡   What?

Magpie   All of us from up there, why don't we just go outside into the yard and get sucked back up into our universe?

REPLIES OF 'OH YEAH', 'OF COURSE', 'IT'S OBVIOUS', ETC.

Magpie   Come on then, let's go.

Alex   Wait, wait, wait.

You can't just go outside and get pulled back up.

Sam   Why not?

Alex   Who knows where you'll end up?

Billy   Yeah, Sam, it's not safe.

Sam   We'll end up back home.

Jay   Not necessarily.

This might not be the only breach.

If universes are colliding there could be tears all over. They might be moving and shifting all the time. You might get pulled up and land in a universe where the dinosaurs never got wiped out or which is entirely submerged in water.

Sam   Or we might end up back home.

Jay   Are you willing to take the risk?

And if it's that easy, why have none of our people up there just jumped back down? Or maybe they've tried and ended up in a different universe entirely. One where cats make the rules and keep humans as pets.

Sam   I don't want to be a cat's pet but I wouldn't mind seeing a dinosaur.

Alex   Let's all just wait for now until I work something better out.

ASH APPEARS, FURTIVE. SHE BECKONS TO **MAGPIE**.

Ash   Come here.

Magpie   What?

Ash   Here.

MAGPIE DOES. **ASH** HOLDS OPEN HER BAG – **MAGPIE** SEES INSIDE.

Magpie   Where did you get all that?

Ash   Everyone's bags are just lying about. No one's paying attention.

Magpie   You stole it all?

Ash   Yeah. It was easy.

Magpie   You should put it back.

Ash   Why? I thought you'd be pleased.

Magpie   Why would I be pleased?

Ash   I thought it would be fun.

Magpie   Was it?

Ash   Not now it isn't, you've spoiled it.

Magpie   You don't want to be like me, Ash.

You're good. People like you, respect you.

Ash   I'm boring.

Magpie   I'm jealous of boring. Being boring means your parents don't look so tired and disappointed all the time.

Ash   Being boring means my parents expect everything to be perfect. Top of the class, good at everything.

Magpie   The first thing I stole was two eyeshadows and a blusher from Topshop.

I was with my friend Katie. She took a denim jacket – walked out wearing it – but I was too scared to take anything that big. We got out of the shop and a security guard appeared. Katie legged it but I was too slow. The security guard brought me back inside and rang my mam.

Ash   I remember Katie.

Magpie   Yeah?

Ash   Her and her dad moved away years ago.

But I remember going to town with her most Saturdays, she was always trying to get me to nick stuff.

Magpie   You didn't, though.

Ash   No.

Magpie   Well, I did.

Mam came. She kept asking why I'd done it, I didn't have to steal. The shop didn't call the police, and she took me home and grounded me. But that time we spent, from the shop to home, it was the most time we'd spent together in ages.

I liked it.

I kept stealing. Sometimes I'd get away with it, sometimes I wouldn't. When I'd get caught Mam or Dad or both of them would come and shout at me.

They don't now, though. They've given up. But I can't stop myself cos maybe, maybe next time I do something wrong they'll be bothered again.

Ash   I'd love my parents to not be bothered about what I do, to leave me alone.

Magpie   You wouldn't if it happened.

Ash   Were they nice – the eyeshadows and blusher?

Magpie   No. Horrible.

Ash   You can still change.

Magpie   I don't know.

Ash   Do you want to?

Magpie   I think so. I don't really like who I am.

Ash   I don't think we're meant to, are we? Not yet.

LOU APPROACHES, ANGRY.

Lou   Oi, Ash. I saw you in my bag. Give me my money back.

Ash   I haven't got your money.

Lou   I saw you.

Ash   It was her. (POINTING AT **MAGPIE**.)

Magpie   What? No it wasn't. It was her.

Ash   It was her.

Magpie   It was her.

Lou   I don't know which one's which.

Ash   She took it. Magpie. The clue's in the name.

Magpie   Don't do this, Ash.

Ash   She stole your money, Lou.

Lou   I've told sir.

Ash   Good.

Lou   You lot, the Them. You can't be trusted.

≡   *And so it started. The divide.*

≡   *Suspicion.*

≡   *Accusation.*

≡   I've got money missing, too.

≡   And me.

≡   And my phone.

≡   And my headphones.

≡   Me too.

≡   And me.

Lou   Magpie can't be trusted. She needs to be separated from the rest of us.

Magpie   I didn't take your stuff.

Lou   Ash says you did.

Magpie   She's lying.

Lou   Ash wouldn't lie. She's not like that.

Put Magpie in a classroom on her own.

Sir says. Sir says you're to sit in there on your own and he'll guard outside.

≡   *The Year 7 boys from up there started to cry that they wanted to go home. It was really sad.*

≡   *It was really annoying.*

≡   *We were all getting tired.*

≡   *Cold.*

≡   *Bored.*

≡   *Scared that this wasn't stopping, that things weren't going back to normal.*

≡   *The novelty had worn off and it wasn't exciting anymore.*

≡   *These people, these strangers.*

≡   *Outsiders.*

≡   *Aliens.*

≡   *Asking so many questions and looking lost. Moaning. Complaining.*

≡   *Eating our snacks and drinking our drinks.*

≡   How long are they going to be here?

≡   Are they going to have to come home with us, cos we haven't got any room.

≡   What about the new ones – where will they go?

Mack   What will I tell Ali and Remy's parents about where they've gone?

≡   Are our people okay up there? Will your lot be treating them well?

≡   Our lot?

≡   Why did you have to fall into our school yard? Why us?

≡   I just want things to go back to normal.

SAM STARTS TO COUGH.

Billy   Are you okay?

Sam   Yes.

BUT SHE KEEPS COUGHING.

Billy   You don't sound okay.

Sam   There's just a tickle in my throat.

≡   *Then they all started to cough. Just a little at first, a tickle in their throats, but it didn't stop.*

≡   *Then another started.*

≡   *And another.*

≡   *And another.*

≡   *And another.*

≡   *Until all of them from up there were coughing and coughing and coughing.*

Billy   I'll get you some water.

EXIT **BILLY**.

Jay   I was worried this might happen.

Alex   Me too.

≡   What's going on?

Jay   The first clue was Cam's rotten orange. It was the first sign that our atmosphere isn't compatible –

Alex (INTERRUPTING)   It isn't compatible –

Jay   That's what I was saying.

Alex   I know.

Jay   Then why did you butt in? You never let me do the explaining.

Alex   I do. Loads.

Jay   You're always saying 'I'. I did this, I worked out. It's never 'we'.

Alex   Sorry, I'm not used to working with someone else.

Jay   Neither am I. But it's nice to have someone who understands, who 'gets it' like I do. Don't you think?

Alex   I don't know. It's . . . different.

Jay   Fine. Go ahead.

Alex   What?

Jay   Explain it.

You tell everyone what's happening and then you work out what to do if you're so amazing.

Alex   Jay . . .

BUT **JAY** TURNS AWAY.

Alex   Our atmosphere and their atmosphere having exactly the same mixture of nitrogen, oxygen, carbon dioxide and argon is really unlikely. Similar, maybe, but not the same.

Something in our atmosphere isn't compatible for them. Is bad for them, even.

≡   Are they going to be okay?

Alex   I don't know.

≡   Are they going to rot like Cam's orange?

Alex   I don't know.

≡   What's their atmosphere like up there?

Alex   I don't know.

≡   Are our people okay?

Alex   I don't know.

Jay   You don't know much, do you.

BILLY RETURNS WITH A GLASS OF WATER FOR **SAM**.

Billy   Here you go.

Sam   Thanks.

SAM DRINKS.

Billy   What's this?

Sam   What?

Billy   On your arm, let me see.

It's a rash. All red spots up your arm. Does it hurt?

Sam   It's itchy.

Magpie   Really itchy.

Alex   You're having an allergic reaction to the atmosphere.

Our air is irritating your skin.

≡   A rash is worse than a cough.

≡   A rash is contagious. Are we going to catch it?

Alex   Probably not.

≡   Probably isn't very certain. Are you sure?

Alex   Well, no.

≡   She said we're going to catch it.

Jay   She didn't.

≡   She said it's contagious.

Alex   I didn't.

≡   It's definitely contagious. Stay away.

≡   Move away.

≡   Get over there. Further.

Mack   Further.

Cam   Help me.

Mack   Don't touch me.

Cam   I helped you.

Mack   So?

≡   Further.

≡   Further.

≡   Further.

THE SIDES SEPARATE AGAIN INTO US AND THEM.

FRANKY IS RESISTING BEING PUT WITH THE THEM.

≡   You too, Franky. Get over there with Them, where you belong.

Franky   I'm not one of them.

≡   Yes you are.

Franky   I'm not.

≡   You said you are.

Franky   I lied. I'm Here Franky, not There Franky. I'm from here.

≡   There is no Here Franky.

Franky   Yes there is, just none of you notice me.

≡   Impossible. You're lying.

Franky   I'm not.

≡   That's what a liar would say.

Franky   I swear. I'm not coughing, I've not got a rash. Look.

≡   Why would you say you're from up there if you're not?

Franky   For a fresh start.

≡   What?

Franky   A do-over.

You don't know me cos I'm off school so much looking after my dad. He needs so much help.

I look after him and my little brother – I do the washing, the shopping, cooking, cleaning, all of it. And no matter how hard I try there's always more to do, it never stops. And if they think I can't cope, if they think I'm not doing well enough, we might get split up and I can't let that happen.

I love my dad and I know it's not his fault, but when you thought I was from up there it was such a weight off my shoulders. Other Franky doesn't have all that responsibility.

She said – Sam – she said it's not my problem.

I just wanted it not to be my problem for a little bit. Just so I could have a rest.

≡   I'm so sorry, Franky.

≡   I don't believe him.

≡   What?

≡   He's lying. He's one of them.

Franky   I'm not. Please.

≡   I believe him.

≡   So do I.

≡   I don't.

≡   Me neither. And do we really want to take the risk?

FRANKY IS PUSHED ACROSS WITH THE REST OF THE THEM.

BILLY IS IN WITH THE THEM, WITH **SAM**.

≡   Billy, come away.

Billy   No.

≡   Come over here to us where it's safe.

Billy   I'm staying with Sam.

Sam   They're right. You should go over there.

Billy   No.

Sam   You might catch it, whatever it is.

Billy   I don't care.

Sam   I'm scared.

Billy   So am I.

THEY WRAP THEIR ARMS AROUND EACH OTHER AND WON'T BE PARTED.

≡   *We didn't take our eyes off them.*

≡   *We didn't blink, didn't dare.*

≡   *How could we trust them? One was a thief.*

Magpie   It wasn't me.

≡   *One was a liar.*

Franky   I'm not lying.

≡   *Who knew what the rest of them were capable of?*

≡   *They cowered in a corner and we took turns to stand guard. Teachers too, it wasn't just us wanting to make sure we were kept apart.*

≡   *They coughed their dry coughs. Their skin got paler. Their eyes drooped.*

≡   *Outside it was starting to get dark but we could still hear the pull and the rattle from the tear in the sky.*

BILLY CRADLES **SAM** WHO – ALONG WITH THE REST OF THE THEM – HAS GOTTEN PROGRESSIVELY WORSE. SHE'S PALE, WEAK.

Billy   I'll get you some more water.

HE GETS UP TO GO BUT IS STOPPED BY **LOU**.

Billy   Let me past.

Lou   You can't leave. You might have it, might spread it.

Billy   I haven't.

Lou   You might.

Billy   I can't let her die again. You have to let me through.

BILLY TRIES TO BARGE PAST **LOU** BUT IS PUSHED BACK.

SAM IS ITCHING HER ARM.

Billy   Try not to scratch it. You're making it bleed.

Sam   Tell me the story about the chicken.

Billy   What?

Sam   Sorry, I forgot. My head's a bit fuzzy.

Mam used to tell me and my Billy this story when we were little –

Billy   About the chicken who felt *cooped* up so went on an *egg*-cellent holiday?

Sam   That's right.

Tell it to me.

Billy   It was silly, for babies.

Sam   Please.

Billy   I don't know if I can remember it very well.

Sam   Try.

Billy   It was a cold and rainy day on the farm –

Sam   On Sunnydale Farm.

Billy   Yes, Sunnydale Farm. It was cold and rainy but out in the field Farmer Giles was –

BUT **SAM** DESCENDS INTO ANOTHER COUGHING FIT.

Billy   I don't know what to do.

What do we do?

We can't just sit here doing nothing.

Alex   He's right. We have to do something.

Ash   But what?

Alex   Think. Think, Alex, if you're so clever.

Cam's orange was the first sign. Where is it? Can I see it?

ALEX TRIES TO GO TO **CAM** BUT **LOU** STOPS HER.

Alex   This could help them. Help all of us.

Cam   Here.

CAM THROWS THE ORANGE ACROSS TO **ALEX**. SHE STUDIES IT.

Alex   What do oranges have? Vitamin C. What does Vitamin C do?

Jay   Fights infection.

Alex   Yes. Fights infection.

Go to the kitchens, look for anything full of Vitamin C – oranges, broccoli, cauliflower, Brussels sprouts –

Jay   Urgh, no Brussels sprouts.

Alex   Yes Brussels sprouts. Go on, quickly.

≡   Not all of it, though. We need to keep enough back for us. Just in case.

≡   *The fruit and veg worked. A bit.*

≡   *It perked them up. A bit.*

≡   *But they were still coughing. Still had a rash.*

≡   *They needed to get back to their universe. And quickly.*

Alex   Okay, let's think.

Jay, can you help me? I really need you to help me.

Franky   We can all help.

Jay   Let's go back to the beginning.

What do we know for sure?

Sam   That there's another universe.

Ash   With different versions of us in it.

Billy   Or people we lost here.

Cam   Or people who aren't here at all.

Alex   That's right. Yes.

Magpie stole something, Ash didn't.

A driver texted, a driver didn't.

A school built a new science block, a school didn't.

Jay   Our mam met my dad. Our mam met someone else.

Alex   And so on.

Different outcomes from different choices.

Jay   And for every choice we make, the option we don't take happens in another universe that exists in its own time and space.

Mack   Okay, so how does that help us now?

Alex   I don't know.

Magpie   Can we undo what we did today? The choices we made? Stop it happening?

Ash   How?

Magpie   I don't know.

Jay   The choices we've made can't be undone.

It's not what we _did_ that matters –

Jay & Alex   It's what we do now.

Billy   And that shouldn't be us sitting here separately glaring at each other.

Ash   He's right. It needs all of us, together.

THE TWO SIDES MERGE. THEY'RE TALKING ANIMATEDLY, THROWING AROUND IDEAS.

≡   *We got all of the whiteboards out of the nearby classrooms and put them around the hall.*

≡   *We got all of the Bunsen burners and microscopes.*

≡   *All of the art supplies.*

≡   *All of the textbooks we could find, library books too – fiction and non-fiction, desperately looking for ideas.*

≡   *Crash mats.*

≡   *Music stands.*

≡   *One of those clicky wheels for measuring distance.*

≡   *Everything we could find to try and help us work out what to do.*

FROM ALL OF THE ACTIVITY, **CAM** EMERGES. BUT NO ONE CAN HEAR HIM.

Cam   All of us together.

≡   What about –?

Cam   All of us together.

≡   What if we –?

Cam   All of us together.

Mack   What are you saying? Shhh, Cam's saying something.

Cam   All of us together.

Ash   Yeah, it needs all of us working together. That's what I said. And we are.

Cam   A human chain.

Jay   Explain.

Cam   We make a human chain, one long enough to reach right up to the tear.

Then someone can climb up it and go through.

Magpie   I suggested going up through the tear earlier.

Cam   Yes but if the person is attached to the human chain and there's dinosaurs or giant cats it means they're not stuck in that universe with no way back.

THERE IS A BEAT AS EVERYONE THINKS ABOUT THIS, THEN A CLAMOUR OF 'NO', 'NO WAY', 'NOT A CHANCE', ETC.

Jay   Has anyone got a better idea?

THAT SHUTS EVERYONE UP.

Jay   Okay. We'll make the chain and then I'll go through.

Alex   You're not well enough.

Franky   I'll do it. I've let my dad down and my brother, wanting to be away from them. I'll go through, it's the least I can do.

≡   Franky, your dad needs you. And your brother. You can't risk it.

Franky   Who can risk it? We all have people who need us, who'll miss us.

Ash   I'll do it.

Alex   Why?

Ash   It's the least I can do.

Jay   What do you mean?

Ash   Magpie knows.

CREATION OF THE HUMAN CHAIN –

≡   *We started by creating the anchor, two teachers in the Assembly Hall tied to a pillar with bicycle chains.*

≡   Secure?

≡   Secure.

≡   *From there we snaked out to the door, gripping each other around our waists and tied together by whatever we could find – jumpers, tights, headphone cables. Anything to help us stay together.*

≡   *As soon as we edged the door open to outside we felt the pull.*

≡   Deep breath. We can do this. We have to.

≡   *The chain continued to right under the tear where we started to be lifted off the ground. Grips tightened.*

≡   *It was hard to tell how high we'd need to go. On and on we went, each new link crawling over the ones in front to add themselves to the human chain.*

Cam   Mack, your turn.

Mack   No way.

Magpie   We need everyone.

Mack   I can't.

Billy   You can.

Mack   I'm scared.

Sam   We're all scared.

Mack   I can't do it on my own.

Franky   You're not on your own, look at everyone.

You're next after Naz.

NAZ HOLDS A HAND OUT TO **MACK** BUT **MACK** DOESN'T TAKE IT.

Mack   I can't.

≡   *Up and up we went – Us and Them, one after another – reaching up towards the tear in the sky.*

Ash   Is it high enough?

Cam   I don't know, but there's no one left but us two.

≡   *Cam crawled up first, Ash close behind.*

The nearer they got to the tear, the stronger the pull.

Cam   It's still not quite long enough.

Ash   I could jump?

Cam   No. We need to all stay connected for this to work.

≡   *All seemed lost, but then –*

Cam   Mack!

Mack   It was boring down there on my own, there was no one to talk to.

≡   *Finally everyone was connected and Ash was able to stick her head up through the tear.*

All   Well?

Ash   It looks like our yard. It's not submerged in water. There's no dinosaurs or giant cats.

Hang on, someone's coming. They've got . . . it's a rope. They've got a rope. Why didn't we think of that?

≡   *Ash took the rope, pulled it through the tear and passed it down the human chain to the teachers at the bottom who tied it to the pillar in the Assembly Hall.*

≡   Secure?

≡   Secure.

≡   *The human chain climbed down and the rope held fast, joining our two universes together. It was time to swap back.*

Ash   I'm really sorry.

Magpie   Forget it.

Ash   I should have admitted it was me.

Magpie   You should, yeah. Maybe I'm not the one who needs to change.

≡   *As they climbed up the rope we smiled, waved, said bye, but we struggled to look them in the eye.*

Mack   See you.

Cam   Yeah.

Mack   You can do it, you know. You can speak up. I've seen it.

Be braver. Remember how it felt standing up for yourself.

Cam   Be kinder. Remember how it felt being scared.

≡   *As ours came down there was hugging and crying.*

≡   *Ours had a rash too and a cough. We asked how they'd been treated.*

≡   Really well.

≡   They were so kind. So worried.

≡   They really looked after us.

≡   *No one said anything.*

≡   *I looked at the floor.*

≡   *I looked at my shoes.*

Alex   Bye then. I couldn't have done it without you.

Jay   I know you couldn't.

Ali   Hiya.

Remy   Hi.

Mack   I missed you.

Both   Did you?

Mack   Yeah. It's good to have things back to normal.

Ali   Yeah, about that.

Remy   We're not going to walk two steps behind you all the time anymore.

Ali   Or agree with everything you say.

Remy   Or do everything you tell us to do.

Mack   Okay.

Both   Really?

Mack   Yeah.

ALI AND **REMY** WALK AWAY TOGETHER, LEAVING **MACK** BEHIND.

Mack   Hold on, wait for me.

MACK FOLLOWS THEM.

≡   *Eventually everyone was back where they started except for –*

Billy   Please don't go.

Sam   I have to.

Billy   No you don't. Stay. Come home with me and we can be a family again.

Sam   But what about my Billy? What about my mam?

Do you want them to lose me too, when you know what it feels like?

BILLY SHRUGS.

Sam   I know this is hard.

But let me go so my Billy doesn't feel as bad as you do.

Billy   I'm your Billy.

Sam   You're not. You know you're not.

You are like him, though. Kind. Annoying. Always looking after me.

Billy   I didn't look after you well enough, though.

Sam   It wasn't your fault.

Billy   I want my Sam back.

Sam   I know you do. But you can't have her, she's gone.

What you can do is give the Billy up there his Sam back.

Billy   I love you.

Sam   I love you too.

THEY HUG.

Alex   *And just like that, everything was back to normal.*

≡   *Normal apart from the swirling, yawning tear in the sky.*

Alex   *Apart from that, yeah.*

≡   *We blocked the tear up with a trestle table briefly. Mr Chandra and Miss Moore lugged it up the rope. It lasted long enough to evacuate everyone from the area.*

≡   *The police and ambulance and fire engines and parents and neighbours and carers and mysterious figures in black suits were waiting at a cordon far back from the school gates.*

≡   *The mysterious figures in black looked quite annoyed when they heard we had saved the day with some rope and a trestle table.*

They swarmed on the building while our worried loved ones enveloped us in more hugs and tears.

≡   *School was closed for ages which was great at first and then it got quite boring.*

Ash   *I think about Magpie all the time. About what she's doing up there. If she's okay. Will I see her again, if it happened again? Could it happen again?*

Alex   *At least we know the signs to look out for. Remember – tiredness, headaches, weird behaviour, odd decisions.*

≡   *The official announcement was that the strange sky was some rare, freak weather phenomenon.*

≡   *Climate change.*

≡   *Anything we tried to post on social media disappeared straight away.*

≡   *There was nothing on the news or in the papers, and we never found out if it was worldwide or just us.*

≡   *No one believed us about what really happened.*

Billy   *I haven't told Mam about Sam. Not without any proof. But I know. And it helps me feel better that she's happy and thriving up there, and at least one Billy hasn't lost her.*

Mack   *I wonder about my choices every day now. Everything, even as simple as what to have for breakfast. If I have porridge rather than toast, is a whole new universe created? A porridge-verse? And is that better or worse? What if me in the porridge-verse is having more fun than me here?*

Franky   *I started to doubt that it had ever happened at all. It all seemed so far-fetched. That I would even think about leaving my dad. Cos when I saw him outside the school, so worried, I realised that I need him as much as he needs me.*

Billy   *And if you ever need a break, want to hang out.*

Franky   *I'd like that, thanks.*

≡   *When school finally re-opened we all ran straight into the yard and looked up into the sky. We squinted.*

≡   *Peered.*

≡   *Stared.*

All   *Gasped.*

≡   *It was normal. Totally normal.*

≡   *Blue.*

≡   *Calm.*

≡   *Serene.*

≡   *Still.*

But if you looked really closely –

Alex   There, can you see it?

≡   Where?

Alex   There. If you look you can see a faint line, where the sky's been stitched back together. The two blues don't quite match up.

≡   Can you see it?

≡   Yeah.

≡   Me too.

≡   Where?

≡   I can see it. So it did happen?

≡   Definitely.

≡   100 per cent.

≡   We were right.

≡   *It happened on a Tuesday.*

≡   *At Lane End School.*

≡   *And it was really, really weird.*

END

Tuesday

BY ALISON CARR

*Notes on rehearsal and staging, drawn from a workshop with the writer,
held at the National Theatre, October 2019*

How Alison came to write the play

Alison said that this was not only her first play for NT Connections but her first play for young people in general. She said that when she got the brief it felt at first a little daunting but she knew she had a jumping-off point with her research into the 'Mandela Effect'. She said there was no great lightning bolt moment that created this play but that it grew from research over a period of time.

Alison mentioned that she often gets really interested in different things; for example, there was a point where she was really interested in wind farms but there was never really a suitable play or project to apply this new-found knowledge, but then three years later along came a project in which she could. The 'Mandela Effect' was another example of something she became interested in while researching for a different play, but it didn't quite fit with that piece. Researching the 'Mandela Effect' led her down a rabbit hole of reading about parallel universes and multiverses and when she was asked to write a play for NT Connections she thought that big groups of young people could possibly get quite invested in a piece about multiverses, so she brought that into the piece along with lots of other ideas.

She really wanted to write a piece that could potentially have a lot of people involved or just nine people, that it could accommodate a whole different range of groups and, most importantly, a piece that could be really flexible. She didn't want to make the play too prescriptive or patronise the young people or the directors but give them a framework, plot and structure where the young people could explore their strengths and challenge themselves. She wanted to see how the groups might approach the physical imagery in a play where huge things can happen, which the young people and directors could make themselves by filling in the gaps.

She ended by saying: 'The play is yours.'

What is the 'Mandela Effect'?

It is the phenomenon of collective misremembering of facts or events. The term refers to Nelson Mandela and the memory shared by many that he died in prison in the 1980s (he actually died a free man in 2013). People who believe in parallel worlds or multiverses might argue that in one universe he died in the 1980s, in another he died in 2013, and the collective misremembering is proof of people moving between universes without realising. Another example is: What colour is chartreuse? Magenta? Or a greeny yellow? Many (including Alison) would have sworn it's a magenta/maroon colour but it has always been a sort of neon green. Another is how many people were in the car when JFK was shot? Three? Four? There were actually six. Also what does the stepmother say to the mirror in *Snow White*? 'Mirror, mirror on the wall'? Nope, it's 'Magic mirror on the wall'. Some theorists believe that déjà vu is also proof of parallel worlds as it signifies the breakdown of cosmic walls between other existences.

This phenomenon of collective misremembering was a path for Alison into the idea of multiverses and there being more than one possible timeline of events. This felt like an interesting framework, structure and plot device to explore the decisions we make, decisions that others make for us and the effects that those decisions have in regards to leading us down different paths and having major repercussions in the future. There is something quite exciting about meeting a version of yourself who has made a different choice.

Because of different worlds and different timelines they could be taken down (e.g. shoplifting or not shoplifting) Alison felt that this could be an interesting subject matter for young people to look at. At an age when people are making big and small decisions, it would be good to think about the consequences of those choices: could a whole different universe exist as a result of a decision?

Text and movement

Lead director Adam Penford led a workshop that focused on the play as a whole and some of the challenges and opportunities it presents. In a parallel room, movement director Vicki Manderson focused on the many opportunities for physical storytelling in a movement workshop. These notes document both workshops, starting with the text workshop with Adam.

Approaching the play

Adam mentioned that he was aware of the varying length of rehearsal periods for different groups and of all the stuff that can make rehearsing complicated (people dropping in and out, etc.) so wanted to give a clear, effective way of how to approach the play from the beginning.

He said his first day would start with a read-through of the text, then they would discuss what the play was about. What are the themes? These are the first things he would look at when approaching the play with any group of actors and how much time you spend exploring these things depends on your time constraints, but it is definitely a great place to start.

Themes

Adam said that he always starts a process thematically, even with professional groups, and adapts how he does so depending on the size or age of the group. He finds that these thematic conversations can really grab their imaginations, particularly with a theme like the 'Mandela Effect'.

Adam asked the group to brainstorm themes in the play. The group found the following:

- Us and them
- Prejudice
- Loss
- Responsibility
- Family
- Self-interest
- The environment (which is killing them)
- Consequences
- Hierarchy
- Friendships/relationships
- Bullying
- Division
- Grief
- Conflict
- Loneliness
- Parallel universe
- Opportunities
- (Self-)reflections
- Crisis management

He asked if Alison could select five from the above which she felt were most important. She said:

- Responsibility
- Consequences
- Us/them (with prejudice tied in)
- Family/friendship
- Crisis management

Adam then split the group into five or six to discuss a theme for three minutes. First, he asked them to talk about the theme in relation to their own lives, e.g. 'What is family to me/us? What is responsibility to me?' This can help young people to think about the wider picture and their own personal response, which can lead to them being more invested in the work. Then to discuss that same theme in the context of the play, thinking about how this theme is approached in the text and how it relates to the characters. Here is an outline of what each group discussed.

Us/Them

The group found the following sub-themes:

Identity: the idea of what makes you you. Who are the Us and who are the Them?

Conflicts: two sides, division. Relevant to society today. Brexit is not going away anytime soon and even within families there are differing opinions.

Brexit and Cambridge Analytica.

Labelling: Instinctively we label each other and ourselves, e.g. I am white, female, with a hearing difficulty. I have lived experiences that shape how I see the world. In this play, you can look the same but be different. Someone on the other side of the world could look just like you but have experienced a totally different life.

Violence: Humans innately veer towards violence and being cruel to one another – we are more violent than we are friendly. What is refreshing in this play is that they end up working together rather than tearing each other apart.

Subgroups: Even within the Us group and the Them group there are even smaller subgroups. Sam and Billy become a separate Us group.

Prejudices

We have a concept that someone across the other side of the world wouldn't be able to do what we do; e.g. asylum seekers have such different lives to us. It would be easier in a way to accept a parallel universe if the 'Them' looked totally different. Because in this play they look like us, it's a lot scarier and more uncomfortable because they are so close to us but not quite there. We automatically have a fear of someone who is different. This therefore breeds prejudice which we see in the play; e.g. they steal, they have the infection, they will be a bad influence.

Family

Billy and Sam are family.

School family: closing ranks when they see something they don't understand.

Family groups: what are they? Blood, or social structures?

Mack loses her family as they disappear.

Friendship

The group discussed relationships in the play and a little bit about families too, and how that resonated with people they work with. One thing that struck them was how realistic the character friendship groups are. There are relationships and groups that they think their students could relate to such as outcasts, loners and bullies; also, that some people can get on quite happily without friends.

When the friends of bullies such as Mack leave it makes them feel unsettled but also makes them realise that their relationship is built on something not healthy and that's not a good thing. The group observed that young people can be really horrible to one another, telling someone where to sit or which group to be in and are quite willing to leave someone out.

The play explores positive change in relationships. That we have to work together as friends, because if we don't then we can't save the world. This involves teamwork.

Sometimes we don't want to work with people we don't like, but you don't have to be friends to work together, and through crisis someone can find a friendship like Franky.

Consequences

This group started by talking about if they believe in parallel universes and how their minds would cope if they discovered the existence of them.

They discussed the consequences of people's larger actions within the play, e.g. shoplifting.

They talked about the smaller actions we take and the effects they could have; e.g. if you had something specific for breakfast, could that change the world? If you were angry at someone, that anger could pass onto someone else and then someone else, etc.

They thought it would be interesting to explore morals in this respect and get the young people to ask that question; not 'What is the right or wrong choice?' but maybe just 'What might be the consequences of that choice?' We make decisions, wanting to make the right ones, but it depends on what people think is right or wrong. If there is a parallel universe for right or wrong choices then it doesn't matter what we choose, other than the fact that the *you* in this universe still has to live with the result of that decision.

Crisis management

First, the group recognised that the natural hierarchy was lost at the beginning of this play as the teachers are not there to take the lead. So then there becomes a bit of a contest, fighting each other to be leader. In moments of crisis someone has to come out and take the lead and generally a consensus arises out of a crisis. They also discussed what the crisis was: the event of the tear in the sky or the breakdown of human niceties? Was it the event that was the crisis or the reaction/humanity?

They thought it was interesting that the crisis was covered up at the end and asked the question: did it really happen at all? Was it an example of another parallel universe? Alison said that it definitely did happen but was just covered up.

Responsibilities

This group also started by thinking about how the natural leader/responsible adult is lost at the beginning of the play by being sucked up into the sky so the young people are left to take responsibility. When a teacher's presence is taken away then they have to take on 'grown-up' roles.

They looked at the relationships in the script and noted down that all of the pairs have a responsibility before and after the split; e.g. Franky as carer, Billy responsible for letting go of his sister.

Once they have realised that there are two worlds depending on what decisions they make, they have the knowledge that their actions do make a difference and it's their responsibility to apply that knowledge or not.

Adam said that he would then turn these discussions about themes into practical tasks; e.g. if one of the themes that arose was about people labelling themselves, then he'd get them to individually label themselves. This helps them think about the script in relation to themselves before relating it to any character they are playing.

Structure, style and transitions

Alison said that she wanted to just give a framework for the groups to work within, so the style is entirely up to the groups of young people and directors to take ownership of and discover/create together. She wanted to write something that could be quite fun and playful in regards to missing people and doubled people, but at the same time also think about bigger issues.

One moment that was mentioned was a stage direction that read: 'Do they tighten around Mack? Do they start to push and jostle her?'(p. 87) Alison said that she wrote this for the director and company to decide what they want to do here.

The most important thing is that the play flows, which is why she hasn't written in scene changes or been prescriptive with setting. Also characters seem to 'appear' or 'emerge', suggesting that they may always be present in the background but just come into focus for their scenes/moments. She said that keeping the pace up, particularly in the ensemble moments, is really key to motoring the drama along.

Language

Alison mentioned that though she is from the North East and has used words such as 'Mam', she doesn't imagine groups performing it with Geordie accents and encourages everyone to just use their own vernacular and accents.

Characters and characterisation

Adam said that as a director he gets asked a lot about how performers can practically approach character and characterisation. He suggested starting by using Stanislavski questions. These questions are:

- **What do I say about myself?** Write in bullet points everything the characters says about themselves . 'I say . . .'
- **What do others say about me?** As above, write in bullet points everything that is said by other characters about your character. 'A says that I am . . .' 'B says that I am . . .' (Sometimes it might be that no one says anything about your character but this can be quite interesting too.)
- **What do I say about the other characters?** As above, write in bullet points everything that you say about other characters. 'I say that A is . . .', etc.
- **What does the playwright say about me?** This may be in character descriptions or within stage directions. Write in bullet points: 'The playwright says that . . . I fall asleep', 'The playwright says I storm in angrily', 'The playwright says I have ginger hair', etc.

He gave small groups one character each. They all had a minute on each of the questions. He asked them not to diagnose any discoveries but just be factual, keeping an objective analysis to aid building a character. When we jump to conclusions immediately or make any interpretations from this information we might be influenced by our own life experiences. This exploration can be done as a secondary layer throughout the process.

They looked at Billy, Sam, Mack, Ash and Cam. An example looked like this:

Billy

What do I say about myself?

I say it's been nearly a year since they saw Sam.

I say I love Sam, twice. And that I want her to know that.

I say I wish I'd told Sam I loved her more often. Everyday.

I say I left Flopsy's cage open when he escaped that time but I let Mam blame you.

I say I do need to apologise. I say I always felt bad about that.

I say I was feeding him and I didn't close the door properly.

I say pins and needles are horrible.

I say I'm sorry to Sam.

What do others say about me?

Sam: I'm glad you're ok.

Jay: Billy and Sam are related.

Sam: He's in a mood.

Sam: Are you crying?

What do I say about the other characters?

I ask if Sam is warm enough.

I ask if Sam is hungry.

I ask if Sam is thirsty.

I ask if Sam needs the toilet.

I say I just want to make sure Sam is ok.

I ask where Sam is going.

I ask if Sam's foot is ok.

I say that when his mum sees Sam she will cry. And swear loads.

I say that Franky is barging around like an idiot. Like he owns the place.

What does the playwright say about me?

The playwright says I am male.

The playwright says I am one of Us.

The playwright says I am paired with Sam.

The playwright says I shrug.

The playwright says I am anxious.

The playwright says I am protective.

The playwright says I get upset.

The playwright says I overreact and square up to Franky.

The playwright says I walk away.

The playwright says I reappear.

The playwright says I cry.

The playwright says I am quiet.

The playwright says I hug Sam tight.

The playwright says Sam is my sister.

The playwright says I cradle Sam.

Casting

Alison had no set ages in mind as she knew there would be lots of different groups involved. This is why she didn't separate casting into years at school. The only reference to school years is the group of year 7s who get sucked up into the sky. She said she didn't mind if you wanted to change the year reference there, but that there is something quite funny visually about this group as quite a small, younger age group.

She said that she recommends people sticking to their own ages. It's useful for them not to have to be acting older or younger as there are quite a few issues like grief and death to explore and it is more interesting if coming from their own life perspective rather than imagining how they would deal with those issues if older or younger. Think about the emotional maturity of your young people when considering your casting options.

The only ages that should be stuck to are that Billy is older than Sam. It doesn't matter too much what this age gap is but she said it didn't want to be huge. None of the ages were set in stone.

Gender also isn't set in stone. She has given everyone gender neutral names so that they can be swapped around. She doesn't think that girls should play boys and vice versa so change the gender of the character to fit the performer. The description at the top of the play is the ideal and if you can do that split in the group then go for it, but if not possible then it's not gospel.

Production, staging and design

Costume wise, the action is taking place during a school day so it would be in uniform but you can decide what that might be. The science block is also referred to, but who knows what is going on in there, so costume could be different for any characters coming from there. It could be useful having something different between the Us and Them so you can define who is who onstage. It could be something really simple or subtle; for example, the Them have hoods up and the Us don't.

Alison suggests the play has no set, though there is a school setting. Adam tried an exercise using chairs (see 'Script Exercise' under 'Exercises for Use in Rehearsals' below) which was useful in regards to how you can use simple object/furniture to change the setting/scene.

Exercises for use in rehearsals

Warm-up

Exercise: Shower

Physicalise having a shower: rubbing soap together on your hands and then rubbing all over your body but not touching your body, keeping hands 1 cm away from body.

Then do the same but this time keeping hands 5 cm from your body.

Then do the same again but this time 30 cm from your body.

Exercise: High ten

Teach the group six simple moves; e.g. lift left arm up to side, lift right arm up to side, lift both arms up at sides, touch left shoulder with left hand, touch right shoulder with right hand, touch both shoulders at the same time.

Then split the group into pairs and ask them to face one another. They each should continuously do these movements in any order they like, facing their partner and getting into a rhythm so each doing a movement at the same time. At any moment they both happen to do the same movement at the same time, like in a mirror they can give each other a high ten to celebrate and then go back to continuously repeating the moves in any order until they mirror each other again, high ten, etc.

Exercise: 1, 2, 3

In pairs count to three with each person taking alternate numbers. Keep repeating over and over until it feels natural time to stop it/they have got the hang of it.

Then swap the 2 out for a clap and repeat the exercise.

Then swap the 3 out for a stamp and repeat the exercise.

Then swap the 1 out for a nod and repeat the exercise.

Exercise: Sign name

In a circle each individual performer thinks for a second about what their sign name might be. Usually this is based on an activity they do a lot or a significant descriptive feature; for example, kicking a ball if they play a lot of football, a drinking action if they like drinking a lot of tea, painting nails if they have colourful painted nails, typing if they spend a lot of time on the computer.

One at a time, go around the circle with each person saying their name and doing their action and then everyone copies.

Once you've got around the circle once, go again but this time have everyone say the name and do the action of the person at the same time rather than repeating after them.

Next get the group to get as close together as possible, shoulder to shoulder, and say the name and do the action as quietly and as small as possible, again doing them all together.

Finally move the circle much further apart and do the same but saying the name as loud as they can and doing the action as big as they can.

Character

Exercise: Developing character

Walking around the space, think about a character of your choice (this group took whichever character they did their Stanislavski questions for).

While walking around, think about what colour this character would be.

Continuing walking, think about what sort of animal this character would be. Think about how this might affect their physicality. You can subtly let this bleed into the way in which you walk around the space.

Next think about which verb might describe your character.

Next think about how fast they move on a scale of 1–10.

Next make eye contact with the others walking around the space, if your character would make eye contact; some might not, but certainly become aware of those around you.

Next greet one another while walking around; vocalise if it feels appropriate for your character.

Next definitely vocalise a greeting that feels suitable to this character.

Next sit in the space, however you think your character might sit: on the floor, on a chair, against a wall, or maybe they would refuse to.

Next think about how suggestible this character is to new ideas on a scale of 1–10. Are they someone who is easily influenced or not? This might depend on what point in the play you are thinking about as their suggestibility might change, so pick a point in the play to make this choice.

Still in character, take a chair and make a circle to then lead into the next improvisation exercise.

Exercise: Group improvisation 1

Direction

In the circle, Adam asked one of the performers to start a conversation in character. Someone playing Magpie started a conversation about biscuits and raised the question of whether there is more chocolate on a chunky or a normal Kit Kat.

Depending on their level of suggestibility, the other characters in the circle reacted in different ways. Some argued quite vocally, some took a back seat, some removed themselves from the group entirely.

Reflections

In a group of young people they may be less open to improvisation and keeping it active, and might be more likely to shut things down. It's then a case of encouraging them to say 'yes' to ideas. It doesn't mean they can't disagree in character but just that they focus on contributing rather than shutting the exercise down.

This situation talking about biscuits felt quite low stakes so there wasn't somewhere with high drama to go with it.

Adam then asked a person to come with him out of the room to give them details of a much more dramatic situation to deliver to the group.

Exercise: Group improvisation 2

Direction

Adam told this person to inform the group that there was an Armageddon-like situation; school was in lockdown, lots of police outside, explosions, army, etc. She was panicky and upset, and tried to get them to react, to get out safely. Staying on the same level of 'suggestibility' the group left in the room were asked to react in character.

Reflections

This one felt a lot more dramatic and the stakes were definitely higher. It divided the group a lot more and the divisions were a lot clearer. This is something that Adam would do with his group quite early on to put themselves in another situation, something quite close to the play's own drama. This exercise could also be left for later on in the process once performers had worked a little more on character. It might also depend on how well people in the group know each other as to how comfortable they feel playing this sort of improvisation early on.

Stakes

Exercise: Lost items

This is an exercise Adam does when he feels like a group isn't grasping the notion of stakes.

He took a group of ten outside with him while the others set up a little audience. The group of ten re-entered, jumbled themselves up and set up in a line in front of the audience.

Outside, he had told them all to have lost something with a value of 1–10. They did a short improvisation for 15–30 seconds. As the audience watched each improvisation they put the line in order of stakes from low to high and guessed what it was that they had lost. After each improv they said if they thought they were higher or lower than the previous ones.

Once everyone had done their improvisation, they went along the line seeing how accurate the audience were in ranking the stakes and in guessing what it was they had lost. Items ranged from a dirty hanky, pencil, 20p, phone, wallet, passport, train ticket, luggage, etc.

Reflection

Losing a train ticket might not be so scary if it didn't cost much and the trains go every five minutes. So even within a lost item there might be variation of the stakes that would be played. Adam finds that young people really enjoy this exercise as it gives a really specific thing to improvise with. If doing it with a young company, try to avoid them getting too far into a back story about the object (e.g. 'Oh I reacted really dramatically about losing the pencil because it was one my grandma gave me on her deathbed'), otherwise that can mess the stakes up.

Script

Objectives and tactics

Adam said that when watching productions it is often clear whether work has been done with actors on character objectives or not.

The group read the conversation between Naz and Mack (p. 86) and then asked: 'What is it that Mack wants? What is her objective?' They decided her objective was to maintain status. Then, 'What is her tactic to achieve this objective?' They decided it was to belittle or undermine others.

Adam then paired everyone off and asked them to look at the scene and perform it thinking about their objectives and tactics.

Reflections

Stillness worked quite nicely.

This interaction feels pre-planned so physically Naz feels more confident.

Physical size is interesting here – if an actor is smaller can they still be intimidating?

Redirection

Adam then gave Naz a gang to circle Mack, which enabled Naz to have more physical presence to help achieve the objective.

Reflections

Naz felt more powerful in this version.

They realised it could be a tricky moment to stage as you'd want the group to be around Mack but would also need to let an audience in.

Line runs

One thing that Adam noted from his years of working on NT Connections is that learning the lines and the cues for the performers can be one of the hardest things. He said that the great thing about these ensemble scripts is that parts can be spread evenly to create a strong group dynamic, but the difficult thing can be keeping the pace up as there is no thinking time. The design and performances, etc. might be great, but certain pieces have a rhythm to them which can get broken by people not picking up cues.

Adam suggested that if you can find the time, it is a really useful thing to do a line run before a performance, but to also factor line runs into the process. You don't need staging or props to drill lines, but the more you find time to just focus on the lines, the more confident everyone will be. With this in mind, it is also helpful to assign lines as early as possible in the process to maximise learning time.

Script exercise

Adam also noticed that sometimes pieces can become quite static when there are a lot of voices onstage, which is linked to pace. It can be helpful to attach a certain physicality to lines to help with learning, as well as encouraging actors to keep active and not get stuck in certain positions.

He asked the group to read the first two pages of text, just taking one line at a time rather than one character. He then asked them to move their chairs back so they could walk into the space with their line and, on entering, they could either sit or stand.

Reflection
Saying the line at the same time as the move made it feel more alive.
There was a clarity of what was going on and they knew where to look.

Redirection
Adam then asked them to go back to their spaces and made the rule that not only could they move on their own line, but on other people's lines too they could react to what is going on or being said.

Reflection
This seemed messier and more distracting.
It felt more anarchic.
In the first version it was clearer where the focus was.

Redirection
Adam them asked them to only direct their lines to the other performers onstage.

Reflection
Delivering to each other felt less focused as it is written like direct address. When performing direct address, actors naturally feel a little awkward making eye contact with an audience. Even if the lights are bright and they can't see an audience member, it needs to feel like they can.

Redirection
Adam then asked each of the performers to grab a chair and bring it into the space, though it didn't need to be in a 'chair' position. He asked the performers to start in the space. They could stand, lie, sit wherever they wanted. He added one more rule: it's definitely direct address and, when speaking their own line, they should always speak to the audience, but when not speaking they can be looking at other performers as an ensemble storyteller. They can move on their own line and on other people's lines. Adam asked them to have a physical action linked to what they were saying and deliver this to the audience by looking them in the eye.

Reflection
Because the lines are so short and snappy it takes a while to tune in, so you might want to slowly build something like this so it doesn't feel like a bombardment from the top.

You could give other directions to the group; for example, they all have to enter the space and just sit on the floor facing the audience, which might almost look like an assembly.

There were gaps between lines as you could tell performers were thinking about the action they were going to give before saying a line.

Redirection
Adam asked them to do exactly the same again, but this time without any gaps between cues. He encouraged people to stand up ready to go over the top of someone else's line.

Reflection
The rhythms started becoming clear because the air was taken out of it. It became snappy.

Redirection
Adam asked them all to read the script all together, as a whole group at the same time.

Reflection
This felt much quicker and you could hear the natural rhythm.

Redirection
Repeat with the same pace.

Reflection
It felt like they all had a collective responsibility to keep the rhythm going.

Question and answer with Alison Carr

If the company are all boys and wouldn't naturally steal eye shadow, could they potentially steal something else?
They can, but something small that would fit in a pocket and not be too significant, like a chocolate bar.

Can 'Mam' be changed?
It can and I don't expect anyone to be doing the show in Geordie accents.

What is your picture or vision?
I totally appreciate it is a difficult text, even just the practicality of learning it. In earlier drafts it was even more broken up and I've now tried clumping it together more. But I like the pace of it. It needs that pace and rhythm with twenty people or five people. It's part collective storytelling to the audience and part scene moments between the characters. If it doesn't have pace then it will drag. This is why I didn't want scene changes or set and why I wanted it to be just one collective piece. There is an element of radio drama to it as it is a narration of what is happening, so it's more about telling than showing.

Can you tell us a little about your writing process?
My process is very different for every play. As I haven't written for young people before it was about writing for lots of people and thinking about relationships that exist between young people. There wasn't much redrafting but I just sat and went down the rabbit hole of what multiverses are, but eventually decided that this was my version of what a multiverse could be. Then I concentrated on deciding what the most interesting duos were. The pairs do exist in isolation and then come back in collection at the end.

Do you think it should be performed in a naturalistic or more abstract style?
Because of the direct address those moments can be performative. The scenes that happen on the day are naturalistic but there is scope for a bit of everything. Lots of flexibility. The stage directions do give a clue as to how it could be performed – are they always there and then just 'emerge' or 'appear'?

Did you visualise it as a busy space?
I'd say it would be a very fluid space which helps with pace as well.

Is it a private or state school?
State school, as that is my experience.

Movement workshop with Vicki Manderson

Movement director Vicki Manderson commented that, as an ensemble piece, *Tuesday* has many opportunities for physical storytelling, and that if you want to explore this in your piece, bring it in right from the beginning of your rehearsals. Vicki told the group that she would take them through how as a movement director she would approach a number of moments in the play and invited them to take what's useful; even though it might not be how they would approach things, it might provide them with a way in.

Exercise: Physical warm-up

It is a good idea to start your movement sessions with a physical warm-up as it prepares the body for work and helps to prevent injuries.

Step 1: Start by standing in a circle.

Stand with your feet underneath your hips, take a breath in and then exhale on a sigh.

Inhale again, lifting the shoulders towards the ears and then exhale on a sigh, dropping the shoulders back down.

Repeat.

The third time you repeat the sequence develop the movement further in the body by bending your knees as you drop the shoulders and sigh.

Keep the body loose and open.

Step 2: Go around the circle, each person saying their name loudly and clearly.

Leave space after each name is said, allowing a chance to really listen and learn each other's names.

Repeat, but this time you're going to make eye contact with someone in the circle and smile at them as you say your name.

This is a really simple way to start to connect as a group, in this case by looking at each other and giving someone your attention.

Step 3: Roll the shoulders back twice. Make sure you are breathing, then add your arms making full arm rotations.

Then start to roll the shoulders forward, think about getting space into your back, take the movement into your arms allowing them to circle forward. Then bend your knees at the start of the movement and allow your head to follow, creating a full body undulation.

At the top of an arm circle leave your arms up there. Grab your right wrist with the left hand, pull up and across towards your left side. Breathe into this space on the right side of the body, breathe in through your nose and out of the mouth.

Drop arms to side and shake out.

Repeat from the start of step three, grabbing your left wrist with the right hand towards the end of the sequence and pulling across to the right side.

Step 4: Take your feet out to the side slightly wider than hip distance and place your hands on your knees.

Inhale, arching the spine and drawing the shoulder blades together, sending the stomach towards the floor, opening your chest up, head lifts towards the ceiling and lifting the eyeline forwards.

Then exhale and curve the spine, dropping your head and eyeline in towards the stomach.

Repeat both stages three times. Think about your breathing: one movement is an inhale, one is an exhale.

Step 5: Let your hands go towards the floor, resting your hands on your ankles or the floor, allow your knees to bend and gently shake your head, releasing any tension in the neck and shoulders.

Then walk up through the spine, using your hands to walk up your legs.

Inhale, take your arms up, then exhale and, letting the head lead, roll back down through the spine to the floor and repeat step five again.

Step 6: Stand with feet together. Stand on your left foot, lifting your right foot in the air and circle the ankle in one direction and then the other.

Then shake the whole leg out to the front, side and behind you. Let your body and arms move around to balance you.

Repeat standing on the right foot.

Bring the feet back together, bend your knees down towards the floor, and circle the knees to the right and then to the left five times.

Step 7: Take your feet out to the side slightly wider than hip distance. Interlace your fingers holding your arms out in front of you, and invert your hands so that your palms are facing away from you. Curve the spine and drop the head. Take the arms to the right and to the left, stretching through the sides of the body. Then release your fingers, take your arms up and circle them forward twice, exhaling as the arms fall forward.

Shake everything out.

Exercise: Building an ensemble

It is important at the start of rehearsals to take the time to develop a sense of ensemble, choosing exercises that help your cast to become physically comfortable and trusting with each other. You can build exercises up in stages; for example, if a hug as part of this exercise is too intimidating, maybe start by standing back to back and then work towards the hug as rehearsals progress.

These exercises will help you to create an ensemble, building a sense of awareness and connection between the performers and the space.

Start walking around the room, and look for the open spaces to move into.

Let your eyes lift away from the floor and start to see each other and connect in the space.

Acknowledge each other – you can smile! Check your breathing – make sure you're not holding any tension.

Vicki then added the following words and instructions for each action. Each instruction was added one at a time and then given in a random order.

GO

Move around the space, keep making eye contact, relax the shoulders.

CENTRE

Move quickly into the centre of the room and see how closely you can stand as an ensemble. Put your hand on someone's back or shoulder. Be purposeful with this gesture. Contact is through the hand, not the fingertips.

CLEAR

Clear to the side of the space as quickly as you can.

SWAP

Swap to the opposite side of the space. The goal is to arrive at the same time as each other.

This may take a few tries – ask your group how they might achieve this. It becomes less about their journey alone and more about their journey together. You should feel a sense of movement and then everything settling at the same time.

PERSON 1

Grab the person closest to you and give them a big hug; squeeze them close to you. This is your person number 1; each time 'Person number 1' is shouted out, find them, and give them a squeeze!

PERSON 2

Find a different person to hug. Remember them, this is your person 2.

FAVOURITE

Point to your favourite area or object in the room. This needs to be a dynamic, sharp gesture, think about sending all your energy in that direction.

Once you have run through these instructions a couple of times and the group are familiar with them all, give a final instruction – CENTRE.

Vicki explained that the group would now explore how they might breathe together as an ensemble.

Inhale as a group and take a few steps out keeping some sort of physical contact within the group.

As the group exhales contract back to the original formation.

Repeat, placing the emphasis on the exhale/contraction of the group.

Keep looking at each other and having an awareness of the whole group.

Observations

- After just fifteen minutes the group felt much more physically relaxed and connected to each other.

Vicki commented that when you start to look at each other and breathe together you begin to get a sense of an ensemble, a sense of complicity within the group.

Building a sense of ensemble with your company right at the beginning of the rehearsal process is really important and will allow the rest of the rehearsal process to open up.

Exercise: Physical improvisation

This exercise further explores ensemble dynamics and the use of space, rhythm, tempo, breath and physicality, and how you can play with these to create different atmospheres. Vicki explained that she was going to take the group through an improvisation and that she would give very clear rules. She asked the group to always make clear decisions, to keep their eyes up, to keep seeing each other.

Step 1: Walk around the space. Look for the open spaces. Have a check-in with your body: how is it feeling after warm-up?

You have the choice to:

1 Walk around.

2 Be still. Keep it 'alive'; you are still actively part of the room.

3 If a space between two people appears you can move through it as if it's a door, moving through at a quicker pace.

4 Vary your speed. You might decide that you want to walk really quickly, or slowly. You have a choice to vary your own speed now.

Once you have played with these four instructions you can continue on:

5 React to someone's energy. You can go with their energy or against it. It should feel like a physical conversation.

Vicki reminded the group to never let their eyeline touch the ground, to stay connected to each other and the play.

Step 2: Vicki asked the group to keep all the same rules but to lighten the atmosphere in the room. (Don't let your group talk about it, just ask them to keep playing.)

- How can you change your physicality?
- Your tempo?
- How do you relate to each other in the space differently? When you find something go with it.

Have an awareness of how this feels physically in the body.

Vicki then clapped her hands and asked the group to create a more threatening atmosphere.

- What changes in your body now?
- How has your focus changed?
- How has your breathing changed?
- How has the tempo of the group changed?

Step 3: Vicki asked the group to listen to each other and come to a stop altogether.

Observations

When lightening the atmosphere:

- They moved freely, body language was open, they smiled!
- They moved quickly and lightly.
- Breathing was faster and deeper.
- There was more eye contact.

When creating a threatening atmosphere:

- They felt physically more tense, body language was closed.
- They felt more grounded.
- Breathing slowed down and became shallower.
- They slowed down.
- Still lots of eye contact, but maybe shifted from person to person quicker.

Vicki suggested that it might be useful to think about how you change the atmosphere at various points in the play. What is the atmosphere in the opening scene and how does this contrast with the moment of the sky tearing? How can you show this change in atmosphere physically?

Exercise: Flocking

Flocking exercises are an excellent way to create an ensemble and to encourage listening with the whole body. This exercise is also useful preparation for creating the physicality of Ash and Magpie.

Vicki split the group into two groups.

Step 1: As a group you form a clump. Vicki asked the person at the front of the clump to start leading the group around the space. Keeping the form, the rest of the group follow the movement and speed of the leader as accurately as they can. When the leader decides to change the direction a new leader emerges. If you cannot see anyone else, you have become the leader!

Vicki reminded the groups to try and keep equal distance between themselves, so that the leader doesn't pull away too much from the rest of their group. The leader can take their group to different areas of the room, exploring all the available space.

If you take over as leader from someone, how do you change the quality and dynamics of the movement?

Leaders need to be clear in their movement; the rest of the group shouldn't be in doubt as to what they are being asked to follow. The clearer and bolder you are the better.

Step 2: The leader can start to add a simple action, something that the group can repeat easily; for example, lifting your arms and dropping them by your side.

Simple actions work best. Explore using different levels, dynamics and tempos.

Step 3: Vicki asked the two groups to start listening to each other, to start talking to each other physically. To split their focus between their group and the other group.

- Don't be afraid of stillness, stillness might be better.
- What happens if you take the energy up a bit? Try and build the energy, intensity and relationship between the two groups. Does it become more of a confrontation?
- How does one group pass through the other group at speed?
- How do they find their way to becoming one big group?

Step 4: Shout 'NOW' and everyone becomes individuals again and moves away from each other.

Observations

- It was interesting finding the connection between the two groups and the importance of eye contact during this part of the exercise.
- That you didn't have to be able to see the leader during the flocking, that you could listen with the whole body and keep your eyeline forward.
- Feeling a sense of pressure when at the front of the group to be interesting.

Vicki reminded the group that there is no right or wrong way to do things and that everything helps us find the answer, that when devising we need to get things wrong in order to get things right. Vicki suggested that the more you do these exercises with your company the more relaxed and playful they'll become. If your groups are hesitant, then start with smaller groups and build towards larger ensemble groups.

Physicality of Ash and Magpie

You can use this exercise to explore the similar physicalities of Ash and Magpie and how they might move together.

Step 1: Find a partner and label yourselves A and B: A is active, B is the observer.

A:

Create yourself a simple pathway through the space.

Find three points that you go to within the space.

Each time you repeat the pattern make it more accurate and clearer for yourself. For example, if you walk to the wall and lean against it folding your arms, know which part of your body makes contact with the wall first. How do you turn into the wall? How do you fold your arms? Where is your eyeline? Make it simple and precise.

B:

As you watch A, really start to notice their focus and physicality. If they're holding any tension in their body notice that. Be clear with your observations; remember as much as you can about their pathway in the space. Notice their speed: does it change at all? Where is their eyeline at each moment? How long do they stay at each point? What do their arms do as they walk? Try and observe as much detail as you can.

Step 2: Once A is sure of their sequence, B follows A on their journey, but just behind them so they can still observe. B is like A's shadow.

See if you can really accurately copy their pattern.

Step 3: Now perform the sequence as a pair. Try and move at exactly the same time as each other. Tune in to each other's movement, to each other's breathing. Repeat this a couple of times, aiming to work as one.

Step 4: Next, in your pairs have a conversation with each other and find the moments that aren't quite working yet and fix them. Together, try and pinpoint the detail, qualities of movement and the exact timings.

Step 5: Vicki then split the pairs into three groups to observe each other, noting when things worked and when they didn't.

Observations

What happens when it works?

- There is detail and confidence in the movement.
- There is a good use of focus.
- There is an accurate level of detail.
- There is an ease of physicality and sense of fluidity.
- There is detail in the transferring of weight.
- There were purposeful moments of stillness.

Vicki concluded the exercise by saying that if you want to look at two characters who are similar in their behaviour, then it's useful to start from one person's perspective as it tends to create something that feels more natural and truthful. You might like to ask each character to make up a movement sequence separately and then put them together. This approach is more versatile, with more dramatic and staging possibilities than two characters standing opposite each other, mirroring each other.

Creating the sky and the tear

In the absence of a large set and budget, Vicki suggested that there is something useful about the performers becoming the sky. This exercise explores how you can create the sky, the changing colours, the different dynamics and the moment the sky tears apart with just the bodies of the performers.

Vicki split the group into smaller groups of five or six and gave them fifteen minutes to create the following six moments starting from being a group of separate people:

1 **The moment a group of individual people become the sky.** What is the moment where they all come together? How does this happen?
2 **Gear change – colour change.** How do you show the colour changes in the sky? Think of it as gear changes, very clear, abrupt changes in movement.
3 **Swirl and pulse.** How does the group show the swirling and pulsing? Find something physical to represent this.
4 **Rhythm.** Create a rhythmical movement that comes from the swirl and pulse.
5 **Fracture.** How do you show moment the sky fractures?
6 **Tear.** How do you show the tear? Think about the speed of the tear and the quality of it.

Each group shared their six moments.

Observations

- It worked well with the addition of vocalisation and sound.
- The most effective pieces were the ones with a sense of anticipation. An audience needs to feel that something is about to happen and to feel the release as the sky tears.

Vicki suggested that there are many opportunities for physicality within the piece and that these moments don't have to be very long but that you might create moments like this throughout the piece alongside the text.

'Us' and 'Them'

It is often useful to use words and images to generate movement. These might be words that you come up with in the rehearsal room or words that come directly from the script or stage directions. In this instance, Vicki asked the group to suggest contrasting words that might evoke moments, words that are easy to physicalise.

The group come up with:

Free/Bound
Line/Circle
High/Low
Heavy/Light

Bright/Dark

Small /Large

Fast/Slow

Squidgy/Rigid

Bold/Meek

Air/Fire

Rough/Smooth

Neat/Untidy

Open/Close

Hard/Soft

Out of control/Controlled

Vicki split the group into two.

Task 1: You are going to create five different group formations. There needs to be a feeling that you are a unit somehow.

Task 2: Vicki asked the group to create transitions between each of the five different formations, using a different word each time from the above list to inform the quality of movement as they transition between positions.

Task 3: Each group shared their piece with an additional instruction from Vicki to keep their eyes on the audience the whole time they are performing.

This next stage might be helpful in informing how the group discover that there is an 'Us' and a 'Them'.

Exercise: Creating an 'Us and Them'

Step 1: Choose one of the five actions that your group has developed in the previous exercise and remember it. (In this workshop it was a shuffle motion and a tapping of the chest with the hand.)

Ask the two groups to mix up and stand spread out as one big group of strangers.

Ask them to look around – in this scene they are a group of people who aren't normally in a space together, they don't recognise anyone in the group.

Gradually invite everyone to start making their sound or movement; the physical language starts to emerge, you begin to hear and see your tribe and find your way towards each other creating the two groups, always keeping your attention on the other group.

Now you can start to explore moments of action and reaction. What does one group do that triggers the other group to react with something?

This is a way of exploring the physical language of the text; you might choose to layer this onto the text, or find moments of physical storytelling alongside the text.

Step 2: During this improvisation, ask the two groups to perform their five formations again but this time, rather than being separate from each other, stop and rework how each formation might relate to the other group. Find interesting dynamics, patterns and pathways between the two groups, moments of action and reaction, develop each group's physical vocabulary and the unfolding story between them.

The workshop's improvisation went as follows: When Vicki said 'go' both groups started to build their first formations, keeping their focus and attention on the other group. Vicki then instructed both groups to take a step towards each other. Then they created their second formation. One of the group's second formation was a circle. Rather than making this circle separate from the other group, Vicki directed them to circle the group, thereby creating a relationship between them. The inner group made a triangle. The outside group took a step in. Vicki asked the inner group to allow this push from the outside to force them to contract as a group from their triangle formation into two lines back to back. Then the outer circle started to stamp their feet, closing in on the inner group who at the last minute exploded through the advancing group to form an outside circle.

Observations

- The clarity of focus is really important.
- There was a tribal quality to it.
- It allows you to think about different formations and ways of staging.
- The change in dynamics is really effective. What moments can you explode physically?
- It was really interesting to watch the story unfold and how the status of the groups kept changing.

In your improvisations there might be a movement or gesture that you find, like the shuffle or body tap, that you use to differentiate between the two groups helping you to find a physical vocabulary for 'Us' and 'Them'.

Vicki added that these moments don't have to be very long – it could be a fifteen-second burst of movement. If the sense of ensemble is created from the beginning then you can return to it throughout the piece.

Creation of the human chain

Vicki split the group into smaller groups of five or six.

Task 1: Start with one person in your group and work out how the next person can link onto them to start creating a human chain. Keep going until you have added all the members of your group.

- Decide what the anchor point is. How does that first person anchor themselves?
- Think about where and how you link with another person's body. Explore using the whole body, not just linking by hands.
- Explore using different levels. This will also help give a sense of the vertical and journeying to the sky.
- Your link might have a story. What is the story of that link? Maybe you can't quite grab onto their wrist before you finally get a grip.

Task 2: Once the group found their formations, Vicki asked someone in the middle of the chain to remove themselves and find somewhere else to go. The broken chain then had to quickly work out how to fix itself. This breaking and fixing of the chain can keep happening.

Observations

- An audience has to understand the sense of urgency and fragility of this chain, that there is a sense of tension, that something is going to happen.
- A sense of focus is really important for the storytelling. Looking at a single point above might help give a sense of elevation and moving upwards.
- Removing the centre person and disrupting the chain creates a sense of urgency – it keeps the action and storytelling alive. Keeping things moving is useful for both small and large companies.
- Creating a sense of urgency, effort and risk is key. When you can't defy gravity you need something else.
- An audience needs to understand that their efforts might fail and that they need the final character, Mack, to join in order for it to stand a chance of succeeding.
- It was effective using a piece of furniture or the wall as an anchor and starting point. There was a feeling of starting in the real, physical world and ending up in another world.

Vicki suggested that creating the human chain should be the last thing you do as a company as it takes a lot of trust.

Music suggestions

Working with music can really help create the right atmosphere in the rehearsal room, aid focus and help generate ideas. When selecting music for the performance be wary of using music with lyrics: the music should not dominate the text or movement. Below is a list of music used in the workshop and other suggestions that you might like to try:

Rival Consoles
Jon Hopkins
Nils Frahm
Underworld
Aphex Twin
Deadmau5
Four Tet
Interpol
Colleen
Peter Broderick
Peter Gregson

Further suggested references

Google the 'Mandela Effect' and 'multiverses'.

One workshop member mentioned *Counterpart*, an American TV show about parallel universes that collide, which could be interesting to watch.

From a workshop led by Adam Penford and Vicki Manderson
with notes by Anna Girvan and Lizzie Wiggs

A series of
public apologies
(in response to an unfortunate
incident in the school lavatories)

by John Donnelly

This satirical play is heightened in its naturalism, in its seriousness, in its parody and piercing in its interrogation of how our attempts to define ourselves in public are shaped by the fear of saying the wrong thing. Presented quite literally as a series of public apologies this play is spacious, flexible and welcoming of inventive and imaginative interpretation as each iteration spirals inevitably to its absurdist core. This is a play on words, on convention, on manners, on institutions, on order, online and on point.

Cast size
8–100, any gender
Recommended for ages 14+

John Donnelly's plays include *The Pass* (Royal Court Theatre), a version of Chekhov's *The Seagull* (Headlong/UK tour), *Little Russians* (Tricycle Theatre/First Blast: Proliferation Season), *The Knowledge* (Bush Theatre), *Encourage the Others* (Almeida Projects), *Songs of Grace and Redemption* (Liminal Theatre/Theatre503), *Bone* (Royal Court Theatre) and a version of Molière's *Tartuffe* (National Theatre).

For television John has written the short film *Henry* for Channel 4's *Coming Up* and an episode of *Glue* (Channel 4/Eleven Films), and co-written two episodes of *Utopia* (Kudos/Channel 4). Most recently, John adapted his stage play *The Pass* for screen, produced by Duncan Kenworthy/Toledo Productions and starring Russell Tovey. The film opened the BFI Flare Festival in 2016 and returned to the BFI later in the year for the London Film Festival. John and the film's director, Ben A. Williams, were nominated for a BAFTA Award for Outstanding Debut by a British Writer, Director or Producer.

Thank you to the pupils of Addey & Stanhope School Deptford, Tinuke Craig, Ola Animashawun, Michael Bryher and the NT Studio.

Notes on production

To be performed by as many or as few

Of any age, shape, race, gender; people with or without disabilities

Gender pronouns may be changed

Dialogue to be allocated by the company

Dashes (–) are sometimes used at the start of cues where it may be desirable to create consistency of character by having the same actor(s) speaking the lines. For instance, the Questioner/Alan/Guilty Party sequence may be best played by three people

Dashes are also sometimes used to indicate that a new cue completes a thought started in a preceding cue

Impersonations of real people are neither necessary nor forbidden nor do they have to be any good

Projection, live recording, live streaming, pre-recorded footage and so on may all be used

Unless you don't want to

Is this all a bit much?

Sorry

Thank you all for coming we will be as brief as possible your time is valuable

This won't take long

It won't take long at all

Obviously a minor incident occurred in the school lavatories which may have caused some distress

Something was written

Scrawled

On the walls

There's been a lot of speculation around this which we would – obviously – like to nip in the bud

But that's all we're going to say at this point

Except to say the school neither endorses the message, nor the medium through which the message was conveyed

Nor do we accept responsibility for the incident or its effect on members of the school or indeed wider community

The wider community occasionally have access to the lavatories when they use the school sports hall

All part of our drive to improve the school

So we wish to apologise for any offence caused, assure you that lessons have been learned and that we now intend to draw a line under things and move on

Obviously

Thank you for coming. That is the end of our statement

*

Thank you all for coming we will be as brief as possible your time is valuable

Apparently some of you found the previous statement unsatisfactory

By saying that the incident *may* have caused some distress, it may have been taken to imply that no distress was caused

Distress was caused

We're not trying to minimise or undermine the integrity of anyone's lived experience

We take this seriously

We take our responsibility very seriously

We acknowledge that distress was caused

We didn't mean to throw more fuel on the fire

Pour salt on the wound

Throw acid in the eyes

That's inappropriate, so

We're sorry for any distress caused and wish to make it clear that this statement constitutes an apology for the incident and draw a line under this whole sorry business

What was the incident?

And move on

What was the incident?

Thank you. No questions at this time

*

Thank you all for coming we will be as brief as possible your time is valuable

In our previous statement we attempted to draw a line under the matter

It has since come to our attention that this was inappropriate

And there was some lack of clarity over the incident itself

Accordingly we wish to clarify the incident in the hope of drawing a line underneath the incident

And providing closure

Some words were written

Scrawled

On the lavatory walls

By whom we don't know

Words which may have been deemed offensive

Were deemed, *were* deemed offensive

Mr Laurence, our wonderful caretaker, found the words, cleaned the words and that was that

I hope that clears everything up

What were the words?

Sorry

What were the words?

I hope that draws a line under this

*

Thank you all for coming we will be as brief as possible your time is valuable

Apparently some information was omitted from our previous statement

We weren't trying to underplay the seriousness of the incident or the message that was smeared on the walls

Did you say smeared?

No

You did, you said smeared

I mean scrawled, I meant scrawled on the walls

In the spirit of openness we wish to share with you the message that was smeared sorry scrawled on the walls

And we hope that means we can then draw a line under this whole sorry incident

The message was as follows

EAT MY SHIT. EAT MY SHIT ALAN

Why are you shouting?

It was written in capitals

In capitals? My gosh, we're dealing with an insane person

Who is Alan?

We don't know

What do you mean you don't know?

We don't know any Alans

We're not aware of an Alan

All we know is that someone smeared this on the walls

You've said it again. You've just said smeared again

Scrawled, I mean scrawled

What was the message scrawled in exactly?

Human excrement. And blood we think

It was written in

In shit and blood, yes

All of it?

That's a lot of shit

It was spread quite thinly

Hang on, was it spread or smeared?

Smeared, it was smeared

Mr Laurence the caretaker spent his entire weekend cleaning it off

EAT MY SHIT. EAT MY SHIT ALAN

Thank you, we get the idea

Poor Mr Laurence

The staff have had a whip round

Forty-one pounds, Amazon vouchers. And a pound

The thing is, someone had already taken photographs

Images, there are images?

Some of which are now in the public domain

Images of the –

Shit, yes, and the blood

Can we stop saying shit?

Shall we bring back excrement?

Actually, I think shit is better

Let's stick with shit and see how we get on

What kind of person smears shit and blood on the walls?

Clearly whoever did it was psychologically disturbed

That's an offensive statement. Not all psychologically disturbed people smear shit and blood

Why else would you smear shit?

A protest

I'm not sure it was a protest

It could have been

'EAT MY SHIT. EAT MY SHIT ALAN'. That's not a protest

Perhaps it's a metaphor

For what?

About what?

Any number of things

The government

Climate Change

The final season of *Game of Thrones*

Speculation is not helpful

There are questions we need answered

Who is behind this?

Who is it intended for?

And who is Alan?

*

We need to issue an apology

But we weren't responsible

It happened on the premises of our school, a school with children

Someone has to take responsibility

We need to shut this down

Can we contain this? Can we contain the shit?

It's too late. The shit is out there

And the blood

It's already on Insta

Oh my gosh

Have you seen Twitter?

Twitter is angry

Reddit is angry

Upworthy is angry

Mumsnet is furious

There's a meme

There's a meme of the shit and the blood

And it's getting good ratio

It's out of hand

It's getting very good ratio

The shit and the blood is out of hand

Can we stop talking about shit and blood, can we just say smears?

Is everyone happy with smears?

I can live with smears

*

Thank you for your tweets

Thank you for your emails

Thank you for your texts

Thank you for your online petitions

Thank you for the YouTube takedowns

We are now very much aware that we should not have been attempting to draw a line at all

It was never our intention to shut down the conversation

It seems closure was not desired

Which is why we're here today

To open up real dialogue

We want to hear divergent voices

Not just the normal voices

We want to hear other voices too

The abnormal ones

No, no, not abnormal

No, God, we're not saying they're abnormal

We're simply saying we invite all voices to be heard

To this end, we will be holding a meeting to be broadcast online in order to make it as fully accessible as –

We'll be live streaming the event

The real meeting will also be accessible

We have a ramp

That's right

This meeting is an opportunity to air grievances

And for a plethora of voices to be heard

Dialogue created

And bridges built

We have a ramp

And for those of you affected by any words or images you have seen there will be a helpline

Thank you

We have a ramp

Oh and please use the hashtag

*

#EATMYSHITALAN

#WEAREALLALAN

#SOLIDARITYWITHALAN

#FREEISALAN

#FREEALAN

#ALANISDAMAN

#ALANLIVESMATTER

#SHITBLOODALAN

#REMEMBERMRLAURENCE

*

Thank you all for coming we will be as brief as possible your time is valuable

We wish to acknowledge the issues raised concerning yesterday's meeting

We value your feedback and we recognise the immense courage it took you to speak out

Both about the initial incident as well as any and all distress caused by our subsequent statements or indeed yesterday's meeting

Regarding yesterday's meeting

We are grateful for your feedback

And in the light of your feedback

We regret the inflammatory nature of yesterday's meeting

We could have managed yesterday's meeting better

Had we been aware of the demonstrations that would take place outside yesterday's meeting

And inside yesterday's meeting

As well as the counter-demonstrations

And the counter-counter-demonstrations

We may not have proceeded with yesterday's meeting

We were unaware of the strong sentiment both pro- and anti-Alan that existed

We regret subsequent events

The eye gouging, the decapitation, the maiming, the ligament scarring, the tendon scarring, the serious injuries that occurred

We regret all of it

We regret that some of the injuries were life changing

Not least the decapitation

The decapitation was definitely life changing

The decapitation was regrettable

We're not saying people with life-changing injuries can't live fulfilling lives

We're not saying that

We're not trying to undermine the contribution to society of people with less than the normal number of heads

Don't say normal

The conventional number of heads

They are full members of society in some cases contributing more than people whose lives haven't been changed by decapitation-related injuries

In fact, one could possibly even say that in some cases those life-changing injuries have inspired such a radical rethink of purpose that for some individuals those injuries might even be seen in hindsight as life improving

*

Thank you all for coming we will be as brief as possible your time is valuable

We wish to apologise for the wording of yesterday's statement pertaining to the previous day's meeting pertaining to the previous statements pertaining to the original incident

Some of which was less than clear

In particular the inference that certain injuries –

Up to and including but not limited to decapitation

– can be seen as life improving

We wish to retract that statement

We will now embark on a time of reflection during which we aim to clarify the processes by which the decisions we made were made

In order to ensure all future decisions are sound

Which isn't to say we didn't have processes in place before

Oh no

We don't want to give that impression

We had processes

Coming out of our arses

Not literally

That would be inappropriate

Especially given the nature of the original smears

But rest assured there were processes

If there were processes, why were the decisions made not sound?

Sorry?

If there were processes, why were the decisions made not sound?

There's a perfectly rational, reasonable explanation for that

Yes, we're perfectly rational, reasonable people as I expect, as I hope is –

We like clarity

Too much fuzziness in the world

Too much chat

Too many people trying to avoid responsibility by talking their way out of things

That's why we are taking responsibility

We are owning our decisions

Our mistakes

And that's rare

*

This is getting out of hand

It's affecting the brand

What brand?

Our brand

We don't have a brand

Everyone has a brand. Everything has a brand

Where do you think the school gets its money from?

The government?

The government!

Who do you think pays for the sports hall?

Who do you think pays for the drama studio?

Who do you think pays for the food?

Do you think we just conjure paper and pencils out of thin air?

We need to raise funds for books, we need raffles, cake bakes, fancy-dress days, parents playing the trombone, bouncy castles, fun runs, we need the support of the community

And how is that going?

Why r ppl so SICK? 2 many H8rs #FreeAlan

Alan is ma boiiiiiii!!!!! #FreeAlan

Canot believ u suport this [poo emoji] &blood what is the world coming 2 dissGUSTING!!!! #LOCKHIMUP

Who is funding you? #DeepStateAlan #StopSmearingAlan

I'm not convinced these are real people

I think this is the work of bots, I wouldn't worry

Yes, Russian bots and conspiracy theorists

It'll all just blow over

Russian bots and – yes, conspiracy theorists, grown men sat in airless rooms in Greater Manchester or Clapham or Hove, trolling people like us

Innocent people like us

Night and day – exactly, yes – pausing only when their mums come in with a sandwich and a mug of tea and clean underpants

It'll all just blow over, I wouldn't worry

No, it'll all just blow over, you'll see

*

Celebrities are calling us out

What?

There's a hashtag

#StopSmearingAlan is catching on

#StopSmearingAlan is trending

Tess Daly has called us out

Lorraine has called us out

Gary Lineker has called us out

But Piers Morgan has tweeted in support

Benedict Cumberbatch on the other hand is appalled

Cumberbatch?

Cumberbatch is shocked and appalled

Cumberbatch is distancing himself from us

Sherlock is distancing himself from us

He's donating all payments from his next television to the fund

What fund?

The #FreeAlan fund

But there is no Alan

There must be, there's a fund

Where is this money coming from?

Where is it going?

Is Alan exploiting the situation for his own personal gain?

I think we need to be cautious not to scapegoat

We need to find Alan

We don't want this turning into a pile-on

We're not suggesting a witchhunt

But we don't want a cover-up

We can't be seen to allow a cover-up

We have to be seen to do something

We have to kill this, now, before it gets out of hand

*

We now go live to Downing Street where the lectern is out and the prime minister will shortly be giving a statement

Look, it would be anti-democratic of me to go against the will of the people, and if voters are against the smears it's not our role to nanny or mollycoddle, we're here to say, If that's what you want, chaps, full steam ahead, right behind you

The Leader of the Opposition has released a statement

My position is clear. I don't approve of these smears, I'm not personally a fan, but if we take time to reflect properly on the underlying causes of the smears –

Breaking news, according to a new opinion poll, the public is now against the smears, we're going live to Downing Street and – yes – the lectern is out. The lectern is out. The prime minister is standing behind the lectern, the lectern is out!

If you look at what I actually said, the point I was making – if you'll let me finish –

No one's interrupting

Yes, if you'll let me finish

But no one's interrupting

Yes, the point I was making is that smears are part and parcel of daily life, the public is frankly sick of hearing about smears and people just want to get on with their lives

The president of the United States is tweeting about the smears

The biased mainstream media has been trying to SMEAR me since day one. All of them FAILED! Someone needs to do something about these LOSER smears. SAD

According to a phone in, 84 per cent of *Good Morning Britain* viewers blame Raheem Sterling

And yes, yes, the lectern is back out. The prime minister is releasing a new statement, clarifying his position

When I said people are making too much of these smears, it's clear what I meant is that most ordinary decent people just want to be part of a society where small business can flourish and children play on the streets free of the fear of the smear. I do not shirk this challenge. Those who live by the smear will die by the smear. They shall not prosper. That's why – to quote Shakespeare – or someone – we will crack down on the smear menace with a velvet fist wrapped in an iron glove – or is that the other way round?

We now go live to CarpetWorld in Croydon where people are rioting

An angry mob in yellow vests is throwing milkshakes at CarpetWorld. Someone's attempting to set a low-shag carpet on fire. We're on fire! We're on fire! Water cannons are being deployed as we speak!

The water cannons have failed! The water cannons don't work! It's anarchy! JD Sports is on fire! Mothercare is on fire! Primark is on fire!

And according to a new poll, 87 per cent of voters believe the European Union is responsible for the smears

Society is collapsing!

There are riots in the streets!

A man was decapitated!

I saw his head on a spike

You saw footage of his head on a spike

It may have been doctored footage

The footage was probably doctored

You can doctor footage on an ordinary phone these days

It looked very real

I don't think it was real

This has gone too far

And finally some good news, the footballer Raheem Sterling is not responsible for the smears, it turns out he was playing football at the time

*

Thank you all for coming, brief as possible, time is valuable

We would like to begin by apologising for any misunderstandings that arose from our previous statements

We have examined ourselves

We have undergone a period of further reflection

And following that period of reflection we have changed

Who we were at the time of both the initial incidents and all subsequent statements does not reflect who we are now

We are no longer ourselves

We are literally different people

As a result we wish to distance ourselves from our previous statements

Because those statements we made

We didn't make them

No, we didn't make them, because we were different people then

We were unaware of the strength of feeling those decisions would arouse

Had we been aware, obviously, we would not have made those decisions

It goes without saying, we would have made different decisions

And I don't need to tell you we're not afraid to be seen to be wrong

Being wrong is actually a sign of being right

In a show of strength and leadership, we have therefore decided to act decisively by reversing that initial decision. We are no longer apologising and we will shortly be releasing a statement

*

Thank you brief time valuable

We've listened and we've heard your protests and your objections

And while you have every right to be angry

Frankly we think you should be more grateful

We're simply not responsible for everything that goes on here

It's too big

There's too much

I mean what do you expect?

We can't apologise for all the incidents because we'd never stop apologising

Because it's not really a series of incidents is it?

It's a culture

We can't apologise for a culture

We're not responsible for a culture

We didn't create the culture

Some people would say we perpetuate it

But they're wrong

We're not perpetuating a culture

We're challenging a culture

By our actions and our words

Which is why we're here

On Twitter

On Facebook

On Instagram

On YouTube

On BuzzFeed

On CNN

On Fox News

On Russia Today

There's even an opinion piece in the *New Yorker* magazine

Have you read it?

No, but I hear it's very good

And what we're saying is, what we're saying is, what we're actually saying is –

We're saying what we did was wrong

We're taking responsibility for the things we did

But we can't take responsibility for everything

There are limits

Our actions

Our specific actions

Our specific and limited actions

The way we talked to you for instance

Our tone

We'll take responsibility for our tone and even possibly some of the content

If our language was belittling or triggering or any of those things

We'll take responsibility for that, for those specific things

But not the entire culture, we can't take responsibility for that

Yes of course it's our building, we technically run the building, we technically built the building

Well not us but the people before us

That's the thing isn't it, it was the people before us

They laid the foundations of all this

And we're the ones having to clean up after them

Well, Mr Laurence is the one doing the cleaning up

Anyway, it's their fault really

So don't be angry with us

We're making the best out of a tricky situation

And yes, in the meantime, there may be some upset, some minor unrest

Some anger

Some of you it seems are very angry

Yes, people are angry and that's okay

You have the right to be angry

And that's valid

Within reason

Yes, within reason of course

You have the right to be angry, you have the right to be angry, you have the right to voice an opinion

Until they start throwing things, well then you've crossed a line

It's the line crossing we have a problem with

What we're asking for is patience

For you to bear with us

As we all pull together to solve this through dialogue

If we can just talk it out

Well that's what democracy is about

And that's why we're here to state our intentions

Yes, about the future

About – going forward – how this is going to work

And of course we apologise for anything the people before us may have done

Or may not have done, we're not here to judge

And assure you from now on –

Going forward

– that things will be different

Because we're in charge

And if you trust us, if you trust us

If you put your future in our hands

We'll take care of you

Going forward

Who are you exactly?

What?

Who are you exactly?

That's all we have time for

*

Thanks time valuable

It seems some of you weren't happy with the previous statement

It seems some of you weren't happy with the previous statement and have done some very silly things

Some very silly things indeed

Some of you it seems have smashed some things up

Some of you have taken to the streets

Which is silly

It's showing off

What we need is constructive dialogue

What we need is a time of healing to air our grievances

Not just air them

I'm talking about a sharing, a sharing of stories, an empowering sharing of stories

We'll get together and we'll share stories and we'll talk and we'll cry

What's important is we keep talking

That's right

Because as long as we're talking, you won't notice we aren't actually doing anything and everything is still the same as it was

That was a joke

It wasn't a joke

It was a joke, a funny joke to lighten the mood

It wasn't a joke

Going forward, I thought we could share some stories

About the incident

No, no, no, we've moved on from that, let's not dwell on that, let's not live in the past. I mean positive stories

Inspirational stories

Inspirational stories of the kind you get at the theatre

Exactly, of the kind you get at the theatre

I saw a play which, well I forget what it was about, it was about, well people were doing things, well they were talking mainly but they were doing things and these things made them happy or sad

Sometimes happy and sad at the same time which is of course the most sophisticated form of theatre

It is, yes, and then towards the end someone gave the most terrific speech in which he or was it a she, I can't remember

It was probably a he

It's usually a he

In which he basically said what life is like, and he spoke truth to the audience and they sat and they listened while the actor playing the character – because they're not real, these actors, they're not real, it's all made up, it's all just pretend – he articulated in the most extraordinary way these profound truths about life

They were profound

They punctured our souls

They did, my soul was punctured

And there was even – get this – there was even a school trip, a school trip of the kind of kids, who, well – you don't like to stereotype or cast aspersions, but there was a school trip of the kind of kids who when they walk in, they make you, they make you

Nervous?

Yes, nervous, they make you nervous and you wish they didn't, you wish they didn't make you nervous because you don't want to be the kind of person who gets nervous when kids go to the theatre

Because it's good they go to the theatre

Yes, it's good they go to the theatre

It's morally improving

They need the theatre, the kids, they need to know it's for them

Because it's about life

It's about empathy

Empathy!

It's about putting yourself in someone else's shoes and listening and actually really fucking listening and sorry for my language, I apologise for my language, but I'm really getting quite worked up by this, and sometimes, I admit it, I swear for emphasis, I swear to make a point, I know some people don't like swearing

But it happens

It does happen and it's somehow more truthful when people swear, it's more truthful isn't it, it feels more truthful, because people do swear don't they, in real life people do swear because in real life, well some of us are really actually very angry indeed at the way things are and we don't feel listened to or understood, we just feel patronised and talked over and even the people who tell us they're listening and they care –

Teachers, politicians, parents, people in power, even writers who write for the theatre, they don't actually listen do they, they don't actually listen, they tell you they do, but you know they don't cause nothing ever changes does it and – sorry, what was I saying?

The play

The play, yes, the play with the uplifting speech about life it contained so many truths about life and it really made me think, it really made me think and you know how you could tell?

Because the audience was quiet

Because the audience was quiet

Because we'd achieved catharsis

Which is a Greek word meaning – what does it mean?

It means everything is okay again

That's right, because of the truths we'd heard

That's right, because of the truths contained in the speech

And what were the truths contained in the speech?

Well I don't think we need to go into all that, I think my point is clear

*

Time val

Good news. We have found the individual responsible for the initial incident

We have found them and asked them to explain themselves

To Alan and to us

To Alan?

Yes, we found Alan

But I thought there was no Alan

No, there is an Alan and we found him

This is definitely Alan?

Of course this is Alan, of course it is, why would we tell you it was Alan if it wasn't Alan

And you're sure you have the right person, the person responsible for the smears?

Yes, stop asking such silly questions

And now this person will apologise to Alan and to us and then we can finally draw a line under this whole sorry business

This event will be live streamed

Please use the hashtag

*

#AlanForgivenessLive

*

Questioner, **Alan**, **Guilty Party**, *others to join.*

– Sorry

The **Questioner** *looks at* **Alan**. **Alan** *shakes their head.*

Sorry

The **Questioner** *looks at* **Alan**. **Alan** *shakes their head.*

Sorry

– Like you mean it

– Sorry

– Like you mean it

– Sorry

– Like you mean it

– Sorry

– Like you mean it

– Sorry

– Like you mean it

– Sorry

– Like you mean it

– SORRY

– LIKE YOU MEAN IT

– SORRY

– LIKE YOU MEAN IT

– SORRY, SORRY, I'M SORRY

The **Questioner** *looks at* **Alan**. **Alan** *nods.*

– Now if only you'd said that earlier you'd have saved us all so much bother

A fourth speaker.

– That's not Alan

– Of course it is, are you Alan?

Alan *hesitates, then nods.*

– And that's not the person who did it

– How would you know?

– Because I did it

It was me

Whoever speaks next could be anyone apart from the fourth speaker.

– Stop the show

Stop the broadcast

Cut the live feeds

*

The fourth speaker and at least one other.

– Why did you smear the shit and the blood so Mr Laurence the school caretaker had to give up his weekend?

– I don't know

– Why did you write 'EAT MY SHIT. EAT MY SHIT ALAN'?

Why did you write it?

– I was upset

– What about?

– Everything

– Can you be a little more specific?

– I don't know, I just did it

– Was it your shit?

– Yes

– And your blood?

– I had a nose bleed

I meant to write 'EAT MY SHIT. EAT MY SHIT ALL OF YOU', but I ran out of shit and blood and I changed 'ALL OF YOU' to 'ALAN' partly 'cause of running out of shit and blood but also' cause it seemed a bit daft

– And you thought writing 'EAT MY SHIT. EAT MY SHIT ALAN' would be less daft?

– It seemed less daft at the time

– But why did you want to write 'EAT MY SHIT. EAT MY SHIT ALL OF YOU'?

– I told you I was angry

– ABOUT WHAT?

– I trusted you and you broke my heart. Dashed it into a million pieces

– Have we met?

– I trusted you with my future

– Sorry, this is quite awkward

– I was born into a world where I was told things would be okay, that there would be jobs and houses and I would be safe and I could grow up and go to uni maybe and better myself and I could travel and I was told to respect other people that they would respect me

I was told to work hard, sit up straight, say please and thank you

I was told whatever I put in I would get back

I was told the world is fair

I was told there is such a thing as justice

I was told to believe in the future

And it turns out these things were not true

The world is not safe and not fair

You don't get to do what you want in your life by working hard people tell you that but it's not true

And the more I think about it the more I feel despair

– Don't feel despair

– I do I feel despair

– Yeah, but don't feel despair

– People can't afford to eat

People are going out for an evening and not coming home to their mums at night

People don't feel safe to go to sleep in their own homes

People are scared

And no one is doing a thing about it

None of you

You talk and you talk and you talk

You say these things and none of them makes a difference to me or to any of us

Who are you to tell me you're dealing with this?

– Well I'm sorry but that's not my fault

I'm not responsible for this

– You don't care what I say

You don't listen

Well you'll listen when I burn your house down

You'll listen when I riot in your streets

You'll listen when I make it so you can't sleep in your beds at night

You'll listen then, won't you?

– Well these are very serious accusations you're making

I have to say though, you're being very negative

Maybe some of these things are true

Maybe there was some loss of life

Maybe some people did starve to death

Or die in their beds

Or experience life-changing injuries

But that's life

And the thing you have to remember

The thing we all have to be grown up about and remember is there are far worse places to live

So it's actually all okay

It's certainly no excuse for smearing shit on the walls so nice Mr Laurence has to give up his weekend to clear it off

We don't riot, that's not what we do, that's just silly and counterproductive

We believe in the power of talking

We believe in dialogue

We listen to dialogue

And before you get carried away on this, on this, on this witchhunt – because that's what it is – before you get obsessed with ruining the lives of the people you think are responsible, it's important to bear in mind the character of those people

That's right, because these people you're branding monsters

They have families

They do, they have families and cherished pets

Some of them, many of them, most of them in fact are respected businesspeople

Government officials, teachers, nurses, vets, some of them are sports coaches, some of them drive minibuses and pick children up from broken homes to play sport on a Saturday

Some of them run the country

Some of them may be former prime ministers or even the current prime minister

Or future prime ministers

And we can't arrest them all, can we?

That's just silly

Like all this silly stuff you did for attention because that's what it was, it was for attention

Smearing shit and blood like a silly

No one cares

Everyone has moved on

Twitter has moved on

Benedict Cumberbatch has moved on

Lorraine has moved on

Gary Lineker has moved on

Piers Morgan is still tweeting but no one pays him any mind

So it didn't work, did it?

Still it's good to talk, isn't it?

In forums like these

Because if we can't talk to each other and learn to love and forgive and heal and help one another move on, what hope is there? If we can't do that. Forgiveness is what makes us human

How else can we grow? How else can we develop? How else can there be hope?

If we can just focus on this

Your apology. To all of us. For wasting our time

And can I just remind you if you're tweeting or on Insta, please use the hashtag

*

We wish to apologise for what you just heard

We're concerned it may not have been as uplifting as you hoped

We're concerned it may have been unsatisfactory

We're concerned it may have left you angry and unfulfilled

And that won't do

So we have taken the decision to cancel the person responsible

We've cancelled him

Permanently?

For ever, we have cancelled him for ever. He is now cancelled

So he won't be troubling any of you again

What, *cancelled*?

Yes, cancelled

What *cancelled* cancelled?

Oh gosh, no, not *cancelled* cancelled he's just gone to the place where cancelled people go

And where is that?

Probably somewhere in the North or Wales or Scotland or Basingstoke, somewhere like that

Somewhere away from us

And any suggestion that we manufactured this entire incident ourselves to distract from something bigger, well we refute that entirely

Entirely

*

Time

We can't pretend it's a one-off anymore

This is endemic, it's not about a few rotten apples, one or two bad eggs, it's systemic

We need to own this

That's why this time it can't just be about the individual. We need to acknowledge we have a corporate responsibility, all of us, to make these things right, together

Accordingly the head of our organisation has decided to take full responsibility and will shortly be making a brief statement

When I say head, I don't mean the actual head

That simply isn't possible, he's far too busy

However a member of staff will now read out a statement on behalf of the head taking full responsibility for any incidents that may have occurred

—— #Alan [Various hashtags including #AlanIsAGender, #NeverForgetAlan2019, #Alanspiration] ——

It was not me

What I did was not me

I am not the person who did those things

That is not in fact my behaviour

My behaviour at the time in no way reflects who I am

I take full ownership of my behaviour while at the same time wishing to reassure you that my behaviour was not in fact my own

It was someone's else's behaviour and even though that behaviour is not mine, it does in fact belong to the old me, a me that no longer exists, I take full ownership of that behaviour

And of course any and all future behaviours that may result

Are you happy?

Are you satisfied?

We hope you're not left feeling uneasy or unsure or excluded from the process

A series of public apologies

BY JOHN DONNELLY

Notes on rehearsal and staging, drawn from a workshop with the writer, held at the National Theatre, October 2019

Opportunities and challenges

Lead director Lyndsey Turner gave each participant two post-it notes and asked them to record:

Something that excited them about the play.

Something that frightened them about the play.

Lyndsey collected all the post-it notes and read out a couple of the now anonymous responses. Example responses included:

Something that excited us:

The fact that the text is so open.

The play's relevance to young people.

Something that frightened us:

Blocking the scenes so the play doesn't come across as being predictable.

Helping everyone to engage with character when they are not fully defined.

How John came to write the play

'Any value in what I say is whether it's useful to you or not. It's not about the answers or creating a tick list of what you must or mustn't do. It's just my take on the play. Please don't feel like you need to convey any of this. But take what is useful to you.

'I was interested in the idea of apologies in public spaces, having seen people and public organisations get statements really wrong. I became interested in the immediacy of speech and the response cycle surrounding anything you do or say on public forums. People's thinking time is really diminished on the social media channels. That idea got me thinking about how we respond to these public apologies and how language is used in them. It also got me thinking about how we get used to thinking about what the right terms are for certain things or situations. On Twitter, what are the right terms for things? Choosing the right language and what weight the words have becomes the primary objective. Being careful with words is a good thing, but the priority begins to shift from that impulse to be kind and inclusive, into the importance of getting the language right. And suddenly, getting the language right overrides, to the extent that we reward people for choosing the right combination of words, rather than necessarily because they have changed the underlying thinking.

'There's a pressure that we instil in children, that you need to use the right words, regardless of the intention behind them. I do think the words are really important but I think sometimes the addressing of the words in themselves can become slightly strange and not match the behaviour. And it happens on mediums like Twitter. You get people who become very good at using the right language but their behaviour doesn't change at all.

'So all of these things were in my head, and I wanted to write a play about this. At the same time, I've worked in schools quite a lot and I've written some plays for young people and I've wrestled with how you come up with text for them.

'You get the words of a forty-three-year-old man and put them into the mouths of teenagers. It can look odd and can feel a bit manipulative and I'm always a bit wary of that. So I wanted to create a form where it sort of just allows you on some level to draw attention to the fact that these can't literally be the thoughts of the young people. Having adults' language in the mouths of people that are a little bit too young to speak like that is quite useful in terms of exploring those ideas of how we bring children up to say the right thing.

'I wanted to create a form that would allow a range of possibilities. One which would allow a collaborative process. Where the actors could join in the development of the piece and the production themselves. That would be the ideal scenario. I'm also aware of the pressure of time within schools so the form allows you to address that and create a shortcut. Saying that, I do think that this is the type of text that requires a buy-in from the young people. There isn't time for a several month-long devising process, so they need to come on the journey of creation with you. I've written a play with a similar form before and it had a really galvanising effect on the group in terms of the ownership of it. They really enjoyed the process they went on. It contained something of themselves because they were part of creating it. That's something that I really like about theatre, that idea of process that you're engaging in as a group, and I wanted that to happen with this play.'

The form of the play

Because the play has such an 'open' quality, it's important to conceive a production which has quite a tight structure along with clear rules and parameters.

In this play, language is used to shut down dialogue rather than to invite it. The idea being that, 'If I can just phrase this apology in the right way, we will never need to discuss this again'. The ideal scenario for the speakers is that the play finishes on page two!

Even though the actors playing the parts will be young, the characters are written as adults.

Lyndsey asked the group to think about events we have witnessed in popular culture which really speak to the play. A few ideas that the group discussed included:

The moment when Harvey Weinstein attempted to brush off the initial allegations of sexual assault by saying 'it was another time back then'.

The NBA manager Daryl Morey's controversial tweet in support of anti-government protests which has caused huge conflict between major Chinese sponsors and the NBA. Which caused the NBA to distance themselves from Morey, which then resulted in certain groups of people insisting that the NBA should be standing by Morey's so-called moral positioning.

Scarlett Johansson's controversial casting in *Ghost in the Shell*, which ignited a row on an international scale regarding Hollywood 'whitewashing' stories originating in Japan. Subsequently Johansson distanced herself from the producers claiming that it wasn't her fault. Then the film company got someone else to play the part.

Justine Sacco's 2014 inappropriate AIDS tweet just before she boarded a flight. The post blew up whilst she was in the air resulting in her very public sacking even before she had landed. Her belief was that no one ever could have read that tweet as being serious but, unfortunately for her, that wasn't the case.

The 22,000 people who monitored Priti Patel's flight from Kenya as she was summoned back to the UK by the prime minister following the allegations that she had been involved in secret meetings with the Israeli government.

One of the things that John discussed was how immediate everything feels on platforms like Twitter. There isn't the thinking time for anyone to respond more thoughtfully. If there was, it's unlikely that this game of correction ping pong would be necessary. Both Lyndsey and John suggested that the series of events in the play are unlikely to span over more than one week. Possibly less.

John also added that it's worth remembering the scale of the play. If the tweet or message was sent by someone with ten followers, there would be mini ripples of trouble. But if it is sent by someone with ten thousand followers, then there is real trouble and a greater sense of risk and therefore drama for the production.

Why is the play a series of public statements?

How do we account for the fact that the characters haven't structured these sessions as question and answer forums? If the aim of the play is to shut conversation down, then the characters want to steer clear of 'town hall' and 'question time' moments in order to finalise this conversation.

An exciting opportunity

John expressed that the form is designed to allow participants to feel a sense of ownership over the piece that they are making. This is a piece of writing that has been specifically tailored to young actors. Due to the play's form, it suits any size of company. And its openness allows for a nearly infinite number of playing choices, meaning that no two productions will feel the same.

Lyndsey spoke about one of the other joys of this play is that the young cast will have a level of expertise around the subject matter that adults might not have. The internet is more their domain than ours.

Because of the fact that the characters are written as adults, each young company will have a chance to hold up a mirror to this moment in our shared history. It wasn't teenagers who created this 'sorry' culture.

Lyndsey referenced the fact that the play breaks the fourth wall. She spoke about the relish and enjoyment that the actors can have in taking over the space that they are performing, speaking directly to their audience.

Directing opportunities and challenges

The group discussed some of the following challenges and opportunities that they might encounter during the rehearsal and staging of this play:

OPPORTUNITY: There's so much opportunity in creating your production in terms of making a decision about who says which line. For example, do you have the same person saying the opening line of each scene or not? This decision would already start to paint a clear story about who is in control within the group.

CHALLENGE: The play does not rely heavily on character back story. The writer gives us very little information about who these characters are.

CHALLENGE: All the events (from the incident itself to whatever it is that makes the group return when they come back onstage) happen offstage. There are of course micro events (an interruption from the audience), but if you are looking at this through a Stanislavskian lens and exploring the 'beats' of the play, what happens onstage are responses to things offstage. Which means that it's important to establish what actually happens between the scenes.

CHALLENGE: The language. Not any particular words or the fact that it's in some sense a play about language. A world in which the speakers are aware (and sometimes dangerously unaware) of the words they are using. The playing of this language to be precise, as that's where the drama is.

Getting to know the play

Before you can start work on your casting and conceptual ideas, it's important that you spend a moment considering the nature of the play you have in your hands.

Exercise: Describing the play

Lyndsey broke the group up into twelve smaller groups. Each group was given a style or topic in which to describe the play:

January: Describe the play as if you were describing it to a nervous passenger on an aeroplane.

February: A Waterstones recommendation.

March: A movie poster.

April: Describe the story of the play as a lift elevator pitch.

May: As if you were describing it to a small child.

June: A BBC News headline.

July: Tell the story in one minute.

August: Pitching to a headteacher.

September: Describe the play using only five words. There were two versions of this challenge. One for the beginning of the play, one for the end.

October: As if it were the ingredients on a cereal packet.

November: Describe the play in one breath.

December: Describe the play with no words.

Creating the characters

Who are the people within the play? Lyndsey suggested they could be the following:

Teachers – senior management team

Governors – the school's board

Parent teacher association

A PR firm

Local education authority

Local councillors

In an academy setting, it could be the CEO of the trust

Friends of the school – people who have a strong relationship with the school

Powerful alumni of the school

You may want to use just one of these groups or potentially a mixture.

There was a suggestion that it could be the student council, but with that comes a huge challenge: How do you present to an audience 'a young person, playing a young person'? Of course, there is a chance that the school might want to make actual students submit the apology on the school's behalf, but this feels hugely unlikely and may steer away from some of the more exciting opportunities the play has to offer.

What and why are these characters doing what they are doing in the play?

They are attempting to apologise for an incident and then attempting to apologise for the apology for the incident, with the super-objective of shutting the whole event down.

Why do they have to do it so many times?

Lyndsey described this question as being like the 'snake in the tube' prank. As soon as you pop the lid off the tube where the snakes are stored, they leap out at you. No matter how hard you try to get them back in, they keep on leaping back out. It feels like an endless cycle of attempts to get it right.

Why does the piece end where it ends?

John said that it felt right at the end that someone comes in and says that they are refusing to take any more responsibility. They are not talking about this anymore and they are finally drawing a line under it. This is not a conversation that they are willing to have anymore.

The story on pages 156–7

These are the only pages in the play where John has assigned actual lines to characters. Within all the openness of the script, Lyndsey and John have requested that this bit of text should stay consistent in order to preserve the story. This is what they described as a non-negotiable. The four main characters within this section are:

Actor A: (**Questioner**)
Actor B: (**Alan**)
Actor C: (**Guilty Party**)
Actor D: (**Fourth Speaker**)

Details on who should say what:

Questioner, Alan, Guilty Party, others *to join.*

– Sorry (**Guilty Party**)

The **Questioner** *looks at* **Alan**. **Alan** *shakes their head.*

Sorry (**Guilty Party**)

The **Questioner** *looks at* **Alan**. **Alan** *shakes their head.*

Sorry (**Guilty Party**)

– Like you mean it (**Questioner**)

– Sorry (**Guilty Party**)

– Like you mean it (**Questioner**)

– Sorry (**Guilty Party**)

– Like you mean it (**Questioner**)

– Sorry (**Guilty Party**)

– Like you mean it (**Questioner**)

– Sorry (**Guilty Party**)

– Like you mean it (**Questioner**)

– Sorry (**Guilty Party**)

– Like you mean it (**Questioner**)

– SORRY (**Guilty Party**)

– LIKE YOU MEAN IT (**Questioner**)

– SORRY (**Guilty Party**)

– LIKE YOU MEAN IT (**Questioner**)

– SORRY, SORRY, I'M SORRY (**Guilty Party**)

The **Questioner** *looks at* **Alan**. **Alan** *nods.* (**Alan**).

– Now if only you'd said that earlier you'd have saved us all so much bother (**Questioner**)

A fourth speaker

– That's not Alan (**Fourth Speaker**)

– Of course it is, are you Alan? (**Questioner**)

Alan *hesitates, then nods.* (**Alan**)

– And that's not the person who did it (**Fourth Speaker**)

– How would you know? (**Questioner**)

– Because I did it (**Fourth Speaker**)

It was me (**Fourth Speaker**)

Whoever speaks next could be anyone apart from the fourth speaker. [John clarified this stage direction by saying that there is no reason why this line couldn't be said by the questioner or even Alan or, of course, it could be said by absolutely anyone else, including a new person altogether. As long as it's not the fourth speaker.]

– Stop the show (**Anyone except fourth speaker**)

Stop the broadcast (**Anyone except fourth speaker**)

Cut the live feeds (**Anyone except fourth speaker**)

The section that follows this, which begins with the stage direction '*[The fourth speaker and at least one other]*', should also follow the same strict, clear structure in order to preserve the story as it has been written. This structure acts in a similar way to a jazz rhythm. Jazz acknowledges the existence of bar structure. The rigid drum beat supplies you with the spine and structure in order to give you the freedom to play and riff elsewhere.

   It is worth adding that the questioner could of course be played by multiple people. It doesn't just need to be one person. But whoever that person or people are, they should remain consistent throughout this section.

Casting

The cast sizes for the participating groups ranged between six and forty-one actors.

For those with larger groups or groups who need to split the cast up (because of actor availability/rehearsal constraints) this play can legitimately be performed with two separate casts:

On page 149, John has written the lines:

We are no longer ourselves
We are literally different people

For those that didn't want to take the lines literally, there was a question about how else you could highlight that moment. Someone suggested that it could be a moment when everyone switches characters. The challenge with that idea is that this isn't a character play. It is a work play. Everyone is at work. Your primary lever isn't, 'Who are you inside? How prepared are you? How ambitious are you?' It's more a question of, 'What is your function?' For example, how would an audience clearly notice the switch between those who had been part of the PTA group who were now being the famous alumni?

Casting hierarchy

Lyndsey offered the following three different types of casting structures from three different types of plays:

Shakespeare

Tier 1: One person, after whom the play is usually named. They get around 30 per cent of the lines.

Tier 2: Here two or three characters who are instrumental to the plot, each with a decent amount of lines.

Tier 3: Here we find five or six smaller named characters.

Tier 4: Shakespeare fills the rest of the cast up with people of a lower rank (servants, messengers, attendants, etc.). These people are useful in order to tell the story.

Chekhov

Tier 1: He tends to focus on the ways in which three or four characters have an impact on each other's lives.

Tier 2: He then places four or five characters with far fewer lines beneath them.

Tier 3: And then a much smaller group of servants and workmen, some without any lines (Yakov in *The Seagull* for example).

Ensemble

The text is divided pretty equally between all the characters: they share the story

When it comes to casting this play, you might want to use any of the distribution patterns mentioned above – although the Shakespearean model doesn't feel very Connections! How you choose to organise the casting of the play will inevitably have an impact upon the story the audience receive.

Casting idea 1

You might want to start with only part of your cast onstage at the beginning. Potentially a group of senior managers. Then when things get worse, they draft in a larger number of people to help clear up the mess that has been caused. As the problem gets worse, the play grows.

Casting idea 2

You could look at the idea of reshuffling the hierarchy during the play. You could set up a clear status hierarchy at the beginning of the play: a group of people or person that becomes clearly recognisable as the leader. And then when you hit Scene Eight, for example, that person or group of people are shifted to the outskirts of the stage and replaced with someone new.

Casting idea 3

An actor or a group of actors who have been at the centre of the story for a large chunk of the play are then completely absent from the final four scenes. This isn't just a reshuffle but someone being completely axed.

Casting idea 4

What happens if the spokesperson is constantly getting cancelled? Or there has been someone there all along and then they disappear? An audience will start to ask the question: where did she go to?

These are all things you can play with and discover from rehearsals. See what happens when you are with your actors and note what it is that you allow to emerge.

Of course, you can have everyone on stage all of the time, but the option of building and decreasing your cast at different times is a choice you are making as a director for your production; it isn't just logistical. Therefore, start by thinking about what casting shape you'd like to work with and then think about what you want to do with the story and then work from that. For each scene you will then start to think about:

Who has the highest status?

Who's there against their will?

Who's got what specialism that is going to aid the group?

Who's naturally shy?

Who keeps to their talk plan?

Simply the sheer allocation of lines will start to make an audience think and read things into the production you are making.

Collective responsibility

Lyndsey said that if she was directing this play, the idea of collective responsibility would be something that she would be putting a lot of weight behind in her rehearsal room.

In order to explain the idea of collective responsibility, Lyndsey referenced the cabinet. In cabinet meetings there can be a whole variety of opinions. Some people will agree with the idea or bill that is being tabled, some people won't. By the time that the meeting is over and ministers are going out into the public, whatever has been agreed in that meeting must be the line that is toed in public. This is also known as 'the party line'.

Example: In the fictitious cabinet meeting for the culling of hamsters, there are MPs who are for the proposed bill and MPs who are against it. In the meeting, each MP can argue freely for their point. However, once you leave the cabinet and the decision has been made regarding the direction that this bill is taking, at that point it is a case of 'we are all in this together' and everyone must agree irrespective of what people's first proposals were.

Exercise: Collective responsibility task

Due to a marketing error, Pret a Manger are only able to offer one flavour of sandwich. Discuss in your group which flavour of sandwich Pret are going to offer. By the end of the task you need to lobby for that flavour as a group.

Lyndsey then asked one person from each group who started off the task strongly proposing for a very different type of sandwich to then advocate for the chosen sandwich.

The tension between your own personal opinion and the party line is dynamite when dealing with character. It's where so much drama lives. Which characters are having to go along with the collective responsibility despite their own personal views? You could look at improvising the moments in between the scenes. Who agrees with the decision that they come up with? Is there anyone who is struggling to toe the party line? How did they get to the decision that we are hearing today?

Throughout the play, Lyndsey suggested considering to what extent the speeches are planned. Have they been scripted? Are they improvised? Have they been workshopped and developed? This could change throughout the piece and even within sections. Is there development within this?

Exercise: Character tarot cards

The group were asked to create ten index cards and write one of the below titles on each of them. Once the cards have been created, each person in the group should pick one card at random. That title determines how they then play each of the lines in a particular section of the play.

Spokesperson

Deputy Spokesperson

The Lawyer

The PR

The Dissenter (someone who has not bought into the idea of collective responsibility)

The Corrector/Fact Checker

The Optimist

The Joker**

The Calmer

The Genius

Fire Starter*

The Humaniser*

The Amateur*

* These got added to the list during the exercise.
** The usefulness of The Joker was questioned and more helpfully replaced by the * words.

Groups were split into three and each chose two pages of text. Instructions were as follows:

First of all, read the play neutrally, swapping lines line by line. The second time, read the scene neutrally and line by line again, but this time play your card when you think the line could work for the tarot card you are holding. Read the scene a third time, but this time the lines are given to whoever played their card at that time. Allow your chosen tarot quality to colour what you are saying. If more than one person plays their card on a certain line – try both options and see which works best/most successfully for the production you are making. What stories emerge? It's not a game to win the most lines nor is it a game about being the best sharer. By allocating lines this way, you start to be able to steer what the story is rather than just randomly selecting who says what. There's a logic or story to the process. Here is what the group discovered:

Group 1: the section beginning on page 141

After hearing it once through, Lyndsey asked the group to imagine that this scene was a backstage moment and not one of the more common public moments. She asked the group to redo the scene as if the mics are no longer live. This is not something that is going out to the public but a more private, group consultation meeting. She then repeated the scene for a third time: having played the scene as if it was behind closed doors, they are now trying to solve the situation but this time they are having to sort it out in public. The first time the group read the scene, when they were in private, it felt easy. The second time was far more anxiety inducing. It felt like they were having to come up with ideas on the spot.

There's more information about these 'backstage' or 'bunker' moments later on in the notes.

Group 2: the first smear section on pages 139–41

The group looked at the idea of potentially planting someone in the audience for this section. A heckler. Someone who doesn't feel like they are in the world of the play. In order for this to really work, we must really buy into the idea that they really are an outsider. So it's less about characterisation in these instances, but more about really asking the questions and demanding an answer. This really increases the stakes of the meeting and gives the group something really dangerous to deal with. It automatically makes them work harder because things aren't going well.

Group 3: the first smear section on pages 139–41

This time lines were assigned for this group, allocating different tarot cards to the different lines. This version felt really clear. It had a very clear story. It was incredibly clear where the power in the scene was. This version was far less evenly spread and therefore highlighted the people who weren't speaking. It revealed the collective responsibility of the bodies in space. Who stands behind the spokesperson is a choice that can be made. They are advocates of these words.

Tarot card summary

At the end of the exercise the group noted the successes of this exercise. Lyndsey commented on how smooth and easy the process of making and selecting the cards was. The conversations that were taking place around the room felt extremely high quality. Furthermore, it seemed to take the pressure off the participants. Simply playing a card rather than having to fight your corner felt far less ego bruising. The disagreements felt less personal.

Getting the actors to choose those characters also felt like the most efficient way of establishing who says what and why, resulting in getting lots of directing done.

This exercise felt like a great way to start thinking about the roles and energies of the different Tarot cards when assigned to different lines. With larger groups, you could have whole tribes of lawyers or a whole agency of PR people. The only multiple that wouldn't naturally work as well would be a tribe of spokespeople.

The scenic shape: sliders

Lyndsey offered the idea of sliders to the group. These are exceptionally useful when repetition is kind of the point. Like in music, repetition changes slightly – you repeat with a change in tension, variation of tempo or relaxation. Suggestions of different sliders included:

Order – chaos

Relaxation – tension

Optimism – pessimism

Together – separation

Written – improvised

Using the text on pages 142–3, the group were split into two and assigned lines. The objective for one group was to take the scene from a place of 'togetherness' at the beginning to a place of separation at the end and the reverse for the other group.

Different modes within the play

As discussed earlier on in the notes, Lyndsey and John suggested that there are a number of 'private' or 'bunker' scenes that don't follow the usual Q and A pattern of the play. The scenes that don't necessarily start with 'Thank you for coming'.

The following scenes seem to encourage a slightly different mode on how the companies might engage with the play:

Page 141 – As discussed previously.

Page 143 – Starting with hashtags. These could be presented in any way you like. Referring to the stage directions at the top of the play, this could be an opportunity for companies with technical students to explore projection. It could become a non-spoken scene. Alternatively, Lyndsey suggested an idea of reading out the hashtags as if they were reading from phones.

Page 145 – Same mode as page 141.

Page 146 – Same mode as page 141.

Page 148 – This isn't exactly a bunker scene but its mode feels different to the majority of the play. For those with bigger cast sizes, Lyndsey suggested this could be a great opportunity to introduce a new cast member. The surprise of seeing someone we've never seen before. It could give the idea that we're in a new world. There was also a suggestion that this section doesn't just have to be one single news report. It could be news reports from all over the world. For example:

'We now go live to Downing Street' – BBC News

'Look, it would be anti-democratic of me' – Channel 4 News

'Breaking News' – Sky News

Page 155 – The Hashtag

Page 156 – The Question and Answer

Page 156 – The Apology

Structure

John broke down the structure of the play in the following way. This might become a really useful way of structuring your rehearsals. To begin with you will want to rehearse the play asterisk to asterisk but eventually you will want to weave them together and work act to act.

Act One (pages 137–42): A group of people are fairly sure that all they need to do is make one statement and it will go away. This proves incorrect. The pressure of their wrongness leads to fighting within the group. This leads to the first 'bunker moment'.

Act Two (pages 142–9): The Problem Gets Bigger. The Spokesperson starts again but with renewed energy. We've had our meeting. We've spoken about what we got wrong. Hopefully now people will see that we have changed. However, the problem only gets bigger. The outside world starts to become an antagonist. Leading to: we've got a problem of scale. We haven't just made an error but a monumental one.

Act Three (pages 149–53): Open Warfare. It's actually your fault. The group reincarnate and become something different. They're ready to fight.

Act Four (pages 153–7, up to and including the live stream): The Search for Closure. How on earth is this ever going to end? 'Cut the live stream' ends that search for closure. Lyndsey described Act Four as being the moment where you are throwing red meat to the audience in an attempt to make them stop fighting you. The biggest piece of red meat is the live stream.

Act Five (page 157–end): The big problem in Act Five is not who wrote what on a wall. The big problem in Act Five is the world. When the red meat/live stream doesn't work, they really are out of options. The audience has a lot of the power here and the play ends with a pulling back of responsibility. No. This has gone too far. We are not willing to discuss this anymore.

Working in this way will support you when you're looking to find the ups and downs, the peaks and troughs of the play.

Stakes

Exercise: Marble game – building a sense of stakes with language

Lyndsey referenced the board game Operation. In order to win at that game, there has to be a real sense of care with each and every one of your actions. There is a huge similarity with language in John's play. It's instant stakes. If anyone gets this wrong, the consequences are huge. The words that the speakers choose are chosen with care and real consideration.

The game

Three people are holding a tray with one hand. A marble is placed on the tray. Behind each person holding the tray is a line feeder. Their role is to feed the lines to the person trying to keep the marble on the tray. The people holding the tray should say the words whilst trying to keep the marble on the tray. Note what effect this level of care has on the voice and text.

Lyndsey upped the stakes of the exercise and told the groups not to find it funny when the marble dropped. Keeping the marble on the tray represents this matter coming to a close once and for all. When it threatens to fall off, it becomes a problem and you need to concentrate on getting it back into the middle.

The final challenge to this exercise was to get rid of the tray and marble (but keep the feeding of the lines). Lyndsey asked the participants to replicate the quality of the speaking without the exercise keeping them in the game. This resulted in the really specific and conscious choosing of certain words. It started to bring out the importance of the language and how well those characters chose them.

Exercise: Blue and green boxes

Lyndsey drew a chart with a series of blue and green boxes.

Blue box – this is a solution, the written scene that is seen and heard onstage.

Green box – this is the event that took place offstage which the scene onstage is responding to. The what happened/what is the problem before this scene. It is also the what happened in between the scenes.

The group looked at page 137 for this exercise.

The green box for in between the first two scenes identified that the word 'may' that was used in the first scene was the problem. Therefore, the solution for the following scene was to admit distressed *was* caused.

The group then reread the scene on page 137 but with the idea that they are now solving a problem that they had identified in between the first and second scenes. This reading brings the problem of 'may' to the forefront of the scene. The scene becomes the only logical response to the problem.

Inventive ways of dealing with the swearing in the play

John requested that the companies who might find the swearing challenging in their group/school find a way of covering the expletives up, but not changing the words.

Lyndsey offered the character of The Censor. This is potentially a sound that goes over the swear word. A character who exaggeratedly mouths the word but does not vocalise it. An accidental noise that covers up the swear word each time it is said. A cartoonish piece of cardboard that is raised in front of the actor's mouth each time an expletive is about to be said.

Lyndsey also drew the group's attention to the idea of neutralising the swearing. It's about passing through the word in the line rather than leaning on it. It is highly likely that it is not the most interesting word in the line and, by not drawing attention to it, the audience are far less likely to be concerned by it.

Staging the transitions

There is a chance that this play could easily run longer than one hour. This will happen if the moments in between the scenes are longer than the scenes themselves. Lyndsey's advice was to keep these moments short wherever possible.

Lyndsey gave the example of a production of Mike Bartlett's *Cock*, which is also a play with many short scenes. The sound design in between each of the scenes was just the beep of an answering machine. Could the sound for these transitions be something similar? The sound of social media alerts for example?

Do you want to see characters and actors arrive and leave? Characters/actors just being in their position is one choice. Them arriving/leaving the space is a choice. Do you see them arriving before the camera is rolling? Do you see a studio manager counting down before the scenes go live? Do you see characters leaving when they think the cameras have stopped rolling? Do the transitions start in a place of disorder and get more organised as the story unfolds? What happens if the play is continuous action? Thinking about how you get your actors on and off stage is a real choice for your production.

Think about characters' behaviours. What habits do characters in the play have? Is there someone who has a habit that needs managing throughout the play?

Set design

This isn't a play that relies heavily on huge set design. It is all about finding a simple or singular gesture. A selection of ideas included:

That gesture could be a company who are never allowed to sit down throughout the duration of the problem.

A singular door where everyone enters from.

An onstage and offstage wing space.

A set of blocks or seat raking that could work as a podium.

A projection of the school crest with the school motto that keeps changing.

Are they just in one space throughout? Does the play move when they are in different modes?

The task of this design is finding the one thing that works or goes on a journey, rather than lots of things. This is not the play that needs to win the award for best set design. Doing one little gesture is what the play is asking for.

Pre-recorded moments?

There was a conversation within the group surrounding the possibility of recording certain moments of the play. For example, could the broadcast in the middle of the play be pre-recorded reports, potentially performed by different members from within the wider school or college community? Could it potentially be recorded by other staff members? John said that as long as this was very much a choice and part of the world of the play, this should be OK. If possible, use other students, but for those with a really small cast, this could be an option.

Costume

In a school setting you could keep them in their school uniform but get them to play the serious business manner that was discussed earlier in the notes. It's as if you are giving the transcript of the events to a group of students and getting them to act it out.

In sharp business attire.

Could the world be slightly off-kilter? Like *The Handmaid's Tale*?

What is the bottom half of the costume compared to the top half (as if they were on camera and we are only meant to see one half of them)?

If you were to do the version with two casts, what is the difference between the two casts? Are the first half dishevelled and unprepared, in comparison to the second half who are slick and ready?

What is the journey of the costume? Does the costume sharpen? Or do they look a mess and have to correct it throughout the play?

Line learning

For groups who have additional needs and may struggle with the word-heavy nature of the play, this is actually one of the few plays that could handle a stage-manager figure where certain lines are fed to actors – as if an earpiece has failed. Groups could utilise cue cards as if it were a presentation. Some scenes could be read from the sides as if it was a prepared statement, whereas other scenes could feel improvised.

In this circumstances, it might be worth thinking about the Chekhov casting structure where certain actors who can manage it take the lion's share of the spoken word.

Suggested references

David Cameron leaving the podium whistling

Theresa May walking onstage for the Tory Party conference

Harvey Weinstein's initial response to the allegations against him

Little Britain: the politician apologising for the sex scandal

Borat – his interviews where really inappropriate questions are asked to people in power

TV programme *Sex Education* – the different hierarchical groups within that series

#Brexit on Twitter

Monty Python: Four Yorkshiremen sketch

Spinal Tap – band trapped under the basement

BBC – Naga Munchetty's disciplinary hearing

The articles in the US about Prince George doing ballet

Kids Meet YouTube series

Timeline of Kanye v. Taylor Swift

Donald Trump's Twitter feed – a good example of someone never apologising

Harry Enfield: Tory Boy

Monty Python: Spanish Inquisition

TV programmes/film: *The Thick of It, In the Loop, Veep*

Jonathan Pie's opinion on politics

Footage of politicians walking through crowds

Politicians approaching podiums

BBC series *W1A* and *2012* – great examples of people stuck in language

The Active Text by Dymphna Callery

TV programme *Spitting Image*

Alan Partridge

The Play That Goes Wrong by Mischief Theatre Company

Katie Hopkins' Twitter feed

Piers Morgan – 'Have you got a TV?' moment on *Good Morning Britain*

G7 Summit – Boris Johnson's aide walking away with a coffee cup

Ed Miliband eating a bacon sandwich

The letters falling behind Theresa May at Tory Party conference

Montage of David Cameron walking out of shot

The Cut, YouTube

Waiting for Godot by Samuel Beckett

Aaron Sorkin – opening of Studio 60 (YouTube)

West Wing – Toby's first attempt at being press security

Political cartoons

The expert trying to keep his children out of the room during a live interview

From a workshop by Lyndsey Turner
with notes by Alex Thorpe

The IT
by Vivienne Franzmann

The IT is a play about a teenage girl who has something growing inside her. She doesn't know what it is, but she knows it's not a baby. It expands in her body. It starts in her stomach, but quickly outgrows that, until eventually it takes over the entirety of her insides. It has claws. She feels them. Does it have teeth, skin and hair as well, or is that feathers or spikes she can feel, butting up against her organs? What is it? It makes a noise, like a lizard or a snake. No one must know about it. She has to keep its presence, its possession of her, concealed. She pulls away from her friends. She refuses to speak in case the It is heard. Then the It tries to escape from her body. She can't let that happen. She cuts an isolated weird figure at school, trying to live her life normally, but battling to keep the It inside of her. But she can't contain it for ever – sooner or later something's got to give . . .

Presented in the style of a direct-to-camera documentary, this is a darkly comic state-of-the-nation play exploring adolescent mental health and the rage within, written very specifically for today.

Cast size
8–100, 1F and all other characters any gender
Suitable for all ages

Vivienne Franzmann won a Bruntwood Playwriting Award in 2008 for her first play *Mogadishu* and was awarded the George Devine Award for Most Promising Playwright in 2010. Her next play, *The Witness*, premiered at the Royal Court Theatre in 2012. In 2014, her play *Pests*, written for the theatre company Clean Break, was performed at the Royal Exchange and the Royal Court. In 2016, *The Snow Queen* was staged at the Bristol Old Vic. In 2017, *Bodies* premiered at the Royal Court. She has written for Channel 4, BBC One, Radio 4 and Radio 3. In 2014, she was awarded a BAFTA for her short film for children *Lizard Girl*. Vivienne has taught playwriting nationally and internationally.

Twenty-seven speaking parts. Can use multi-roling.

Chorus is minimum of five people. No maximum.

The Chorus represents all the information that Grace sees and hears.

Members of the Chorus take on the roles of Grace's Mum and Dad, Barrister, etc.

Grace is written for a girl.

All other parts can be played by anyone and pronouns changed accordingly.

The song that is referred to in the pizza scene, the classroom scene and penultimate scene can be any song you think fits.

The **Chorus** *makes its presence felt.*

The **Chorus** *buzzes. It fizzes. It hums. It is here.*

*

Student 1   She was quiet.

Student 2   Yeah.

Student 1   Didn't really notice her.

Student 2   Nah.

Student 1   Not shy exactly.

Student 2   No, not shy.

Student 1   But not loud either.

Student 2   No, not loud.

Student 1   The sort of person that if someone at school said 'You know Grace?', you'd say 'Who's Grace?'

Student 2   Who's Grace?

Student 1   And they'd say 'Grace Freemantle'.

Student 2   Grace Freemantle.

Student 1   And you'd say, 'Who's Grace Freemantle?'

Student 2   Exactly.

Student 1   And they'd say, 'She's the one in 11F'.

Student 2   The one in 11F.

Student 1   And you'd say, 'Oh, the one with the hair and the glasses'. And they'd say, 'No, that's Miriam'.

Student 2   That's Miriam.

Student 1   And then after a few tries, you'd get it.

Student 2   Yeah.

Student 1   You'd remember who she was. You know the sort, not that good-looking.

Student 2   Nah.

Student 1   Not bad-looking though.

Student 2   Nah.

Student 1   Not clever. Like clever clever.

Student 2   Nah.

Student 1   You know, not in the top sets or anything like that.

Student 2   Nothing like that.

Student 1   But not the bottom sets either.

Student 2   Nope.

Student 1   Not a joker.

Student 2   Nah.

Student 1   Or a trouble-maker.

Student 2   Nah

Student 1   Or a loner.

Student 2   Nope.

Student 1   She had friends.

Student 2   Yeah, she had friends.

Student 1   They weren't popular.

Student 2   Unpopular.

Student 1   No, not unpopular.

Student 2   No, yeah, no, yeah, not unpopular.

Student 1   Grace was just kind of . . .

Beat.

Student 1   You know those American kids that go into high schools and shoot everyone dead. And the teachers go, 'No big surprise, he hasn't spoken for two years and he's been wearing the same black sweatshirt for eleven months and his Chemistry book is full of drawings of guns'.

Beat.

Student 1   Well, Grace wasn't like that.

Student 2   She wasn't like that.

Student 1   She was average.

Student 2   Yeah, average.

Student 1   Grace Freemantle was totally average.

Student 2   Totally average.

Grace   I am Grace Freemantle. I was totally average.

Chorus *buzzes.*

*

Student 3   My dad is mates with Grace's dad Paul. My dad always says Paul is a good bloke. My dad's a twitcher, which means he's a bird watcher. Yeah, cringe. Totally. I hear you. Paul, Grace's dad, is also a twitcher. The pair of them go down the Marshes every Sunday with their binoculars and then they go for a fry-up at Pauline's cafe and chat about sparrows and bob-tailed tits. That's a real bird. That's its real name.

Last year, Paul, Grace's dad, posted this video of Grace having a tantrum when she was little.

Chorus   46 likes. 15 thumbs up. 27 tears of laughter emojis.

Grace   I am five years old. I am wearing my 'Little Miss Sunshine' t-shirt. Dad is playing with his new phone. We're supposed to be going to the park. I ask him. He says he's busy. But he promised. Before, he promised. And that is not fair.

Student 3   It is a funny video. I can't deny that. She's screaming on the floor, little arms and legs all over the place.

Grace   I am fire and fury inside.

Student 3   Then she gets up and she falls onto her Lego. And if you've ever fallen on Lego, you'll know that it hurts like hell. And Grace's dad, Paul, films it all on his new phone, giggling away. Not in a horrible way, just, you know, like a dad way.

Grace   I am red and blood and pus inside.

Student 3   Grace's mum, Jen, comes in to see what's going on. She tries to reason with Grace, but there's no point.

Grace   I am blast and yellow and clash inside.

Student 3   Jen tries to cuddle her and Grace kicks her.

Grace   I am rupture and burst and storm inside.

Student 3   And Paul, Grace's dad says:

Student 3 and Grace's Dad   'Your behaviour is completely inappropriate for a young lady.'

Student 3   And Grace roars in his face. Like actually roars. Like properly roars. And she's sent to her bedroom to think about what she has done. And Jen turns to Paul and says, 'What did we do to deserve her?' and they burst out laughing. And the video stops.

Paul found the video last year and he put it up on Facebook with the title 'EPIC Dis-Grace'. Which is kind of funny and clever because it's a pun on her name, Grace. Dis-Grace. Epic Dis-Grace. But also a bit, you know, crap of him. All the parents thought it was hilarious, my dad included.

Chorus   Comments.
Epic: Dis-Grace. Lol. Emoji thumbs up
Little Miss Sunshine. Lol.
Give me that over a teenager any day.
Preach. Emoji fist bump
The roar! Emoji love heart eyes.
Yes! The roar! The roar! Five emoji love heart eyes.

Student 3   FYI, I'm not saying that Paul, Grace's dad, posting that video on Facebook has got anything to do with Grace and that day in PE and what happened and everything. I mean it probably didn't. It's just, you know, I wouldn't like it if my dad did that. It's not a very responsible adult grown-up thing to do.

*

Grace   It's December. Cold. Evening. Seven o'clock. I am at home. My dad is still at work. Mum has just got back from her shift and is eating a sandwich with some chutney she found at the back of the cupboard.

I am in my bedroom, staring at my GCSE revision time table. My revision time table is colour coded and covered in fluorescent post-its that Dad nicked from work. My parents are big on revision and working hard and me being the 'best possible version' of myself. My revision time table is a work of art.

Mum takes a bite of her sandwich and shouts up the stairs:

Grace's Mum   Grace, are you revising?

Grace   I like the way the pink and the yellow post-its look next to each other.

Grace's Mum   Grace, did you hear me?

Grace   They remind me of sweets.

Grace's Mum   Grace?

Grace   Like Rhubarb and Custards.

Grace's Mum   I hope you're revising, Grace.

Grace   Like the Rhubarb and Custards I had when we went to the seaside when I was seven.

Grace's Mum   It's Maths and Physics tonight, isn't it?

Grace   When we walked along the beach and found shells and Dad ran into the sea and I had a 99 ice-cream and Mum ruffled my hair and snuck a bite of my flake, but I didn't mind cos the sun was shining and the sea was wavy.

Grace's Mum   Grace, I'm not going to nag you. Remember, it's your future.

Grace   And that's when I first feel it.

Grace's Mum and Chorus   Your future.

Grace   In my belly. I feel . . .

Grace's Mum and Chorus   Your future.

Grace
A presence.
A gnawing.
A squirming.
It is small.
Like a cherry pip.

Or a baby shrimp.
It is really small.
Whatever it is.
But it's here.
It's definitely here.

*

Student 4   Grace Freemantle?

--

Student 4   Grace Freemantle in PE?

--

Student 4   More like Grace Freemental.

--

Student 4   Grace Free-mental?

--

Student 4   D'you get it?

--

Student 4   You don't get it.

*

Sam   I met Grace on my first day at primary. We were best friends. We are best friends . . . were . . . are . . . I dunno . . . it's hard to . . . since . . . Anyway, I loved primary. We all loved primary. Every Thursday, our teacher, Mrs Drake, took the whole class onto the school field and told us to look up at the sky. She told us about cumulus clouds and stratus clouds and nimbus clouds. She asked us to close our eyes and listen to the music of the wind in the trees. She asked us to lie on our stomachs and feel the heat of the earth on our skin and look at the grass and count all the different things we could see. She said, 'Isn't the world a wonderful place?' And we nodded, belly down on the hot soil. One Thursday, I counted seventeen things in the grass. Grace counted seventeen too. We both saw an iridescent bug with bright green wings. It was beautiful. I miss being seven. I miss counting interesting things in the grass.

*

Grace   I am in the library. I am reading a book about . . . I don't know what it's about, because I'm not reading it really. It's for English and it's boring and I'd rather read my own books than the books that someone else tells me I have to read. I flick through Insta on my phone.

Chorus   A young woman stands in a bikini on a beach.

Grace   My insides feel hot.

Chorus   A young woman stands in a bikini on a beach. The beautiful orange sun sets behind her.

Grace   I feel . . .

Chorus   The palm trees are a vivid green.

Grace   My stomach feels wormy.

Chorus   She is tanned.

Grace   Like the night before an exam.

Chorus   The orange sun makes her glow.

Grace   Or when your friends don't respond to your post.

Chorus   Her body is slim and curvy.

Grace   Or when a teacher says, 'Can I speak to you after class?'

Chorus   Her bikini is the brightest white.

Grace   It is pulsing in my body.

Chorus   Her hair is windswept and natural.

Grace   I can feel it pulsing in my body.

Chorus   She is having the best time.

Grace   Pulse.

Chorus   Post: Didn't want to leave our little place at @greenpinesibiza today.

Grace   Pulse.

Chorus   Thank you to everyone @greenpinesibiza for such a gorgeous two days . . . Emoji waves,

Grace   I'm not pregnant if that's what you think.

Chorus   Emoji sun, emoji pink hearts x2,

Grace   I've never had sex. Never been near any sperm.

Chorus   Emoji white hands preach. Hashtag Ditsy Bikinis.

Grace   And it's not another Jesus, just to be clear.

Chorus   Hashtag Seawater shampoo.

Grace   I don't know what it is, but it's not that.

Chorus   Hashtag EasyJet.

Grace   Pulse.

*

Student 5   Grace Freemantle was a normal person. Until she wasn't.

*

Grace   There's a special school assembly with a special guest. The special guest is a famous barrister who went to the private school across town, which has its own theatre and a cricket pitch and ancient oak trees. Our school doesn't have its own theatre or cricket pitch or ancient oak trees. Our school has one between two books and teachers who go off sick. The barrister is very passionate.

Barrister   I want you to look around you. I want you to look to your left. Now look to your right.

Beat.

Barrister   Welcome to your competition.

Grace   My womb contracts.

Barrister   You will sit your GCSEs at the same time. You will sit your A levels together. You will apply for university at the same time.

Grace   My womb judders.

Barrister   And what I want to know is what are you doing to stand out from everyone here?

Grace   It expands in my womb.

Barrister   You are at a crucial point in your lives.

Grace   It expands.

Barrister   Every choice you make now will impact on your future.

Grace   It grows to the size of a chestnut.

Barrister   Let's get real here, do you want to own your own house? Well, how are you going to get it?

Grace   It's not painful. But not not painful either. It feels sort of . . .

Barrister   How are you going to manage that? Because houses are expensive.

Grace   Unknowable.

Barrister   You should be thinking about the things you want in the future now. What is your plan?

Grace   It feels like the worst is yet to come.

Barrister   What is your five-year plan?

Grace   Or the best is yet to come.

Barrister   You are in charge of your destiny.

Grace   It grows to the size of a mouse.

Barrister   With hard work and determination you can make your dream come true.

Grace   It grows to the size of a hamster.

Barrister   Harness your power.

Grace   By the end of the assembly, it is the size of a new-born puppy.

Barrister   You can make it happen.

Grace   A small one.

Barrister   The hard work starts now.

Grace   A Jack Russell maybe.

Barrister   The competition started yesterday.

Grace   Or a West Highland Terrier.

Barrister   Welcome to the real world.

Grace   Yes, like a West Highland Terrier puppy scrabbling around inside me.

*

Student 6   My memory of Grace Freemantle before that day in PE, before it happened, is kinda hazy . . . She was in a couple of my classes and yeah . . . nothing much really . . . just kind of . . . no nothing. . . . Oh yeah! Actually, no that wasn't her. . . . Oh, yeah, I remember something! There was this one time, right? It was break and my lot were by the Art block. My mate Ali was laughing and looking at his phone. And I said, 'What's that?' and Ali passed it over. Someone had posted a video of Janice Leavy, who's in the year below, winning the 100-metre sprint in the borough championships.

Just so you know, a bit of context and that, Janice Leavy was the fastest runner in our school. She was, like, super-human. She broke all the running records all the time. She was in the local paper and some famous coach came from Manchester specially to see her and there was some chat about the next Olympics.

Anyway, so in the video, Janice Leavy is running this race for the school in the borough championships, really fast, obviously. And in the video, you can see quite clearly that Janice isn't wearing a sports bra. She's just got her normal bra on and her boobs are really bouncing and cos she's so fast and her boobs are big, they're flying all over the place. And someone has put up a title that doesn't say 'Super-human Woman Slays all the Competition in the Borough Championships'. Instead they've written, 'The Fastest Tits in the Borough'.

And all my lot are creasing. I don't think it's funny but I don't want to seem . . . I dunno . . . I sort of half laugh because . . . I don't want to . . . Anyway, Grace Freemantle walks by and Ali shows it to her. Grace looks.

Chorus   Fastest tits in the borough! 609 tears of laughter faces. 110 green sick faces. 42 thumbs up. 37 aubergines.

Student 6   She doesn't say anything, but doesn't laugh either. She gives the phone back to Ali and goes into her Art class. (*Pause.*) I told my form tutor about that video cos I thought an adult should know what was going on, but I don't know if he did anything. And that's my Grace story. Sorry, it's a bit of an anti-climax, isn't it? (*Beat.*) Janice refused to come to school after that. Yeah, it's more of a Janice story than a Grace story. Sorry. Yeah. Sorry.

*

Grace   When it is asleep, it throbs in time with my heartbeat. It's like we're one thing.

I know we are not one thing.

It plays around.

Sometimes I think it has feathers. Sometimes I think it has fur. Sometimes spikes like a porcupine. It wrestles and tumbles inside my body. I can feel its spine up against my kidneys.

*

Student 7   It was February when I first noticed Grace being an oddball. My mum had just got engaged to John, AKA The Dickhead. She was trying to get me on side so she'd given me ten quid to get some dinner as a treat.

Me and Grace was in Pizza Town waiting for our pizzas. Mine, an extra hot Hawaiian with olives, cos I'm half Italian and I love pineapple, so sue me. Grace was having a Margherita. Classic. Pizza Town is not a place that is bothered about cleanliness. The tables are bare sticky and the floor . . . well, you don't want to think too hard about that. Let's just say the mop is a stranger to that floor, but the pizzas are banging, so swings and roundabouts, innit. There's this TV in the corner, right up by the ceiling. It's not a flat-screen, it's one of those old ones with a big bum at the back. Some bare boring news was on. Grace was watching it.

Chorus   There are children and women and men in an inflatable boat on the sea. The waves are enormous. The boat is sinking.

Grace   It scuttles down from my belly, across my pelvis and into my thigh.

Student 7   The sound was off. Ed Sheeran was blaring out at a million decibels making the news look like the most boringest music video ever.

Chorus *sings a line/lines from the song.*

Student 7   And Grace just kept watching.

Chorus   A woman slips from the boat. She has a baby in her arms. She tries to keep the baby above her head as she is dragged into the water.

Grace   Its body quivers inside my thigh.

Student 7   Mum met The Dickhead through her mate Sally who used to go out with him but dumped him because he was 'high maintenance'. When I met him, I didn't like him one bit. He was cold to me when Mum went out the room and a bit nasty to her when she didn't do what he wanted.

Chorus   A terrified man reaches for the screaming baby and passes it to a terrified teenage girl.

Grace   It pushes its tiny skull up against my kneecap.

Student 7   I tried to say something about it to Mum, like 'Look at the warning signs', but she said, 'Don't you want me to be happy?' And there's nothing you can say to that and then she gave me ten quid. So, there we were, in Pizza Town waiting. Me, worrying about my mum and The Dickhead, and Grace staring at the TV liked she'd never seen a TV before.

Chorus   The woman disappears under a crash of foam and bubble.

Student 7   I said 'Grace, what are you going to do next year?'

Grace   It taps at my kneecap. Tap.

Student 7   I said, 'Are you going to stay on at school?'

Grace   Tap. I put my hand above my knee. I massage the skin. I try to soothe it.

Student 7   I said, 'Grace?' (*Beat.*) 'Grace!'

Chorus   The boat upturns. The children, women and men scream and shout. They cling to the inflatable, which grows soft under their touch.

Grace   My leg violently jerks, hits the underneath of the table.

Student 7   And you'll never believe what happened next. She just got up and left. She left me in Pizza Town without even a goodbye. I'm like are you joking? Are you actually joking? Who does that? She weren't even my first choice to get pizza with. I only asked her cos everyone else was busy.

Grace   I crouch behind the bins out the back. I take a deep breath. I look at my leg. Just above my knee, it is straining against my skin. I can see the outline of its face. There's a beak. It has a beak. It has a beak and it is straining against my skin.

Student 7   My mum went ahead and married that dickhead.

*

Student 8   Grace was in my Maths class. I liked her. I think she liked me too. Sometimes she'd catch me looking at her and she'd smile over at me. And sometimes I'd catch her looking at me and I'd smile over at her. There was something between us, I could feel it. You can, can't you? You can feel it when there's something there. I was going to ask her if she wanted to go out somewhere or come over to mine or hang out or whatever. But then she changed and I didn't. (*Beat.*) I wish I'd . . . She was nice . . . I really wish I'd . . . I wish I'd said to her, 'You can talk to me if you want. No pressure. I'm here if you need to talk.' I wish I'd done that.

*

Student 9   We were in Geography.

Student 10   It was proper boring.

Student 11   Grace was sat on our table.

Student 9   Seating plan.

Student 10   Between. (*Points at the other two.*)

Student 9   The teacher, Miss Jarvis, loves a seating plan.

Student 10   Miss Jarvis is scary.

Student 9   Innit, the way her eyes bulge out of her head when she's annoyed.

Student 11   That lesson, Miss Jarvis was going on about carbon emissions.

Student 10   Miss Jarvis is always going on about carbon emissions.

Student 9   Miss Jarvis really hates carbon emissions.

Grace   It is asleep. It is curled around my heart

Miss Jarvis   It's important to understand that the earth's climate is changing at an unprecedented speed . . .

Grace   It wakes up.

Student 9   I don't even know about a carbon emission is. (*To* **Students 10 and 11**.) Do you?

Students 10 and 11   Yeah.

Student 9   Oh.

Miss Jarvis   We can see this in higher temperatures all over the world along with rising sea levels.

Grace   It wants something.

Student 9   Geography isn't my thing. Art is my thing.

Student 10   You're sick at Art.

Student 9   Thanks, hun.

Miss Jarvis   We can see this in more frequent and severe floods, droughts and storms.

Grace   I don't know what it wants.

Student 11   Miss Jarvis was droning on so I got my phone out to show the others this bag I liked. I passed my phone to Grace under the table.

Chorus   ANNABEAUTY 1.1 M followers.

This beautiful clutch makes the perfect travel bag! And it's only £42.99.

Miss Jarvis   We can see this in species extinction . . .

Student 9   Grace looked at the phone really close. I remember cos I wanted to see it, but I couldn't get to it.

Chorus ANNABEAUTY

Hashtag clutch, hashtag retro vibes, hashtag bring on summer!

Miss Jarvis   The vaquita is the world's rarest marine mammal.

Student 10   Grace was gripping the phone like (*does it*).

Student 9 (*laughs*)   Yeah, like (*does it*).

Chorus   PixieDream22. AnnaBeauty, I want your bag!! I want your life!!

Miss Jarvis   The vaquita will be extinct in the next five years.

Grace   Its body tenses.

Student 11   She had her head right down like (*does it*).

Student 9 (*laughs*)   Like (*does it*).

Student 10   Yeah, and then Miss Jarvis put up a picture of the sea fish thing she was going on about.

Miss Jarvis   This small porpoise was only discovered in 1958 and here we are, sixty years later about to lose them for ever.

Student 9   And Grace suddenly looked up.

Student 11   But she was still gripping my phone like (*does it*).

Grace   It scuttles along the length of my torso.

Student 11   And I wanted my phone back.

Miss Jarvis   Climate change is a catastrophe in waiting. For all of us.

Grace   Its body bristles.

Student 9   Yeah, cos here if the teachers see your phone, they take it.

Miss Jarvis   And the consequences for humans can already be seen.

Grace   It starts climbing up my rib cage.

Student 10   Yeah, they lock your phone in a safe.

Miss Jarvis   Around the world we see wars and starvation.

Grace   It pulls itself up inside my rib cage. I think it has teeth.

Student 9   And your mum or dad or older sister or whoever has to come and collect it.

Miss Jarvis   Around the world we see desertification and forced migration.

Student 10   My dad had to come and get my phone. He was livid.

Miss Jarvis   And this is only going to get worse.

Grace   There's a noise.

Student 11   I really wanted to get my phone off of her before Miss Jarvis saw it.

Grace   There's a noise inside of me.

Miss Jarvis   We have twelve years to do something before catastrophe is inevitable.

Student 11   So I reached over and I grabbed it out of Grace's hand.

Grace   I can hear it inside me.

Miss Jarvis   Just twelve years.

Student 10   Yeah, that's when she went really weird.

Student 11   It wasn't my fault.

Student 10   Not saying it was.

Student 11   Oh, I thought you were –

Student 10   It was no one's fault. Or it might have been somebody's fault but, well, we don't know, do we?

Grace   I can hear it from inside me.

Student 9   Then Grace leaned right over the desk and held her stomach like (*does it*).

Students 11 and 10   Yeah.

Miss Jarvis   Twelve years for global leaders to take action.

Student 10   And I said, 'What's up Grace?'

Miss Jarvis   And my question to you is . . .

Grace   It's making this noise like –

Miss Jarvis   What can we do about it?

Student 11   And I said, 'Grace are you alright?'

Miss Jarvis   Does anyone have any ideas?

Grace   I pull my jumper round me so no one can else can hear

Student 9   And then Grace did a very unGrace thing.

Grace   I don't know how to stop it from –

Student 11   Very unGrace.

Grace   I can't make it –

Student 10   Totally unGrace.

Grace   They're gonna hear.

Student 9   She started –

Grace   They're all gonna hear.

Student 11   Yeah, she started (*laughs*)

Grace   I can't let them hear it.

Student 10   She started (*laughs*) singing.

Grace *sings quietly some Ed Sheeran song/or any other you think is better for this moment, but should be the same as the one in the pizza scene and penultimate scene.*

Miss Jarvis   What on earth is –

Student 9   And it was proper funny seeing Miss Jarvis's eyes popping out all over the place, so I (*sings*)

Miss Jarvis   Why are you –

Student 10   And me (*sings*)

Miss Jarvis   I'm warning you –

Student 11   Until we were all (*sings*)

They sing.

Miss Jarvis   Stop it!

They sing.

Miss Jarvis   Stop this right now!

They sing.

Miss Jarvis   I said stop!

They stop and burst out laughing.

Student 11   And that's when we realised.

Grace   And that's when I realise.

Students 9 and 10   Yeah, we realised.

Grace   I realise –

Students 9, 10 and 11   There was something seriously up with Grace.

Grace   The IT wants to be heard.

*

Student 12   Grace?

Grace   The IT hisses and spits and growls.

Student 12   Grace Freemantle?

Grace   When I speak, the IT cracks through all my words.

Student 12   Grace Freemantle in 11F?

Grace   I stop speaking.

Student 12 *looks at* **Student 13**. *They burst out laughing.*

*

Sam   Me and Grace just got each other. Right from the start, that first day that we met in Year 1. She was really kind . . . is really . . was . . . is, yeah, . . . She always made me feel like it's ok to be me. And a lot of times, I feel horrible being me. I hate my body.

Grace   I keep my mouth shut.

Sam   And when I look around me, I see loads of other people hating their bodies too and their bodies look just fine to me.

Grace   I keep my mouth shut.

Sam   After school we'd always go to Grace's house and make macaroni cheese, which was our thing. We love . . . loved macaroni cheese.

Grace   I keep my mouth shut.

Sam   But then she just, kind of disappeared. Not literally. She was still around, but she wasn't, if you know what I mean. She stopped communicating.

Grace   I keep my mouth shut.

Sam   She started staying after school in the library and getting the bus home when everyone was long gone.

Grace   I keep my mouth shut.

Sam   She stopped asking me to come over to her house. She stopped texting, Snapchatting, Whatsapping, Insta-ing. All of it. Everything. Finished.

Grace   I keep my mouth shut.

Sam   I missed her . . .

Grace   I keep my mouth shut.

Sam   I still miss her.

Grace   I keep my mouth shut.

Sam   One day at school, I said to her, 'Do you want to walk home together today?'

Grace   I keep my mouth shut.

Sam   I said, 'We can walk home and then go to yours to make macaroni cheese'.

Grace   I keep my mouth shut.

Sam   I said, 'We can just hang out'.

Grace   I keep my mouth shut.

Sam   And she didn't say anything. I took a big breath and I asked her what I've been wanting to ask her for weeks.

Grace   I keep my mouth shut.

Sam   'Grace, don't you like me anymore?'

Grace   I keep my mouth shut.

Sam   And she didn't say anything.

Grace   I keep my mouth shut.

*

Grace   I am at home. I am standing at the kitchen sink getting a drink of water. The IT is resting. It occasionally rolls over and stretches along my abdomen. My mum comes in and puts on the radio to listen to the news.

Newsreader   The latest victim of knife crime has been named as fourteen-year-old David Sanderson.

Grace   The IT tenses.

Newsreader   Witnesses say they saw David Sanderson being chased by a group of three or four other youths.

Grace   I don't know why, but I go right up to where the radio is.

Newsreader   The victim is thought to have run into a local shop for help.

Grace   Suddenly, without warning, the IT moves up over my shoulder and squeezes into my arm. I turn up the radio. A local mother comes on.

Local Mother   We're scared for our children.

Grace   There is a sharp pain in my hand.

Local Mother   We're scared when our children go to school.

Grace   There's a tiny cut in my hand.

Local Mother   We're scared when our children are out of sight.

Grace   There's blood in the palm of my hand.

Local Mother   We need someone to do something.

Grace   There's something sticking out of the palm of my hand.

Local Mother   He was fourteen. Just a kid.

Grace   It looks like a thorn from a rose, but it's bright blue.

Local Mother   That poor boy lying in his own blood.

Grace   It's a claw.

Local Mother   Why is no one doing anything?

Grace   There is a claw sticking out of the palm of my hand.

Local Mother   Why does no one care?

Grace   I try to push the claw back in with my fingertip,

Local Mother   That boy terrified, screaming, knowing he's going to die.

Grace   It won't go back in.

Local Mother   Screaming for his mum.

Grace   I go to the bathroom. I close the bathroom door. I take my shoe off.

Local Mother   The fifth teenage boy to be killed round here.

Grace   I hit the palm of my hand with the shoe like a hammer.

Local Mother   And no one in charge seems to give a toss.

Grace   The claw resists.

Local Mother   That poor boy.

Grace   The claw resists.

Local Mother   That poor poor boy.

Grace   I wrap gaffer tape around my hand.

*

Student 14   Remember those lessons we had in History about the Middle East?

Student 15   Yeah, boring.

Student 14   With Mr Logan.

Student 15   Yeah, dickhead.

Student 14   Remember that test?

Student 15   Yeah, easy.

Student 14   When I was sitting next to Grace Freemantle?

Student 15   Yeah, Freemental.

Student 14   That's not nice.

Student 15   True though.

Student 14   Grace didn't answer one question in that test. She just sat there staring at the paper. She didn't even pick up her pen.

Student 15   Maybe it was hard to pick up a pen with them woolly gloves on.

--

Student 15   Joke.

Student 14   That's not funny

--

Student 14   I don't think you should joke about her.

--

Student 14   I don't think we should be making jokes about her.

--

Student 14   I wouldn't like it if that happened to me and everyone –

Student 15   Ok, ok. God.

Silence.

Student 14   You know that photo of that little boy in Syria who was bombed?

--

Student 14   When Grace saw that photo, she started to shake.

Grace   The pain inside is . . .

Chorus   A four-year-old boy sits on an orange chair. The chair is too big for him. Aleppo has been bombed. The little boy is dusty from the exploded buildings. His hair is matted and chalky. One side of his face is covered in blood. The little boy sits neatly with his hands on his knees. He is silent and traumatised.

Grace   The pain inside me is unbearable.

Student 14   The whole desk started moving. Her whole body was shaking. I asked her if she was alright, but she didn't say anything. I tried to get Mr Logan's attention, but Grace looked at me in a way that, I don't know, made me feel that I shouldn't.

--

Student 14   I should have told Mr Logan.

--

Student 14   Maybe if I'd told Mr Logan then that thing in PE would never have happened.

--

Student 14   It's obvious that something was going on with her.

--

Student 14   She was in trouble and I didn't do anything. I should have done something.

Student 15   Yeah.

Student 14   Do you think?

Student 15   Yeah. No. I don't know.

*

Grace   I can't stop watching the news. I can't stop reading the news. I can't stop listening to the news. I don't want to. I shut my eyes. I cover my ears. I don't want to know.

Chorus   Food banks, cyclones, arms dealing, famine, plutocrats, benefits cuts, luxury yachts, suicide, extinction.

Grace   The IT crawls up through my chest. Its spikey head reaches my throat. It wriggles up. (*Coughs.*) Its beak is stuck in the back of my throat. (*Coughs.*) Its beak opens like a baby bird wanting to be fed. It speaks. The IT speaks. The IT speaks and it says, 'What is next?'

Chorus   Disaster.

Grace   I gulp and I gulp and I gulp it back until it is forced back down my throat, back down into my body, pulsing and vibrating back in the pit of my stomach. I put tape over my mouth.

*

Student 16   Grace, man, Grace.

Student 17   Yeah, Grace, man.

Student 16   With the (*mimes gloves*) and the (*motions to head*)

Student 17   Balaclava.

Student 16   Nah, that's a pastry thing.

Student 17   No, that's –

Student 16   Nah, that's a Greek Turkish Arabic pastry thing.

Student 17   That's baklava.

Student 16   Nah that's definitely . . . Oh yeah, you're right.

Student 17   My Year 4 teacher used to bring baklava in at the end of term. Sick.

Grace   I cover my face.

Student 16   So one day Grace comes to school wearing this . . .

Student 17   Balaclava.

Student 16   And it wasn't winter or nothing.

Grace   They all take the piss. I don't give a shit.

Student 16   I don't know how she got away with it. They me put in isolation when I wore my trainers two days in a row and I had a proper reason. My school shoes were getting fixed.

Student 17   Yeah, I remember.

Student 16   Just cos I didn't have a note.

Student 17   Yeah, I remember.

Student 16   It was an extreme reaction.

Student 17   Yeah, I remember.

Grace   At break time, I go to the toilet, I take my clothes off. I watch the IT move around inside my body, bumping and poking and pushing at my skin. It has grown so big. A long low growl rumbles through my blood, muscle and gristle. What is next?

Student 16   And then Grace Freemantle comes in wearing her baklava.

Student 17   Balaclava.

Grace   What is next?

Student 16   And she's allowed to wander round willy-nilly wearing her . . .

Student 17   Balaclava.

Student 16   Happy as Larry in her . . .

Both   . . . balaclava. (*High five/fist bump.*)

Grace   What is next?

*

Chorus   Rich people hunt giraffes and tigers and lions and rhinos. Rich people follow the animals in jeeps. They stalk them and watch them and raise their guns as the giraffes and tigers and lions and rhinos stop for a drink at the river in the burning sun. Bang.

*

Grace   I fall asleep on the floor of my bedroom.

Chorus   There are people in a camp in Calais. There are people in a camp in Kos. There are people in a camp in Bangladesh –

Grace   My dreams are infiltrated,

Chorus   They've run away from their own countries. They've run away from hunger and war and terror.

Grace   My dreams are infiltrated.

Chorus   The people used to live in peace with grandparents and friends and neighbours.

Grace   I wake up.

Chorus   They used to sip tea and break bread with smiles and love. They used to bicker about parking spaces and the music that next door played at 3 a.m.

Grace   I have a terrible pain just below my belly button.

Chorus   They used to sing the old songs and dance to the new songs and laugh about silly things like the way grandma eats pomegranates.

Grace   There is a trickle of blood.

Chorus   The children used to go to school and learn their one two threes. Then guns and bombs and helicopters arrived.

Grace   There is a rip in my stomach.

Chorus   The women and men gathered up their children and started to run. They travelled miles with their possessions on their backs.

Grace   I peel back the skin.

Chorus   The women and children and men are not wanted in the camps of Calais and Kos and Bangladesh.

Grace   There is an eye.

Chorus   They dream of home.

Grace   A yellow eye.

Chorus   They dream of grandma eating her breakfast in the pink light of the morning. They dream of banging on the wall at 3 a.m. and shouting at their neighbour to turn his music down.

Grace   A bright yellow eye.

Chorus   There are women and children and men in a different type of camp in the south of France.

Grace   A bright yellow eye with a thin black pupil.

Chorus   They wake up in the morning and have croissants and jam and coffee. They stretch their legs and yawn into the glimmering sun.

Grace   The IT blinks up at me.

Chorus   They think about the day ahead, which will be full of giggles and sandcastles.

Grace   We look at each other.

Chorus   And swimming and sun-cream and cool bubbly drinks.

Grace   I think I know what it wants.

*

Student 15   Grace. Yes. Grace. In PE. Weird. 100 per cent weird.

*

Sam   It was after school and I'd been at Science Revision. I'd left my coat in the lab so I was running back to get it when I saw Grace in an empty classroom. She was there all on her own, sitting very still, very upright, very neat. She was staring into space. I went in and I said, 'Is everything ok Grace?' But she didn't look at me. I moved closer to her. I saw something flicker in her eyes.

Grace   The IT is flexing its wings.

Sam   I thought she was going to say something.

Grace   Stretching its legs.

Sam   I touched her shoulder.

Grace   Grooming its fur or its feathers or its scales.

Sam   She flinched and she got up.

Grace   I can feel all of its muscles.

Sam   She moved to the door. I reached for her arm.

Grace   I can feel its strength

Sam   And I said, 'Grace, tell me what's happening'.

Grace   I can feel its power.

Sam   She shrugged me off.

Grace   It is preparing.

Sam   I grabbed hold of her blazer.

Grace   It's nearly ready.

Sam   I grabbed her and she turned round and she pushed me so hard that I fell over. I hit my head on the side of a desk and it started to bleed.

Grace   I am scared.

Sam   I said, 'Look what you've done'.

Grace   I am so scared.

Sam   And she turned around and walked away. And I shouted after her. I shouted, 'I hate you!'

Grace   I am so so scared.

Sam   And that was the last time I saw her.

*

Student 18   My auntie's friend knows Grace's neighbour and he told my auntie's friend that when Grace started wearing all those clothes that the teachers thought she had a special condition, which meant she was cold all the time. Apparently Grace's parents contacted the school and said she had some autoimmune thing. I have no idea what an autoimmune thing is, but it doesn't really matter because she didn't have an autoimmune thing anyway, and her parents didn't contact the school either. It was Grace. Grace sent an email pretending to be them.

Grace   The inside of me is heating up. I can hardly breathe. I can hardly move. I tape my whole body up to make a barrier. I wear a layer of clothes under my school uniform and an old puffa jacket over the top. My mouth is covered. My hands are covered. My head is covered. It cannot get out. I cannot let it get out.

Student 18   My auntie's friend says that Grace's neighbour said that Grace's parents are really nice. He said they are 'switched on'. I think that means they know what's going on. Although they didn't seem to know what was going on with Grace and she's their daughter. Not that I think it's their fault. I don't tell my parents a bean about my life. They say, 'What happened at school today?' I say, 'Nothing'. They say, 'What are doing in your bedroom?' I say 'Nothing'. They say, 'What are you looking at online?' I say, 'Nothing'. They're so nosey; they get on my nerves. Grace's neighbour said Grace's parents are devastated. He said that they had no idea what was happening to her. That if only they'd known then that day in PE could have been avoided. They could have helped her or stopped it or I don't know, but they could have done something, which I'm sure is true. Someone should've been able to do something to help her before . . . you know. Don't you think?

*

Student 19   I was in PE when it happened. It was mental. The whole thing was, like, total madness. It was a boiling hot day and we had a supply teacher. The supply teacher wanted us to run 100 metres. I shouted out, 'That's against our human rights!' and everybody creased. I'm a joker, innit. Everyone was in shorts and t-shirts apart from Grace who was dressed in all her gear looking like a colossal nutter.

Grace   Pulse.

Student 19   Um, I'd like to take that back. She didn't look like a colossal nutter; she looked . . . unusual. Yeah, that's right, she looked unusual in her . . . unusual . . . apparel. Anyway, we were outside on the field, which was as dry as the savanna cos of the heat wave and we were all lined up to run the first race. Grace was on the other side of me. The supply teacher woman blew a whistle and we all set off. No one could be arsed, so there was a lot of dawdling and chit chat.

Grace   Pulse.

Student 19   The general lack of effort pissed the supply teacher off and she proper shouted at us.

Supply Teacher   You are supposed to be competing!

Grace   The IT freezes.

Supply Teacher   Whoever's last gets a detention!

Student 19   The supply teacher was a wild one. You know how some supply teachers are; a bit unpredictable, so everyone started running.

Grace   The IT darts its head.

Student 19   And then someone shouted something about Janice Leavy.

Student 20   Fastest tits in the borough!

Student 19   And everyone started laughing.

Grace   The IT clenches its jaw.

Chorus   609 tears of laughter faces.

Grace   The IT arches its scaly back. Its spikes flicker.

Chorus   110 green sick faces.

Grace   The IT's claws retract and protract.

Student 19   I finished the race and turned back to see if I was last, which I wasn't, which was surprising to me cos I usually am. Running is not my forte. Grace was way behind me, standing dead still in her lane. And the supply teacher was lining up the next race to go.

Barrister   What I want to know is, what are you doing to stand out from everyone here?

Grace   The IT opens its beak and bares its teeth.

Chorus   There are children and women and men in an inflatable boat in the sea.

Grace   The IT plunges and heaves and dives inside me.

Student 19   The supply teacher spotted Grace and marched up to her and was all (*gesticulating*), but Grace didn't even look at her.

Grace's Mum   Remember, it's your future.

Grace   The IT whirls in a fever of blistering heat around my organs.

Chorus   The waves are enormous.

Student 19   And the supply teacher was shouting her head off, right in Grace's face and Grace was standing still as a statue, ignoring her, which was making the supply teacher apoplectic.

Chorus   Hashtag Ditsy bikinis! Hashtag EasyJet!

Grace   It twists my liver.

Grace's Mum   Grace, are you revising?

Grace   It snaps at my kidneys

Chorus   There are people in a camp in Calais.

Grace   It claws at my lungs.

Student 19   Eventually, the supply teacher got fed up and stomped off back to the starting line to have go at someone else.

Chorus   There are people in a camp in Kos.

Grace   It starts to shred my muscles.

Student 19   Grace stayed where she was. In the middle of the lane in the middle of the track in the middle of the school field on a boiling hot day.

Chorus   There are people in a camp in Bangladesh.

Grace   You know when you see a dog digging? It's doing that to the soft flesh inside of me.

Local Mother   The fifth teenage boy to be killed round here.

Student 19   And the supply teacher started the next race. The runners pointed at Grace and the supply teacher motioned they should run round her.

Local Mother   And no one in charge seems to give a toss.

Grace   I am filling up with blood.

Student 19   The girl who was running in Grace's lane looked a bit worried about the human obstacle and said something to the teacher who looked like she was gonna explode at any moment and suddenly started shouting:

Student 19 and Supply Teacher   Just F-ING RUN!

Student 16   And instead of cracking up with laughter or saying they were going to report her to the headteacher, everybody just started to f-ing run.

Chorus   The woman disappears under a crash of foam and bubbles.

Grace   Its talons scratch up at my larynx. I cough up blood.

Chorus   Food banks, cyclones, arms dealing,

Grace   It crushes my heart.

Student 19   But the girl who was running in Grace's lane veered so far into the other lane that she tripped up whoever who tripped up whoever tripped up whoever and so on until there was a whole pile of them and they all started cracking up.

Chorus   Rich people hunt giraffes and tigers and lions and rhinos

Grace   It snaps off my ribs and pushes through. The pain.

Chorus   Bang.

Student 19   And we all started cracking up.

Miss Jarvis   The earth's climate is changing at an unprecedented speed.

Grace   The pain is . . .

Student 19   Everybody was cracking up.

Chorus   The little boy is dusty from the exploded building.

Grace   It burrows its face up through my throat.

Student 19   It was so funny.

Chorus   Food banks.

Grace   I gulp down.

Chorus   Plutocrats.

Grace   I gulp down.

Chorus   Benefit cuts.

Grace   I gulp down.

Student   We were literally rolling around on the floor in hysterics.

Grace   It forces my mouth open.

Chorus   The children used to go to school to learn their one two threes. Then guns and bombs and helicopters arrived.

Student 19   And suddenly there was this noise. Like someone was being murdered.

Grace   Its head rams my teeth.

Chorus   Hashtag bring on the summer!

Student 19   And we looked at the just 'f-ing run' supply teacher and it wasn't her.

Grace   My teeth shatter and crumble from my mouth,

Local Mother   That poor boy. That poor poor boy.

Student 19   The supply teacher was staring at the third lane of the running track.

Grace   My cheeks split as the IT hauls itself out of me.

Student 19   All our eyes swivelled to where she was looking. It was Grace.

Grace's Dad   Your behaviour is completely inappropriate for a young lady.

Grace   It's scaly feet kick at the sides of my throat.

Student 19   Grace was standing in exactly the same position.

Chorus *sings a line from previous song.*

Grace   It uses my windpipe as a launch pad.

Student 19   But her mouth was open.

Grace's Mum   It's your future!

Grace   It wrestles itself out of me. It is slick and wet, covered in blood and pus. Its tail slaps my face as it launches itself into the sky.

Student   Her head was tilted right back.

Miss Jarvis   Floods, droughts and storms.

Grace   Its enormous wings unfurl mid-air with blast and yellow and clash.

Student 19   Her face turned up to the sky.

Miss Jarvis   Desertification and forced migration.

Grace   The wings are bright green and iridescent.

Student 19   And her mouth wide open.

Chorus   Anna Beauty! I want your bag! I want your life!

Grace   Flecks of fire spin off its scaly body like a Catherine wheel.

Student 19   The noise was unbelievable.

Chorus   The boat upturns.

Grace   It stinks of fire and demons and rupture and storm.

Student 19   The noise was so loud.

Grace   The sky is filled with red and orange and clot and guts.

Chorus   The boy's hair is matted and chalky.

Student 19   It was frightening.

Grace   The whole world heats up.

Grace's Mum   It's your future!

Grace   The adults in charge run for safety.

Student 19   The noise that was coming from her was so frightening.

Grace   It is all their fault.

Chorus   Luxury yachts, suicide, extinction.

Grace   The IT is coming for them.

Student 19   I'll never forget that.

Grace   The IT blinks its bright yellow eyes. The earth shudders.

Miss Jarvis   War and starvation

Grace   It opens its beak, full of howl.

Student 19   She was . . .

Chorus   Bang.

Grace   It cuts out the sunlight

Student 19   She was . . .

Chorus   Bang.

Grace   We descend into darkness.

Chorus   Bang.

Grace   Full of fury and brilliance –

Student 19   She was. .

Chorus   Bang.

Grace   And fever and magnificence

Student 19   She . . .

Chorus   Bang.

Grace   The IT stops the world with a –

Student 19   She . . .

Grace *roars.*

*

Student 21   They tried to get Grace Freemantle off the school field, but she wouldn't go. It was awful. Eventually, three teachers carried her off. They took her to the medical room. Her parents arrived. They put a blanket around her and walked her to their car. Her mum was asking her loads of questions, but Grace wasn't saying anything. She looked exhausted. Her whole body was sagging and, at one point, she stumbled and they had to catch her and hold her up. She didn't come back to school. I don't know where she went. No one knows where she went. Even Sam doesn't know. No one told us anything. Everyone has different theories about why it happened; exam pressure, drugs, eating disorders, boy trouble, girl trouble, friend trouble, parent trouble. I don't join in. I don't say anything. When they're all gossiping and giggling and talking in whispers, I don't say one word. Because when they all saw Grace Freemantle lose her shit on the PE field that day, when they all saw her open her mouth and scream and scream and scream up at the sky, I saw something different. I probably shouldn't say this. I'll regret saying it but . . . I saw it crawl out of her mouth and open its wings and cover the sky. I saw it open its beak and roar. I saw it shower flames of yellow and gold and rust all over us. I saw what was inside her, the fury, the blood and the gore. I saw it, because it's in me too. I know it is, I can feel it. It's just here . . .

I feel . . . a presence.
A gnawing.
A squirming.

It's small.
Like a cherry pip.
Or a baby shrimp.
It is really small.
Whatever it is.
But it's here.
It is definitely here.

[*Optional*: **Grace** *watches* **Student 17. Grace** *smiles.* **Grace** *offers her hand.*]

The end.

The IT

BY VIVIENNE FRANZMANN

*Notes on rehearsal and staging, drawn from a workshop with the writer,
held at the National Theatre, October 2019*

How Vivienne came to write the play

'Everyone who works with young people knows that there has been a huge explosion in mental health issues. The reportage of this crisis often blames social media. I was thinking, that can't just be it. I'm sure that social media plays a part, but that can't be the beginning, middle and end of the story. I started thinking about the world and young people within it. I thought we are in such a terrible state in terms of things like the environmental crisis, the migrant crisis, global poverty and inequality as well as national poverty and inequality. Everywhere we look feels like there's looming catastrophe. I started thinking about the amount of information young people receive and what the pressures of having access to all that information must feel like. It seems to me totally appropriate to feel overwhelmed, particularly about the future. It is such a difficult and turbulent time. And I really wanted to write a play to excavate that. I wanted this "overwhelming" feeling to be realised in the play as an anger. I feel like young people have every right to be furious about our current situation.'

Vivienne wanted to explore an anger through the IT which grows inside of Grace. The IT is fed by the constant information about the world that Grace receives.

Approaching the play

Lead directors Polly Findlay and Hannah Joss began by explaining to the room that the purpose of the day was not to give any answers about how to 'do' the play. Instead the day would be about looking at the questions that would help them unlock what their production could be, whilst unravelling and understanding a very complex, hard and brilliant play.

Polly split the room into small groups and asked them to discuss the challenges and opportunities presented by the play in terms of staging it.

These can be summarised as:

Opportunities

- Deepening the young people's political understanding of the world
- Using the Chorus in exciting ways
- Working out what the IT is
- It's an exciting story

- Complex characters
- Embracing the dark and light within the story
- Sound and lighting design is open

Challenges

- Creating the IT – creating the sense of fear/the sense of dread/the impending doom
- How do you stage the scream? How do you deliver a big theatrical moment like that?
- Pace management/creating tension
- Pastoral care – controlling a safe conversation
- How to keep the audience focused on all the different narrative threads
- Storytelling clarity/creating and maintaining the clarity of the different realities of the play
- Finding variety in the Chorus
- Narrative discipline

Themes

- Adolescent mental health
- The pressures of contemporary living on young people
- The impact of social media on young people
- The access to an abundance of information
- The bombardment of information

Creative discipline

Polly discussed that the opportunities for ensemble work and physical theatre presented by the play are endless and exciting, but the challenge is to maintain the clarity of the story. A good production must find a narrative discipline that is detailed and not prescriptive. It is vital to be selective and avoid the temptation to throw everything (and the kitchen sink!) at the play. These additional elements should not distract from or cause the audience to lose the story. For example, in the idea of how to create 'the IT' itself, it is vital to guard against self-indulgence. With each production choice, make sure the audience is understanding something new about the story and characters on the stage.

With a play this big, where the need for imagination is so great, how do you impose discipline? What are the rules and parameters for your individual production? And then how do you keep them clear and useful in telling the story?

Exercise: One sentence

Polly asked everyone to write one sentence that encapsulated the play. Ideally it should be short enough to fit on a post-it note and get to the heart of what they wanted to do with their production of *The IT*. This sentence will allow you to be specific and focused when rehearsing and creating your production. It allows for the pursuit of storytelling clarity which is very much needed when directing *The IT*. The sentence is the inherent gesture of your production written down. All of the choices you make when creating your production must in some way support the sentence.

The sentence can be rewritten later if, in rehearsal, you find that it's not quite right, but it will serve to give a focus to the work. The aim is to find the clearest, most unambiguous sentence.

Examples of sentences:

Struggling with the pressures of the world, a girl is forced to roar.

The overwhelming something explodes.

Example for *The IT* from writer Vivienne Franzmann:

A girl whose fury (at the world and the adults in charge) cannot be articulated, until one day it erupts.

Fury is hugely important as it leads to the roar at the end.

Her lines at the end, beginning 'the IT is coming for them', are hugely important and must be heard. The adults are responsible for the world that has been created.

This feels like Grace v. the adults.

Structure, style and transitions: The three narratives

There are three different narratives or story planes throughout the play that are weaved and spun together, often shifting between audiences (whether characters are speaking to each other, to the Chorus, to Grace or to the audience) and time. You need to make each narrative clear so that you can craft the audience's experience throughout the whole play and lead them where you need to, whilst still building to the final moment.

The challenge of this play is that there are different realities in different times that coexist at the same time. You are asking the audience to stay on top of which reality they are watching and so you need to be certain of what reality you are in, what its function is and how it serves the purpose of the text.

Polly suggested breaking these different realities or storylines down into different families as a way to make it clear structurally. You can use any language or rules for each that you like but you do need to know them.

The three different story planes are:

1   The Aftermath. Or PE and what happens afterwards.

   How the world pre-PE affected Grace to make the event of the roar happen.

2   The world of the Chorus.

   The Chorus is the personification of the forces that affect Grace. The Chorus is separate and distinct from the IT.

3   The world of Grace and the IT.

The IT lives within Grace's world. They are intertwined. Remember Grace's experience of the IT gets bigger throughout the play. Her description of it begins as very small, growing and growing until she can no longer contain it within herself.

Polly asked a group to attempt to stage pages 188–9 from Grace's line 'It's December', focusing on finding a way to differentiate between the different story planes. From this exercise, the room discovered it's important to you make sure you focus your audience's attention where it needs to go. How do you get everybody looking at the right place at the right time? Polly referred to the transitions between the story planes and between scenes as 'turning corners'. How you stage and navigate those corners will ensure clear storytelling and an exciting evening.

Timeline

A useful timeline of important moments in *The IT*:

- Using the day in PE as the pivotal event.
- Posting of the Grace video on Facebook.
- December – Grace feels the IT at home.
- Grace in the library.
- Special school assembly – barrister comes to speak.
- Grace being shown the video of Janice Leavy.
- February – Pizza Town.
- Grace sings in the Geography lesson.
- Sam approaches Grace and Grace rejects them.
- At home the It pushes its claw through Grace's palm.
- Grace shakes seeing the video of the little boy in Syria.
- The IT speaks: 'What is next?'
- Grace finds the eye of the IT in her stomach.
- Grace pushes Sam over.

Discovering the world (story plane) of the Chorus

Polly asked the different groups to think of one word that fits for their production on 'what the Chorus is'. The groups had the following suggestions.
    The Chorus is:

- Fuel
- Information
- Essence

- What Grace sees and receives
- The adult fuck-ups
- Provocateur
- Pressure

The words that seemed to 'fit best' for the participants were that the Chorus was provocative, pointing, a catalyst, feeding the rage and journey of Grace and the IT. The Chorus represents the wider world which feeds into the micro world. The Chorus is information, factual, specific and contemporary, *and* it is pushing all this information onto Grace. A general agreement was that if the Chorus was passive as opposed to either aggressive or active, it would place a greater restriction on staging for the director and do a disservice to the text.

A good question to ask with your company is: what is the function of the Chorus? If you removed it, what would the play be missing? You can use the Chorus to goad Grace and push her along, it can also guide her and support her.

A very important note is that the IT is *different* from the Chorus. This idea came up a few times throughout the day. The IT is the rage and the Chorus is the thing that causes the rage to bubble up and then be released, therefore they have to be separate.

Polly then asked the group to take 'the Chorus is . . .' exercise one step further and come up with a sentence to define the Chorus this time using the following structure:

The Chorus is a **[blank]** which **[blank]** the growth of the IT.

Polly's sentence as an example:

The Chorus is a **social force** which **feeds** the growth of the IT.

The groups were then asked to have a think about rooting the specific personality of their individual Chorus into the stage direction of the opening of the play:

The Chorus makes its presence felt. The chorus buzzes. It fizzes. It hums. It is here.

Polly asked the groups to think about how they could make their Chorus 'perform' within that stage direction and what effect they would want it to have on the audience. The following ideas came out of those explorations:

- The clearer the verb the more detailed and distinct the work
- The verb can change
- The target (who the Chorus is interacting with) can change (throughout this moment, throughout the play). In fact a good general note is to check who the target is for any interaction with any character as it often changes

Soundscape

In another variation, using the word from 'the Chorus is' exercise, the groups spent ten minutes finding a soundscape that made the Chorus 'present'.

- Using p. 188 of the text, how could they combine the pieces of text that the Chorus have with the soundscape they created?

- How could they activate the physical language of the Chorus? Take the discoveries into physical action.

Clarify what the rules/requirements of your Chorus are. Test your rules on other sections of the text where the Chorus speaks.

The Chorus as a gesture or as a personality

How does the Chorus exist without Grace? The Chorus's presence opens the play, but Grace's first line isn't until page 186. The Chorus is information that goads/provokes/forces/feeds Grace's rage (the IT). The Chorus pushes Grace out of shape. But does the Chorus only feed and provoke Grace? Is Grace onstage at the start? If the Chorus only exists with Grace, why does she not speak until page 186 when she says, 'I am Grace Freemantle. I was totally average.' It is important to remember that the information (of the world) exists whether Grace has learnt about it yet or not.

Suggested ideas to think about when staging your Chorus:

- A version of the Chorus could be a gang who are always winning at life as opposed to just fuelling Grace's rage. However, if their nature never changes and they are always winning, then it will be hard to find ways for them to push Grace along and fuel the IT.
- What is the Chorus doing to Grace over time? You may want fifty people actively doing something to her in one moment, and in another moment you may want only one.
- The Chorus is always performing an action, maybe on the audience or on Grace.
- The challenge of the Chorus is balancing the role of being an abstract theatrical form with its essential storytelling feature.

Casting and characterisation

Grace

Grace is the merging of the three worlds. She exists in the present – always with the audience – as she is describing something as it's happening. Of course, we know the event during PE has happened. But the way the storytelling works in the play means that Grace is experiencing it all in the moment in front of the audience. She is standing there telling them. Find the emotion and the live-ness in that experience – it is happening to her in the here and now – in the present.

Grace and the IT

Thinking specifically about the IT and the relationship with Grace and how it affects her *totally* – how can you physically represent this? Do you manifest it individually, or through using a group of actors? Again, it is vital to remember that Vivienne intended the IT and the Chorus to be separate as the Chorus is the agent that forces the IT out of Grace.

How do you cast and encourage authentic acting for the part of Grace? Can you multi-role the part? How do you define and pull focus to Grace's separate relationships and storylines as part of the audience experience, keeping each clear in its storytelling? To multi-role the character of Grace would present both opportunities and challenges. In particular, with so many realities and narratives already in play, how could you keep focus and narrative clarity if you had multiple Graces?

Within the story of Grace and the IT, it is a good idea to work through her timeline and work out the moments that lead up to 'that day in PE' and the roar. Polly emphasised that there is a danger with Grace that the way she speaks is internal, but yet the audience needs to focus on her all the time and understand her struggle, so it's worth thinking that all her needs and wants have to reach the back of the theatre. Be bold about pushing her out as opposed to making her too introspective.

The students

The time world they operate in is after the PE lesson, after the event.

The Chorus

The Chorus is a part of Grace's present tense action that has already happened. It is really important you understand the time world you are trying to present.

Staging exercise 1

Polly suggested a staging exercise to think about the world of Grace and the IT.

Groups looked at p. 193 from **Student 6**, 'It was February,' down to p. 194, **Grace**, 'it's straining against my skin'. And then also p. 200, **Grace**, 'I am at home' down to p. 201, **Grace**, 'I wrap gaffer tape around my hand'.

Useful ideas from the exercise:

Who is Grace speaking to?

Why is she speaking?

What's her need?

What is her journey with the audience?

You could play the stakes of the IT so that Grace becomes embarrassed, and you see the effect on her physically using a rhythmic pulse, getting stronger until she can't squish it down.

Volume, space, breath feels important.

Keep thinking of how the audience receives the information – keep it as simple as possible.

Very difficult section as multiple narratives are in play.

From a pure storytelling perspective, what is the most important thing that is happening at the scene? The central object is Grace and her changing relationship with the IT. All the other elements are there to serve the most important aspect. So put that downstage central as a starting point and see where everything goes from there. Be clear with what Grace's focus is and how she is being pulled.

A small note on style

The play flips between direct address to the audience, characters speaking to each other, the Chorus acting as provocateurs. Part of this was inspired by the TV programme *24 Hours in Police Custody*. The set-up is always someone speaking to camera after the event has happened, but the audience does not know what the actual event is; they are drip-fed information throughout until the reveal. Vivienne chose to follow a similar framework to build tension. Therefore, it's imperative the audience is led to focus on the information that is drip-fed through the play.

The world of the aftermath of that day in PE/talking to the audience

Polly and Vivienne discussed that the world of the aftermath has a different 'feeling' or style (see above). In these direct address moments, it's helpful to think about who you want your audience to be.

Staging exercise 2

Two groups were asked to look at the world of the audience using the aftermath timeline, in particular thinking about the relationship to the audience of the production. They were asked to stage a section in three ways. Each way needed to focus on who the audience was as a way of shaping the text and how the scene played out.

They were asked to look at p. 185, **Student 1**: 'She was quiet' down to p. 186, **Student 2**: 'No, yeah, no, yeah, not unpopular.'

What if the audience was . . .

your friend, and are you worried that they might not believe you?

a police investigation room?

your parents who are really anxious about what happened at school that day?

your teacher whilst you are all meant to be sitting an exam?

a TV documentary crew (it is interesting to consider what the student's priorities might be here, i.e. telling the truth or looking cool!)?

This is a really nice exercise to create an immediate effect. It helps to give shape to an ensemble and create more detailed individual characters. However, you do need to be careful that you keep the audience your central focus – make sure that they feel included in whatever choice you make.

Actions and actioning

Polly offered actioning as a useful tool for trying to identify the effect you want to have either on the audience or on the person someone is talking to. Actioning means giving each sentence or thought an action or transitive verb that describes what you want to do to the other person and attaching it to the line to give it a very clear direction, e.g.:

I embrace you

I reward you

I attack you

I prod you

Note that a character's intention is what a character wants to achieve or where they want to end up. Smaller actions (how they go about achieving their intention) will need to be employed to get another character to do what they want, in order to reach their goal. Add into the mix how the characters feel about each other and their status to each other, as well as an obstacle, and you will create a very fine, detailed, focused scene for an audience.

When Grace talks to the audience she is hoping that she is talking to someone who will finally understand what she is going through. When the students talk to the audience, they are perhaps seeing a TV crew who they want to impress.

Staging exercise 3

Polly split the room into two groups, asking for one person within each group to be the director, but as a team starting from p. 194, 'We were in Geography', to p. 198, 'The IT wants to be heard'.

Participants were split into two groups of fifteen, each with a director in charge of directing a section. The challenge was to find the clearest, most dynamic, most interesting way of differentiating/turning the corner between the different realities. Building on choices found throughout the day, now they had to try to work out how they might all work together to create an exciting and surprising piece of theatre.

In order to do this exercise they had to pick an interpretation of each reality first, and then begin to tackle where they may exist onstage. The challenge here was to differentiate the realities existing onstage while ensuring they exist *alongside* one another; because of the nature of the scene, more than one reality exists onstage.

The items to focus on included:

Pace

Spacing – in terms of creating interesting, clear stage pictures and also creating room

Actions and targets

Intensity – how strong is the action?

Singular or collective action/text/focus

Turning corners – what is the most exciting and dynamic way of changing from their relationship to the audience and the relationship to Grace, or switching between the narrative threads, or being the Chorus and then the students.

Exercises for use in rehearsal

Exercise: Waking brains up!

Stage 1

- Leader says, 'GO', all the players walk around, filling the space in the room.
- Leader says, 'STOP', all the players must freeze.

Try this a few times until everyone is used to it.

Stage 2

Then add two more instructions:

- Leader says, 'CLAP', all the players should clap.
- Leader says, 'JUMP', all the players should jump.

The leader should mix up the instructions – GO, STOP, CLAP, JUMP – for a while until most of the players are doing it correctly.

Stage 3

Now two more instructions can be added:

- Leader says, 'SKY', all the players should reach up towards the sky.
- Leader says, 'KNEES', all the players should bend down and touch their knees.

Continue now with all six instructions until pretty much everyone gets it right.

Stage 4

To make it tricky, the leader announces that everything is now opposite:

- GO now means STOP
- STOP now means GO
- CLAP now means JUMP
- JUMP now means CLAP
- SKY now means KNEES
- KNEES now means SKY

The leader mixes up all the instructions and does the opposite actions along with the players.

Stage 5

Finally, in the most challenging stage, the leader calls out the actions, and does what the action says, while the players have to keep doing the opposite actions.

You can change/adapt the instructions to serve the production you are working on with your young people.

Exercise: Pass the clap (pace and energy)

Vivienne stressed that the worst production of this play would be a really slow one, so Hannah suggested a game to help work on picking up cues, driving text forward and keeping the pace up, which will then allow you to find the moments that deserve space and breathe or even silence. You could start every rehearsal with a quick game of 'pass the clap' to remind them of the importance of pacing.

Send a clap around the circle once with energy.

Let it go round naturally without anyone 'directing' it. Find its natural ebbs and flows and changes of rhythm and speed, volume and energy, direction and intention.

Then pass across the circle and send in different directions, being very clear where you are sending the clap.

Then use lines from the script (the group looked at p. 208, where there is a real barrage of energy and text, as the Chorus is really operating on Grace).

Lines are split up amongst the circle by reading a line each (then 'saving' that line as theirs) and exploring how fast and energetically lines can be sent around the circle, picking up their cues whilst retaining clarity.

Then move everyone to a different place in the circle, but everyone keeps the same lines. Keep the pace up.

Encourage everyone to think of energy onstage as their responsibility, to pick up the baton and pass it on like in a race or like in this clap game.

Another variation could be all the individuals with 'Grace' lines step into the circle when they say their line and remain inside the circle.

Question and answer with Vivienne Franzmann, Polly Findlay and Hannah Joss

Is the Chorus good or bad?

[Polly] It's not particularly helpful to think this way with your cast or production. Everyone thinks they are right and so that must be looked at – remember in *Othello*, Iago believes he is in a play called 'Iago' where he is the one being wronged. Every character must see themselves as good or 'right'.

Are the students separate to the Chorus?

[Polly] The students are part of the story aftermath, but you can do it through multi-roling. They can all interact and be played by the same people as long as you are aware of the gesture of function they are performing in the moment and what effect you want them to have on an audience.

What if the students are more well-spoken than how it's been written?

[Vivienne] If dialect feels like a barrier, then you can change it to sit within their voices. Do what you need to do including taking out words (within reason) so that it feels natural to them. There is a rhythm to the language, however, so make sure to keep an eye on that.

How do you feel about having Grace being played by more than one person?

[Vivienne] Whatever floats your boat, as long as the storytelling is clear.

Is this thing growing within her like a phantom pregnancy?

[Vivienne] It is growing in her. The whole IT is inside her.

Is there a possibility that the IT could be about finding an inner power or voice? Could it be that everything else is the horror and the IT can be a positive? Could it be about a young woman finding her voice, finding her opinion on the world?

[Vivienne] Yes.

Grace's roar feels like the impassioned speech by Greta Thunberg, and the situation feels like the older generation shouting her down and being fearful of her. And actually, this anger is within them all and it is the anger that all the younger generation have been left with?

[Vivienne] I wrote it long before Greta's speech but when I saw her make it and the anger fuelling her, I thought of Grace.

Why does Grace smile at the end?

[Vivienne] She smiles in an 'it will all be ok' kind of way to the other student to offer support. She has found some peace now that the IT has been released. In taking ownership of her situation, there is a catharsis, especially in being allowed to be angry at the world rather than pushing it down. So this thing has happened and now she is free of this thing – so yes the roar is a good thing, but don't play it like a good thing throughout!

[Hannah] The roar has been suppressed for eight years and so there is relief when it is finally released – much like migraines which are horrific but if you are able to be sick, which is violent and horrible, the moment after the headache begins to lift and relief starts to happen.

Has the IT been passed onto the student at the end after it leaves Grace?

[Vivienne] No, it isn't passed on – it exists already within young people. The other student recognises it's in them already, not that it has been passed on. It has become activated.

Is the character of Sam stand-alone or is she part of the Chorus or students?

[Vivienne] Sam belongs to the aftermath world; she is reporting what happened.

You mentioned earlier that 24 Hours in Police Custody *influenced the direct address aspect at the beginning. Are there any other influences?*

[Vivienne] Mainly documentaries that interview the friends of someone something has happened to. I think of the students almost as if they are giving footage to an imaginary TV crew, some of which will be edited out.

There are elements of self-harm raised in the play. Could you advise on safeguarding, especially if you have young people involved who have experienced self-harm?

[Vivienne] Your job is to keep everyone safe. So it is an important question to ask how you take care of your students in the creation of this piece.

This last question about safeguarding was opened up to the room. The group were split up into smaller groups and asked to each come up with actionable ways to safeguard students working on this play. Below are some of the suggestions:

Possible safeguarding measures that can be taken (as offered by the companies in the room)

- Having policies and procedures
- Providing a safe breakout space
- Knowing your students as best you can
- Transparency; sending the script out with themes to students and parents
- Create a rehearsal contract
- Remaining focused on the play and the characters, preventing talk becoming personalised or being treated like therapy
- Give names to nameless characters to stop self-identifying
- Modelling as a teacher the world of the play as opposed to making it personal
- Use the Equity safe space statement as a starting point – read the statement at the beginning of rehearsals (point out it is used for professional actors as well)
- Allowing time within your practice to check in and check out
- Keep information in the room about who they can contact if they need anyone to talk to
- Anger management – the anger in Grace is a theme for all students, so going macro rather than thinking micro
- Focus on the humour in the play, not just the darkness
- Discussing what other things Grace could have done instead of keeping silent until the roar
- As leader, be clear on the journey that you want to take your students on
- Keep rehearsals positive and fun, and focus on the play's and the student's strengths
- The play is a good springboard to discuss society not letting Grace speak out

Final tips from Vivienne Franzmann

- Create your sentence that sums up the play for you.
- Always return to serving that sentence or idea.

- Less is more – you don't have to throw everything at it.
- Kill your darlings; if it doesn't serve the story get rid of it.
- Clarity is key in this piece.
- Pace is also key.
- Remember Grace is experiencing it in the moment – be wary of a 'storytelling' Grace rather than her experiencing it happening in the moment.

Suggested references

TV programme *24 Hours in Police Custody*

Greta Thunberg's speech to world leaders about climate change: https://www.youtube.com/watch?v=TMrtLsQbaok

Equity safe space statement: https://www.equity.org.uk/getting-involved/campaigns/safe-spaces/safe-spaces-statement/

From a workshop led by Polly Findlay and Hannah Joss with notes by Jemma Gross and Emma Baggott

The Marxist in Heaven

by Hattie Naylor

The Marxist in Heaven is a play that does exactly what its title page says it's going to do. The eponymous protagonist 'wakes up' in paradise and, once they get over the shock of this fundamental contradiction of everything they believe in, they get straight back to work, and continue their lifelong struggle for equality and fairness for all – even in death. Funny, playful, provocative, pertinent and jam-packed with discourse, disputes, deities and disco-dancing by the bucketful, this upbeat buoyant allegory shines its holy light on globalisation and asks the salient questions: who are we and what are we doing to ourselves, and what conditioner do you use on your hair?

Cast size
20 speaking parts, plus unlimited non-speaking parts, any gender
Suitable for all ages

Hattie Naylor's plays include *The Night Watch* (Manchester Royal Exchange, 2016), *Going Dark* with Sound&Fury (Fuel/Young Vic, 2014), *As the Crow Flies* (Pentabus, 2017) and *Bluebeard* (Gallivant/Bristol Old Vic, 2013). *Ivan and the Dogs* (Soho Theatre/ATC, 2010) was nominated in the Olivier Awards for Outstanding Achievement in an Affiliate Theatre and won the Tinniswood Award. The film adaptation of the play, *Lek and the Dogs*, premiered at the London Film Festival in 2018.

Other theatre productions include her gender-swapping *The Three Musketeers* (The Dukes, nominated for National Theatre Awards 2018); *Weighting* (with Extraordinary Bodies, national tour 2015/16); *What Am I Worth?* (Extraordinary Bodies national tour and National Theatre River Stage 2018); and *The Puppeteer* (with Blind Summit, international and national tour 2018/19).

Her work as a librettist includes *Picard in Space* with Will Gregory (Goldfrapp) for the Electronica Festival at the Southbank 2012 and Radio 3. She has also written extensively for BBC Radio 4, notably: *Lullaby* (2019), *The Diaries of Samuel Pepys* (nominated Best Radio Drama 2012) and *The Aeneid* (nominated Best Radio Adaptation, BBC Audio Awards 2013).

I would like to dedicate this play to: the unknown female aged twenty-three who committed suicide by throwing herself off a Foxconn building in Shenzhen, China, in 2013; to Víctor Hugo Daza who died at seventeen when he was shot while demonstrating against the privatisation of the city's water supply in Cochabamba, Bolivia, in 2000; and to the 117 piece workers who died in the fire in Dhaka, Bangladesh, at a fast-fashion factory in 2012.

I would also like to dedicate this play to Brett Davies for the inspiration with a little help from Woodie Guthrie and Joe Hill, and to all union reps around the world who continue to fight the good fight.

Casting

This is a non-gender specific, non-racially specific, non-people with and without disability specific play, i.e. any part can be played by any person of any orientation, gender, with disability, etc. This applies to all roles including the Angels and God. Disability is present in Heaven where the play is set, and its representation is to be encouraged within casting. All names including Valerie are male or female. Heaven is inclusive. Bob is likewise a male or female role. Occasionally the direction refers to she or he but this is only for grammatical reasons. The Angels are not dressed as Angels until the finale, allowing for a fabulous visual treat at the end of the play. '. . .' denotes an interruption which should begin at least two words before the dots in the previous line. The musical tracks, their length and where they begin, are specific and carefully chosen and are very much part of the play and are not to be deviated from. The Multitude refers to any character that is not an Angel or God, and can include infinite and additional cast members with non-speaking parts.

Characters

Valerie	**Jade**
Nanael	**Keanu**
Bob	**Umut**
Hofniel	**Raz**
Muriel	**Daza**
River	**Xu**
Ayo	**Michael**
Bailey	**Mighty Metatron**
Chandra	**God**
Fara	
Chen	

Scene One

Valerie *is terrified and in panic.* **Nanael** *is seated and is reading* Hello! *magazine and barely looks up.* **Nanael** *is used to this panic and is very bored.*

Valerie   What? Where? This? What?

How? Where? Where? Where?!

Nanael *without looking up nonchalantly turns a page.*

Valerie   So I was on my bike.
On my bike, cycling. Yeah. I was cycling.
And then. And then.

Nanael *continues to read.*

Valerie   It goes black.
And then I'm here. I'm here.
With, with. You. Whoever you are.
Do I know you?

Nanael *looks up, thinks about the question, and then answers.*

Nanael   No.

And goes back to the magazine.

Valerie   Ok. (*With mounting panic.*)

So, I'm on my bike. I'm cycling along.
And, and. And then I'm. I'm.

Nanael   Dead?

Valerie   I'm cycling along. It goes black. And then. I'm.

Nanael   Dead.

Valerie   I'm cycling and then I'm.

Nanael *makes a hand gesture across the throat to suggest 'dead'.* **Valerie** *takes this in and continues.*

Valerie (*with anger*)   I'm cycling along. It's a great day, the sun's out and everything is great apart from the political system we live in. And then. And. Then I'm.

Nanael *makes a more grotesque version of someone dying.*

Valerie   That's not possible.

Nanael (*indifferent*)   If you say so.

Nanael *goes back to reading.*

Valerie   I can't be can I, because I'm here.

Nanael (*reading magazine*)   You got me there.

Valerie   Yeah, here talking to you.

Nanael   Right?

Valerie   Talking to you. (*Pause. On the edge of tears.* **Valerie** *has just died!*)

So, I'm on my bike, I'm on my bike!

Silence. **Valerie** *unable to continue.*

Nanael (*not looking up*)   Yeah it's a bit tough.

Valerie   What is?

Nanael   Dying?

Beat.

Valerie   I was on my bike! I was on it! And then.

Silence. **Valerie** *looks towards* **Nanael** *in hope of help/guidance/sympathy even.*

Nanael   This isn't really my job.

Valerie   You're reading Hello! magazine.

Nanael   I mean *this* isn't.

Valerie   This?

Nanael   I'm covering.

Valerie   For who?

Nanael   Well, they're late.

Valerie   I can't be here, this isn't here or real because I'm a Marxist you see and here, if I'm dead, and I'm only saying 'if', because obviously I'm not because I'm here talking to you, 'if', well here, doesn't exist because there is no after life, Heaven or Hell and I know this, I know this because I'm a Marxist and we are atheists and don't believe in guff.

Nanael (*groaning*)   Oh. What was that word you just said?

Valerie   Heaven?

Nanael (*sighing*)   No a word after that?

Valerie   Hell?

Nanael (*sighing*)   No.

Valerie   Guff.

Nanael   No.

Valerie   Marxist?

Nanael   Yeah, that one.

Nanael *gets up.*

I don't know how you got in.
I better go and tell him.

Valerie   Him?

Nanael   Her then?

Valerie   Him or her?

Nanael   Doesn't matter here does it, him, her, it's all the same.

Valerie   And who is him, her?

Nanael (*ignoring* **Valerie**)   Where is your.

Bob *explodes onto the stage, rushing on.*

Bob   Guide! Sorry, so sorry, I was just finishing a blow-dry.

Bob *bows to* **Nanael**. **Nanael** *barely acknowledges him, and exits.*

Bob (*whispered/mouthed*)   Sorry.

Valerie   A guide?

Bob   Yes everyone has one. But you can call me Bob.

Valerie   Right. (*Referring to* **Nanael**.) And who was that?

Bob   Nanael.

Valerie   Nanael?

Bob   They're a Principality.

Valerie   What's that?

Bob   Or maybe a higher tier, they might have been promoted.

Valerie   But what is a Principality?

Bob *makes the BSL sign for 'halo'.*

Valerie   Is that the international sign for halo?

Bob   Lower Order.

Valerie   Lower Order?

Bob   Lower Order in The Great Angelic Order. It's in tiers.

Valerie   What?

Bob   Principalities and Archangels are at the bottom with Angels. Then it goes to the second tier which is Virtues, Powers and Dominions, and then above that is your

Thrones, and of course your Cherubim and then Seraphim at the top. (*New thought.*) If you can get chosen . . .

Valerie   Chosen.

Bob   Yeah, if you're, like, well good, you can be chosen. Sometimes, if you're, like, really, really good, you don't have to go in at the bottom, you can go like straight in at the top.

Valerie   Right.

Bob   I'm hoping to get chosen one day.

Bob *repeats the BSL sign and then points to himself and smiles.*

Valerie (*incredulous*)   As an Angel.

Bob   Yeah. You can help me if you like.

Valerie   How?

Bob   There's a feedback form.

Valerie   Ok. (*Beat.*) I get you, I get you. Who put you up to it?

Bob   No one.

Valerie   Was it our new union rep?

Bob   No. (*Beat.*) What sort of conditioner do you use? Your hair looks very limp.

Valerie   What?

Bob   So, Valerie. It's a nice name.

Valerie   Who told you my name?

Bob   They told me.

Repeats the BSL for halo. Beat.

Valerie   So, I was on my bike and.

FX loud disco – the introduction to 'September' by Earth, Wind and Fire. All cast members enter (apart from Angels and God) and dance with exuberance. The music is too loud to hear any dialogue but **Bob** *clearly shouts at* **Valerie** *to dance.* **Valerie** *awkwardly begins to dance towards the end. The music lasts for exactly thirty seconds and then abruptly (with no fade!) ends. All the cast slowly exit, smiling as they do so and chatting.*

Valerie   What was that?

Bob   Thirty-second disco. We love it.

Valerie   Who's we?

Bob (*announcing*)   'The Great Multitude of Heaven'. Keeps the world spinning.

Valerie   What?!

Bob   The world rotating.

Beat. **Valerie** *is on the edge of tears again, confused and afraid.*

Valerie   I'm finding this all just really upsetting now.

Beat.

Bob   Come on, it'll get better. It's your induction next.

Valerie   My what?

Bob   Your induction, you'll feel better after that. Really it's very wonderful here, just a bit confusing at first.

Valerie (*overwhelmingly sad and confused*)   I was on my bike.

Bob (*gently*)   We're you.

Valerie   I was going to join a picket line.

Bob   Come on.

Valerie   At an Amazon fulfilment centre. I think I hit a tree.

Bob   I know.

Valerie   You do?

Bob   Of course. (**Bob** *takes* **Valerie***'s hand and leads* **Valerie** *off looking at* **Valerie***'s hair.*)

Bob   What conditioner did you say you use?

Valerie (*very sad*)   I didn't.

Bob   Are you from the no-conditioner school of hair washing?

Brave. Maybe a little too brave. It's very dry.

An **Angel** *(NB not in their kit) enters carrying a tray of sandwiches.*

Bob   Have you ever thought of using Argan oil?

Valerie   No, what's that.

Bob   It's for dry hair.

Valerie *refuses a sandwich.* **Bob** *takes one and eats.* **Angel** *exits.*

Bob   The hospitality in Heaven is always excellent. Though there's usually crisps. Mmhhm. These are delicious. 'Heavenly'. Cheese! Not hungry?

Valerie   There wasn't a vegan option.

Bob   Cheeeeseee!

Valerie   Cheese isn't vegan.

Bob   It is in Heaven. Everything's vegan in Heaven. I love cheese.

Hofniel *enters looking at his smartphone, He is listening to music (which we never hear) through headphones.* **Bob** *does the BSL sign for halo and bows, encouraging* **Valerie** *who also awkwardly bows.* **Hofniel** *does not notice.*

Valerie   Who's this?

Bob   Hofniel. He's an

Bob *makes the BSL sign for halo and mouths 'Angel'.* **Hofniel** *takes his headphones off and hands them to* **Bob.**

Hofniel   So, fam.

Bob *puts the headphones on and nods his head in time with the music.*

Hofniel   What's app?

Valerie   I was on my bike..

Hofniel   Shoot, bruv. You say it how it is.

Bob *takes the headphones out and hands them back to* **Hofniel**.

Bob (*referring to music through headphones*)   Excellent.

Hofniel *goes back to looking at the phone, searching for another track.*

Valerie   Is this a trick?

Hofniel (*not looking up*)   Awesome.

Valerie   Did someone put you up to it?

It's our new union rep isn't it? She looks like a joker.

Hofniel (*not looking up or listening*)   Sure thing. Yeah. Yeah. I get you, fam.

Hofniel *puts the headphones on and holds up a hand to silence* **Valerie**. *We wait till* **Hofniel***'s head is bobbing up and down, then they take the headphones out and hand them to* **Bob**. **Bob** *takes them and listens.*

Valerie   I knew it. Where is she? Ok. The game's up.

You can come out now.

Hofniel (*still not listening*)   Sure thing, I'm down there with you, bruv.

Valerie   Down where?

Hofniel   Viva da Revolutionary.

Valerie   What?

Bob (*referring to music through headphones*)   Excellent.

Hofniel (*agreeing*)   Pounding watts. (*Looking for another track on his phone.*)

You're trocking, fam.

Valerie   Trocking? Fam?

Hofniel (*not looking up or listening*)   Sure thing. Yeah. Yeah. I get you.

Valerie   Do all Angels talk like this?

Hofniel   Picked it up from the kids, din I? Like I'm down with them.

Valerie   It doesn't sound patronising?

Hofniel   Cool it, bruv. Allow it. You're the man, woman. Whatever.

Valerie   I am (*whatever sex they are*) a man/a woman!

Hofniel   It's no fuss here, fam. You need to relax.

Bob   Yeah relax.

Valerie   I AM RELAXED! (*Pause, takes a breath.*)

So, if, let's suppose, if this is Heaven.

Hofniel   The peak.

Valerie   'The peak'. Why am I here then?

Hofniel   Coz you're trocking's well sick . . .

Valerie   If this isn't a trick.

Hofniel   Be some trick, bruv. I mean we've got everything here. Magazines, conditioner, that wax stuff you put in your ears to pull the hairs out with.

Valerie   What?

Hofniel *takes one of the headphones from* **Bob** *and they listen together, bobbing their heads up and down.*

Hofniel (*referring to music, shouting over music*)   Eargasm.

Bob (*shouting*)   Oh yeah. Eargasm.

Bob *and* **Hofniel** *remove headphones.*

Hofniel   You, my fam, have worked all your days for the other brothers and the sisters. When everyone was out, you were in, well in; marching with the sisters, and the brothers, you stopped by, dug them out, went on the line, stared down the bosses, you fought the good fight, it was you, you took one for the boys and girls, innit? And that's why you got into The Peak. Got me?

Valerie *looks blank.* **Hofniel** *looks for another track.*

Bob   Hofniel means you worked for the benefit of others all your life, you put everyone else before yourself. That's why you're here.

Valerie   But I have no faith. I don't believe.

Hofniel   You do believe.

Hofniel *hands the headphones over to* **Bob** *once more.*

Valerie   There is no God.

Hofniel *and* **Bob** *burst into laughter, verging on hysterical.*

Hofniel   Yeah, well, you don't have to be perfect to get a look in on The Peak.

Valerie   But you have to have faith?

Hofniel   You do, bruv, you do.

Bob *puts the headphones back in, listens.*

Valerie   In what?

Hofniel   Marxism, bruv.

Valerie   That's not a belief system.

Hofniel   Yeah, bruv, it is. Allow it.

Bob *hands the headphones back to* **Hofniel**.

Hofniel   Yeah?

Bob   Banging.

Hofniel   Yeah, banging.

Bob   Banging.

Hofniel *puts the headphones in and exits, listening to the music as he goes.*

Valerie   Was that a smartphone? Doesn't she (*or he*) know how they're made?

Bob   They know most things up here.

Valerie   The assembly lines . . .

Bob   Most things.

Valerie   Twelve-hour shifts, timed bathroom visits, bullying and shouting by the bosses, no unionisation and workers driven to suicide.

Bob   Yeah. Sounds awesome.

Valerie   Awesome?

Bob   Not awesome?

Valerie   No not awesome. In 2016 a group of just under a hundred workers threatened to commit mass suicide in a Foxconn factory in China. Can you imagine the working conditions that drive a hundred men and women to do that? They went to the top of a building and threatened to jump off.

Bob   Yeah, but it doesn't matter here.

Valerie   What?!

Bob It doesn't matter.

Valerie Your Angel is using a smartphone!

Bob Do you think a good haircut with some high-quality conditioner would help? Just a fresh look can change a person's outlook. I do a great head massage.

Valerie A head massage.

Bob Yeah, (*holding up hands*) look at these fingers.

Valerie What?! I'm talking about an industry that is diabolical, literally! And yet this technology is being used in Heaven, or wherever we are.

Bob Yeah, The Peak. Have a sandwich, I think a sandwich would help.

Valerie That's a cheese sandwich. Like I said. I'm a vegan.

Bob (*waving the sandwich in front of* **Valerie**) Mmhmm.

Valerie Is that cheese even organic, free range?

Bob Well, no because.

Valerie Milk production, do you know about milk production?

Bob Have you tried hair-straighteners, they can change the quality of your hair making it more . . .

Valerie Cows, do you know what happens to cows?

Bob The oils rush to the surface of the hair, making it softer and more manageable and shinier leaving a glossier finish.

Valerie Cows!

Bob Cows?

Valerie Yes cows! Are artificially inseminated to make them lactate all year, hooked up to machines, milked twice a day, often developing mastitis, you should look at the pictures online. They live for as little as five years until their milk yield drops, lifespan normally twenty, then their crippled bodies are sold for dog food. Let alone what happens to their calves. Do you know what happens to their calves, Bob?

Bob No.

Valerie Within a day of them being born, they're torn away from their mum. Have you heard a distressed cow calling for its calf? (*Beat.*) Well, have you?

Bob No. I was a hairdresser, trainee. I lived in the middle of Manchester. (*Or nearest big city.*) There aren't any cows in Moss Side. (*Or urban area in local big city.*)

Valerie It's a sound that never leaves you. The calves are then shoved into cramped boxes and turned into veal after a short life of unimaginable suffering.

Bob That sounds, well that sounds.

Valerie Bad?

Bob   Bad.

Valerie   Pretty diabolical again I'd say, and as we're supposedly in Heaven.

Bob   The Peak.

Valerie   The Peak, I would have thought all crimes against humanity, and animals would be, well at least off limits. That's where your cheese is from, Bob. Eat up!

Bob   Only that.

Valerie   Only what?!

Bob   Well, everything's imagined here, so nothing is real, like, so there is no farm, organic or otherwise. You can just have what you want, even animal-tested shampoo because it's not real. You see. It's Heaven. 'The Peak'. Abundance and all. Lots of lovely things and Kentucky Fried Chicken whenever you want it. I love a bit of Kentucky. Heaven wouldn't be Heaven unless you could have whatever you wanted. I mean you wouldn't want that austerity stuff in Heaven would you.

Valerie   A capitalist Heaven.

Who makes the rules?

Bob   That'll be the Great Angelic Order, the high-ups, the rule, The Authority.

Valerie   So, it's a hierarchy. Of course.

Bob   Yeah, there's like I said, different tiers. Yeah, I mean it's great, coz one day I'll be made an Angel. I'm at the bottom now, but I can see myself as a Cherubim. Can't you?

Valerie   Not really.

Bob   Why, do you think my cheeks need to be fatter? (**Bob** *puffs out his face.*) See it now?

Valerie   And that one we just spoke to?

Bob   What Hofniel?

Valerie   Yeah.

Bob   He's a lower one.

Valerie   He didn't look like an Angel.

Bob   No. They only dress up for big occasions. (*Beat.*) It's the wings. They get in the way. (*Pause.*) Anyway it's nice to have all the stuff you want, whenever you want it. I remember once my mum got me this lamp right, when you blew on it, it came on, all on its own. It was dead amazing. (*Blows. Holding up sandwich.*) You sure you don't want a bite?

Valerie   No. I don't want a sandwich.

Bob   Mmmh. (*Waves sandwich in front of* **Valerie**'s *face.*)

Valerie   Get that thing out of my face.

FX 'You Make Me Feel Mighty Real' by Sylvester from beginning.

Bob   Oh, I love this song!

Multitude enter and dance with joy. **Bob** *clearly shouts at* **Valerie** *to dance.* **Valerie** *will not dance. The music lasts for exactly thirty seconds and then abruptly (with no fade) ends. Multitude remain on stage, chatting quietly.* **Muriel** *and* **Hofniel** *enter. The room falls silent, everyone bows.* **Bob** *attempts to get* **Valerie** *to bow by doing the BSL sign for halo.* **Muriel** *has a clipboard and never smiles as she recites the standard greeting, as if reading a shopping list. NB she has been saying this for thousands of years.*

Muriel (*so bored*)   This is fantastic. You, fantastic people. Well done for getting here. Look at your beautiful faces. You all look great. Well, it doesn't get much better than Heaven. (*Sighs – it's a joke she's been made to tell for aeons.*) My little joke, of course it doesn't get any better than here.

Hofniel   This is The Peak!

Muriel   The Peak. Thank you, Hofniel.

Hofniel   The Peak!

Muriel   Yes. This is a meet and greet session. We have a mixture of newbies and oldies here, so we can all get to know each other.

FX 'Word Up!' by Little Mix, thirty seconds, from the beginning. **Muriel** *groans. Everyone dances.* **Muriel** *dances particularly badly and reluctantly.* **Hofniel** *dances madly.* **Valerie** *does not dance. The music abruptly stops, and everyone stops dancing.* **Hofniel** *put his headphones on and half-listens.*

Muriel   So, where was I? Has everyone had plenty to eat and drink?

All nod.

Actually I'm a little thirsty. Bob, would you?

Bob   Of course, Muriel.

Bob *'imagines' some water for Muriel which 'appears' and hands it over.*

Muriel: Thank you.

Bob (*explaining*)   Angels can't imagine.

Muriel   That's right, (*proudly*) 'we only know TRUTH!'

Bob   And on account of Cindy.

Valerie   Who's Cindy?

Muriel   Right, let's get started.

Valerie *puts their hand up.*

Yes?

Valerie   I'd like to speak to God.

Muriel   That's not possible.

Bob   Sorry, Muriel, he's a newbie.

Muriel   Newbies always take time to adjust, Bob. It's Valerie isn't it?

Valerie   Yes. So, who gets to talk to him?

Muriel   The Great Angelic Order of course.

Valerie   Which ones?

Muriel   The Seraphim or the Cherubim.

Valerie   So the lower orders like you, they don't get to speak to him either?

Muriel   Well, no.

Bob   I'm so sorry, Muriel. Will this count against me . . .?

Valerie   So not only are the Angels better than us, you're better than each other. There's a chain of command, and a chain of better-ness. You do know that I'm a Marxist?

Muriel   I thought we didn't let Marxists in?

Hofniel   We do, fam.

Muriel   Since when?

River *puts their hand up.*

Hofniel   Since my bruv here, Valerie. Can I call you Val?

Valerie (*no*)   I suppose so.

Hofniel   My bruv Val stared down the bosses, fought the good fight, took one for the boys and girls, he's trocking, so he got in. I looked at his stats, it's all there. He put everyone else first.

Muriel   Does *he* know about it?

Hofniel   He? She?

Muriel   He *or* she.

Hofniel *shrugs.*

Hofniel   I saw Nanael running like he was well feared, chaffing about Cindy . . .

Muriel (*looking afraid*)   Cindy . . .?

Valerie   So, this chain of command.

River *is now stretching their arm as high as possible.*

Muriel   We don't look at it that way.

Valerie   What other way of looking at it is there?

Muriel   Yes, River?

River   Will Messi get to heaven?

Bob   Messi?

Muriel   The footballer?

River (*very serious*)   There's only one Messi.

Muriel   We don't know yet.

River   Is it dependent on how well he plays?

Muriel   Nooo, River. This is Heaven.

Hofniel   The Peak!

Muriel   Thank you.

Hofniel   The Peak!

Ayo *puts up his/her hand.*

Valerie   Surely Heaven should be perfect?

Muriel   Yes, Ayo?

Ayo   And Neymar?

Beat.

Muriel   Neymar?

Ayo   Will Neymar get to Heaven?

Hofniel   The Peak!

Muriel   We just don't know yet.

Ayo   But if he plays really well?

Muriel   Getting into Heaven is to do with being good, it's not to do with sporting achievements. Any more questions?

Valerie *puts his hand up.* **Muriel** *ignores* **Valerie**.

Muriel   Anyone else?

Reluctantly **Muriel** *defers to* **Valerie**.

Yesss?

Valerie   How can I get to meet God?

Muriel   You can't.

So, in this meet and greet session I'd like you to look around the room, spot someone you don't know, go up, say hello, and then tell them something about yourself. Oldies maybe you can take the initiative to help the newbies. Don't be afraid, you're in Heaven. Go on, go right up.

All apart from **Muriel***,* **Bob** *and* **Valerie** *look for a partner to shake hands with. They continue to talk quietly among themselves. FX 'Funky Town' by Lipps Inc. Everyone dances. Music abruptly stops at about thirty seconds. The Multitude then go back to shaking each other's hands and talking among themselves. Some sit in the corners and chat.*

Bob   Happy?

Valerie   No, I'm not happy with the regime.

Bob   It's not a regime.

Hofniel   But this is The Peak. Everyone's well happy at The Peak.

Valerie   It's a power structure isn't it. With top guys and bottom guys, winners and losers. Those deemed worthy to speak to the high-ups and those not, the Cherubim or whatever.

Muriel   Well, I don't think you'll ever get to speak to a Cherubim.

Valerie   I'd say that's a regime. And I don't like the music.

Bob   How can you not like Little Mix?! I'm so sorry, Muriel, this has nothing to do with me.

Hofniel   They won't be sending you back if you don't chill.

Valerie   You threatening me with Hell?

Bob   No, they can't send you below once you've got in.

But everyone goes back.

Hofniel   Yeah, fam.

Bob   Yeah everyone returns.

Valerie   What so this isn't even eternity?!

Muriel   It's too much all at once, Bob, sometimes they just can't take it in.

Valerie (*now very upset*)   No. 'They' can't!

Hofniel   Is my bruv about to cry?

Bob   I don't know.

Hofniel   Have you offered my bruv one of your head massages? (**Hofniel** *nudges* **Bob***.*) Go on.

Bob *attempts to touch* **Valerie***'s head.*

Valerie   Get off. (*Beat.*) And who *decides* when you go back?!

Bob   God.

Muriel Well, not really. It's the one down from God.

Valerie And you don't get to meet either of them?

Muriel No.

Valerie And that's not even a discussion?

Muriel No.

Valerie So it's a dictatorship?

Hofniel But God's well good.

Muriel Like, universally good.

Hofniel So like what's the problem, fam?

Valerie Let alone the shitting music.

Bob Did you just swear in front of an Angel?

Nanael *enters, spots* **Valerie** *and heads straight for him/her.*

Hofniel Angels!

Bob I'm never going to progress. I'll never be an Angel . . .

Nanael So, you. (*Pointing at* **Valerie**.) We can fast track you.

Bob Fast track?   **Muriel** What?   **Hofniel** Woe, mama!

Nanael Yep.

Hofniel Is that a thing?

Nanael Yep it's a thing, Hofniel. 'It has always been and always will be,' (*beat*) a thing.

Bob Fast tracking.

Nanael Yep. So you can continue the revolution and stuff.

Isn't that what you want to do, you know, change the world? You can't do it from here.

Valerie No.

Nanael I mean, if you're a Marxist.

Valerie Yeah.

Bob What is a Marxist?

Nanael A follower of Marx. Shouldn't you return pronto?

Bob Who was Marx?

Nanael A nineteenth-century philosopher and economist. It's not very political stuck in Heaven where you can't do anything, is it?

Valerie   And socialist revolutionary.

Nanael   What?

Valerie   And socialist revolutionary, primarily concerned with working-class emancipation.

Bob (*smiling*)   Oh! I'm working class!

Nanael (*to* **Valerie**)   Well?

Bob   That sounds lovely.

Valerie   I don't know.

Bob   Is he the beard guy?

Nanael   Don't you want to continue the revolution?

Valerie   Of course.

Bob   On the mugs.

Valerie and Nanael   What?

Bailey *gets up and approaches* **Muriel**.

Bob   The beard guy on the mugs, that's Marx.

Valerie   He had a beard yes. (*To* **Nanael**.) Ok. I'll be fast tracked.

Nanael   Great. Let's go.

Muriel   Don't you need to tell him, her, first?

Nanael   It was her, his idea.

Bailey *puts his hand up.*

Valerie   Who's her, his. (*Beat.*) Him, her?

Muriel   Yes, Bailey?

Bailey   I don't like the music much either . . .

Bob   You can't be serious?

Bailey   I am.

Muriel   But it's the way it's always been. Disco is the music of Heaven.

Valerie   It was invented in the seventies?

Hofniel (*still on their headphones*)   The Peak!

Muriel   Thank you, Hofniel.

Hofniel   The Peak!

Muriel   It was here well before that. (*Announcing.*)

'Disco has always been and always will be.'

Bailey   Yeah, that's what people always say, 'It's just the way things are'. So no one ever questions it because it's always been so. I just don't think I can listen to it anymore.

Nanael (*to* **Valerie**)   Come on we're leaving. You're being fast tracked.

Bob (*to* **Bailey**)   How can you not like the music?

Bailey   I never have. I just didn't think we could change it. But now Valerie has said . . . can I call you Val too?

Valerie   Of course.

Nanael   Come on!

Bob   You need to go with Nanael.

Bailey and Valerie   Why?

Bob   Because.

Hofniel   You'll ruin his chances of being an Angel if you don't.

Bob   Hofniel?

Hofniel   What? It's the truth! I'm an Angel! Only speaking truth, bruv.

Bailey   It can't be Heaven if we're not all happy, can it? Can it, Val?

And . .

Bailey *addresses the rest of the* **Multitude** *that are seated.*

Bailey   We should all be happy if this is The Peak.

Valerie   Yes, you should.

The seated **Multitude** *begin to stand and move to listen.*

Bailey   You hear that? We should all be happy.

Chandra   I've never liked the music either. I thought I was the only one.

Fara   Me too. What about some progressive rock? It's always disco. We don't even get to listen to any ELO.

Chen   Toto, what about some Toto?

Chandra   'Hold the Line', why can't we listen to 'Hold the Line'?

Muriel   IT'S ALWAYS BEEN DISCO!

Hofniel   Yeah, always, bruv.

Valerie   It's a bad choice whenever it was made. It should be a consensus.

Bob   We had to replace the singing with something.

Valerie (*baffled*)   Right.

Bob   To keep the world in motion.

Keanu   And I hate the bowing.

Chen   So do I.

Keanu   It's oppressive.

Muriel   I didn't start the bowing.

Jade *puts up their hand.*

Valerie   We have no power and no say.

Nanael   I thought we were leaving?

Muriel   Yes, Jade?

Jade   I think I agree.

Muriel   Aren't you happy?

Jade   Yes, Heaven's very nice.

Hofniel   The Peak.

Jade   The people are great. I mean really friendly and kind.

General ad-lib 'Thanks, Jade', 'We think you're great too'. **Jade** *might respond with a 'Thank you'.*

Muriel   That's Heaven for you.

Jade   It is nice. But it would be nice to make it really nice. We're never consulted. The music's just part of it. I agree with Valerie, Heaven should be perfect, and it can't be perfect unless we're all equal. There should be consensus and what we decide should be acted on.

Valerie   Otherwise it's just a dictatorship.

Jade   Exactly.

Keanu   Yeah, you'd expect Heaven to be perfect.

Chen   You'd expect some Toto.

Fara   Or at least some ELO.

Jade   And I'd like to meet God too.

Chandra   Yeah, and God.

Jade   Yeah, and God. We'd all like to meet God.

Bob (*to* **Valerie**)   This is your fault.

Bailey   I really hate disco.

Muriel   Look, I don't choose the music.

Valerie   Well, who does?

Muriel   I don't know. Someone above me.

Chandra   Part of the hierarchy, The Authority.

Jade   Yeah, part of The Authority.

Muriel   But it's the order of things. No one questions the system because we all prosper within it and we're happy!

Valerie   Clearly not.

Bob   I thought you were going?

Nanael   Yes, so did I.

Umut *puts her/his hand up.*

Muriel   Yes Umut?

Umut   Will Ronaldo get to Heaven?

Muriel   I don't know!

Raz   You don't get into Heaven because of goal average.

Umut   Course you can.

Ayo   Yeah, course.

Valerie   You know I think I might stay for a bit.

Chen *chants 'Toto! Toto! Toto! Toto! Toto!' leading the Multitude.*

Bob (*to* **Valerie**)   Look what you've done.

A banner appears with 'Toto' at its centre as the Multitude chant.

Scene Two

Hofniel *is massaging* **Daza**'s *head.* **Xu** *and* **Valerie** *are watching.*

Xu   Do you think your demands will be met?

Valerie   To meet God?

Xu   Yes.

Valerie   I believe it's in discussion. You'd think heaven wouldn't be afraid of the negotiating table

Daza *groans.*

Hofniel   I miss the singing, it was well good. You know when there were loads of us here. Keeping the world well oiled.

Valerie   So let me get this right. The Angels sang to keep the world rotating?

Hofniel   Got it, fam.

Valerie   What happened to them all?

Hofniel   Cindy weren't it.

Daza   Who's Cindy?

Hofniel   Goes by loads of handles, Satan, Lucifer, Beelzebub, though that's some other Mother, like technically. But no one like says his real handle here, they all call him Cindy. God took imagination away from the Angels after Cindy led a rebellion, like large, like well large, when he imagined he was greater than God and took a whole load of Angels with him below, so we lost almost a third of the choir then, mostly the altos.

Daza *groans*.

Valerie   Good?

Daza   Very.

Hofniel   And then, like, coz he was down there, you know with nothing to do like, and like this well big imagination and stuff, he created the world, in'it?

Valerie   What, Satan?

Hofniel (*correcting him*)   Cindy.

Valerie   Created the Earth?

Hofniel   Yeah.

Valerie   So, it wasn't God?

Hofniel   No. Course not. The world is made up of matter right? And matter by its very nature is corrupt, get it? So, course Cindy created it. I mean look at it. (**Daza** *groans*.) All that stuff, all the things. Like plastic, or coal.

Valerie   Coal?

Hofniel   Industrial revolution, don't work without coal. Leads all the way, don't it, bruv, to where the world is now.

Who put it there, you gotta ask yourself. Durr.

Valerie   O.K. Wow.

Xu   That's what our local factories were run on. Coal. You couldn't breathe the air.

Hofniel   He's a mean dude.

Daza   So, they went to Earth?

Valerie   But not all of them?

Hofniel   No, we managed to keep hold of the basses, sopranos and tenors till the Tamagotchis.

Daza   Those pet things?

Hofniel   Yeah. Well, by then the Angels, we, couldn't imagine nothin', and there was like this wait between people arriving at The Peak who could imagine new technology because they'd lived with it, and the Angels actually getting their hands on it.

Valerie   The demand outstripped the supply.

Hofniel   Yeah something like that, so loads were just too impatient to wait and went down to get the Tamagotchis themselves. That was mostly the tenors. Then the basses went for the smartphones, and then finally we lost like most of the sopranos coz of Pokémon. And that's when they came up with getting the Multitude to dance to keep the world in motion.

Valerie   I see.

Daza   Do they get to come back?

Hofniel   Shouldn't think so, my fam got terrible memories, none of them, like, will remember who they were by now.

Valerie   And if we were to stop dancing?

Hofniel   Well the world would stop, like everything would stop.

Daza *groans.*

Xu   When do you think they'll let you know?

Valerie   If I can talk to God? (**Valerie** *shrugs.*)

Xu   The bosses never listen, Valerie.

Valerie   They can be made to listen, Xu.

Beat.

Xu   No they can't. (*Beat.*) I made smartphones, fastening the chip boards, one every minute.

Daza (*groans*)   Oh that is good.

Hofniel   Bob taught me.

Xu (*serious/sad*)   I was shouted at for not being fast enough.

The factory had dorms that we rented. They were expensive and cramped, as many as twelve in one room. I couldn't sleep, they were hot, and always noisy.

Hofniel *stops the massage as* **Xu** *continues – truly moved, they all listen.*

Xu   As I got more tired, I got slower, and I fell behind, so the bosses shouted at me in front of everyone on the line. But I couldn't leave because I was in debt to them because of the rent for the dorms. I tried standing up for myself, but they called the police, who beat me with sticks. But still I fell behind, so then they made me read out a letter to the line promising that I would never fall behind again. I couldn't take it anymore, I couldn't see any way out, so I went to the top of the dorm block and jumped.

They have nets there now to stop people from killing themselves. It cost them five dollars to make one phone but they sell for hundreds.

Silence, as they absorb the horror of what **Xu** *has said.*

Hofniel *touches* **Daza** *on the shoulders signalling that they should move and when* **Daza** *gets up* **Hofniel** *pats the seat for* **Xu**. **Xu** *sits.*

Xu   Thanks.

Bob *enters.*

Bob   You're not moving your hands right. Allow me.

Hofniel   'Course.

Bob   I charged a lot for those you know, back in Moss Side. (*To* **Valerie**.) You still here then?

Valerie   Looks like it.

Bob   You've ruined my chances.

Valerie   For what?

Hofniel   For becoming an Angel, bruv. They're not like completely ruined, Bob.

Valerie   How did you get in?

Xu   His head massages are really good.

Bob   I was great with the customers.

Valerie   People that paid you?

Bob   You don't know anything about hairdressers do you?

Valerie   Never thought about them.

Bob   We listen. I made literally hundreds of unloved men and women feel and look fantastic. A high-quality conditioner, a bit of chat and a good haircut is all most people need in the world. (*Beat.*) There are loads of hairdressers up here.

Hofniel   I love a permanent wave.

Valerie   And tell me about your boss, Bob? How much did they make from the happiness you gave? From your labour?

Bob   I dunno. It was a good job, everyone was happy there.

Valerie   Everyone?

Bob   Well, apart from Jess.

Daza   Who was Jess?

Bob   She tried to unionise us.

Xu   If you tried to unionise at my factory, you were beaten up and dismissed.

Valerie   Why did she try to do that, Bob?

Bob   I think she wanted a toaster?

Valerie   It would have been the working conditions.

Bob   I got the minimum wage, and there were tips on top.

Valerie   And where did your boss get the money to set up the shop?

Bob   I think he said his dad was a postal worker and he re-mortgaged his house.

Valerie   Due to rates agreed by unions. Would you have been able to buy a house from *your* wages?

Bob   No.

Valerie   Imagine if you could, imagine if you all went on strike. Maybe you could have bought your own home, if your wages were better. (*Beat.*) And were there other investors in your hairdressers?

Bob   Well, there was this Tora, I think she put some money in.

Xu *groans.*

Valerie   And she didn't work there, but took the profit? Yes?

Bob *nods.*

Daza   Doing nothing.

Valerie   And where was her money from?

Bob   I don't know. She lived in some mansion in Cheshire.

Valerie   So maybe slavery?

Bob   No. Tora was lovely . . .

Valerie   If she's from old money. Very likely. Do you know they were compensated?

Bob   The slaves, well you'd hope so.

Valerie   No, the slavers when the Anti-Slavery Act came in. Millions of pounds, setting themselves up for generations. It's inherited wealth that maintains the ever-widening gap, not working hard. Ill-gotten money from ill-gotten gains; gains that are now classed as criminal but money that stayed in their pockets forever. All the way down to little Tora.

Bob   She wasn't like that.

Valerie   I think you're missing the point, the *money* she gave you *was* like that! So who kept the real wealth? Your labour?

Bob   You've lost me.

Valerie   Marx said that the money created in the labour of the workers should be owned by the workers.

Xu (*to* **Valerie**)   So the profit?

Valerie   The capital.

Xu   The capital, the labour in the phone?

Valerie   Yeah, that's it. Your labour in the phone.

Xu   Five dollars a phone, and I made seven hundred phones a day.

Valerie   And they sell for five hundred dollars, maybe.

Hofniel   Woe, mama! A profit of one thousand per cent.

Valerie   Yep. 'Woe, mama'.

Bob *stops massaging* **Xu**'*s head.*

Daza   They banned the collection of rain water in my city and then they raised the price of water.

Bob   How did you wash your hair?

Daza   We couldn't afford to drink. I was protesting when they came, men with guns. (*Beat.*) After (*beat*) everyone stopped work: factory workers, street vendors, students. The US trained the man who shot me, so no one would take on the case because they were afraid. (*Beat.*) How can you charge for rain water? How can you own rain water? Doesn't rain water belong to God?

Xu   It's like charging for sky, or air, or the view.

Valerie   Exactly. And so the likes of Tora just get richer and richer.

Bob   But she was so nice to animals . . .

Daza   And it's not questioned.

Xu   Because it's always been and always will be.

Valerie   No it hasn't. It hasn't always been. That's another myth.

The way we consume, the endless more, is new.

Daza   We just went along with it?

Valerie   Yeah.

Xu   Or didn't see the end-point. Didn't see the assembly lines.

Companies that don't care about human rights, don't care about the planet or anything.

Valerie   That's right, Xu.

Bob   Oh get a grip. What's this to us now we're here?

Valerie   So not caring about the masses is just fine once you're in Heaven?

Bob   No, that's not what I meant . . .

Muriel *and* **Nanael** *enter.*

Muriel   The music stays the same.

Bob *bows.*

Valerie   Then we'll have to take action.

Bob, **Nanael and Muriel**   Action?

Hofniel   Now you're talking, bruv.

Nanael   Who's side are you on, Hofniel?

Hofniel (*not getting it*)   Sides, yeah are there sides?

Valerie   Yeah, organise.

Hofniel   Trocking.

Valerie   Yes, 'trocking'.

The dancing is to keep the world in motion, that right?

Muriel   Yes?

Valerie   What if we refuse to dance?

All Angels   What?!

Muriel   You can't do that.

Nanael   No, you can't.

Valerie   Can't we?

Daza and Xu   Can we?

Valerie   We can.

Muriel   Right.

Muriel *exits.*

Bob   What are you trying to do to me?

Valerie   It's not personal.

Bob   How is it not personal?

Valerie   It's called collective bargaining.

Bob   What's that?

Hofniel   But if you stop dancing everything stops.

Valerie   It's all that we have to negotiate with.

Daza   The Peak should be perfect.

Valerie   Exactly.

Xu   I don't *like* Toto.

Valerie   It's not about Toto, Xu.

Muriel *re-enters.*

Nanael   Did you get to talk to him, her?

Muriel   Yes. He, she is furious.

Hofniel (*going pale*)   Furious, bruv?

Nanael   Yes furious, 'bruv'. (*Beat.*) He's sending someone.

Muriel   Who?

Michael *enters.* **Muriel** *and* **Nanael** *exchange a look.* **Michael** *carries a sword in one hand and a burger in the other which he hands to* **Xu.** **Michael** *repeatedly plunges the sword into the air as if in an imaginary fight.*

Valerie   Who's that?

Michael (*in time with blows*)   Swish, bosh, bash.

Hofniel *makes a bad attempt at BSL for halo.*

Hofniel   Hi, Mike, what's app?

Bob   It's Mike.

Nanael   It's the Archangel Michael to you lot.

Hofniel   He's always, like, well hungry. Hi, Mike.

Nanael   The Archangel Michael.

Michael   Not anymore, Nanael. I've been promoted. I'm a Seraphim now. Top dog! Swish, bosh, bash!

Bob   We're very honoured. (*To* **Valerie.**) Bow!

Valerie   No.

Michael *snatches the chicken burger back from* **Xu** *and eats it.*

Valerie   Is that the end of a chicken burger?

Michael   Yep.

Valerie   Fed on cheap soya feed from cleared Amazon rainforest!

Bred in tiny cages with their beaks chopped off so the birds don't peck each other to death!

Bob   Don't you ever switch off?

Valerie   No.

Michael   It's imagined. Well, someone else imagined it for me. Though there are more and more vegans in Heaven, so it is a bit disappointing taste wise. (*Beat.*) You got anything else?

Xu   No.

Michael (*to* **Bob**)   Head massage?

Bob   I'd be honoured, your greatness.

Valerie   You're greatness?

Bob   Please be seated.

Michael *sits in front of* **Bob** *who proceeds to massage his head and moans.*

Valerie   And what are you, middle management?

Michael   No, I'm a Seraphim. One tier down from God. Hey, I got promoted, is no one listening?!

Valerie   You don't think there's a problem with a hierarchy?

Michael   Everyone's happy.

Muriel   Not everyone.

Hofniel   They'd like some Toto, bruv.

Michael   Who are Toto?

Valerie   They're an American rock band from the eighties.

Michael   Oh yeah, I got you: 'Hold the Line', 'Africa', 'Rosanna'.

Valerie   But it's more than that, actually I've made a list of demands.

Hofniel   Demands! Woe, mama!

Valerie   We would like (*reading from a list*) discussion, consensus and everything voted on, we'd like to choose when we return, and we want to meet God. And then there's the Toto.

Michael   No one gets to talk to God.

Valerie   Why not?.

Michael   You're not even Angels!

Bob   Yeah, you're not!

Daza   So?

Xu   So?

Michael   Well, that's the whole point of a hierarchy.

Daza   So, we're not equal?

Michael   Heaven is not concerned with equality.

Valerie   Then how is it holy? It can't be if you're saying that you can have access and I can't. You can make decisions about my time here and I can't. You can decide when I begin again, when I am ready to return and I can't and I have no vehicle through which I can contribute to that discussion. I have no say, no power, no authority.

Michael   I can't believe you didn't get me a feast.

Valerie   What?

Michael   There is one isn't there? Just tucked around the corner?

Daza, Xu and Valerie   No!

Valerie   This is because you believe you are better than me, better than all of us, we are lesser than you and through this logic you decide what is best for us. That is a definition of fascism.

Daza   Yeah, you're a fascist.

Xu   A fascist.

Bob   You can't say that.

Nanael   You can't call him that.

Michael   I'm a Seraphim, an Angel of the first tier. I'm part of the Heavenly Hierarchy. You can't call me a fascist.

Valerie   You're all fascists.

Muriel   No, we're Angels.

Nanael   We didn't make the rules.

Michael   No. We didn't. We are not responsible.

Valerie   Then let us speak to who is. Because it's time for a regime change.

Nanael, Michael, Muriel and Bob   What?!

Daza   And some Toto.

Valerie   We demand to meet God or we'll stop dancing.

Bob   THAT'S IT, THAT'S IT! I won't have it, you hear me, I just won't. I resign as your guide.

Hofniel   You can't do that, bruv, you can't like just resign as a guide.

Nanael   Yeah, that's never allowed Bob.

Muriel   No, never.

Bob   Oh! (*To* **Valerie**.) You have personally ruined my life.

Valerie   Well, I haven't done that, have I?

Bob   You have!

Valerie   You're dead already?

Bob   Oh! Oh! Oh! May your hair, always, always be dry!

Bob *storms off.*

Michael   Why's he so upset?

And just before he exits.

Bob   And split ends, just, just loads of them!

Muriel   He wants to be an Angel.

Valerie   Yeah, part of The Authority! The first premise of Heaven should be equality.

Michael   There'd be chaos without The Authority, without the rule.

FX 'Give Me the Night' by, George Benson. Music runs from the beginning. **Valerie** *shouts over the song. Multitude and* **Bob** *rush on.*

Valerie (*to* **Multitude**)   Don't dance.

Daza (*to* **Multitude**)   Don't.

Chen   What?

Michael   No! Dance!

Valerie   Don't.

Chandra   We don't have to dance?

Keanu   What really?

Muriel   Yes, you do.

Daza   No, you don't.

Nanael   You do.

Daza   Not if you want some Toto.

Keanu   I hate George Benson.

Xu   And consensus!

Daza   And choose when you return.

Keanu   We can get to choose!

Chen   Then we're not dancing.

Chandra   No, we're not.

They all sit. **Michael**, **Nanael** *and* **Muriel** *shout over the music.* **Hofniel** *thinks it's funny.*

Muriel, Michael and Nanael   Get up!

'Give Me the Night' slows to a slurring stop.

Michael   Get up! Get up! You've got to dance. Get up.

You have to dance. You have to.
The world will stop. You can't do this. Get up! Get up!

Fx Trumpets. **Mighty Metatron** *enters in full* **Angel** *kit, halo, wings, long gold dress, etc. All the* **Angels** (*mostly in fear rather than respect) dive to the ground lying flat, arms stretched towards* **Mighty Metatron***.*

Mighty Metatron (*slowly*)   What is happening here?

Some of the **Multitude** *bow, some don't.*

Valerie   Is that God?

Bob   I don't know.

Mighty Metatron   Explain yourselves.

Michael   They want to meet God.

Mighty Metatron   God?

Chen   And some Toto.

Mighty Metatron   What did he say?

Michael   Toto, they're a rock band from the eighties, 'Rosanna', 'Africa', 'Hold the Line'.

Mighty Metatron *holds up his hand to silence* **Michael***.*

Mighty Metatron   What did you say?

Valerie   We don't want to dance.

Mighty Metatron   Am I being addressed?

Valerie   Yes.

Mighty Metatron   I am The Authority and you will dance.

Valerie   We don't accept your authority.

Mighty Metatron   Are you addressing me again?

Valerie   Guess so.

Mighty Metatron   I am the Mighty Metatron, I only speak to the highest tier of the Great Angelic Order.

Valerie   You're who?

Hofniel   He, she.

Valerie   This is he, she?

Hofniel   Yeah, bruv, the one before God.

Nanael   The Mighty Metatron, the greatest Angel that ever existed.

Your greatness.

Valerie   We won't dance.

Mighty Metatron   Who is this?

Valerie   I'm Valerie.

Mighty Metatron *refers to* **Michael**.

Michael   It's Valerie.

Valerie   Valerie.

Mighty Metatron (*to* **Valerie**)   Silence.

Valerie   Exactly an example of fascism.

Mighty Metatron   What?

Valerie   You silencing me? This is where it comes from, isn't it?

Inequality, the lack of consensus, it's all from here.

Mighty Metatron   I said silence.

Valerie   The inspiration for creating a system so cruel that . . .

Mighty Metatron   Be quiet, you've been told . . .

Valerie (*an idea*)   I know, I know! (*Turning to address the* **Multitude**.) How many of you died as a direct or indirect result of some corporation's greed?!

Mighty Metatron   SILENCE! I said SILENCE!

Pause. **Valerie** *takes a breath and then continues quickly.*

Valerie   Due to an accident at work or suicide due to working conditions, poverty, lack of a proper home, water pollution or air pollution?

Mighty Metatron   I am the Mighty Metatron.

Umut   I died in a fire at an unregulated factory. Does that count?

Valerie   'Course.

Mighty Metatron   And I will be obeyed.

Fara   I died in an air raid in a hospital in a war started over oil.

Raz   I died in an asthma attack due to pollution. Does that count?

Valerie   Yes.

The **Multitude** *think for a moment and then one by one put their hands up apart from* **Bob**. *General: 'That's me too', 'Me too'.*

Mighty Metatron   Shut up, SHUT UP, SHUT UP, SHUT UP!

Valerie *continues and shouts over* **Mighty Metatron**.

Valerie Make him be quiet, make him.

The other **Angels** *don't know what to do, and shrug as* **Valerie** *continues.*

Valerie   Your 'Cindy' took it all from here. The belief in hierarchy and that everything on the planet is ours for the taking regardless of the hurt it causes to people and the planet itself. And it's all the result of the ordinary people on Earth having no say. Exactly like it is here, in The Peak.

FX 'Promised Land' – Joe Smooth. From the beginning (7 inch mix). All the cast resist. **Mighty Metatron** *continues to shout manically.* **Nanael**, **Muriel** *and* **Bob** *dance wildly, attempting to keep the world in motion.*

Mighty Metatron   DANCE! DANCE!

Valerie   WE WILL NOT!

Muriel   YOU CAN'T BE SERIOUS . . .!

Nanael   YOU CAN'T LET THIS HAPPEN . . .!

Bob   WHAT ABOUT THE WORLD?!

Muriel   YOU'LL DESTROY EVERYTHING. EVERYTHING. THE WORLD WILL DIE.

Valerie   IT'S DYING ANYWAY.

Daza   THIS IS THE ONLY WAY TO STOP IT.

Umut   WE'RE TAKING A STAND.

Chandra   WE'RE SAVING THE WORLD.

Xu   WE'RE ALL WITH VAL.

The world begins to judder towards a stop. FX trumpets, thunder, screams, and then an almighty crash. Silence. No one moves. **Angels** *and* **Bob** *one side of the stage,* **Multitude** *on the other. A Mexican face-off. A tired, small and unassuming figure enters quietly at the back and wanders around looking disorientated. This is* **God**. **God** *has a cold, carries a handkerchief, sneezes occasionally.* **Mighty Metatron** *stops shouting once he has seen the figure. The music abruptly stops.* **Michael** *bows.*

Mighty Metatron   What are you doing out of bed?

God   I was woken up by the juddering of the world, is it stopping?

Why's there no singing?

Hofniel   Pokémon.

God   Who? (*Sneezes.*)

Bob   Bless you.

Mighty Metatron   You need to rest.

God   Do I? (**Mighty Metatron** *attempts to usher* **God** *back to bed.*)

God   I sense I have been sleeping for some time.

God *sneezes.*

Multitude   Bless you.

God   Thank you.

Michael   My Lord.

God   How long have I been sleeping?

Mighty Metatron (*lying*)   Not so very long.

Michael   Since the Seventies.

Valerie   The Seventies!

Hofniel, Nanael and Muriel   The Seventies?!

God   Since 1979 I think.

Hofniel   You didn't tell us he was, like, ill, Mighty Metatron.

Nanael   Yeah, you never said.

Mighty Metatron   I didn't want to worry you.

Muriel   Worry was it?

Nanael   That's not cool Mighty Metatron.

Hofniel   Like well not cool, Fam.

God *sneezes.*

Multitude   Bless you.

God   You can stop blessing me. I'm, you know. I'm the one that blesses.

Michael   God.

God   Exactly. So how has everyone been?

Valerie   Not great.

Mighty Metatron   Silence.

God   No, do speak.

Mighty Metatron   Bow.

God   It doesn't matter about the bowing, Metatron.

Tell me, what has been happening?

Valerie   Well, globalisation happened?

God   And how was that?

Valerie   Bad?

God   And that started in the seventies?

Valerie   Yes, the deregulation that permitted it started then.

Daza   I was murdered.

God   Well, that's always happening.

Daza   For collecting rain water?

Valerie   Deregulated markets meant unsafe environments, exploitation of labour without union protection and the cheapest energy, so fossil fuel, land, air and communities devastated, society fragmented, poverty and so on. Companies took their business to the cheapest and therefore most unregulated markets they could find, so the devastation went global with a tiny minority at the top, just getting richer and more powerful. That's what happened while you were sleeping.

God (*to* **Metatron**)   And people suffered?

Valerie   Terribly.

God   Why didn't you wake me?

Mighty Metatron   I didn't think there was anything we could do about it. And you had such a bad cold. And anyway there have always been bad people.

Valerie   But not on a global scale, not within a world order that no one can escape from, in which cruelty is justified in the name of financial gain and as an end itself. That is new. (*Beat.*) You need to step down, show a different way forward. You weren't even awake.

God   No.

Mighty Metatron   He's been ill.

Valerie   A cold that lasts five decades?

God (*to* **Metatron**)   I still don't understand why you didn't wake me?

Mighty Metatron   Like I said, your cold was terrible.

Hofniel   And you liked the power, dude.

Mighty Metatron   I did not like the power.

Hofniel   He did.

Mighty Metatron   I didn't.

Nanael   You did really.

Muriel   You did. It's why he didn't tell us.

Mighty Metatron   It wasn't like that.

Hofniel   Dude, it was.

Nanael   We know truth.

Hofniel   Yeah, truth, bruv.

Valerie   The rules, The Authority, have to change.

Mighty Metatron   They'll be chaos.

Valerie   They'll be chaos anyway unless the world is re-imagined.

You should step down.

God   Me?

Mighty Metatron   You can't ask that. With a snap of my fingers I could send you back, and land you in the middle of a murderous war. Or I could give you an immune system that has no defence against any disease out there, you could die horribly, painfully of malaria, typhoid, ebola, or, or (*getting excited*) you could be born into a place where you cannot breathe, where there is death on every corner and where.

Slowly as **Mighty Metratron** *speaks the others stand aghast.*

Hofniel *mouths 'Power' and makes the BSL sign for halo and makes a face.*

God   What are you saying?

Mighty Metatron   I just, just. He was disrespectful.

God   And you weren't?

Valerie   And he's in your employment? (*Beat.*) You should step down and let us decide. You're a dictator.

God   I don't see myself as a dictator.

Valerie   Well, what else are you?

God   But I am good aren't I? I mean I've always thought of myself as good.

God *looks about the room for affirmation. All the* **Angels** *ad lib agreeing with him: 'Yes, you're very good', 'Very, very good', 'Really good', 'Apart from your middle-management'.*

I mean if your dictator is utterly good and eternal I don't really see the problem.

Valerie   Without everyone taking full responsibility there can be no change and when we return we will simply accept the order once more, The Authority, the Rule, the System.

God   I've never thought about any of it like that. A dictator, really?

Michael   But it has always been this way.

Valerie   And it has led us to here, to the end of everything. True freedom is only possible when we all take responsibility, as it is only then that real change can happen.

Silence.

God   Well, we could try it for a bit. Maybe it will help my cold clear up.

Mighty Metatron   You can't step down.

God   Why ever not? I'm God, I can do anything.

God *clicks his fingers. FX 'Hold the Line' by Toto. Everyone dances with joy, and a reprise of the 'Toto' chant. 'Hold the Line' leaks into the next scene and fades.*

Scene Three

The **Multitude** *are in pairs giving each other head massages.* **Hofniel** *goes down the line occasionally changing hand positions.* **Muriel** *sits with them.*

Fara   I got the vote.

River   I voted for you.

Fara   An evening of ELO, all their greatest hits.

Keanu   I love ELO.

Fara   'All Over the World', 'Livin' Thing', 'Mr Blue Sky', 'Horace Wimp'.

Xu   I was you know happy before, well quite happy.

Jade   So was I.

Raz   And me.

The **Multitude** *all agree.*

Xu   But now I'm ecstatic! Heaven is just brilliant.

Chen   Awesome.

Jade   Equality is just great.

Bailey   It's perfect.

Keanu   Perfect.

Chen (*to* **River**)   Are you going back?

River   Thinking about it.

Chen   Me too.

Umut   Me too.

Fara   And me.

Valerie *enters and sits with* **Muriel***.*

Valerie   You coming back with us, Muriel, to take the revolution to below?

*The **Multitude** join in to encourage them: 'Come with us, Muriel', 'You're so welcome'.*

Muriel   No, I don't think I'd be a very good revolutionary.

Valerie   You'd be brilliant.

Bob *enters and attempts to walk past.* **Valerie** *blocks* **Bob**'s *way.*

Valerie   Bob?!

Bob   I'm still not talking to you.

Valerie   Why?

Bob   Because I will never be an Angel thanks to you.

Valerie   Can't you just imagine you're an Angel?

Bob   What?

Valerie   Imagine you're Angel.

Hofniel   Yeah, you could do that, fam. You could so do that, like now there's no hierarchy.

Muriel   He's right, Bob.

Bob   What, really?

Valerie   Like I imagined I wanted to change things, I imagined I wanted the world to be different. I imagined that it can be.

Bob   You imagined you were a revolutionary leader?

Valerie   No, I didn't imagine that. I am that.

Bob   But you had to imagine it first. You had to imagine a different system before it could happen.

Valerie   Yeah.

Bob   So, it's the system itself that makes us think we can't change anything, but if you change the order, and change the system, you change the people.

Valerie   You were listening.

Bob *takes a deep breath and repeats as he exits.*

Bob   I'm an Angel! I'm an Angel! I'm an Angel!

Valerie (*to* **Muriel**)   You sure you don't want to come with us?

Muriel   No, thank you.

Hofniel   It's Cindy, bruv.

Muriel   Cindy. It's Cindy's world.

Hofniel   So, like, the revolution can work here but in the big below, it'd be well hard, coz of all the bad brothers and sisters being under the spell of Cindy.

Muriel   For many the system is Cindy.

Valerie   Capitalism.

Muriel   A God. Their God.

Hofniel   Be some awesome revolution though, bruv.

FX trumpets. **God**, **Nanael** *and* **Michael** *enter in full* **Angel** *kit.*

Muriel   Oh goodness we're not dressed.

Hofniel   'scuse us, bruv.

Hofniel and Muriel *exit.*

God   The vote. Valerie, you wanted to say a few words?

Valerie   Yes. I do. (*Pause.*) Having created a perfect Heaven, I move that you return with me to continue the revolution below and work with me to create a perfect world for all. A world of justice, equality and friendship. Come with me, comrades, the revolutionary Multitude of Heaven, let us go together.

Mighty Metatron *enters in full kit and bows to* **God**.

Valerie   No bowing.

God   Yes, no bowing, Metatron.

Mighty Metatron (*angry*)   Ok.

God   We're just waiting for the vote.

Valerie   Who's with me?

The **Multitude** *(not the* **Angels***) raise their hands and then clap.*

God   Time to go.

All sing 'The Red Flag'. **Hofniel** *and* **Muriel** *enter halfway through.*

All   The People's Flag is deepest red,
It shrouded oft our martyred dead,
And ere their limbs grew stiff and cold,
Their hearts' blood dyed its every fold.

(*Chorus*) Then raise the scarlet standard high.
Beneath its shade we'll live and die,
Though cowards flinch and traitors sneer,
We'll keep the red flag flying here.

It well recalls the triumphs past,
It gives the hope of peace at last;
The banner bright, the symbol plain,
Of human right and human gain.

Chorus.

Bob *enters in full Angel kit and interrupts the song.* **Bob** *cannot believe it and plays to the audience and to the cast, and then rushes up to* **Valerie**.

Bob   I'm an Angel. I'm an Angel.

Look! Look! It's me a trainee hairdresser from Moss Side. (*Or equivalent area in the nearest big city.*) I'm an Angel.

'The Red Flag' continues, **Bob** *joining in and beaming as he does so. the* **Multitude** *begin to leave.*

All   It suits today the weak and base,
   Whose minds are fixed on pelf and place
   To cringe before the rich man's frown,
   And haul the sacred emblem down.

Chorus.

   With head uncovered swear we all
   To bear it onward till we fall;
   Come dungeons dark or gallows grim,
   This song shall be our parting hymn.

Chorus.

Valerie *is the only one of the* **Multitude** *left on stage.* **Valerie** *and* **Bob** *hug. Then* **Bob** *waves* **Valerie** *off.*

Bob   Go, go, you've got work to do!

Valerie *exits, leaving only the* **Angels,** **Bob** *and* God *on stage. FX 'All Over the World' by ELO from opening chords.*

Muriel   They've all gone.

God (*happily*)   Yes.

Nanael   They've all gone?

God   Oh yes. We better dance. DANCE! DANCE!

All the **Angels** *dance, coping with their wings as best they can.* **Mighty Metatron** *is particularly resentful of having to dance and is a fantastically terrible (dad dancing) dancer.* **Bob** *dances superbly and with utter, utter joy; maybe a solo, a routine might emerge which* **Mighty Metatron** *clearly cannot do. All back on stage for bow. All join in the routine.*

Music fades.

The End.

The Marxist in Heaven

BY HATTIE NAYLOR

Notes on rehearsal and staging, drawn from a workshop with the writer, held at the National Theatre, October 2019

How Hattie came to write the play

The inspiration for the play came when writer Hattie Naylor was thinking about singer-songwriter Woody Guthrie and labour activist Joe Hill and people who worked towards the benefit of others, battling against injustices. She thought that surely they would get into heaven, regardless of their atheism. So the question at the heart of the piece is: what if a Marxist got into heaven? Hattie had also been reading Naomi Klein's book *This Changes Everything* and that influenced the writing of the play. So she wanted it to include all of that but also for it to be really enjoyable, really funny and to include the joy of change. Hattie didn't want it to be 'a saga of pain', so she included disco music!

Read-through

Participants introduced themselves and were asked to talk about an artist that inspired them.

The group then read through the entire play, with each person reading one line or stage direction before passing to the next person. Lead director Justin Audibert encouraged strong, bold choices for a first reading, reminding the group that it doesn't have to be right first time.

Pronunciation

Xu = Shway

Umut = Oo-mutt

The 'ael' at the end of angels' names is pronounced 'ay-el', which means 'shining one'.

You can pronounce Muriel like the contemporary name because it is funny.

Use of language

Hattie spoke about adhering to a rule when writing fantasy worlds of being aware of powerful words and avoiding their overuse so that you don't lose the believability of the world you're crafting. For this reason, she included BSL for 'Halo' instead of having the word 'Angel', spoken. This is also why she has characters refer to Heaven as 'The Peak'. The only sign language that the characters use is for 'Halo'. You can add sign language if you like but be sensitive to its inclusion, as well as to its impact on your running time.

Ensemble work

Exercise: Clear the space

Justin demonstrated a Frantic Assembly warm-up that has several rules introduced one by one as an ensemble move around the space. The possibilities for more rules are endless and adaptable to your own group. Group ownership is possible once the rules have been established.

Centre: move to the centre of the space

Clear the Space: move to the edges of the space

Audience: stop and look towards the audience

Sky: stop and look towards the sky

Victim: everyone stops and one person falls to the ground

Survivor: everyone falls to the ground and one person remains standing

Wither: everyone slowly corkscrews to the floor

Bloom: everyone comes back up to standing, even larger than they were before

Stop/Go

Characteristics can be added to these rules, for example:

Centre: gliding as if there is no gravity

Wither: as if melting

Clear the Space: in panic

Go: in slow motion

Sky: as if Metatron is arriving

Go: in serene bliss

Go: as if at a protest

Exercise: Flocking

In this exercise, the ensemble stand all facing in the same direction. The person at the front leads, moving around the space with the rest of the ensemble copying their movement. The slower the movement is, the more effective it becomes. Slow arm movements are particularly effective. When the flock turns, the leader shifts to the person now at the front.

Analysing the text

Justin split the participants into five groups and each group took a section of the script. Working on their section they created lists of Facts, Questions, Words/Concepts and

Challenges:

> **Facts:** A fact is not an opinion. It is something that has clear evidence in the text. These can be facts in relation to the world of the play; for example, 'disco is the music of heaven'.
>
> **Questions:** These are questions provoked by the script. For example, they could be costume design (what do the Angels look like?) or character questions (why does Bob desperately want to be an Angel?).
>
> **Words/Concepts:** These are things to research (keeping your company in mind). Justin recommended that as soon as you can in rehearsal, define the concepts on a wall. He also encouraged honesty with your company about having to look things up – even the director does not know everything!
>
> **Challenges:** These are theatrical challenges presented by the script. Moments that provoke the question: how do I stage this? In making the list you simply need to acknowledge the challenge – you don't have to solve it in the moment.

Lists from the workshop

Below are the full lists from this workshop, but you are encouraged to make your own versions of these lists with your company.

Facts

Multitude = everyone except God/Angels

We never hear Hofniel's music

Heaven is inclusive

Angels only present outwardly as Angels at the end

Valerie has bad hair

Valerie was unionised

Valerie is a vegan

Valerie died in a bike accident

Valerie and Nanael don't know each other

Valerie is dead

Heaven has an induction process

Valerie died on their way to a protest

Archangel = glory and splendour

Principality = Angel of victory

Angel is signed rather than spoken

Heaven is a hierarchy

Valerie is a Marxist and an atheist

Nanael is covering for someone

Nanael is reading *Hello!* magazine

Heaven = genderless

Bob was a hairdresser in training

Bob is a guide

Bob is lower than Nanael

You can be chosen to be an Angel

Bob wants to be an Angel

There are stats that are looked at to get into heaven

Hell is a place

Metatron decides who goes back

Muriel is bored

The multitude are dissatisfied with dancing

You can't speak to God – only the great angelic order can

They have smartphones in heaven

Some people don't know each other in heaven

Everything is imagined in heaven

Angels only dress up for big occasions

Muriel is thirsty

Angels can't imagine: they only know truth

You have to have faith to get into the peak

Marxism is a belief system

There is a hierarchy in heaven

Valerie worked for the benefit of others

The multitude want to meet God

Michael loves food – they are always hungry

Valerie doesn't care for the higher Authority

Toto are an American rock band from the 1980s

Seraphim is one down from God

People in heaven see those higher up as better

Valerie exposes heaven as a fascist idea

People trained by the US shot Daza

Ritual of heaven is important to the angels

Dancing keeps the world in motion

A Marxist is a follower of Karl Marx

Marx is a nineteenth-century philosopher, economist and social revolutionary

Bob is working class

Xu made smartphones

Xu committed suicide

Disco is the music of heaven

Hofniel is an Angel

Bob did massages on earth

There are loads of hairdressers in heaven

Chandra doesn't like the music

Bailey doesn't like the music

Singing was replaced to keep the world in motion

Keanu and Chen hate the bowing

There is bowing in heaven

The multitude are never consulted

There is The Authority

There is God

Heaven used to be more populous

The Angels sang to keep the world rotating

Cindy is Satan

God took imagination away from the Angels

Cindy led a rebellion

Cindy took a load of Angels below – dancing started

Cindy created the world

Angels went down for new technology

Bob is on minimum wage plus tips

The world stops turning when dancing stops

God arrives and has a cold

God has been asleep for forty years

Metatron left God asleep

ELO gets voted for

The Angels, Bob, and God stay in heaven

Bob becomes an Angel

Questions

N.B. Where Hattie offered an answer to a question, that answer is briefly stated in brackets following the question:

What age is Val? (Any age)

What is the BSL sign for 'Halo'? (A video link is included at the end of these notes)

Is there deafness in heaven?

Is it rude to say Angel in the presence of an Angel? (See 'Use of Language' section)

Is Hofniel trying to impress Valerie?

Why is Hofniel trying to be down with the kids?

How did Bob die?

Why include BSL? (See 'Use of Language' section)

Why is Little Mix used?

Why Cindy?

How do you address casting?

Can you imagine a new thing in heaven?

What is the piece of music Hofniel is listening to? (A secret)

Why 'The Peak'? (See 'Use of Language' section)

Can we adapt Hofniel's text to local dialect/localisms? (Only with Hattie's approval)

Are the Angels always present?

What is happiness in heaven?

Do Angels know God is asleep? (No, only Metatron knows)

Who is Archangel Michael?

Why is Bob so desperate to be an angel?

What is trocking? (Behaving in an impish way)

Why is Hofniel a different angel to the others? (Because he has stayed interested)

What is 'the endless more'?

Who is him/her? Is it God or Metatron? (It's Metatron)

What is the purpose of 'The Red Flag' song and what atmosphere is intended to be created from it? (See section about 'The Red Flag')

Do they have accents – particularly Hofniel? (Find a cast member that can deal with 'bruv', etc.)

Can you take BSL further?

Why disco?

Does heaven carry on as normal after?

Words/concepts

Amazon fulfilment centre

Marxism

Atheist

Union/Union rep

Principality

Heaven, hell, reincarnation

Gender

Tiers/Hierarchy

All angelic concepts

Disco

Toto

Veganism

Trocking

Viva da revolution

Eargasm

What is good?

Heavenly power structure

Lower class

Angel names

Fam

Austerity

Mastitis

Artificially inseminated

The Peak

Capitalism

Cherubim

Seraphim

Messi

Neymar

Rebirth/Reincarnation

Disco

ELO

Progressive rock

Hold the line

Tamagotchis

Foxconn suicides

Mass production

Outsourcing

Capitalism

Modern-day slavery

Zero-hour contracts

1979 – context

Inherited wealth

Slavery

Human rights

Cochabamba, Bolivia

Collective bargaining

The ever widening gap

Equality

Change

Globalism

Deregulated markets

Unregulated markets

Fossil fuels

Dictator

Ebola

Malaria

Revolutionary

'The Red Flag'

Comrades

Challenges

Remembering lines

Remembering cues

Cast numbers

Angel costumes

Visual distinction in the hierarchy

Navigating atheism with students of faith

Staging disco sections?

Making Hofniel clearly down with the kids

Repetition of 'The Peak'

The banner appearing

The story of Cindy

Religion and how to discuss this in a sensitive way

The characters' emotional connections to the stories they tell?

Suicide and characters feelings once they are in heaven

How to produce imagined things?

Sensitivity around suicide

Vocabulary of protest (e.g. 'brothers and sisters')

What kind of dancing are the dances?

Size of wings

Ethics of imagined acts/behaviours

How to make a 'meet and greet' clear

Concealing or discovering actor identities in casting (i.e. is identity an issue and
    what statements do casting choices make?)

Young people's musical tastes differing from disco

'The Red Flag'

What does the performer playing God do until they enter?

Angel costumes

Contextual challenges

Accents/dialects

Diversity of casting

Sensitivity towards varying beliefs

Transition between scenes

Likeability of Valerie

Balancing the hard, gritty nature of this section with the rest of the piece

Not getting too preachy

Casting decisions

Justin encouraged the participants to think about the tapestry of their individual
productions and what their chosen casting is saying about power roles, etc. What does
it mean to cast a certain type of person in a specific role, for example God?

A question arose about double-casting and Hattie noted that specifically for the
casting of God it is preferable that it is a performer we have not seen before, or double-
cast with a very minor character if absolutely necessary.

Angels

It's up to you what you want your angels to look like, but Hattie strongly urged that you
don't bring in the wings too early as it will spoil the celebration of the final moment.
Resist that temptation in order to earn the reward.

Hattie reiterated that the Angels are really bored – they have been saying these
things for thousands of years. When asked why the name Cindy was used, Hattie said
that Cindy is a safe name, like when the wizards in Harry Potter avoid using the name
Voldemort – it's safer to use Cindy than to use one of the real names.

Archangel Michael

In some accounts of the angelic hierarchy, Michael is closest to God and is the only
Angel who hasn't fallen. He is always hungry in the play as a reference to his depiction

in Milton's *Paradise Lost*. Michael is often depicted with a sword, which is why he has a sword in the play.

Suicide

While the extremity of Xu's situation is specific and based on a real life event, it is important that your company deal with discussions around suicide in a sensitive manner and in relation to any safeguarding policies you have in place. It may also be appropriate to consider posting content warnings outside your theatre in the same way that you would forewarn audiences of the presence of strobe lights.

It is important to be careful with language around suicide (for example 'died by suicide' rather than 'committed suicide') and Samaritans provide useful guidance on appropriate language: https://www.samaritans.org/about-samaritans/media-guidelines/best-practice-suicide-reporting-tips/

In Hattie's version of justice, if you have a horrible life you can still make it to heaven, no matter how some religious doctrine may regard suicide.

Religion

Hattie stressed that her play is an allegory and not intended as a blasphemous piece of work.

The heaven depicted is allegorical – it is a fictional, imagined world and is constructed to reflect our own world. It is a broken-down system – things have gone wrong here, they are not perfect. There is no religious doctrine in the play and it is a play about a place where everyone is equal. The heaven of this play is a place where you end up if you do good things.

Justin encouraged companies to avoid fluffy clouds and everything literal in their design choices – to find a version of heaven that works for the company.

It may be important to clearly communicate the fact that this is a comedy and an allegory with your audiences (and in particular parents/guardians) early in the process. It is also worth being sensitive to the challenges of the depiction of God on stage that may present themselves in some communities.

'The Red Flag'

'The Red Flag' is a historically left-wing song that has associations with the Labour Party but its historical link is to the trade unions and the broader socialist movement. Hattie said that it is the clearest example we have in the UK of a political song.

In the workshop, the group discussed the fact that the meaning of 'The Red Flag' has shifting resonances depending on its context which makes it a challenging song to stage, and it is therefore worthwhile to discuss the history of the song in the rehearsal room. It's important to consider the context and discover an appropriate theatrical staging that reflects your company's individual response. The director's role is as an interpretative artist, honouring what the writer has written, but this does not mean that you cannot be critical of the ideology underpinning the song in your productions, as our duty as artists is also to explore nuance.

Justin encouraged the participants to focus on the dramatic function of the song, which is to unite the characters around something positive and optimistic happening onstage. Perhaps there are staging solutions that include dissent within the staging of the song. Perhaps the song is not sung but spoken.

Justin also noted that it is not the final moment of the play and that it is undercut structurally by disco.

Hattie was asked if 'The Red Flag' had to be included in the play and she said that it did unless you can find an emotional equivalent that achieves the same dramatic function.

Music

Hattie's musical choices were specifically chosen to fit each moment. The choices are based on what surprises and keeps the ear interested based on the musicality of the song. It is not intended to be a chronological history of disco.

Imagining of things

The play requires things to appear after being imagined. Justin demonstrated a simple way of making this happen using misdirection, using the imagining of water for Muriel as an example.

A third character on stage had the bottle of water and it was passed to Bob during the scene at an opportune moment. Bob held the water behind his back, hidden from the audience. Justin advised that the performer playing Muriel make a big, bold move and gesture while requesting the water to pull focus before the reveal of the object by Bob. Big, bold moves to pull the audience's focus away from the conjuring moment are key to successful imaginings.

Angel wings

One of your key design decisions will be how to present the wings of the angels. It is up to you whether the wings are functional or just for show. Decisions will need to be made regarding the aesthetic qualities and also the practicality of the wings.

There is a possibility that they are metaphorical wings: perhaps they wear capes, boas, lights, glitter jackets. There is also the potential that each character is their own version of what an angel is.

Justin cautioned the use of white costumes as this can cause difficulties for a lighting designer. It's also important to take care over your design decisions before the angels appear in full angel garb so that you don't undercut that final moment.

Performing large pieces of text

There are a number of moments in the play where a performer has to deal with a large complex chunk of text. Justin advised directors to encourage their performers to avoid rushing to the end of every line. Encourage them to pay attention to the importance of every syllable and every word.

An exercise that Justin called 'ghosting' might help with large chunks of text. The performer is shadowed by another performer who holds the script. That shadow or ghost feeds lines to the performer so that they can have physical freedom from the script.

Instructions for the ghost:

Don't whisper

Read flatly, without interpretation

Read so you can be heard

Don't read a bigger chunk than can be remembered by the performer

Ghosting can be a time-saver when it comes to learning lines and also means you don't have to cast the best at learning lines – you can cast the best actor.

Dance

A good way to introduce dance is to lead a circle warm-up game where each member of the ensemble introduces a dance move and it is copied by the group. This will give you a palette of dance moves to draw on. Justin suggested that instead of freestyle dance moves, companies could discover agreed moves for each dance section – perhaps one dance move, or a string of moves, is selected for each thirty-second song.

Recommended further reading

This Changes Everything by Naomi Klein
The Ragged-Trousered Philanthropists by Robert Tressell
Paradise Lost by John Milton – specifically the feast of St Michael
Wild Wild Country – documentary on Netflix
The Good Place – TV show on Netflix
Dogma – film by Kevin Smith
Beyoncé's 'Halo' in BSL: https://www.youtube.com/watch?v=MvRos6_xow0

From a workshop led by Justin Audibert
with notes by Alasdair Hunter

Look Up

by Andrew Muir

Look Up plunges us into a world free from adult intervention, supervision and protection. It's about seeking the truth for yourself and finding the space to find and be yourself. Nine young people are creating new rules for what they hope will be a new and brighter future full of hope in a world in which they can trust again. Each one of them is unique, original and defiantly individual, break into an abandoned building and set about claiming the space, because that is what they do. They have rituals, they have rules; together they are a tribe, they have faith in themselves – and nothing and no one else. They are the future, unless the real world catches up with them and then all they can hope for is that they don't crash and burn like the adults they ran away from in the first place.

Cast size
10: characters are 4F, 5M and one gender fluid, but can be gender swapped
as necessary
Recommended for ages 15+

Andrew Muir is a critically acclaimed writer for stage and screen with works including *Take on Me* (Dante or Die, national tour and nominated for Breakthrough Performance, National Rural Touring Awards 2019); *The Session* (Soho Theatre); *Gaugleprixtown* (The Kirk @ Theatre Row, Studio 42, New York); *Double Sentence* (Soho Theatre); *Anniversary Sweet* (Finborough Theatre); and *Sacrifice* (Soho Theatre). His debut radio play, *A Perfect Non-Starter*, was produced for *The Verb* (BBC Radio 3), and his screenplay *How Soon Is Now* is in development with INRed Films.

Andrew writes extensively for young people and is currently writer-in-residence at Bournemouth & Poole College in Dorset. Recent work for the college includes *Tides of Neglect* and *Life & Death in an Ocean Full of Hope* (Lighthouse Theatre, Poole and Paines Plough Roundabout Tent Arts by the Sea Festival). Other recent commissions include *Beyond that Distant Line* and *The Boy Project* (Haberdashers' Aske's Boys' School).

Characters

(M) – cisgender male
(F) – cisgender female
(GF) – gender fluid

Jack *(M), the democratically elected leader who's afraid of crashing out.*
Jamie *(M), over the top by nature, he has always wanted to be a dame.*
Kerri *(M), loves his nan and is into girls despite never going out with one yet.*
Ellie *(F), a lover of Jane Austen and dreams of one day emulating her heroine.*
David *(M), requires medication to maintain a healthy balance.*
Jordan *(M), does not agree with his dad's opinions.*
Crystal *(F), cool and calm with an addictive personality.*
Anna *(F), liberal minded who fights for equal rights.*
Jade *(GF), prefers to hide behind the facade of Raven, their chosen avatar.*
Chloe *(F), a sibling who needs to deliver a message to her brother.*

Note
This play can be adapted for any space. Every group of players will have different resources at their disposal. Stage directions are in place as more of a guide than a necessity. The creative team behind each production can use as little or as much as they want. A collective imagination is all that matters.

A space.

Music plays. This is their anthem and can be chosen by the group of performers – this piece of music always accompanies the moment of 'break-in'.

Noises from all over the space, as gradually the group start appearing. Very quickly, eight of them gather, with **Jack** *standing centre. There is one missing. There is a sense that someone might not have made it. They start panicking as they run around checking walls, windows, doors and so on. Nothing. This has not happened before. Suddenly, out of a trap door in the floor,* **Jamie** *appears. [NB: this does not need to be a trap door, just somewhere Jamie can suddenly appear from.] They roar. A celebratory roar that signifies victory.* **Jack** *places his hand in the centre and they all one by one place theirs on top of his. There is an order to this. A routine. They have done this before and it shows. They close their eyes. They take a deep breath. As they exhale the music fades. The music is created through a collective imagining of what they all want to hear at that particular time. In the silence that follows they start to look around the space. It is smothered in drop cloths.*

As a group there is a huge sense of relief as well as euphoria about completing their task. Except **Jack**. *For some reason, he is slightly preoccupied.*

Kerri   I didn't think we'd make it.

Ellie   I was literally hanging from an old wire at one point.

David   There was so much barbed wire I had to cut through.

Kerri   Have you ever seen so many cameras?

Jordan   It's a test.

Kerri   We did it, captain.

Jordan   We always do it.

Crystal   Didn't we, Jack?

Jack *doesn't answer.*

Crystal   Jack?

Jack   Huh?

Crystal   Mission accomplished, captain.

Jack (*unconvincing*)   Mission accomplished.

The celebratory roar. During the roar, **Anna** *notices the cuts on* **David***'s body.*

Anna   Wow, look at those cuts –

David   – I told you, there was a lot of barbed wire.

Anna   You need to be more careful.

David   Why, if we're invincible?

Crystal   You're not, none of us are.

David   Speak for yourself.

Jamie   This is real, David, remember? (*Referring to his frock.*) Despite what the dress might suggest.

David   Even when we bleed, we're safe.

He roars. He's a little out of control.

Jack   David, stop –

David   *ignores him.*

Jack (*grabbing* **David**)   Stop.

Silence.

Jack   Listen to me.

There is tension in the room.

As a team we're strong. But that's all. As individuals we become weak again. You are not invincible. You're young. We all are. But that does not make us invincible. It makes us vulnerable.

Beat.

(*To* **David**.) Do you understand?

Beat.

Do you understand? This isn't a game anymore.

David   I know that.

Jack   This is real.

David   I know that, stop speaking to me like I'm an idiot.

Jack   You chose the red door, remember?

David   I know what I did.

Jade   We all chose the red door.

Crystal   That feels like a lifetime ago now.

Anna   Can anyone actually remember even making that choice?

Ellie   I can. Like it was yesterday.

Jamie   I remember my parents were watching TV, my sister was listening to her music, and I was staring at the red door, and I just thought . . . I'm going through.

Ellie   So, I was walking back from school, and I saw this old woman sat at a bus stop and she was crying because someone had stolen her shopping. I don't know why but when I saw this bus appear and the door open, I just thought, I'm going to choose the red door.

Anna   What about you, Kerri?

Kerri   Yeah, uh . . . I got told in class that it would probably be best if I just didn't say anything, because what I said was going to be useless anyway. Took one look at the red door, and I thought, I'm walking out.

David   I know what I did, alright?

Jack   All of us. Something. Our very own 'red door'. The moment we all chose to live. Truly live. That is the moment we all came together. I don't know how that happened, none of us do, we did. A moment. Together. Same thought and the same time. We suddenly found ourselves, a bunch of strangers, outside an abandoned building and so began our new life. And now look at us.

David   I understand, captain.

Jack   Think of all the rest. At home, in their rooms, on their beds, playing *God of War* and *Fortnite* and *Soul Calibur* and *FIFA* –

Kerri   Yes!

All look at **Kerri** *with disdain.*

Kerri (*embarrassed*)   I mean 'no'.

Jack   Their parents, quietly content that upstairs their loved ones are at least safe. But they're not, because it's not real. None of it is. But this. Us. This is real. We are not online, David. We no longer have three lives. This is this. And when we bleed, we need to stop that bleeding. Because if we keep bleeding. We die. We're on our own now. We've been on our own since we broke into that first building and started dancing. We think differently now. We now think how we were always supposed to think. For ourselves.

Jordan   And that, my friend, is why you're the captain.

They all cheer.

Jack   Anna, can you see to his wounds please?

Anna   Of course.

She takes a first-aid pack from the rucksack and gets to work on **David** *who takes a pill from his pocket and stares at it.*

David   Adderall, you beauty. (*He swallows the pill.*)

Jack   Okay . . . the rest of you, (*teasing*) I think we know what to do, don't we? Or do we need to think about it for a minute?

All (*rising in volume and in intensity*)   We want to feel afraid . . . We want to feel afraid . . . We want to feel afraid . . . We want to feel . . .

Jack   . . . Something other than safe.

They close their eyes to summon the next piece of music. They inhale and exhale. As they slowly exhale music begins softly and builds slowly.

Jack We have chosen this building.

All Aye, captain.

Jack As we have chosen to live only by our means.

All Aye, captain.

Jack What we see.

All Is all that we see.

Jack What we hear.

All Is all that we hear.

Jack There is no truth beyond what we are. On our own we will be happier.

All Aye, captain.

Jack And we will only ever speak the truth.

All Aye, captain.

They all look at **Jack**. *There is more, but he isn't saying anything.*

Crystal (*whispering*) Jack?

Beat.

Jordan Captain?

Jack And the truth that we speak is a truth created by us.

All And only ever by us.

Jack Good. Remember, keep vigilant, don't talk to strangers and always remember that the helicopters you hear outside of this building are merely over-protective adults hovering overhead. Shout them down, warriors.

They all shout out loud like a tribal roar. Music is loud now.

Okay, let's do this.

They spread out to check out the building. **Anna** *continues to attend to* **David**.

Kerri *searches for the best place to be look-out.*

Jamie *and* **Ellie** *empty out everyone's rucksacks of food and make a small pile somewhere.*

Crystal, **Jade** *and* **Jordan** *set out some mouse traps around the space.*

After a short while, **Jack** *calls out like a wolf.*

Jack I hereby declare this building ours.

They cheer.

Jordan There's a smell.

Jack   What sort of smell?

Jordan   Like I know it, but I don't.

David   I get that feeling a lot.

Anna (*still tending to* **David**)   I think we are all starting to smell a bit.

David   Speak for yourself.

Anna   I am.

Ellie   Oh, for a warm bath full of bubbles, a candle and a good book.

David   I hate baths. Way too boring.

Kerri   With you on that, dude, shower for me every time.

Jack (*speaks like a leader*)   Enough of this talk of clean skin and sweet smells. Look at us. We smell because we care.

Jamie   We smell because we haven't washed properly, captain.

Jack   We don't need to wash. Washing is for the oppressed. We're free, remember? Remember?

All   Yes, captain.

Jack   All mouse traps set?

Crystal/Jade/Jordan   All set.

Jack   Thank you. I'm sorry, but as you know I'll stand up against giants, but I cannot stand up against mice. (*To* **Kerri**.) Kerri?

Kerri (*pointing to an area somewhere in the space*)   I found a good view of the world from just over there.

Jack   And how does that world look?

Kerri   The oceans are full of plastic and the air is filled with poison.

Crystal (*frustrated*)   When will they learn?

Anna   Once we have re-educated them.

Crystal   But when will that be?

Jordan   It takes time.

Crystal   But we don't have time, that's the whole point.

Jamie   There's no way I'm going back into that world, no way.

Jade   You've no choice. The minute any of us turn eighteen, we're out. You know the rules. Section one of the manifesto. As soon as anyone turns eighteen they will be asked to leave the group and start spreading the truth. Our truth. The truth that is real and based on what we see and feel and not on what we read and hear. That's right isn't it, captain?

Jack   That's right.

David   I never want to be eighteen. I want to keep breaking into buildings for the rest of my life. Way more fun than being an adult.

Jack (*to* **Jamie**)   Right. Provisions? Jamie?

Jamie (*shrugging his shoulders*)   We have a bag full of apples.

Jack   Better than nothing.

Suddenly a bell rings, like the sound of a bell that rings in a pub. Only **Jack** *hears it.*

Jack   What was that?

David   What?

Crystal (*to* **Jack**)   Are you alright?

Anna   You're pale, Jack.

Ellie   Like you've seen a ghost?

Jack   Did anyone . . . A bell?

Crystal   What bell?

Jack *looks at them all individually and realises that he's the only one to have heard the bell. He takes them in.*

Ellie   Is everything alright?

Jack *looks around the group.*

Crystal   Jack?

Jack   Ellie, are you ready?

Ellie   Of course.

Anna *fixes the final cut.*

Anna (*to* **David**)   All done.

Kerri   Why can't I ever say the 'welcome' address?

Jack   You can.

Kerri   At last.

Jack   Just not now.

The group chuckle except **Kerri**.

Kerri   I could do a football chant or something?

Anna   You could, but I don't think this is a football stadium.

Kerri   I know that, I'm not stupid.

Crystal   Well . . .

Jack   Crystal –

Kerri   – I'm not.

Jack   You're not stupid, Kerri.

Kerri (*to* **Crystal**)   You see.

Jade   You're just gender predictable.

David (*under his breath*)   Oh dear.

Jack   Brilliant, thanks, Jade.

Kerri   What's that supposed to mean?

David   Don't worry about it, mate –

Anna   – It means you speak how a male has always been programmed to speak since the days of caves and spears and very little clothes.

Jamie (*dreamily*)   The good old days . . .

Jack   Ellie?

Kerri   What's wrong with being a man when I actually am one?

Jamie   Absolutely nothing as far as I'm concerned.

Kerri   I'm not asking you.

Jack   Kerri –

Anna   – He's asking me aren't you, Kerri?

Kerri (*to* **Anna**)   You know you want some.

Crystal   Oh my God –

Ellie   I bet you don't even know what that 'some' is.

David *tries not to laugh.*

Kerri (*offended*)   I do.

Anna   I may be the one with the foreign tongue but I'm not desperate.

Ellie   What does you 'being a man' even mean anyway?

Jade (*referring to herself*)   Raven and I prefer being neutral.

Kerri   You do know that a raven is actually a big black bird that flies over graveyards?

Crystal   Leave it, Kerri.

Jade   I do know that, and I also know that Raven completes me.

Kerri   But what does that even mean?

Anna   Why does everything have to mean something?

Jordan   Shouldn't we be preparing to dance, captain?

Jack   That is precisely what we should be doing.

David (*to* **Jade**)   I'm not going to lie, I am also a bit confused when you talk about Raven.

Jade   And that's okay.

Kerri (*to* **Anna**)   I'm just saying I am a male, and I'm proud of that.

Anna   On what grounds?

Jack   We need to get on.

Kerri   Listen, you need me, and you know it.

Crystal *and* **Ellie** *laugh out loud.*

Jamie   Amen.

Kerri   So why Raven?

Jordan   Oh please.

Jade   Why not?

Kerri   You see, I hate that sort of response? It's like . . . it's like it's actually not even a response.

Jade   Why not?

Jack (*interrupting them*)   Thank you, everyone, right, Ellie, please . . . let us celebrate this new building before we dance.

They adopt 'their' positions around the building. They wait for **Ellie** *to speak.*

Ellie   'There is nothing I would not do for those who are really my friends. I have no notion of loving people by halves, it is not in my nature.' It's from a book called *Northanger Abbey* and I love it because it's about a young girl who is trying to work out the world. Like me. A bit. Maybe?

Jack   Thanks, Ellie.

The bell rings again, but only **Jack** *hears it.*

Jack (*annoyed*)   What is that?

Crystal   Jack?

Kerri (*to* **Ellie**)   Was that the same bird as before?

Ellie   Same what?

David (*under his breath*)   Oh, that's not good, Kerri.

Ellie   Jane Austen is a female novelist not a bird.

Kerri   You do know that 'bird' is another name for woman?

David (*under his breath*) Oh God.

Jade Raven takes offence to that, Kerri.

Jordan If you can try and avoid taking offence, Jade, that would be a big step forward as far as this group is concerned.

Jade Do you mean Raven?

Jordan Yes. Raven. Sorry.

Jade Are you going to say that to Raven then?

Jordan If you can try and avoid taking offence, Raven, that would be a big step forward as far as this group is concerned.

Kerri Well, I take offence to Raven, who isn't even a Raven, because Raven's a bird.

Jamie Yep, I think you lost me on the first 'Raven'.

Anna Kerri –

Kerri – Why is everyone still so sensitive?

David That's not great, Kerri.

Jordan Remember to work on your resilience everyone, in these moments of heightened banter.

Jade This isn't banter.

Anna This feels like war.

Jordan Really?

Crystal I really don't think it's war, Anna.

Kerri (*to* **Jade**) All I'm saying is, what gives you the right to walk around as two, all neutral, with one of you being a big black bird from a graveyard and the other . . . well you? And I can't be a male? What's that all about?

Jade It's my choice.

Kerri And that's fine, but it's a weird choice.

Anna Kerri –

Jade And that's offensive.

Kerri It's not though, it's an opinion.

Jordan (*to* **Jade**) Try and work through the feeling of being offended and turn that instead into something positive. Section six of the manifesto if I remember correctly?

Jack Good work, Jordan.

Jade I'm sorry.

Jack   It's going to take time.

Jade   – I'm sorry, it's just –

Jack   – I know. And that's okay. Early stages yet, but we'll get stronger. We all will. We're here to build up our resilience, remember? So, when it's your time to leave the group, you're ready to prove to the world that we are not weak, and we do care, and we will stop our planet from imploding. I believe we're stronger than we've ever been. We are the new generation and we will not be offended, and we will not cry, and we will not be told we cannot go somewhere because it isn't safe. Okay? Jade?

Jade *gives* **Jack** *a look.*

Jack   Jade and Raven? Okay?

Jade   We're trying.

Jack   That's okay.

Kerri   Yeah, well . . . very trying if you ask me.

Anna   We're actually not.

Ellie (*to* **Kerri**)   And for your information a bird has feathers and cannot write novels.

Kerri   Which is actually a bit presumptuous I reckon.

Ellie   What bird do you know has written a novel?

Kerri   That Jane one for a start.

Ellie *groans in frustration.*

David   Shall we get on, Jack?

Jack (*a little distant*)   Absolutely.

He walks back into the centre of the group.

Ellie   Sorry, Jack, but Kerri just winds me up.

Jack   I know he does, he winds us all up, but we can trust him with our lives, and that's what really matters. The rest you'll have to turn to section six of the manifesto.

They all look at **Kerri***, who smiles back at them.*

Crystal   I can't argue against that.

Kerri (*teasing* **Crystal**)   So, you do admit you need me?

Crystal   Don't push it, Kerri.

Anna (*to* **Ellie**)   You have to learn to not raise to him.

Jordan   I think you'll find that's 'rise' to him.

Anna   Sorry, my tongue is tripping up again.

Crystal (*to* **Anna**)   Don't worry about it.

Jordan   It's not your fault your foreign.

Jade (*offended*)   What? Damn, I found that offensive, sorry, captain.

Jack   Yep, that's not great either, Jordan.

Jordan (*remembering his dad*)   It's him, I told you.

Crystal   You have to stop saying the stuff your dad would say, remember?

Jade   Sorry for being offended earlier.

Jack   Thank you, Jade.

Kerri   What about Raven?

Jack   Thank you both.

Jordan   I'm sorry, Anna, it's in my blood, it's going to take a while, I don't mean it.

Anna   I realise this racism will take time to leave.

Jack   It has no place in this building, Jordan.

Jordan   I know that.

Jack   In any buildings. You have to keep working on it. Section three.

Jordan   I know, I will. I'll go back to section three again.

Ellie   So, I have a question?

Crystal   Brilliant, I love your questions.

Ellie   Do you think us breaking into all these buildings and dancing and shouting and making new rules and standing up for what we believe will be a better future, will actually have any effect on future generations?

Jamie   Oh, now that is a question?

Crystal   Wow!

Jordan   If you're having doubts then you need to go home.

Ellie   I'm not having doubts.

Jordan   Then where does that question come from?

Anna   You sound like an outsider.

Jade   Are you sure you came through the same red door as us?

Ellie   I have a right to ask questions. Section four.

Jamie   Questions can be asked but must never with intention to destabilise.

Ellie   It just came to me when I was hanging off that wire outside.

Jordan   What else came to you while you were there?

Ellie   What's that supposed to mean?

Jordan   The sudden urge for a warm bath full of bubbles?

Ellie   What?

Jordan   The candle, the book?

Jamie   Your phone?

Ellie   I forgot I even had a phone.

Jamie   Really?

Ellie   I'm over it.

Jordan   What else have you been thinking Ellie?

Ellie   Just back off alright, I just like to ask questions.

Jamie   I still dream of my phone every night.

David   Fight that urge, Jamie.

Jamie   I do. Every night. That and many other urges.

David   What about a Big Mac, Ellie, do you think about Big Macs?

Ellie   I don't like Big Macs.

David   How can anyone not like Big Macs?

Jade   How about a lift home in your dad's car?

Ellie   My dad never picked me up, that was my mum who did all that stuff.

Jordan   But a library full of new books would probably be one temptation too far, surely?

Ellie   Will you stop?

Crystal   Back off her, Jordan.

Ellie   I do have the right to express my thoughts and ask questions. We all do. Not with an intention to destabilise, but with the intention to find reassurance.

Jack   Ellie's right. It is good to question sometimes.

Jade   So, what's the answer, captain? To the question she asked.

David   Can anyone actually remember it?

Jack   I believe we will make a difference, yes.

David (*impressed that* **Jack** *remembered the initial question*)   Which is what makes you the captain.

Ellie   How?

Jamie   The sucker punch.

Crystal   Just because he's the captain doesn't mean he has to have all the answers.

Jack   We will make a difference because what we're doing is establishing the truth and spreading that truth. Every time we break into a building they search for us and they search harder and harder each time. Trying to save us from ourselves. And each time we escape. Providing more and more of us with the evidence that life is for living. Look around you, Ellie. I thought I was the only one, but then Jordan joined me, and then Crystal quickly came along.

Jamie   Then me I think –

Jack   – And then you, and then the rest of us. You found the red door, Ellie, you *knew*, you didn't have to think how and why, you just *knew*, and others will follow.

The bell rings again, but again only **Jack** *hears it.*

Jack (*clearly distracted*)   Besides, if we don't do this, the world beyond these walls is not going to make it. Trust me.

Jamie (*feels a twang in his ankle*)   Ow –

Anna (*to* **Jamie**)   Are you alright?

Jamie   Ankle's a bit sore, I twisted it I think when I fell down a stupid hole outside. (*Referring to the trap door he appeared from.*)

Jade   You have no right to abuse a hole like that.

Kerri   Do you just defend the rights of anything?

Jade   I believe in equality for all.

Kerri   He's talking about a hole in the ground?

Jamie   Which I happened to fall into.

Crystal   If you insist on wearing those heels.

Jamie   I like my heels.

Crystal   So do I, but if you insist on wearing them even during a break-in?

David (*bending down to look at* **Jamie**'*s ankle*)   Let's take a look, I've had a few sprains in my time.

Jamie (*to* **David**)   Thank you, dear. And watch the tights, they're Asda. Stolen property but, still, I'm sure they'll appreciate the free advertising.

David (*to* **Jamie**)   Lift it up for me.

Jamie   Is that the skirt or the foot dear?

David   Shall we start with the foot?

Jamie   Love a man who knows what they want.

He lifts his foot for **David** *to examine.*

Jade (*to* **Kerri**)   I believe in the legal rights of nature.

Kerri (*to* **Jade**)   What legal rights?

Jade   Because without nature we cannot survive.

David (*looking at the ankle*)   I think it's just bruised.

Jamie   That was quick.

David (*to* **Jack**)   He'd be on the floor by now if it was broken.

Jamie   Happy to get on the floor if you think that might save me?

David   I think you'll be alright.

Kerri   Nature, like animals and that, I get. But we're talking about a hole in the ground.

Jade   I want to save our planet. A hole is not 'stupid'. A hole is part of our world. We should respect that.

Jamie   I'm sorry for referring to the hole as stupid.

Jade   Thank you. Apology accepted.

Jamie   But it was.

A bell rings again. **Jack** *quickly turns to face it.*

Crystal   Jack?

Jack   I can hear a bell.

All look at each other, confused by this remark.

Jordan   You need to eat something, captain.

Ellie   We all do I think.

Jamie   I'll get the apples.

He goes over to a bag and hands out an apple to everyone.

Jack   I can't stop it, can I?

Crystal   You can't stop what?

Jack   My question is this . . . am I resilient enough?

Ellie   For what?

Beat.

Jack (*shouting*)   To the edges, people. The time has come.

David   At last.

They cheer and stand at the edges.

Jordan   Ready, captain?

They all turn to face **Jack** *who is silent.*

Jordan Jack?

Jack *doesn't speak; he takes them all in.*

Jack I think somebody else should start.

Jade Why?

Jack It's somebody else's turn now, I've done it for long enough. Crystal, I think you should start.

Crystal Really?

Jack Let's try it with Crystal starting, and everyone else steps up. Means, Jade, you get to say something.

Jade Really?

Jack Now everyone's involved.

Jade What about Raven?

Jack Not everyone. I mean everyone, except Raven, obviously.

Jade Next time?

Jack Absolutely.

Kerri It's like progress for the sake of progress without actually making any progress.

Anna Was that English?

Jordan You tell us.

Ellie Jordan –

Jordan Sorry.

Kerri I know what I mean.

Anna Why is it such a confusing language?

Jordan At this moment in time, my dad would say, 'We won the war'.

Jamie And at this moment in time, I would say to him, 'Look at where it has got us'.

David How can parents make us think stuff we don't even agree with?

Ellie That's what parents are for aren't they?

Jordan What's that, then?

Ellie They believe in stuff we don't.

Jordan Is that really what they're for?

Ellie   That and picking us up from parties.

A moment as they all think about their families.

Crystal   My dad waited three hours outside a house party once, just so he knew I got home safe.

David   My dad did a six-hour round trip to a chemist once, just so I had my medication for a field trip we went on once at school.

Anna   That's impressive.

Jack   Okay, people, let's remember that red door if we can.

Ellie   Sorry, captain –

Jack   They know we love them. Sort of. But we're here now. Do not lose the faith people.

All   No, captain.

Jack   Right, are you okay to start, Crystal?

Crystal   Sure.

Jack   Thank you.

They turn to face the edges and begin a ritual.

Crystal   We are not special.

Silence.

Jamie (*to* **David**)   David, that's you.

David   We are not beautiful.

Ellie   We are not unique.

Jamie   We are the same organic . . .

Ellie (*whispering*)   . . . and decaying –

Jamie   – And decaying matter.

Anna   As everyone else.

Jordan   We want to feel frightened.

Kerri   We want to be scared.

Jade   We want to experience everything.

Kerri (*whispering to* **Jade**)   You repeat that bit.

Jade (*whispering back to* **Kerri**)   Thank you.

Kerri (*whispering back to* **Jade**)   Go on, then.

Jade   We want to experience everything.

They howl and beat their chests. They breathe in. Music fades in. Suddenly a light comes on from somewhere around the space and the music stops. They all notice it.

David (*confused*)   Captain?

Jordan   Sorry, but did that light just – ?

Anna   – It did.

Jamie   Without –?

Jordan   – Any of us doing anything?

David   Yep.

Anna   Is this a trap?

Jack   No. It's a sign.

Another light switches on.

Ellie   Oh my God.

Jordan   What sign?

David   Okay, so what's going on?

Sound of helicopters in the distance. They listen. Still.

Jordan   They've trapped us.

Jack (*losing it a little*)   It's not a trap, stop saying that.

Crystal   Stay calm, captain.

Another light, then another, before a lot of lights around the space have switched on by themselves causing the group to be constantly caught by surprise. [NB: these lights can be as few or as many as the director chooses. And any light – fixed lights on walls, lights in the ceiling, fairy lights, etc.]

Jack   Stay perfectly still.

After a short while the sound of the helicopters disappears.

Silence. Another light switches on.

Ellie   Is that it, do you think?

Jack   Maybe one more for luck?

One last light obliges.

David   What the – ?

Jordan (*sudden realisation*)   It's a pub.

David   What is?

Jordan   The smell.

Ellie   How would you know?

Crystal   So are we in a pub?

Kerri   So this is what they look like?

Jade   Really?

Jordan (*looking around the space*)   I need to check to make sure my dad hasn't collapsed somewhere.

David   Why would your dad have collapsed somewhere?

Ellie   We don't know where we are, Jordan, how's your dad going to know?

Jordan   Makes no difference. If there's a pub, he'll find it, and then there's every chance he could have collapsed inside it.

They watch as **Jordan** *checks.*

Jordan   He's not here.

David   Well, that's something.

Jordan   But he might have been. I just needed to check.

A sound. It comes from behind a trap door. [NB: this can be any area that is hidden from the main playing area; for example, under the floor, behind a curtain, outside of the building, etc.]. Silence.

Jack   You did say that all traps are set?

Crystal   All except down there.

Jack   Why not down there?

Crystal   I didn't think.

Jack   You didn't think what?

Crystal   I'm sorry.

Jordan   You know that rats love a good pub.

Jack   Oh God.

David   How do you know that?

Jordan   My dad came home once, and he was wearing his old Winter coat and he was drunk, and he had been at the pub all night. He fell asleep in the kitchen next to the radiator. When me and mum found him the next morning he had a rat sleeping in every pocket. He had five pockets in that coat.

Jamie   Is that true?

Kerri   That's disgusting.

Jordan   I'm just saying that rats love a good pub.

Anna   Then let us hope this was never a good one.

Another sound from behind the trap door. Louder.

Crystal   What do we do?

Jordan   Captain?

Jack   All of you close your eyes.

Jade   What for?

Jack   Just close your eyes. Everyone. Now. Close your eyes.

They close their eyes.

Jade (*whispering, to* **Ellie**)   Is this to try and make the rats go away?

Ellie (*whispering, to* **Jade**)   I have no idea.

Jack   Breathe warriors . . . breathe.

Silence.

He opens his eyes.

Okay, everyone, now open your eyes.

They open their eyes.

David   Did that work do you think?

Jack   I think so.

Chloe (*from behind the trap door*)   Hello?

They stare in shock.

Chloe (*from behind the trap door*)   Can you hear me?

Suddenly Elton John's 'Circle of Life' starts playing from somewhere.

Jordan   What's going on?

Jade   It's *The Lion King*.

Chloe (*from behind the trap door*)   Is that *The Lion King?*

Jack (*in the direction of the trap door*)   Shut up.

Crystal   Jack?

Kerri   I hate that film.

Anna   How can anyone hate *The Lion King?*

Kerri   I mean what sort of name is Simba?

Chloe (*from behind the trap door*)   It's Swahili for lion.

Jack (*in the direction of the trap door*)   I said shut up.

Crystal   Jack –

Kerri (*to* **Anna**)   – Why not something less complicated?

Ellie   Like what?

Kerri   I don't know . . . Brian?

Jamie   Brian?

Ellie   It's because it's set in Africa.

Jade   Are you seriously suggesting that it should be 'Brian' the Lion King?

Kerri   Why not? My dad was called Brian and he had a right roar on him when he needed it. Mainly towards me and my younger brother.

David   What kind of pub plays *The Lion King* anyway?

Jamie   An empty one.

Kerri   No surprise if all they play is *The Lion King*.

Ellie (*to* **Kerri**)   That's the first time you've ever mentioned your dad.

Kerri   Left a long time ago now.

Chloe (*from behind the trap door*)   My mum loves *The Lion King*.

Chloe *is interrupted when* **Jack** *suddenly runs around the space screaming trying to locate the source of the music and turn it off.*

Jack   I don't know where it's coming from.

Anna   Does everyone here hate *The Lion King*?

Jade   I don't.

Jack *screams out loudly. Music stops.*

Crystal (*to* **Jack**)   Are you alright?

A random light switches on.

Jack   Will you stop doing that?

Crystal   Jack –

Jack   – It's doing my head in.

Jamie   Have we made a mistake do you think?

David   What do you mean?

Jamie   Is this one building too far do you think?

Crystal   No.

Jordan   We're in this for the long term, aren't we, captain?

Chloe (*from behind the trap door*)   Who's the captain then?

David *is about to tell her but is stopped suddenly by* **Jack**.

Jack   Don't tell her.

Chloe (*from behind the trap door*)   I could guess I reckon.

Jack   Can you just go back to where you came from?

Chloe (*from behind the trap door*)   Do you not think, it's time you went back to where you all came from?

They all look at each other and then all towards **Jack**.

Jack   Stay strong, warriors.

Chloe (*from behind the trap door*)   Do you seriously think you can make a difference?

David   We're renegades.

All (*cheering*)   Yes.

Chloe (*from behind the trap door*)   I bet you don't even know what that means?

They look at each other for an answer. They don't have one.

David (*in the direction of* **Chloe**)   I actually find that offensive.

Jordan (*whispering*)   Section six, David.

Chloe (*from behind the trap door*)   Oh, I'm sorry, I thought you were the new wave of teenager who doesn't get offended. Time to go home, losers. Back to the real world.

Jamie   She's certainly got a tongue on her, I'll say that.

Kerri   How old are you?

Ellie (*disgusted*)   Really?

Kerri (*to* **Ellie**)   What? I'm just checking, you know the rules.

Chloe (*from behind the trap door*)   How old would you like me to be?

Kerri (*embarrassed*)   What? No, I wasn't . . . (*In the direction of the trap door.*) We have rules.

Jack (*losing control*)   You have to go now.

Chloe (*from behind the trap door*)   I'm thirteen.

Kerri   That's good, because we don't allow anyone eighteen or above in this group.

Chloe (*from behind the trap door*)   No adults allowed.

Kerri   That's right.

Chloe (*from behind the trap door*)   And do you – (**Chloe** *coughs.*)

Anna   Are you alright?

Chloe *coughs. Silence.*

Anna   She's struggling I think?

David   Air pollution.

Jack   So?

Anna   So, we should probably help her.

Jack   No way.

Chloe (*from behind the trap door*)   Sorry – (*More coughing.*)

Jack   She's pretending.

Anna   Jack –

Chloe *coughs, more severe.*

Jack   So, turn back.

Chloe (*from behind the trap door*)   The air.

Anna   Jack, please.

Jack   So, go back.

Crystal   What's wrong with you?

Jack   Nothing's wrong with me.

Crystal   So why are you being so aggressive?

Ellie   She must have taken the red door, otherwise she wouldn't have found us.

Jack   She doesn't have the guts.

Ellie   How do you even know that?

Crystal   Ellie's right, she must have taken a risk to be here in the first place.

Jack   Who do we trust?

Jordan   The warriors.

Jack   Who do you choose?

Crystal   What?

Jack   Her or me?

Crystal   What are you talking about?

David   You're the captain.

Jack   So, choose.

Crystal   Jack –

Jack   – Choose.

Beat.

Chloe (*from behind the trap door*)   Please –

Jack (*towards the trap door*)   You're a liar.

Chloe (*from behind the trap door*)   No I'm not –

Jack   Fine, do what you want.

*He turns and finds somewhere to be alone. The rest of them look at each other, not sure how to respond. Eventually **Crystal** goes to the trap door, opens it, and with the help of **Kerri** and **Jade** they help **Chloe** up and into the space. **Chloe** catches her breath. She looks across at **Jack**.*

*Sound of helicopters in the distant. They look towards **Jack**.*

Sound of one helicopter having technical difficulties.

All (*except **Jack** and **Chloe***)   Burnout!

*They grab **Chloe** and run to where they can look out. **Jack** doesn't move; instead he watches the following action.*

Jade   Look at it.

Chloe   What am I looking at?

Jack   She can't see it.

Chloe   Can't see what?

Jack   You see, she's not the same as us.

Chloe   What are you talking about?

David   Do you see the rotating blades of guilt?

Chloe   The what?

Jack   She sees nothing.

Chloe   That's because there is nothing to see, just people going about their lives.

Jack   We have a traitor in our midst, people.

Chloe   Are you actually serious?

Jade   There before you is the engine that never stops.

Chloe   There before me are loads of people doing the school run and going to work.

Jack   She's not like us, I told you.

Chloe   You're not special, you do know that?

Jordan   Each and every one of them fuelled on alcohol.

Chloe   What are you talking about? You're making stuff up that isn't true?

Ellie (*mimicking an adult*)   'Two glasses only mind you.'

Jordan   Only ever two glasses.

Crystal   In front of your very eyes is the millennial burnout.

Chloe   It's just life.

David   Before our very eyes is yet another helicopter, burning from the inside out.

They all react, except **Chloe***, as though having seen it crash before their very eyes.*

All   Woah!

Beat.

Chloe   I don't understand.

Jordan   That could have been my dad.

Jamie   It could have been any of our dads.

Jade   Why do they keep crashing like that?

Crystal   Because that's what happens to adults. They live, they pay, they work, some start a family –

David   Some don't.

Crystal   No, that's true. But no matter what they do, they start to panic, and then they start to regret, then start to spin, and then they burn out, and then and then . . .

David   And then they crash.

Beat.

Ellie   Is anybody else feeling lonely? Right now. Or is it just me.

David *puts his arm around* **Ellie***.*

David   We have to stay strong.

Jack   I don't want to crash.

They look towards **Jack***.*

Jack   I really, really don't want to crash.

Chloe   Right, are you all on some sort of drugs, because I'm telling you, from where I'm standing from, you're all a bunch of nutters.

They turn to face **Chloe***.*

Crystal   Who are you?

Chloe   I came to find out what all the fuss is about.

Jamie   What fuss?

Jack   You came to destroy what we've built because you're not brave enough to handle the truth.

David   Are we famous by the way?

Kerri   Are we?

Jack   Of course, we are.

Jamie   It's all I've ever dreamed of.

Jordan   Are they annoyed they can't catch us?

Chloe (*sarcastically*)   Oh, they are, like, so annoyed.

They all cheer.

You guys are, like, everywhere. There are, like, TV crews chasing you all over the country, going from one building to the next, the prime minster is saying, like, you should all be the next leaders of the country, Netflix, right, get this, Netflix wants to make a new *Stranger Things* but with you guys all in it and you (*pointing to* **Jamie**), you're going to be the one who murders everyone –

Jamie   – An evil dame. Lovely.

Chloe   And apparently, but this hasn't been confirmed yet, Simon Cowell reckons he wants to turn you into a band. That's what's happening in that world, just outside that wall.

They all turn to face out there.

Kerri   Are you serious?

Chloe   Not one word.

Jack   Leave now.

Chloe   I'm joking.

Jack   No, you're not.

Chloe   I was joking.

Jack   Go now.

Chloe   So, what are you doing, then? In here. On your own?

Jack   It's secret.

Chloe   Tell me what you're doing.

Jack (*aggressively*)   No.

Crystal   Jack –

Jack   You wouldn't know how to survive in our world.

Chloe   Yes, I would. And besides, it's the same world as the one out there, only difference is there's no McDonald's in here.

David   Which, I'm not going to lie, is an issue.

Jack (*to* **Chloe**)   You're too small to join this group.

Chloe   I am not too small.

Jack   No?

Chloe   No.

Jack   Really?

Chloe   Really.

Jack   Fine.

Chloe   Fine.

Beat.

Fine what?

Crystal   Jack?

David   What's actually going on here?

Jack   Let's start the party, shall we?

Ellie   Pardon?

Jamie   The party?

Anna   You mean the dancing?

Kerri   With her in the room?

Jack   Why not? She's come all this way.

Chloe   You don't scare me you know.

Jack   Good.

Anna   You really want to start the party already?

Jack   Why not? You said yourself, how else would she have got here, if not through the red door?

Crystal   But what if she didn't?

Ellie   What if she just came here without even knowing?

Jordan   She saw no helicopters, remember?

Jack   So, let's take her dancing, only then will we really know.

Jade   She has to see the stars remember?

Chloe   Will you tell me what you're doing?

Jack   Oh, we'll do more than that.

Jordan   Captain?

Jack   You want to see what we get up to?

Chloe (*a bit nervous*)   You don't scare me.

Jack   Because you think you can handle it?

Crystal   Jack –

Kerri   Perhaps not, captain.

Chloe   Yes. I can. If you can, then I definitely can. Handle it.

Jack   Okay, David . . . let's do it.

David   Now?

Crystal   Jack –

Jack   She's here. Let's dance.

Chloe   What's going on?

Jack   You want to see what we do?

Chloe (*unsure now*)   Yes.

Jack (*persuasive*)   You really want to see what we do?

Chloe   Stop bullying me –

Jack (*raising his voice*)   Do you want to see what we do?

Chloe (*raising her voice*)   Yes.

Jack   David?

David   Absolutely.

Anna   Good luck.

Jack   Let's dance.

Music begins. **David** *starts to hand out some sherbet flying saucers to each person. An air of excitement. Through all of this, there is a strange connection between* **Jack** *and* **Chloe**. **Jack** *takes his sherbet and then* **David** *offers* **Chloe** *one, but she declines. As a group they gather around her and pile on the pressure to force her to have one. Eventually she succumbs to the pressure and accepts.* **Jack** *holds his high in the air. He doesn't speak. Then slowly he places the flying saucer on his tongue. He closes his mouth slowly. They come together, holding hands, they close their eyes and they breathe in. Music starts to play. They all cheer, open their eyes and follow his lead. They start to dance wildly all over the space. It is utterly chaotic and out of control. Eventually the sugar wears off. They collapse in the space and look up towards the ceiling.* **Jack** *goes to the gap in the boards and looks out towards the world outside.*

Silence.

Jamie   Hello, universe.

Chloe   What's going on?

Jade   We're looking at the stars now.

Chloe *looks around at them all lying around the space. She's unconvinced.*

Chloe   Okay . . .

Jade   This is what we do after we've danced.

Chloe (*unsure*)   Right . . .

Jade   They always appear after we've danced.

Chloe (*unsure*)   Okay . . .

Crystal   Can you see them?

Chloe   No, actually, I can't.

Jamie   Shame.

David   You were right, captain.

Ellie   Give her a chance.

Anna   Look up.

Chloe   What?

Ellie (*pointing towards the sky*)   Up there.

Crystal   This is the bit that fills us with hope.

Jade   The bit that makes it all worthwhile.

Chloe *looks up.*

Ellie   They're beautiful, aren't they?

Chloe   I can't see stars.

Jordan   Time for you to go I think.

Ellie   You didn't see them at first, Jordan.

Jade   None of us did.

Anna   It takes time.

Ellie   They're there.

Crystal   You just need to give it some time.

Chloe   This is stupid.

Ellie   No, it's not.

David   Perhaps you should go back to where you came from?

Beat.

Chloe I don't want to.

David Why?

Chloe I just don't want to go home yet.

Crystal Just give it some time. Stars will appear.

Chloe *sits up for a moment.*

Chloe You do know they're just sherbet flying saucers, don't you? The sweets you swallowed?

Crystal It doesn't matter what they are.

Ellie Just as long as we all look up and give it some time, it doesn't matter what they are. Just as long as we're together. Anything is possible if we're together.

Chloe (*still not convinced*) Right.

Eventually **Chloe** *lies on her back and gives it some time.*

Jack You don't see them, do you?

Chloe Shut up, alright? Just shut up.

Jack If you had come here through the red door, then you can spot a helicopter from a thousand kilometres, and you can see what's really going on, you can see through the outward facade of calm and the commonplace and see them spinning out of control until they crash and then they burn. And if you lie back and look up, then you can see the stars. But that's only if you had come here through the red door.

Chloe (*stressed out, under her breath*) I hate you.

Crystal Just give it some time.

Anna (*under her breath*) It took me a while.

Jamie Shhhh . . .

They all look up.

Chloe Oh my God.

Jack She's lying.

Ellie Jack –

Crystal – Just give it some time.

Chloe Are they really stars?

Jack Such a liar.

Ellie Jack –

Chloe I mean, is it not just lights from the building?

Jamie   They really are stars.

Chloe   How?

David   We don't know.

Jade   They just appear.

Chloe   Wow.

Jack   This is what she does.

Ellie   They just shine really bright above our heads.

Jamie   They never let us down.

Crystal   They help us see stuff.

Jordan   Too much stuff sometimes.

Chloe   So, is this what you do? I mean, and I hope you don't take this the wrong way, but all this fuss about breaking into buildings, to eat sherbet flying saucers, dance around a bit and then see some stars? I mean, and don't get me wrong, it's cool that you're doing this together, but . . . why?

Crystal   Jack?

Jack   Somebody else tell her, none of you seem to listen to me anymore anyway.

Elle   What's wrong with you?

Jack   Nothing. Alright. Nothing is wrong with me. Just get on with it.

He sits in a sulk.

Beat.

Jordan   We do what we do because we were fed up with everything out there.

Jack *looks outside.*

Chloe   So, you do this instead?

Crystal   We break in for the buzz it gives us. We create a rulebook because we can, and we follow those rules because we believe in them. We eat sherbet flying saucers because they taste good and we dance because dancing is in all of us.

Chloe   And the stars?

David   They're the reward. For taking the risk in the first place.

Beat.

Kerri (*pointing towards the stars*)   Can anyone see that lion shape?

Jade   Perhaps Brian has come to see you Kerri?

Ellie   Your dad maybe?

Kerri   No, he wouldn't come to see me.

Ellie   You don't know that.

Kerri   I do. I know he wouldn't come to see me, not even in the stars.

Chloe (*feeling her neck*)   My neck hurts.

Ellie   Our neck muscles have become weaker on account of us looking down all the time. We've stopped looking up.

Chloe   Is that actually true?

Ellie   It's true in this group.

Chloe   Is that what you do?

Ellie   What?

Chloe   Rethink what's true and what isn't?

Ellie   It's what we believe to be true. We're starting again.

Chloe   But what if it's not true?

Ellie   We have to start somewhere.

A gust of cold wind rushes through the space.

Jordan   My dad has a box that he keeps in the kitchen. In the box is a medal. It belonged to my great-grandad who died in the war. His dad's dad. He takes it down every now and then and he stares at it. Then he polishes it and stares at it again. And then he puts it back in the box. Sometimes, I'll watch him from the doorway. He doesn't know I'm watching. And he'll be crying. My dad will be crying. Quietly. Softly. I know he will never forget what my great-grandad did. And I know that he's crying because if my great-grandad knew he was going to die for the sake of this world we live in today, would he have still sacrificed everything? The answer is yes. And that's why I sometimes catch my dad crying at our kitchen table. Quietly. Softly.

Beat.

Anna (*still looking up towards a specific part of the sky*)   There. It's a face.

*They all stare at where **Anna** was pointing.*

Ellie   First one.

David   Who is it?

Anna   Jacinda Arden.

Chloe   Who's that?

Ellie   She's a woman who gets stuff done.

Jade   Hi, Jacinda.

David (*pointing*)   There.

They all stare in that direction.

I've got someone, but I don't know her name.

Ellie   What does she look like?

David   She looks young. Got a round face. Kind of. Pigtails.

Chloe   Is it Greta Thunberg?

David   Who?

Chloe   She's amazing. I wish I could see her.

David   No idea.

Chloe   No one is too small to make a difference.

Jamie   So true.

Anna (*pointing*)   There.

Chloe   Where?

Anna (*pointing*)   Do you see?

Chloe   No. Are you all making this up, so I look stupid?

Anna   No.

Ellie   Why would we do that?

Crystal   Just give it some time.

Chloe   Oh my God!

Anna   You see?

Chloe   I do. Hi, Greta. I think you're really cool.

Jack (*to* **Chloe**)   Why are you here?

Chloe (*standing, she hands a voting slip to* **Jack**)   I nearly forgot. Mum said it's from the Government.

Jack *slowly takes it.*

Crystal   Jack?

David   Wait. What?

Ellie (*slow realization*)   Oh my God.

Jordan   What's going on?

David   Jack?

Anna   Wait –

Jade (*working it out slowly*)   Are you two – ?

Kerri   Have I missed something?

Chloe   You have to go home now.

Kerri (*referring to* **Chloe**)   She's your sister?

Chloe   Mum said you need to come home now. She said that's a voting slip. What you're holding. It's really important that you go home, and you vote.

Suddenly **Jack** *runs at his sister and jumps on her. They fight. Others go to help but they decide to let them express themselves.*

Crystal   Leave them.

David   But they'll kill each other.

Crystal   No, they won't. They love each other deep down.

They literally kill each other but don't. The bell rings once again, but this time they all hear it. They stop fighting.

Jordan   Time at the bar, Jack.

Ellie   So, you're eighteen?

Jade   Wow.

David   Let's change the rules.

Jamie   We made them after all.

Crystal   We can't do that.

Jamie   No, fair enough. It would never have sat well in the long term.

David   But we'll lose the captain.

Crystal   We can't start changing the rules.

David   But –

Jamie   She's right. Our captain has to go.

Jack *looks at his sister.*

Jack   How did you find me?

Beat.

Chloe   I'm really sorry but I went into your room. Mum's had the door shut ever since the day you left, but I just . . . I'm sorry. I opened the door.

Jack   Why?

Chloe   Huh?

Jack   Why did you take that risk? Knowing that if ever I found out you went into my room I'd kill you?

Chloe   I was willing to take that risk.

Crystal   Your sister chose the red door, Jack.

Beat.

Chloe (*handing him his iPhone*)   Here. I brought your phone.

They all stare at the phone.

Ellie   Oh my God.

Jordan   Look at it.

Jade   Raven's birthplace.

Kerri   Can I call my nan?

Crystal   No. The most dangerous creature in the world remember?

Jack *takes the phone and stares at it.*

David   Can I hold it?

Crystal   No way.

Jack (*speaking directly to the iPhone*)   I'm rewired now, and you will not own me.

They all cheer.

Chloe   You should record something before you go.

Jack   What?

Chloe   Even the most dangerous creatures in the world have their purpose some of the time.

Ellie   It'll be like your legacy, Jack.

Jack   I don't have a legacy.

Screens suddenly appear all over the auditorium. This is a live feed. And it's already gone viral.

Jack *appears on all the screens. He takes a deep breath.*

Jack (*to the world*)   On their own, snowflakes are lightweight. Whichever way the wind blows, they will be taken with it. But together, it's a different story. A lot of snowflakes at any one time can make a blizzard, or they can make for a very big dump of snow. In which case, people will start to look up. We look out and we see words thrown back at us, which suggest you are simply trying to protect us. We see through that now and understand that in fact what you are actually doing is protecting yourselves.

Chloe (*mouthing the word*)   Wow.

Jamie (*off-screen*)   Jack . . . Jack –

Jack (*looking away from camera and towards* **Jamie**)   I'm trying to lay down our legacy.

Jamie (*off-screen*)   I know, and you're doing brilliantly.

Jack (*looking away from camera and towards* **Jamie**)   So what is it?

Jamie (*off-screen*)   Can you tell my mum I'm gay.

Jack (*looking away from camera and towards* **Jamie**)   Really?

Jamie (*off-screen*)   I'm ready for her to know.

Jack (*looking away from camera and towards* **Jamie**)   Okay, let me finish.

Jamie (*off-screen*)   Thanks, Jack.

Jack (*back to camera*)   This is a message for all the adults who are working hard to remove our right to freedom of speech. Look up now, all of you, because there is an almighty blizzard coming your way. Start telling us the truth and stop lying. Just stop. The lies will only lead us all to a place full of cruelty, inequality, poverty, false entitlement, privilege and hate. Our promise to you is that never again will we think our vote doesn't matter or say we don't care. It does, and we do. We will never think that again. Finally, a message to all children and young people everywhere, this is your world. Use it. And don't be afraid to be offended. Just fight back instead. Don't ban, argue.

Jamie   Jack –

Jack (*to camera*)   Oh . . . and this is a message for Jamie's mum.

Jack *puts the camera on* **Jamie**. **Jamie** *is stunned. Silent.*

Jamie (*to camera*)   Hi, mum. I'm gay.

Silence.

Is that it? (*He smiles.*) Hello, world.

Kerri *grabs the camera.*

Kerri (*into camera*)   Nan. I'm fine. I love you. I really do. You've made me do this. Just you, no one else. Thanks.

Anna (*into camera*)   Hi, Mum and Dad. I hope you are okay. I am fine. Weather here is good. Actually no, it rains too much. But they have pies which are nice. And now I know what an English pub looks like. The English are a funny breed. I will come home soon. When I am ready. And I no longer feel like an outsider. This may take some time. Don't worry. I am safe. Ish. But I am happy.

Crystal (*into camera*)   I'm a captain now. Who would have thought it? Not me. Ever. Well here I am. And it feels good. Natural. Naturally good. Hashtag, we are not afraid.

Ellie (*into camera*)   'I declare after all there is no enjoyment like reading! How much sooner one tires of anything other than a book! When I have a house of my own, I shall be miserable if I have not an excellent library.'

Kerri   *Pride and Prejudice.*

Ellie (*shocked*)   How did you know that?

Kerri   Never presume anything.

Jade (*into camera*)   I've got Raven with me, Mum. You've never met her. Not really. But I think you'll like her. Tell Dad, hi. And tell him to stop smoking if he hasn't done already. And I'm not weird, okay? I'm me. And I'm part of you. So, don't worry.

Jordan (*into camera*)   Dad, I don't share the same views as you. There. Said it. But you're my dad. And I miss you. I really miss you. And I will make you proud one day.

David (*into camera*)   I just wanted some space. I have that now. I feel better. I'm still a bit moody I suppose, and I can still do some weird stuff, but I definitely feel better. Don't crash, okay? Don't.

Camera switches off. Screens blank.

Helicopters suddenly overhead. Very loud. Torchlight from outside streaming through the gaps in the boards. They are under attack.

They all hug **Jack** *quickly one by one. He gets to* **Chloe**.

Chloe   I think I'm going to break into a building.

Jack   Really?

Chloe   Actually, I quite like the taste of those sherbet flying saucers if I'm honest.

Jack   What about Mum?

Chloe   Your turn now. My turn to dance.

They hug.

Jack *takes a deep breath, places the iPhone on the floor, holds up his voting slip and goes.*

They all steer **Crystal** *to the front of the group.*

David   Captain.

Crystal *takes in the group. Slowly she raises her arm. She closes her eyes. They follow. Music fades in. They open their eyes.*

Crystal   To all the young warriors of the world, do not be afraid of choosing the red door. We may well feel scared, fine, let us feel scared. That might mean we won't make others feel so scared in the future. We have to feel what it's like to hurt. Perhaps then we might understand more about not wanting to hurt others. And we have to keep searching for what we believe to be the truth. The real truth. The truth that is born out of lengthy research and time to think. There is only one life.

They all cheer one last time before disappearing back down the trap door. **Chloe** *is the last one. She looks around and then up and then out.*

Chloe   Good luck, Jack. I love you. And tell Mum not to worry, I'll be fine. We all will. We're young. Oh, and don't forget to vote.

Fierce banging from all around the building as the adults attempt to tear down the boards. **Chloe** *disappears through the trap door. She slams it shut.*

Blackout except for spotlight on the iPhone on the floor. Silence. Music.

Spotlight fades to black.

End.

Look Up

Notes on rehearsal and staging, drawn from a workshop with the writer,
held at the National Theatre, October 2019

How Andrew came to write the play

'The characters in this play are based loosely on some of the brilliant young people I
have met during my time as writer in residence at the Bournemouth & Poole College of
Higher Education. Despite the state of the world they inhabit, they remain passionate,
honest and full of spirit, but understand that if certain changes aren't made some time
soon, then there will be no world left for them to feel passionate about. This play is
about how incredibly powerful young people can be when they work together as a
group, and how important it is that they demand change, despite their feeling of never
being listened to. This play attempts to provide a platform on which young people can
start making those demands and finally be heard.'

Themes

Lead director Amy Hodge asked the group to write down the themes of the play and
then collect similar ones together. They then gave them headlines. Some themes overlap
with different headlines. This is not an exhaustive list.

Identity/finding your place in the world

How others see you
Gender
Finding your voice
Racism
Sexuality
Coming of age
Love
Communication
Ownership

Change and the future

Coming of age
Anxiety

Responsibility

Courage

Adolescence

The future

Frustration

Pushing boundaries

Time

Sibling rivalry

Future in the hands of the young

Changing the world

Power

Adult world

Ownership

Leadership

Boundaries

Rules

Trapped

Social structures

Love

Hope

Family

The future

Truth

You can then do improvisations inspired by the themes that resonate for you. What's the outside world like for them? How have the themes affected them? What do the characters and your young people dream of for the future?

You can use themes to find the main super-objective of characters (what they want throughout the play). Finding your main theme could also help you find what the ensemble movement sequences should be.

Characterisation

The following ideas for character exercises were suggested by Amy and the group:

- Ask your actors to write down what their character says about themselves, then what their character says about others, then what people say about their character. What's not being said? You can do this as a group for each character.

- A character sits in the middle and all the characters comment on the character as their character.
- Walking around the room saying hello to others in character.

Question and answer with Andrew Muir and Amy Hodge

About the text

What if our cast doesn't match the specified gender of the characters? For example, can Jack be changed to Jackie?

[Andrew] Yes, the play can be adapted and interpreted to suit the young people in the room.

What about the cultural diversity of the group?

[Andrew] Again, depending on the group working on the piece, this play can be adapted and interpreted to suit that group.

In Scotland you can vote at sixteen, so can Jack's age be changed?

[Andrew] Yes. Absolutely.

How did you choose your 'inspirational people' in the text? And can we add more?

[Andrew] Greta Thunberg was an obvious choice given the time of this play being written, as was Jacinda Arden. In answer to the question regarding additional inspirational people, then my answer again would be 'yes', but only if you felt those names worked within the context of the moment. If your group is keen to add the names of inspirational figures, then my suggestion is that they are added on page 319 after Jade, 'Hi, Jacinda' and before David, 'There'.

[Amy] Be led by your young people by who they want to add in, but it also might be a process thing rather than ending up in your actual show.

What to do with a bigger cast? What can an ensemble do?

[Andrew] A bigger cast could perhaps become one of two things. The first suggestion is that they might form part of the 'break-in' group. They wouldn't have lines to say necessarily, but their presence would be obvious, and they could get involved in all sorts of group stuff including the movement sequence that follows on from the intake of the sherbet flying saucers. They could be 'around' the building and add to the size of the group. My second suggestion is that they could create an outside presence. They could be figures outside of the building who throughout that play let their presence be known. They could be the ones who scare them.

[Amy] They can be a representation of the voice of the young in all of the symbolic moments. They could also represent the outside world. The helicopters, the adults. Or the young people who conform and choose not to go through the red door.

Structure, style and transitions

How long have they been breaking into buildings? Is it always pubs?

[Andrew] Give yourself the most fuel to make the drama the most active it can be. If it's the second time it will be very different to something they've done hundreds of times. No, it's not always pubs!

What should we do with the trapdoor if we don't have one?

[Andrew] No trapdoor needed, just an entrance from which Jamie and Chloe can both appear.

Music

Have you got a piece of music in mind? What's the style of the music? Can the students write music?

[Andrew] My intention with the music was that it should always come from the young people in the group, so directors should be led by that. What speaks to these young people at the time? The reason why the music is throughout is because most of the young people I get to work with are forever plugged into music; there is always something underscoring their life. The music in the play can be live, and it can be original. Their anthem is their collective power, what they are capable of, so should be fluid, slick, conjuring this entire play, the building, the world.

[Amy] How do you articulate that anthemic quality of unity? I would be thinking about whether that's a movement sequence, running on at the same time? How do you embody the gesture of anthem? You need to understand what your themes of the play are in order to make your choice of anthem.

Participant thoughts about the music in the piece

It is a form of expression, a form of identity.

It can help young people collect their thoughts.

It helps them remember what they're from.

Is it music that their parents wouldn't listen to?

Consider the beat, what it says and how it makes you feel.

How do they play music?

[Amy] It's important that they summon it, unified in whatever the beat takes them towards.

Production, staging and design

Why do you end the play with a spotlight on an iPhone?

[Andrew] I believe it's the reason for the title – *Look Up*. But that's also up for interpretation!

What is the thematic function of the flying saucer moment on p. 315?

[Andrew] The characters want it to be something. They are emulating something rebellious and taking it seriously. But bottom line is, it's just a flying saucer with some sherbet inside.

[Note: Some group members thought it was like Holy Communion.]

[Amy] Your own experience is part of the storytelling so if you connect to it through religion rather than raving that's valid. It has to be joyful, free and euphoric.

What is the red door? What is it? What does it represent?

[Andrew] It represents danger according to the adult world. A non-safe space and yet, for whatever reason, they choose it anyway. I never saw it as a real red door. I saw it as a moment where these young people felt compelled to make a change. They want to be heard because they're angry with the state of the world that they've been left with. They're furious with the older generations for letting the world become like this. At that moment, they all think, 'I need to do something different – I don't know what it is'. And so, the first thing they do is break through something they are not allowed to be part of.

[Amy] The gift of the play is that it's interpretable. We should do a list of what it means to these people and what it could be. The material will support all choices.

[The group made a list of what the red door could be:]

Epiphany

Breaking away from parents

Trying to be heard

Trying to find their true self

The door of the pub

Making change

Challenging society

A door into a better world

A protest

Wanting to break out of everything

Coming of age

Trying to find their position in world

Trying to find information for themselves

Wanting to be acknowledged as an individual

Struggling against parent(s)

Questioning the cycle of life and social norms

Is there actually a future for young people? Climate change

Hope – kicked out at eighteen to vote and take responsibility

Is adulthood giving up, a process of giving in?

Over-nurturing of parents to children

Nature versus nurture

All movements are animalistic, anti-adult structure

No phones – I'm not reachable

Could be an online game

'We want to feel afraid' – something other than safe

[Amy] You make your choice for your production. You could choose three, so you don't close it off for your group. You and your company want to be clear about what it is/what it represents, otherwise you'll float in lack of specificity.

What is the manifesto?

[The group looked through the play and pulled out the manifesto rules that they could find:]

Section 1: When you're eighteen you leave

Section 3: Anti-racism

Section 4: I have a right to ask questions

Section 6: Try and work through feeling offended and make it positive

[Amy] They could be making new rules as they go. Get your cast to complete the manifesto. What is the manifesto of your group? And what is the manifesto of the characters?

Approaching the text: facts and questions

Amy asked the group to read the play line by line in a circle and when any facts or questions came up to stop and write them down. Some questions will have no answer, and some will be left to the imagination, based on what you know in the script. For this exercise, it is important to avoid interpreting the material – just keep them as questions.

The group started from the title.

Look Up

Fact

It's called 'Look Up'.

Questions

What does it mean to your production?

Look up at what?

Why should we look up?

Why are children's heads down? It is everyone's heads?

What's the motivation to look up?

Is there symbolism?

How does anyone know that we have to look up?

Is it literal? Or is it looking up stuff? Or to your elders?

Is it in relation to don't look down?

Why not look forward?

Below are a few examples from applying facts and questions to the character breakdowns.

Kerri (M)   Loves his Nan and is into girls despite never going out with one yet

Facts

Male, he's got a nan, heterosexual, has hope.

Questions

Does he fancy anyone in the group?

Where are his parents?

Why hasn't he been out with a girl?

Jack (M)   The democratically elected leader who's afraid of crashing out

Facts

Male

The leader

Voted in

Questions

How did they vote him in?

What is Jack afraid of?

Ellie (F)   A lover of Jane Austen and dreams of one day emulating her heroine

Facts

Female

She loves Jane Austen

Dreamer

Romantic

Wants to emulate her heroine

Questions

Is she missing her books?

Who got her into Jane Austen?

Why Jane Austen?

General questions

Why is it the loved ones that they turn to?

Do Crystal and Ellie have family?

Who starts the live feed? And what does that mean?

Was Chloe planning to stay when she arrived?

Why has Crystal assumed position as leader when Jack was democratically elected?

Are they truly democratic?

Where are they all going now?

What does the future hold?

Where is Jack going?

What is the story of the outside world prior to the play and during the play?

Will Jack change anything?

From a workshop led by Amy Hodge
with notes by Tess Seddon

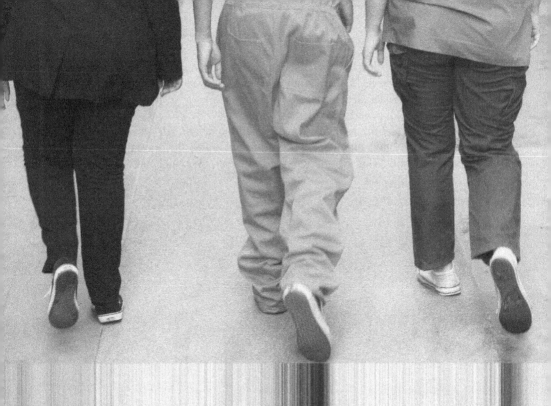

Crusaders

by Frances Poet

A group of teens gather to take their French exam but none of them will step into the exam hall. Because Kyle has had a vision and he'll use anything, even miracles, to ensure his classmates accompany him. Together they have just seven days to save themselves, save the world and be the future.

And Kyle is not the only one who has had the dream. All across the globe, from Azerbaijan to Zambia, children are dreaming and urging their peers to follow them to the promised land. Who will follow? Who will lead? Who will make it?

Cast size
10–100, ideally with a mixture of genders
Recommended for ages 14+

Frances Poet is a Glasgow-based playwright with two decades of experience working as a literary manager and dramaturg for some of the UK's leading theatre companies. Her stage plays include the multi-award-winning *Adam* (Scottish and UK tours, 2017/18 and NYU Skirball Centre, 2019) and *Gut* (Traverse Theatre and Tron Theatre, 2018 and in a French translation as *Madra*, Théâtre La Licorne, Montréal, 2019) which was shortlisted for the Bruntwood Prize for Playwriting (2015), nominated for a UK Theatre Best Play Award and won the Writers' Guild Award for Best Play in 2019.

Frances has also completed a number of classic adaptations including *The Macbeths* (Citizens Theatre/Scottish tour, 2017/18), *What Put the Blood* (Abbey Theatre, 2017 and previously as *Andromaque*, Scottish tour, 2015), *Dance of Death* (Citizens Theatre, 2016) and *The Misanthrope* (Oran Mòr, 2014).

Frances also writes for TV and radio and has had short films screened at national and international festivals.

For Peter and Elizabeth, Noah and AJ, Millie and Max, Hannah and Daniel, Chloe and James. I believe in you.

Casting

The play can be performed by a minimum ensemble of ten actors or up to 100.

The play has been written to be performed by a 50/50 male/female cast. It is possible to change the genders (and associated names/pronouns) of the characters to suit the casting breakdowns of specific theatre groups. If possible Meera, Deborah and Anika/Nadin would be cast as written.

Characters

Kyle, *seventeen/eighteen*
Meera, *seventeen/eighteen*
Kayleigh, *seventeen/eighteen*
Ross, *seventeen/eighteen*
Jay, *seventeen/eighteen*
Demi, *seventeen/eighteen*
Eli, *seventeen/eighteen*
Emma, *seventeen/eighteen*
Sara, *seventeen/eighteen*
Ravi, *seventeen/eighteen*

South American refugee children,
   all ages
Valentina, *fifteen*
Voice of Border Guard Frank
Deborah, *seventeen*
Yafa, *fifteen*
Benjamin, *sixteen*
Nadin, *seventeen*
Anika, *fifteen*
Force of children, *all ages*

Setting

The play is set in locations all over the world. We start in Scotland, where the play was written and workshopped (thank you to Drummond Community High School) but companies are free to relocate to their own home area by changing Highers to A-Levels and Ross's reference to Dundee to a local city/town of their choice. Border Guard Frank could as easily reference the North or South of England, Northern Ireland or Wales in his reference to places where kids have walked out of lessons.

The other locations are fixed but their representation should have a theatrical rather than literal expression. Evoking these worlds will be best achieved by casting according to the strength of the company you have available and focussing your energies on finding the emotional truth of these settings rather than becoming bogged down in questions of ethnicity and accent.

Monday

Scotland. Outside an exam hall. Kids are gathered, waiting to go in. Most are flicking through their French dictionaries/textbooks/notes.

At the centre of them all, **Kyle** *sits alone. He is completely lost in his thoughts, spinning a fidget spinner with almost robotic regularity.*

Meera   I'm actually sweating. Like a cold wet sweat.

Kayleigh   Me too. Totally.

Meera   I've nearly been sick like three times. You know that sick when it sort of like sits in your throat?

Kayleigh   Ugh, mingin.

Meera   That's how nervous I am.

Kayleigh   Me too.

Meera   Yeah but for me it's, like, an actual physical thing.

Kayleigh   You're amazing at French. You're predicted an A.

Meera   Exactly. That is like a lot of actual pressure on me. How can I be sure I'll know the vocab? What's French for headlice?

Kayleigh   Is that going to come up?

Meera   *Anything* could come up.

They flick through their dictionaries with renewed urgency. **Ross** *looks at everybody with their heads in their books – it makes him nervous.*

Ross   What's everybody looking at their books for?

Jay   Revising, I suppose.

Ross   Why? French listening – there's nothing you can do. You either get it or . . .

Jay   You don't?

Ross   You mean me?

Demi   Easy. Bit touchy, Ross.

Ross   Are you saying I'm crap at listening?

Demi   It's true, isn't it?

Ross   Don't need reminding.

Jay   Want to look at my notes? Just some words I thought might come up.

Ross   What's the point? I know what the words mean on the page. It's when they're spoken it's like gibberish. Like it's a different language.

Demi   It is a different language. Duh.

Ross   Shut up.

Eli *enters.*

Eli   *Bonjour tous le monde!* (Hello everybody!)

He high-fives a not very enthusiastic **Emma** *and* **Sara**. **Eli** *moves on to* **Kyle**.

Eli   *Bonjour* Kyle!

Kyle *doesn't register him.* **Eli** *is left hanging. He tries to style it out and heads on over to* **Meera** *and* **Kayleigh**.

Eli   *Ça va pour notre examen?* (How are you feeling about our exam?)

Meera   *Je me sentais bien jusqu'à ton arrivée.* (I felt great until you arrived.)

Ross   What? What are they saying?

Emma   He said something about the exam. Haven't a scooby what she said.

Meera   I said, I felt great until Eli arrived.

Eli   *Es-tu prêt?* (Are you ready?)

Ross   What's he doing?

Eli   *Je pratique.*

Emma   Practising.

Eli   *Je t'aide à prendre ton oreille.* (I'm helping you get your ear in.)

Meera   Actually, I don't think the phrase 'get your ear in' can be translated literally into French like that. Just saying.

Eli   *Merci pour la correction, Meera.* (Thank you for the correction, Meera.)

Ravi *enters and heads over to* **Kyle**.

Ross   You gonna shut up, pal. Stressing me out.

Ravi (*to* **Kyle**)   Thought we were meeting in the common room?

Eli   *Calme toi, Ross. Que sera, sera.* (Calm down, Ross. What will be, will be.)

Kyle *keeps spinning his fidget spinner, lost in his thoughts.*

Ravi   Kyle?

Kyle   What?

Demi (*to* **Eli**)   That's a song isn't it? My gran sings it.

Eli   *Oui, c'est une chanson.* (Yes, it's a song.)

Ross   I asked you to stop, Dog Breath.

Ravi (*to* **Kyle**)   We were supposed to meet at quarter past.

Kyle   Oh. Yeah. Sorry.

Ravi   Phoned you like a hundred times.

You alright?

Eli   *Sois gentille, Ross*. (Be kind, Ross.)

Ross   You're showing off. Just because your mum's French.

Demi (*singing*)   *Que será, será.*

Eli   My mum's Polish.

Ross   Same difference.

Kyle *spins the fidget spinner.*

Ravi   Kyle!

Kyle   I'm fine.

Demi (*singing*)   Whatever will be will be . . .

Eli   *Polonais est une langue très différente.* (Polish is a very different language.)

Ross (*to* **Eli**)   You are doing my nut. I swear.

Demi (*singing*)   The future's not ours to see . . .

Ross (*to* **Demi**)   And you and all. Shut it will you?

Demi (*singing right in* **Ross**'s *face*)   *Que será, será.*

During the following exchange **Kyle** *begins to speak the words his classmates go on to say. He says the words flatly, without emotion and more for himself than for anybody else's benefit.* **Ravi** *is the first to realise what's happening. Gradually* **Kyle**'s *voice cuts through until he has everybody's attention.*

Kyle   *Tu as une belle voix, Demi.*

Eli   *Tu as une belle voix, Demi.*

Ravi (*to* **Kyle**)   What?

Kyle   Do you want a fist in your face?

Ross (*to* **Eli**)   Do you want a fist in your face?

Ravi (*to* **Kyle**)   How do you mean?

Kyle   Knock it off, Eli. Just pissing everybody off.

Kayleigh   Knock it off, Eli. Just pissing everybody off.

Ravi (*to* **Kyle**)   How are you doing that?

Kyle   Ross is the one who needs to pipe down.

Demi   Ross is the one who needs to pipe down.

Kyle   What is your problem with me?

Ross   What is your problem with me?

Ravi (*to* **Jay**)   Have you heard this?

Jay nods, freaked out.

Kyle   Seems to me like you're the one with the problem.

Demi   Seems to me like you're the one with the problem.

Jay   Is he making them speak?

Kayleigh   That is freaky.

Kyle   I just want to wait here in peace

Ross   I just want to wait here in peace.

Emma   What the . . .

Sara   Wow

Eli   *Mon dieu.* (My God.)

Everybody is watching **Kyle** *now, including* **Demi**.

Kyle   You got a problem with that?

Ross   You got a problem with . . .

He has realised.

. . . that?

(*To* **Kyle**.) How did you do that?

Kyle *finally stops spinning his fidget spinner. He stands up and puts it carefully away in his pocket. Everybody's eyes are on him.*

Kyle   We can't do this exam. Sorry but . . . we've got to go.

Ravi   Mate, you're being really weird.

Kayleigh (*to* **Meera**)   Have you got shivers too?

Kyle   We can't sit the exam because . . .

Ravi   Because?

Kyle   Because we're the answer.

A moment in which the assembled receive this information. Then . . .

Ross   What?

Kyle   I had a dream.

Meera   Alright, Martin Luther King.

Kayleigh   Let him speak.

Kyle   I saw . . . I mean, I met . . . it's hard to describe but . . . it was, I think it was /

Ross   Spit it out.

Kyle   God.

Ross   You met God.

Kyle *nods.*

Meera   Yep, he's lost it.

Ross   What did he look like?

Demi   Why do you say 'he'?

Ross   What?

Demi   Could have been a 'she'.

Ross (*dismissing it*)   Yeah right. (*Suddenly unsure.*) Was it?

Kyle   I don't know.

Eli   How do you know it was God?

Emma   Probably just some old homeless fella with a long white beard. Were you high at the time, Kyle?

Sara   Jesus is a homeless guy.

Emma   What?

Sara   That's what my ma says. When you see a homeless guy, it could be Jesus so you've got to be nice.

Ross   Hey guys, why wasn't Jesus born in Dundee? God thought about it but he couldn't find three wise men and a virgin.

Demi   That's not even funny.

Ross   Just 'cause your mum's from Dundee.

Kayleigh   What did God say to you, Kyle?

Meera   Why are you even entertaining this? You don't believe in God.

Kayleigh   You mean you don't.

Ross   Did he speak?

Demi   She. Don't assume it's a he.

Ravi   Everybody just shut up and let him speak.

This unexpected outburst from **Ravi** *silences them.*

Kyle   It was more a feeling. Like you know when you see in movies, doctors holding those shock things over a person's heart and they're like . . .

He demonstrates a body being shocked with a defibrillator.

But not pain. Like . . . the opposite. Like . . . total joy.

Meera   They're going to call us in, any minute.

Kayleigh   Shhh.

Kyle   I saw all time.

Sara   Woah. That's . . .

Meera   Impossible.

Kyle   God led me to a mountain with green trees growing on it, ripe with brightly coloured fruit. It was where God first stood when the world was made.

And I saw the foot of a fallen angel land upon that place turning the green grass to dust. The feathers from his wings fell to the ground and his foot became a cloven hoof. The angel of light became the angel of adversity. And pain poured into the world.

And then I saw war. Thousands of years of war.

Muslim, Christian, Jew – pouring their blood into the dust. The hand and the sword replaced with sniper and bullet, computer and drone. And the spilt blood pours into the land by the gallon. But the earth is never quenched. And when the last man is killed, the only thing left is the dusty footprint of a fallen angel.

And it is there we must travel. To the heart of the Holy Land. The footprint where both stood – Creator and Adversary. For only we can pour our balm into the land and make it whole again. Blood will not quench it. Love will.

A moment. Then laughter. All but **Kayleigh** *and* **Ravi** *piss themselves laughing. Some blatantly, like* **Ross** *and* **Emma***, while others try to hide it. They laugh away all the tension* **Kyle** *has introduced, all the fear about their exam. They laugh and laugh and laugh.* **Kyle** *is crushed.*

Kyle   I'm supposed to lead you.

That's even funnier.

We'll take the school minibus – Jay knows where his mum keeps the keys.

Funnier still.

Passports are a problem. But we'll deal with borders when we have to.

Hilarious.

We are Crusaders. We're going to save the world.

It's suddenly not funny. It's weird and intense and **Kyle***'s clearly unhinged.*

Jay   I'm going to get a teacher. He's not well.

Kyle *is suddenly forceful.*

Kyle   No teachers. No adults.

Jay *stops in his track.*

Meera   Go on, Jay. Go and get Ms Henderson.

Jay *is transfixed.*

Kyle   They've failed. They've made things worse or they've done nothing at all. It's our turn now.

Meera   Jay!

Jay   No teachers?

Kyle *shakes his head.* **Jay** *mirrors him.*

Kyle   I saw all this. I saw you rise and follow me.

Kayleigh   We've got our exams, Kyle. We can't just sack it off and leave.

Kyle   You will.

Ravi   What are you saying, man?

Kyle   I know all of you. I saw all time. Your before and after.

Demi   This is heavy.

Meera   Guys, just stop listening to him. He's going to make us all fail. We have to go in there and sit an exam and there's still a tonne of French words I don't know. And if I don't know it, you lot sure as hell don't. Like who knows the word for tarmac, or lollipop lady, or bus depot?

Eli   Actually I think 'depot' is from the French so /

Meera   I know that! Kyle is confusing me.

Kyle *goes to* **Eli***.*

Kyle   I saw your eyes. Sunken into the face of a shrivelled man, all bones.

Emma   He's definitely high.

Sara   Or ill.

Emma   Or both.

Eli   . . . Papa Ezofowicz?

Kyle   I saw him fall to the earth and take his last breath.

Eli   My grandfather's father. He died in the camps. You saw him?

Kyle *nods.*

Sara   How did he know that?

Meera   Eli told us. Back in S3. He told us his great-grandfather died in the Holocaust.

Eli   But his eyes. My grandfather always said I had Papa Ezofowicz's eyes.

Ross   This is freaking me out.

Meera   You're trying to get out of sitting this exam.

Emma   Is that it, Kyle? You're hoping they'll reschedule if you persuade us all to walk away? Or maybe you just won't feel so bad if we all fail.

Kyle *turns his attention to* **Emma**. *He strokes her arm. She pulls away.*

Kyle   I saw her stroke your arm. In a figure of eight. She did it when you were little. And when she was dying. Soft on your arm. It made you sleepy. I saw her die. I saw you asleep.

Meera   We all know Emma's mum died. This is sick. You're using stuff you know /

Emma (*to* **Sara**)   Did you tell him?

Sara   No.

Emma   I told you that in confidence.

Sara   I didn't /

Emma   I hate that I slept. I hate that I missed her . . .

Sara   I never told a soul. I promise.

Kayleigh *stands up. She places her bag on the floor.*

Kayleigh   We are the answer.

Kyle *nods.* **Jay** *follows suit, placing his bag on the floor.*

Jay   We are the answer.

Meera   You're not going with him? This is our Highers, people. This is important. This is our lives. You don't get to just walk away from /

Emma *puts her bag on the floor.*

Emma   We are the answer.

Sara *follows.*

Sara   We are the answer.

Now **Eli** . . .

Eli   We are the answer.

Ross   Screw it, I'm going to fail anyway.

He puts his bag down.

We are the answer . . . though I'm not sure what the question is.

Kyle   Ravi.

Ravi   This is . . .

Kyle   Do you trust me?

Ravi   We've been friends since we were babies. I've always trusted you. Even when you gave me that backie and I broke my arm. I trust you. But this is . . . I mean everything about this is . . . Fine.

He *drops his bag on the floor.*

We are the answer.

That leaves only **Demi** *and* **Meera**.

Meera   This exam is 33 per cent of our final grade. If you don't sit this, you'll fail. A 'D' is the best you could hope for but you'd have to slay every other exam to even scrape that.

Kyle *walks towards* **Demi**. *She backs away.*

Demi   What is this, Kyle? Is this some sort of power trip or . . .

Kyle *whispers in* **Demi**'s *ear. She reels from what he has told her. She places her bag down on the floor.*

Demi   We are the answer.

Everybody looks to **Meera**.

Meera   No. No way. God isn't even a real thing. It's a construct humans invented to . . . You do what you like. I am sitting this exam.

Kyle   How can you? Your pen doesn't work.

Meera   Of course it does. I bought new pens. A whole pack of them.

Kyle   They don't work.

Meera   They're like brand new. Of course they work.

She gets out a pack of pens.

See for yourself.

She scribbles on a piece of paper. Nothing.

The ink just needs to start, like, flowing.

She scribbles some more. Nothing. She gets out another and another. None of her pens work. She is scraping them against the paper, desperate for one to work.

What did you do? Why don't my pens work?

Somebody give me a pen.

Jay *gets one from his pocket and offers it to* **Meera***. She snatches it and tries it in her notebook. Nothing.*

Meera   This doesn't work. Kayleigh, give me your pen!

Kayleigh   It's in my bag.

Meera *goes to* **Kayleigh***'s bag, empties it out and tries the pen. It doesn't work. She empties other bags, tries the pens. Nothing. Not one works.*

Meera   How are you doing this?

She gives up.

I don't want to go to the Holy Land. I want to stay at home and do my exams.

Kyle *takes a step towards her.*

Meera   Who are you?

Kyle   You're asking the wrong question. Who are we?

Meera *weighs this up. Everybody waits on her reply. Does she even have a choice?*

Meera   We are the answer.

Snap to . . .

Tuesday

America. A giant cage, with make shift beds, mattresses and silver foil blankets. And children. Lots and lots of children.

The children are submissive. Some attempt to sleep under their foil blankets. Others stare into space. They have the lost, hopeless look of people who have no control.

Several of them also wear the signs of a previous scuffle. One or two sport prominent bruises. One, **Valentina** *(fifteen), her top torn from the earlier fight, paces back and forth across the room. She looks fierce.*

A voice can be heard over a speaker. It is **Border Guard Frank***. His voice could be prerecorded. Or it might be performed live on a microphone by an actor or a chorus of actors.*

Border Guard Frank   I'm still waiting.

Nobody responds. A child coughs. Another rolls over on their mattress. **Valentina** *paces.*

Border Guard Frank   I've been too soft on you. They all say so. Joe and Jimmy and Suzanne. Bringing you cookies and sweeties and being playful with you. Trying to make you smile. Guess I'm a mug.

I'll ask you one last time. Who's got it? Who's got my Minion key chain? He's a little yellow guy in blue dungarees with one eye. And he's wearing a tartan hat on his head and playing the bagpipes. My ma brought it back for me from Scotland. I won't be pissed if you give it back now. It probably dropped in the scuffle. I don't think anybody took it deliberate. Just stand up if you got it.

Valentina *pointedly sits down. A couple of the kids might smirk a little. Just a little.*

Border Guard Frank   Never should've been nice to you. Mr M. Pathetic, that's me. I need to stop putting myself in your shoes – thought of you without your folks has always made me think of my kid brother. How lost he'd be. You're not my kid brother. Your parents are criminals. *You* are criminals.

Valentina *hardens at the mention of her parents. She whistles and other kids come to her. They huddle and talk amongst themselves.*

Border Guard Frank   What's got into you? All this huddling and talking. All yesterday too. I can't understand everything you say but I got Google translate so you'd be surprised how much I pick up. *Sueño* is dream. One of you had a dream. And Sante Muerte. You keep saying it. I Googled that too. I know who she is. She's a freaky-ass skeleton goddess of death who can grant you favours. And she visited you in your dream.

They continue to whisper, **Valentina** *leading.*

Border Guard Frank   You lot pick and choose, that's the problem. A little bit Catholic, a little bit Voodoo, a little bit of something going back further than that. Ain't Christian. The dead are dead. They don't come back. They don't visit you in your dreams and tell you to go on a journey. They don't tell you to hurt the one fella who's looked out for you. Grabbing me from behind. Holding them foil blankets over my head. I couldn't breathe.

The kids whisper. Plotting.

Border Guard Frank   Something funny going on. More than just you. Kids disappearing.

Walking out of their lessons, not showing up for their exams. Across the whole country, Russia too, China, Scotland. Like there's some sort of Pied Piper on the loose. Seems to me it's a good thing we got you here in these cages. Keep you safe.

Enough already. Stop whispering. I told Joe to take a long lunch, let me deal with this my way. But I'll get him if I have to. And you know what Joe's like when he's pissed.

They're undeterred. **Valentina** *is drawing something on the floor in the dust.*

Border Guard Frank   Break it up, now. Get away from each other. Hey, I said stop. That's enough. Stand up. Come on now. All of yous, stand up. I said STAND UP!

They ignore him, defiant.

There's other ways to punish you, you know. I can make things difficult on your folks.

This has their attention.

Even those of you who pretend not to, cry for them. I know you do. Think they'll still love you when they found out you caused trouble? Got them more jail time?

This is a frightening thought.

They'll hate you. They won't even ask for you back when they get out.

Leave you here for good and be glad there's one less greedy mouth to feed.

No longer a group, these kids are now a bunch of lonely individuals missing their parents.

When I say stand, you goddam stand.

One by one they stand. **Valentina** *is the last to stand. One of the kids pulls her up.*

Border Guard Frank   See, that wasn't so hard was it.

They are standing, heads low, cowed, defeated.

And now that I have your attention, I want my Minion keychain.

Valentina *speaks in a low, intense voice.*

Valentina   The cage around me is only in my mind.

She and the other children raise their eye-line in unison. Their stance now is defiant and dangerous, and **Border Guard Frank** *knows it.*

Border Guard Frank   No need to keep standing.

Valentina   The cage around me is only in my mind.

Border Guard Frank   You can sit down now. Just wanted you to stop huddling.

Another kid picks up **Valentina***'s mantra.*

Valentina and one other   The cage around me is only in my mind.

Border Guard Frank   All of yous, sit down now.

And another . . .

Valentina and two others   The cage around me is only in my mind.

Border Guard Frank   You've had your fun.

All the kids pick up the mantra now.

Children   The cage around me is only in my mind.

Border Guard Frank   You all sit down now and I'll, well, I'll forget about Mr McMinion. You keep him.

The children start a movement routine, a sort of haka. It's passionate. It's angry. They are a force to be reckoned with.

Children   The cage around me is only in my mind.

Border Guard Frank   Now stop that. No need to get all riled up again.

You, you'll regret this. I'm going go get Joe and I won't be able to stop him getting rough with you.

Children   The cage around me is only in my mind.

The cage walls fall with a clatter. Or they bend and melt, or they cease to exist in a moment, or they transform into flowers or they burst into flames. They're gone.

Border Guard Frank   What did you do? How did you do that? What the . . .

The kids take a step forward.

Now, you need to remember I was nice to you. Real nice. I gave you sweets. I brought in cookies baked by my ma. I was /

Valentina *points out. The loud speaker whistles and then boom. It's gone.* **Frank** *is gone. The kids look to each other.*

Valentina   Ready?

Snap to . . .

Wednesday

Gaza.

Border fence, Israel.

Lights up on **Deborah** *(seventeen), an Israeli soldier on military service, who points her bolt action sniper rifle at the audience.*

Deborah   I've always had a very steady hand.

Lights up on **Yafa** *(fifteen). He is out of breath, panting. He breathes. In and out. In and out. Eventually . . .*

Yafa   Am I alive?

Lights up on **Benjamin** *(sixteen), who also addresses the audience. He has the energy of a stand-up comedian.*

Benjamin   I decided to be funny age seven. I was shorter than all the other kids. I mean really short. So short that people thought I'd have to stand on a chair to reach puberty. The other kids never made fun of my height – they wouldn't stoop that low. I admired them for that – in a way you could say I looked up to them. I just decided if I was going to have a label, 'funny' was better than 'short'. And living where we do, laughter's kind of important.

Yafa   Every day she cries. My *umi*. The sobbing she mostly saves for after I've gone to bed but, day or night, there's always tears wetting her eyes.

Deborah   I don't blink.

Yafa   She says she's grieving for the life I should have had. I tell her. I'm alive, aren't I? What is there to be sad about?

Benjamin   Girls like funny boys. It might not be their pictures they're kissing and hiding under their pillows but we're the ones that win out. Girls like to laugh.

Deborah   I like guns.

Yafa   I shouldn't have told my *umi* about my dream.

Deborah   The weight of it on my shoulder. The cool metal touching my cheek as I look down the sights.

Benjamin   I've set my sights on this girl.

Yafa   Now she won't let me out of her sight. She says her heart is breaking.

Benjamin   She's a heartbreaker this girl – the stuff dreams are made of.

Benjamin and Yafa   Dreams can be confusing.

Deborah   Those guys over the fence, wielding their flags. A flag is not power.

Yafa   In my dream, I'm watching myself.

Benjamin   A kid with kind brown eyes. A gun trained on his head.

Deborah   An M24 SWS 7.62 mm bolt action sniper rifle. That is power.

Yafa   I'm watching myself through the scope of a rifle. Through the crosshair, I see myself.

Yafa and Benjamin   Holding a flag.

Deborah   The red arrow attacking the green. The heavy black sky above. An aggressive flag.

Yafa   My flag.

Benjamin   The Palestinian flag.

Deborah   Not like our prayer flag sporting the star of David. Calm, blue and peaceful.

Benjamin   And this soldier aims for his heart. And she shoots.

Yafa   Bang.

Yafa and Benjamin   And then I wake.

Yafa   Allah gave me my dream.

Benjamin   I don't tell it to anybody. If they asked I'd say it was a dream about a car – that is why I woke up . . . exhausted!

Yafa   In it, Allah showed me many things. Not just my death.

Benjamin   I was swimming in an ocean of orange soda. I guess it was just a Fanta sea!

Yafa   I floated in space and saw His name written in the shape of the land on the sea. I saw Allah's grace and it was everywhere.

Benjamin   It really was orange. Unless it was just a pigment of my imagination.

Yafa   I saw it written in the snow on the highest mountain. In the coral in the ocean. In the heart of the poorest peasant.

Benjamin   But . . .

Benjamin and Yafa   My dream was so clear.

Benjamin   Dreams are always clear if you forget to take off your contact lenses!

Yafa   I woke with this strange feeling of joy and purpose. I wanted to share it with my *umi*. To take the tears from her eyes. But my dream made her more sad, more scared. She says, 'There are three types of dream in Islam, Yafa'. She says that my dream was not *rahmani* – truthful dream. She says it was *Nafsani*, a dream of my own desires.

And when I say, 'No, it was Allah. Allah has chosen me. To save the world.' Then she says my dream was *Shaytani*. She says the devil sent me my dream and that I must pray with her. And for three days I have prayed. But today, I must act.

Benjamin   I'm going to speak to her today. My dream girl.

Deborah   Today my rifle feels heavier.

Yafa   *Umi* is making me *Na'na* tea when I climb out of the window. I run past the broken homes of my neighbours, towards the smoke from burning tyres, towards the guns and the barbed wire.

Benjamin   She's standing outside the synagogue with a group of girls when I stumble up. Practising my joke in my head.

Yafa   I'm amongst the protestors now. I move through the crowd and when I see a kid, my age or younger, I find myself patting them on the shoulder. I stumble into a man, a burning sling shot in his hand. He thrusts a huge flag into my chest. I don't want it. But the hate in his eyes frightens me. I take it and I walk.

Benjamin   'Hello,' I say. 'My name is Benjamin.' She and her friends look annoyed at the interruption. 'Would you like to hear a joke?' Amused now. Intrigued. 'Ok, then, funny boy. Make me laugh.'

Yafa   And the closer I get, the more clearly I can see the soldiers on the perimeter, gripping their rifles.

Deborah   I wanted to do National Service. To protect my people. Each day I sit on my side of the fence and train my gun on Arabs. Mostly they stay more than

350 metres away – any closer, they have our attention. At 300 metres we are primed but we only shoot if we see a weapon. At 100 metres . . . it doesn't matter who you are.

Young, old, doesn't matter if all you hold in your hand is a teddy bear, at 100 metres we shoot.

These people are terrorists. My job is to protect my people.

Benjamin   'Funny boy!' She's smiling. Anticipating the laughter. That's when the burning starts inside my head. The boy with kind brown eyes, the smoke, the bullets, the sniper's rifle. Tell your joke, Benjamin. Tell it.

Yafa   I walk towards the fence.

Deborah   He steps out from the crowd. 350 metres. I raise my rifle.

Yafa   A soldier points her gun at me. I keep walking.

Deborah   300 metres, I scan his body for a weapon.

Yafa   I am unarmed.

Benjamin   'Have you forgotten your joke, Benjamin?'

Yafa   My blood is pounding but I just keep putting one foot after another.

Deborah   200 metres.

Benjamin   'If anyone, um . . .'

Deborah   My finger is on the trigger. I breathe slowly.

Yafa   There's shouting now from both sides. 'Stop. You'll be killed.'

Benjamin   'If anyone needs a . . .'

Yafa   I keep walking.

Deborah   150 metres.

Benjamin   Tell the joke, Benjamin.

Yafa   125.

Benjamin   Make her laugh.

Deborah   110.

Benjamin   If anybody needs an ark . . .

Yafa   100.

Deborah   My finger tightens on the trigger.

Yafa   I step.

Deborah   He steps and I . . .

Benjamin   'If anybody needs an ark, I Noah guy.'

Yafa *and* **Deborah** *look at* **Benjamin** *for the first time – seriously?*

Benjamin (*to the other actors*)   What?!

(*To the audience once more.*) And I'm running away from the synagogue, away from the girl of my dreams. And I'll never know whether my joke made her laugh.

I run for miles, pounding pavements, then earth, scrambling through avocado trees towards the fence and the boy with kind brown eyes.

I see him. Just as he looked in my dreams. And I see the soldier shoot.

Bang.

I was meant to save him. That's what the dream was for, wasn't it?

Deborah   I shoot and I never miss.

Benjamin   Straight in the heart.

As in the opening, **Yafa** *is out of breath, panting. He breathes. In and out. In and out. Eventually . . .*

Yafa   Am I alive?

Benjamin   He's still standing.

Deborah   How?

Yafa   Did it miss?

Benjamin   His body moved with the force of the bullet.

Deborah   I aimed and hit but . . .

Benjamin   He doesn't fall.

Deborah   It's like . . .

Benjamin   A joke without a punchline.

Deborah   It's not possible.

Yafa   I take another step.

Deborah   I aim for his head this time. No room for error. And I shoot again.

Benjamin   No!

Yafa   The bullet tears through my skull.

Benjamin and Deborah   Is he dead?

Yafa   Neither bullet leaves a trace. Allah heals me.

Benjamin   It's a miracle.

Deborah *drops her rifle.*

Deborah   *HaShem* is God; there is nothing besides Him.

Yafa   And He is Allah, there is no god but He.

Deborah   An Arab kid shouts, 'He's a prophet!'

Benjamin   He's just had two bullets tear through him – he's definitely . . . holy.

Deborah   The men and women are routed to the spot, some have fallen to their knees in prayer. But the children. They step forward.

Benjamin   The children are walking towards the boy.

Yafa   Every kid I touched on my way through the crowd.

Deborah   Twenty at least approaching the fence. The fingers of my fellow soldiers twitching on their triggers.

Benjamin   Stay back!

Deborah   One more step and this line of children will be at 100 metres. We have our orders.

Benjamin   I'm over the barbed wire before I know what I'm doing. Arms open – a human shield.

Deborah   My fellow soldiers would die to protect their families. But this – this is one of our own.

Benjamin   And then silence. Everybody's looking at me. Um.

He steps forward, no longer recounting the story but actually in the moment, unsure what he's supposed to say. He gulps, sweats a little, he's looks around for inspiration. And then . . .

An Israeli guy sits between two Arabs on a plane.

He kicks off his shoes and gets settled in when the Arab in the window seat says he wants a coke.

The Israeli offers to get it for him. While he's gone, the Arab spits in one of the Israeli's shoes.

When he returns with the coke, the other Arab says he'd like one too.

Now this Israeli is a good guy and again he offers to get the coke. While he's gone the second Arab spits in his other shoe.

The Israeli returns with the coke and they all relax on their flight. But when the plane lands, the Israeli slips his feet into his shoes and realises what has happened.

He turns to the two Arabs.

'How long must this enmity between our people go on . . . this hatred . . . this animosity . . . this spitting in shoes and pissing in cokes?'

Silence.

Tumbleweed.

Yafa Ten, twenty seconds of silence at least.

Deborah As quiet as I've ever heard it at the fence and then . . .

Benjamin Laughter.

Yafa From both sides.

Deborah I'm laughing. I haven't laughed in . . .

Yafa And the soldier that shot me is climbing down to our side of the fence and she's chuckling to herself.

Deborah A laugh that fills my whole body and . . .

She turns to face **Yafa***.* **Benjamin** *stands between them as if he needs to protect* **Yafa***.* **Deborah** *takes a side step to pass him.* **Benjamin** *sidesteps into her way. She side steps in the opposite direction and again he steps into her path.* **Yafa** *gently guides* **Benjamin** *out of the way and faces* **Deborah***. A moment as they face each other and then . . . they hug.*

Benjamin And we must be in a parallel universe because everywhere you look people are shaking hands, talking together and hugging and it's . . .

He is lost for words. **Deborah** *and* **Yafa** *break their embrace. The three of them look at each other.*

Deborah What now?

Benjamin *and* **Yafa** *look at each other and take a breath. Snap to . . .*

Thursday

Genoa. By the Mediterranean Sea.

The Scottish kids, all but **Ross***, are gathered. They're still in their school uniforms but there's a touch of the* Lord of the Flies *about them now. They look feral. Ties are worn as belts or round their heads Rambo-style, clothes are torn and dirty, and none of them have washed for days. Only* **Meera** *looks neat and tidy still – like she's about to walk into the exam hall.*

They are on the beach, looking out to the sea. **Kyle** *spins his fidget spinner.*

Emma So when will it happen?

Meera When will what happen?

Kayleigh   We just have to be patient. That's right isn't it, Kyle?

Sara   It's not as far as I thought.

Eli   It's quite far.

Sara   Hardly. We can totally walk that.

Meera   Apart from the sea being in the way.

Sara   The Holy Land. Feels better now we can actually see it.

Eli   We can't see it.

Sara   Duh, yeah. It's just there.

Eli   That's Corsica.

Sara   Oh.

Emma   But behind that, Israel right?

Eli   I mean there's Sardinia, Sicily, Tunisia, Libya, Crete. But yeah.

Sara   So quite a long walk then.

Meera   What do you mean walk?

Sara   Don't ask me. Thought that was the plan.

Meera   To walk across the Mediterranean Sea? Tell me you don't think we suddenly have the power to walk on water?

Kayleigh   Course not.

Meera   Thank God for that.

Kayleigh   Nobody's walking on water. The sea will part. Won't it, Kyle?

Meera   What. The. Actual . . .?

Kayleigh   Miracles are happening everywhere.

Meera (*to* **Kyle**)   This? This is the plan?

Kyle *just keeps on spinning.* **Demi** *scrolls on her phone, wide-eyed at what she reads.*

Kayleigh   Lay off him, Meera.

Meera   Because he's a 'prophet'?

Kayleigh   How can you still be so . . . when you know what we are part of?

Demi   Turn on your phone.

Meera   I've read the news. Kids are mobilising. It's a political movement.

Kayleigh   Led by people who were all visited by God on the same night!

Meera   Which God, Kayleigh? Shintoists, Buddists, Jainists, Pagans, Mayans – they're all at it. How many gods am I actually supposed to believe?

Demi   Guys . . .

Kayleigh   I'm not saying I understand it.

Meera   All this is . . . a sort of hysteria. Mass self-hypnosis.

Emma   Not the pens again.

Meera   There was ink in those pens.

Ravi   Why would our brains not let us see it?

Eli   Don't start her on about that documentary again. The woman who was paralysed after a bash to her head.

Meera   She couldn't move the entire right side of her body. Not even when they stuck pins in her. She's sure it's because she bashed the right side of her head and is outraged when the neurosurgeon tells her it's all in her mind. But the neurosurgeon knows she's wrong because /

Eli   / Because the right side of your head controls the left side of your body.

Sara   I don't get it.

Meera   This woman was so convinced the bash to her head would hurt her that her mind made her paralysed. Shame her subconscious didn't know how brains work well enough to paralyse the right side.

Eli   You mean left.

Meera *ignores him.*

Meera   Don't underestimate the power of suggestion. Our minds can do all sorts of mad stuff. But even they have limits. We can't make the Mediterranean Sea part in two. It's just not possible. So *why* are we waiting here?

Demi   Guys! Turn on your phones.

The all get out their phones. All except **Kyle** *who spins.*

Ravi   What the . . .?

Jay   Is this for real?

Eli   Holy pretzel!

Jay   Is everybody seeing this?

Sara   It's . . .

Eli   Yeah.

Sara   It's . . .

Emma   What's the big deal?

Kayleigh   It's another miracle.

Emma   You think?

Meera   It's fake news.

Kayleigh   It's the bloody BBC, Meera!

Meera   A missile can't just melt away into nothing like a Solero in the sun.

Demi   There are thousands of witnesses.

Emma   You guys aren't talking about the *Bake Off* results are you?

Demi   North Korea, Emma!

Emma   Alright! That smug beardy guy winning *Bake Off*'s also pretty miraculous if you ask me.

Kayleigh   Believe, Meera.

Meera   Ok then. Ok. Over to you, Kyle. Make the sea part.

Kayleigh   It doesn't work like that.

Meera   I'll believe. When I see it with my own eyes.

Kayleigh   He can't just . . . just because you tell him to.

Meera   Come on, Kyle. Time to show us why God visited you.

All eyes on **Kyle***. ***Kyle** *stops spinning. He closes his eyes, breathes deeply. Everybody else holds their breath, willing the sea to part. Nothing happens. Finally* **Kyle** *opens his eyes and speaks.*

Kyle   Where's Ross?

Jay   He went for a piss. Chatting to some guys last time I saw him.

Meera   Kyle?

Kyle   We wait for Ross.

Meera *laughs with frustration.* **Ross** *enters.*

Ross   What? What are you all looking at me for?

Meera   Kyle's waiting on you. Then he's going to make the sea part.

Ross   That the plan? You won't need the boat I just got us then.

Kyle *smiles a big relieved smile and hugs* **Ross***.*

Ross   What? What did I say?

Kyle   We go by boat.

Snap to . . .

Later the same day.

Kayleigh *and* **Meera** *sit sopping wet, covered in blankets. They are in shock. Neither speaks for some time.*

Eventually . . .

Meera Did you see what happened to Sara?

Kayleigh Ravi was helping her. Until that big wave came . . . I didn't see them after that.

Meera And Eli?

Kayleigh *shakes her head.*

Kayleigh Kyle knew. When they'd pulled us in, he was the only other person still . . . I saw them reach for him but he just turned away. If he'd reached out, they could have saved him. But he just floated away.

Meera Shhhh. Let's not talk about it /

Kayleigh He knew he would drown.

Meera We all knew we would drown, Kayleigh. That thing Ross called a boat was barely more than a dingy. We got on it because Kyle told us to. If he knew . . .

Kayleigh We got on it because we believed.

Meera Because we were stupid.

Kayleigh *doesn't respond.*

Meera I'll phone home. They'll fly out and collect us.

Kayleigh No.

Meera Kayleigh . . .

Kayleigh Then it's all for nothing.

Meera We should never have come.

A silence. **Kayleigh** *mulls but she can't accept it.*

Kayleigh That woman who thought she was paralysed. We're all her in a way. Insisting the world should work the way we think it should. Maybe God's a doctor or a scientist, trying to show us how things are but we're just not listening.

Meera I'd rather God didn't exist than that he used me as his lab rat.

Kayleigh Sometimes left is right and right is left. Come with me, Meera. Let's finish what we started. For Kyle and Ross and Emma and Ravi and Sara and Demi and Jay.

Hearing their names hits **Meera** *hard. Will she go? Snap to . . .*

Friday

India.

A rudimentary home in a small North Indian village. Propped up on the floor is
Nadin (*eighteen*). *His wrists and ankles are tied with rope. He is gagged.*
Anika (*fifteen*) *sits watching him. Eventually* **Nadin** *wakes.*

Anika   Hi.

Nadin *realises he is restrained and begins to struggle.*

Anika   Sorry, sorry. Sorry. Sorry, I'm . . . I'm so so sorry.

The ropes hold fast. **Nadin** *shouts his frustration but it is muffled by the gag.*

Anika   Please – just stay calm if you can.

More muffled and aggressive talk.

I'll take it all off. I promise. Just. Please. Let me talk.

Nadin *spits out more incomprehensible abuse.*

Anika   Please, Nadin. Just listen. This once.

Nadin *continues to spit muffled abuse and begins to bang his fists and legs against*
the floor.

Anika   Even now?

Every day, I try to get you to talk to me, to teach me about the world but you never
hear my voice. When we were married, I begged you to let me continue to go to
school but it was like I hadn't spoken.

But I learnt anyway, Nadin. From the older women in the village, I learnt about
Brahmi and Shankhpushpi and how they can bring on sleep. Ashwagandha too and
Jatamansi, Vacha and Sarpagandha. And I mixed them up and put them in your food
and I watched your greedy mouth swallow it all down.

Nadin *struggles even more.*

Anika   I begged Matä and Pitä not to marry us. 'But your sister is getting married
and we can afford only one wedding.' I told them there was no shame in letting a
thirteen-year-old remain unmarried even if you know you will never be able to afford
a wedding for her in the future.

I don't know why I have a tongue in my mouth.

You didn't have a choice either. And I know that hurt you. And ever since you have
made all the choices to try to feel better about them taking away that single big
choice. You know how it feels to be ignored.

Nadin *stops struggling.*

Anika   Will you listen now? Please.

Nadin *nods. She takes off the gag.*

Nadin   This is about your dream.

Anika   Yes. You did listen.

Nadin   It's not every day a person tells you Devi Mahatmya visited them.

Anika   I grew a tongue, Nadin. After all these years of not being heard I grew a tongue as huge as Kali's. But it was not Raktabija's blood I licked with my giant tongue. I licked the blood of mortals and I killed their demons. I swallowed war and gave peace.

Nadin   It is blasphemy.

Anika   It is prophesy. I will lead an army to the mountain of my dream.

Nadin   You are a goddess then? And they will write Vedas about you I suppose?

Anika   I know. It is ridiculous. Me! I had the dream five days ago and all I have managed to do since then is to drug my husband.

I tried to speak to the women. They were too frightened even to hear me out – what would the men say if they heard us talking? That is why I need you, Nadin. To speak for me. To persuade others to travel. I need you to lead.

Nadin   Neither of us are going anywhere.

Anika   I have the keys to your *jugaad*.

This is a red rag to a bull – **Nadin** *is furious.*

Nadin   Give them back.

Anika   I will. I just /

Nadin   How dare you.

He tries to free himself. He is pulling at the ropes causing them to tear into his skin.

Anika   You will hurt yourself. Please, don't.

Nadin   You.

Pulling his fists apart despite great physical pain.

Won't.

And again.

Take.

And again.

What's mine.

Anika   I won't touch the *jugaad*. Here.

She takes out the keys and lays them on the floor in front of him.

I won't do anything unless you say we should. I will untie you and put balm where the rope has torn your skin. I don't even have to come. I will pack your bag and make sure you have everything you could possibly need for your journey. If you take my dream on as if it were your own, I will never step out of line again.

Nadin   Untie me.

Anika   Do you believe in my dream?

Nadin   Now, Anika.

Anika   I will. Just say you believe. Please.

Nadin   Untie me!

Anika   Only if you believe.

Nadin   Anika!

She shakes her head, distressed. It is hard for her to disobey him like this.

Nadin *calls out in frustration.* **Anika** *cries and backs away. After a little while.*

Nadin   Ok.

Anika   You believe? You will act on it as your own?

Nadin *nods.*

Anika   Say it. Please, Nadin.

Nadin   I will speak of your dream as if it is my own. If our people don't listen, I will speak out in the next village and the next. I will gather an army.

Anika *could weep with relief. She smothers him in kisses.*

Anika   Oh Nadin, thank you. Thank you. Thank you.

Nadin   Untie me.

Anika   Of course.

She unties his hands. He rubs his wrists and then grabs **Anika** *by the throat.*

Nadin   You are a joke, Anika. You are the last person on earth a deity would ever visit. A giant tongue? I should cut yours out.

Anika *manages to pull away.* **Nadin** *tries to go after her but his feet are still tied.*

Anika   Impatience has always been your worst quality, Nadin. You couldn't even wait until I untied your feet.

Nadin   Get back here. Don't you dare walk away from me.

He tries to untie his legs. The knot is tight and, in his haste, is tightening not loosening.

Anika *takes the opportunity to reach in for the keys before he can grab her again.*

Anika Thank you for the loan of the *jugaad*. I say loan but there's a very good chance I won't bring it back.

Nadin If you walk out that door, Anika . . .

He's trying to untie his legs but she's gone.

Anika!

Snap to . . .

Saturday

Mount Hermon. Night.

Meera *is alone. She is wearing many layers of clothes – we might recognise something worn earlier by* **Kayleigh** *– but she is still shivering. It is freezing.*

She looks at the battery level on her phone and considers. She puts it back in her pocket then, on impulse, changes her mind, pulls it out and dials.

Meera Mum, it's me. I /

It's her mum's answer machine. She is winded by the disappointment of it. She waits for the beep.

Hi. You're working the night shift. I pictured you sitting by the phone waiting for my call but I suppose . . . life goes on. It's me by the way. Meera. Sorry I didn't answer your calls. Maybe you've given up? I'm on a new phone so I don't know if you've been trying me . . . My old one got a bit . . . wet. I can't speak for long because I'm low on battery and this is my only torch so . . . It's so dark here. And cold. I told Kayleigh. I told her it would be freezing at night but she was determined to ditch her layers.

It was so hot and the climb was . . .

I'm on a mountain called Mount Hermon. It's probably where Jesus was transfigured into divine form. It might also have been where Moses was given the Ten Commandments. Lots of people have different theories why we might come here as opposed to, I don't know, Mecca or Machu Picchu or Kashi Vishwanath or Glastonbury Tor. I wish it had been Glastonbury. You could have driven us.

The Arabs just call it Snow Mountain but Hermon has a really complicated meaning in Hebrew. An Israeli guy explained it to me. It's when something changes and part of it is lost. A bit like the food we eat, our body takes nutrients, transforms them into energy and expels the rest as . . . you know. Poo. So there's death but only in the context of transformation, of change. But I googled it and a baby name website said it just meant 'devoted to destruction' which is . . . well, a little worrying.

I'm a bit scared if I'm honest, Mum. I'd really like you to /

She looks at her phone. It has gone black.

Damn it!

She shouts into the void.

Anybody have a charger I can borrow?

She laughs and then she cries but not for long. She pulls herself together.

Bye, Mum.

Snap to . . .

Sunday

Mount Hermon. Early evening.

Meera *survived the night and the many layers of clothes are now strewn around her. She's down to her vest after a swelteringly hot day. She's improvising to the tune 'Dumb Ways to Die' by Tangerine Kitty.*

Meera (*sings*)

　　Run away with your friends

　　Cause the ink's gone from all the pens

　　Use a dinghy to cross the Med

　　Keep on going when all your friends are dead

　　Dumb ways to die

　　So many dumb ways to die

　　Dumb ways to di-ie-ie

　　So many dumb ways to die.

She's stopped singing and all that's left is silence. She calls out into the wind . . .

IS ANYBODY THERE?! IS ANYBODY COMING?!

Nothing.

She sits and looks around her for a bit. Then she bursts into tears. Then big rolling sobs. She gives into it so much that she doesn't notice when . . .

Anika *drags herself forward – a shell of a person.*

Anika (*to* **Meera**)   Water. Do you have water?

Meera *doesn't want to give away the last of her water but doesn't feel she has a choice.*

Anika *drinks deep and long.* **Meera** *almost tells her to stop but swallows the words. When* **Anika** *has revived she asks . . .*

Where is everybody?

Meera *shrugs.*

Anika   But it's Sunday. We're all supposed to gather today. Before sunset.

Meera   I know.

Anika   But the sun is setting . . .

Meera   I know. Are we in the right place?

Anika   Yes. The place of exile where Rakshasas were cast out by Vishnu for Brahma.

Meera   Kyle said it was where God first stood when he made the world, where Satan fell to. Which is it?

Anika   I only know that the goddess told me to come here.

Meera   And did it look like this in your dream? That tree over there, this curve in the rock?

Anika   I think so. Did it in yours?

Meera   Kyle never said.

He should be here. Not me. Only vision I ever had was the telly kind.

Anika   But you found your way here?

Meera   That tree. The one with leaves sticking up like little flames. Felt like I'd seen it before.

Anika   You dreamed it.

Meera   No. Just liked the look of it, that's all.

Did you travel alone?

Anika   Nobody would come with me.

Meera   Not even, like, your best friend? Must have been lonely.

Anika   The goddess was with me.

Meera   My best friend – Kayleigh. She . . . she froze to death halfway up the mountain. I took her clothes, after. Probably kept me alive. I felt bad but she always used to borrow my stuff without asking so . . .

I should be doing my exams. I love exams. The colour-coded revision schedule, guessing what questions will come up and the adrenaline buzz when you come out and most of your classmates have messed it up but you know you've slayed it. I should be at home.

I won't survive another night here. It's too cold.

Anika   We won't die. People will come before the sun sets. Have faith.

Meera *laughs, full of scorn.*

Anika   You don't believe?

Meera   Humans do the worst things to each other in the name of God.

Anika   And some of the best. How did I find the strength to stand up to my husband, to leave my village and travel here? How did I find my voice if it wasn't the goddess?

Meera   Maybe because you wanted to? The sun has set. Look. Nobody's coming.

Anika *doubts for the first time.*

Anika   They must. The goddess showed me.

Meera   Then she lied.

Anika   No. We're both here, at the same spot.

Meera   We got it wrong. The others are all gathering – the Shintoists, the Buddhists, the Muslims, the Jainists, the Sikhs. They're all together on some other mountain while we die here of thirst.

Anika   We're in the right place.

Meera   Then they didn't make it. The others. They died trying to get here. Or gave up. Either way, we die.

Anika   We are here for a reason. You and I were led here to this place.

Meera   I wasn't.

Anika   You'd seen the tree. In your vision.

Meera   No, I . . .

Anika   You pretend you have no faith but without it you couldn't be here!

There's truth in this.

You recognised the tree.

Meera   It could have been any tree. They all look the same. I was tired of climbing.

Anika   Describe what you saw.

Meera   It was a daydream at most. I /

Anika   Describe it.

Meera   I've never had a vision – I just let myself hope! When I'm not raging about coming on this stupid-ass crusade, I close my eyes and I . . . hope.

Anika   Use your tongue and describe it.

Meera *closes her eyes.*

Meera   I'm sitting in a beautiful place, high up with a clear view down to the world below and I'm sheltering under a tree and I'm not sure whether I'm sheltering from the heat or the cold but its leaves look to me like little flames. And all around me it's so quiet but on the wind, I hear an army of kids walking up the mountain. Not an army. A . . . a 'force'. From all over – Azerbaijan to Zambia and every country in between. And I see them walking towards me and they all look and sound different but as they talk and laugh and muck around together, their differences melt away.

The stage fills with children. Every actor in the youth theatre. Every young person who has worked on the production: the set designers, backstage team, the lighting operator. They all gather on stage.

And they're hopeful too. Because they know we hold the power. Here on Mount Hermon. 'Devoted to destruction'. Not to end the world but to change it. And we believe that together we can do that. Because Kyle was right. We are the answer.

But before we do anything, we sit down together and share our food and water and somebody, one of the kids, reaches into the bottom of their bag and pulls out an undamaged packet of jammy dodgers.

Anika It wasn't a daydream. Open your eyes.

Meera *opens her eyes and sees. A hundred children in various states of disarray reflecting the physical demands of their journeys here, carrying blankets, water and food.*

Meera There's hundreds of them.

Anika Thousands.

Meera We're not going to die.

Anika Do you believe now?

Meera *looks at the thousands of children surrounding her.*

Meera I do. I believe in us.

Blackout.

Crusaders

BY FRANCES POET

*Notes on rehearsal and staging, drawn from a workshop with the writer,
held at the National Theatre, October 2019*

Context

Lead director Ria Parry welcomed the participants and asked them to begin by
describing what drew them to the play. Answers included:

- The play has accessible roles which allow young people to develop a variety of
  acting skills.
- The play has a strong ensemble element, so it helps bring young people of
  different ages/year groups together.
- The play contains lots of strong visual moments.
- The 'strangeness' of the beginning: how the play delves into things like magic
  realism.
- The play contains a mix of theatrical styles; e.g. there are fourth-wall moments,
  then moments where it's broken.
- Several people had chosen the play collaboratively with their young people, who
  were interested in the journeys of the characters, themes of the play, and felt the
  language wasn't patronising to young people.

Ria reminded everyone of the importance of remembering why you're doing the
play and what excites you about it. Your personal mission and connection to the play is
what gets you through the sticky bits, when the pressure's on.

How Frances came to write the play

Frances started work on the play eighteen months previously, after having a conversation
with somebody in Glasgow about the Children's Crusade in the Middle Ages. She was
intrigued by this.

The Children's Crusade was a failed, unofficial crusade by European Christians to
regain the Holy Land, said to have taken place in 1212. The crusaders left Northern
France, led by Stephen of Cloyes, and Germany, led by Nicholas. Both children, totally
separately, felt they had been visited by God. The traditional story is put together from
factual and mythical events which include: visions by a French boy and a German boy,
an intention to peacefully convert Muslims in the Holy Land to Christianity and bands
of children marching to Genoa where half were shipwrecked and half sold into slavery.

The idea came before Greta Thunberg though her activism has tied in very beautifully
to make the play resonate. In fact, Frances was influenced by what happened in response
to the Stoneman Douglas High School shooting: The Never Again Movement (Emma

Gonzalez and Douglas Hogg), an American student-led political action committee for gun control that advocates for tighter regulations to prevent gun violence. Young people were standing up against big political movements and corporations, making their voices heard and spreading a message of hope.

Frances knew she wanted to set one scene in Britain and felt the energy around an exam room was a useful moment. She also found herself posing the question: what happens if this kid who agitates the others isn't popular' How might he be able to persuade a group of his peers to abandon their exam for his 'crusade'?

She then undertook a period of research in Drummond High School in Edinburgh, including workshop sessions with a group of thirteen-year-olds. What was interesting was the students' readiness to engage with the darker elements of the text: in terms of where the plotting takes the characters and how easy it was for them, considering current affairs, to go to dark places. As she began writing in earnest, the Greta movement started which allowed the play to grow and become even more current.

Approaching the play #1

Ria split participants into groups and, using A3 sheets and pens, asked them to write down all the big questions they've been burning to ask about the play. She asked them to broadly split them into three areas: The World of the Play, Characters in the Play and the Staging of the Play. After about ten minutes, feedback was given as:

World:

Transitions #1: How do we realise the scene changes?

Accents: If we decide not to do accents, how can we clearly show moves to different countries?

Research: How do we get the aspects of cultural research right?

Big Question: If 'we' are the answer, what is the question?

Characters:

Names, Gender and Diversity swaps: Is this allowed if our cast isn't the right ratio?

Children and Extras: The crowd scene at the end works best with lots of young people onstage, so can we bring more in for this?

Specific Characters #1: Character biographies.

Specific Characters #2: Deborah, Yafa, Benjamin: What happens to them at the end?

Staging:

Moments: Cage and Mountain: How do we stage these?

Transitions #2: 'Snap-to' scene changes: How definite is that, can it be more fluid?

Aesthetics: Did Frances have a visual language in mind for the play? How much visual language can we add to enhance the storytelling without taking away from the writer's vision?

Approaching the play #2

Ria asked the participants to look at a particular section of text, from Kyle's speech '*Tu as une belle voix, Demi*' (on p. 341) to Ross's line: 'How did you do that?' (on p. 342).

Going around the circle, everyone took a line or character section.

Ria remarked that it's useful, whenever working with a living writer, to discover their intentions for a play/scene/section before you are going to direct it.

She then asked: why is this section challenging?

- Something mystical is happening here. The characters need to realise this.
- How do you make sure you communicate this to an audience, without it seeming as though Kyle is just tricking everyone?
- They are two key things to pay attention to here, which you can explore with your company:
  - How does Kyle deliver his lines?
  - How do the other characters react to what is happening?

After reading through the section, Ria asked for suggestions which would technically affect the text. Answers included:

- The actor playing Kyle could deliver the lines 'flat' – without colour/emotion. He needs to be low focus.
- The other actors could do the opposite – delivering their lines as expressively as possible.
- There could be a slight overlap – if a character has a line after a Kyle line, they could slightly cut in before he's finished.
- You could explore physical reaction/movement for the actor playing Kyle.

The group attempted to implement some of these suggestions. Ria said that sometimes notes take a while to work in, so it is sometimes useful to ask yourself if you want to focus on one specific note before adding others in. Too many notes can oversaturate the actors.

Frances noted that Kyle isn't surprised by what is happening. He has seen it all play out. His lack of surprise can be a grounding thing for everyone else. So, this could be confirmation for him. It could be a 'déjà vu journey' for the actor.

One of the participants suggested rehearsing the scene without Kyle in it, doing the conversation with the other characters, and then inserting him afterwards to see the effect.

Ria thought this might be a useful exercise but that it's also important to recognise the vocal score/shifts in the piece. Think about what the audience is hearing. You, as director, need to guide them through it aurally.

Staging, design and transitions

Ria asked everyone to think about a specific moment of ensemble staging: the 'cage' (p. 348). She split everyone into groups and urged them to be playful and engage in the same type of exploration they might do with their companies. Two seconds of this exercise might unlock something when you're working on the sequence with young people. This kind of visual moment is exciting. You might have no idea what the ultimate staging is but it's a challenge to work that out collaboratively.

Ria invited a participant to read out the written stage direction. She urged everyone to think about the sequence in three parts:

- Text – What character/s says during the sequence?
- Movement – What movement might be involved in the sequence?
- Tech – What kind of technology might be available to support the sequence?

Regardless of technology it must work. This is an important story moment, so think about movement before technology. Frances is totally open about this sequence. Do whatever you think tells the best story. Ria urged the group to keep reminding themselves of the beats which Frances has laid down in the text for them. They are a great guidebook through the sequence and prevent ideas becoming too overblown.

What is the 'money-no-object' version of this sequence?

- Projections
- CCTV cameras cutting in and out
- Border Guard Frank as a face on a cinema screen
- Lighted haze to represent the bars
- A physical cage which is lowered

Ria noted that there are lots of brilliant options and it's great to be ambitious. However, she suggested that you work within your means and play to your strengths and the strengths of your group. For example, you might have a young student who's a great sound designer. In which case, base your tech enhancements around sound design.

The ending

How do you stage the ending?

Ria asked the group to explore and improvise another section of the play: the mountain (p. 366). Ria suggested that each group set three rules which make the choreography easier; for example:

- As you enter you must focus on the audience, looking out.
- You must seek physical contact with another person on stage.
- Meera engages with everyone when she opens her eyes.

Ria noted that the key thing with big set pieces like this is preparation. You can move away from an original idea but it's easiest to have a baseline to work from. It helps with the rhythm and timing which you want to achieve.

Frances warned that it's important not to play the ending before it's happened. We need to engage with this moment at the same time as Meera. The audience needs to believe all is lost, until she discovers it's not.

Transitions

How do you manage the transitions?

Frances uses the term 'snap-to'. What does she mean by this? How quick are those moments, and can these be longer transitions?

Ria noted that it can be very easy for directors to get carried away with scene changes. We tend to try and be clever, thereby overcomplicating the story and destabilising the writer's vision.

It is important, whenever possible, to trust the power and reality of the writing. Frances has written it to take us to a different place.

A 'snap-to' slaps us in the face, rather than taking us there gently. Sometimes, there is something nice in an audience having to catch up. Don't add too many extra bits. It puts you in danger of mucking up the rhythm. Frances doesn't think the play can carry long, plodding scene changes. A 'snap-to' adds energy. If the action starts mid-scene, a 'snap-to' can help.

Casting the production

Names, genders and ethnicity

Frances is okay with changing some names and genders and making small changes to pronouns, e.g. 'he said' to 'she said', to accommodate this.

Blind casting is also a possibility. However, this is a nuanced dilemma. How will gender-blind casting shift the texture of the play?

Ideally Deborah and Benjamin would retain their given genders. Frances enjoys the contrast of Deborah's toughness with Benjamin's (mis)understanding about what women like. Frances thinks it will be difficult to cast Nadin and Anika as the same sex, because of placing the world and catching up with it would knock the story off-kilter.

Frances would be disappointed to see Meera become male, as she has deliberately let a young woman carry this important journey.

If your Kyle is a girl, you could change the name to Kyla (Kylie has too many pop culture connotations and doesn't feel like it has the same sort of weight).

One of the participants asked whether the names of the British students could be changed as their names were felt to suggest certain ethnicities. Frances tried to choose names for these characters that could transcend specific ethnicity. Ria urged participants to stick with the names. Frances has already given a lot of licence in the notes at the top of the script.

Border Guard Frank

One of the participants asked if Border Guard Frank could be cast, rather than just being a disembodied voice.

Frances is happy for companies to cast and solve this. However, she thinks keeping him as a voice is useful. He is the only adult in the play and is deliberately 'othered'. If it was visual, i.e. a young person, you'd need to create a clear way of making the audience aware that that young person is playing an adult. You could make a stylistic shift, e.g. mic them.

Characters and characterisation

Ria noted that it's useful to hear Frances's response to characters. You must find a way of adhering to this while allowing your group to put their own spin on the parts.

Frances suggested the actor playing Kyle doesn't need to be your strongest performer. Even though he kicks off the play and has an important role in the story, it might do something to emphasise his lack of command and the fact that it is coming from an unexpected place. However, the roles of Meera and Benjamin, in particular, require strong performers.

Kyle

Kyle is the least attention-seeking character in the play. He's the guy who never speaks in class. If Frances had this dream, she'd be telling everyone. However, Kyle doesn't do this. He gets no enjoyment from freaking them all out. He knows how this will play out and is not relishing it. He is not tricking the other characters. There is a version where Kyle is on the autistic spectrum, but Frances hasn't written this in. The fidget spinner is a manifestation of Kyle's nervous energy. It's not performative. Young people still play with fidget spinners (certainly in Scotland!).

Benjamin

Frances has always seen Benjamin as an Israeli. He is younger than Deborah, so he has not done his National Service yet. He's from the same world as Deborah but he's not at the same stage as her. He's worrying about synagogue and lessons. Non-threatening and safe. Needs a good comic performer. His laughter covers a multitude of pain.

Meera

The protagonist. She is exceptionally intelligent. Vaguely geeky. Rational. She loves exams and learning. A pragmatist. Bound by the rules she's in. Plays by the rules and comes top. Her journey involves realising that sometimes you need to break out from the rules to achieve what is right. Frances likes the fact this responsibility is given to a female character so would prefer her to be cast as a girl.

Kayleigh

Has a much more ready faith. Frances isn't sure what her faith is but she's predisposed to believe. She's a quick thinker and is very perceptive.

Eli

Despite being smart, he is 'a bit of a dick'. The kind of guy you love and find funny, despite yourself. Massively annoying. He forges his own route, knowing that he's going to rub people up the wrong way in the process.

Sara

She's a bit more of a sheep. She's not a leader. Easily led. She tips when everyone else tips.

Ross

A big personality. He's not the brains of the class but is someone to be reckoned with.

Jay

Quite sensitive. A bit like Kayleigh. Nothing is said specifically to convert him, but Jay gets on board with Kyle's message very quickly.

Emma

Very private. Sharing information with her best friend about her mum. Kyle's newfound ability really gets under her skin and into her head. A natural sceptic.

Demi

Really smart. A questioner who sees everything from all angles. A loner but she watches the group dynamic from the sideline. Independent. Sticks up for people.

Ravi

Kyle and Ravi go back a long way, so he's really concerned about his best mate when the weirdness starts happening. Not a leader in the group. He's the one who's not going to laugh at Kyle. History makes him trust Kyle.

Valentina

Representative of all the kids. Older and a slight mother figure. Parenting the younger kids. However, this makes her massively vulnerable. Worried about her own parents.

Yafa

A sensitive dreamer. Gentle. He's not aggressive. He hasn't looked to find this calling but he's comfortable with going on this journey. Willing to risk his life for the dream.

Deborah

Her National Service has taken its toll on her. She's full of repressed trauma at what she has had to do. It's buried deep and has made her hard but there is a softness and sensitivity there too which we see a glimpse of when she hugs Yafa.

Anika (pronounced 'Aneeka')

Frances can't emphasise enough that she has no voice. It's a super steady build in her confidence. She's not instantly confident. Even when offered an opportunity to find her voice, her instinct is to have her husband speak for her. She married very young. There's no pleasure in her tying up her husband and it surprises her that she has had the guts to do it. At no point did she think she could ever be capable of leaving him tied up and going on the journey herself but she finds the strength to do that by the end of the scene.

Border Guard Frank

Frank is a difficult character. He is a wimp, but he has power. So, it'll be difficult to find that balance. You might have an instinct to make him shouty and cross but go for more nuance. Pin down the bits when he's terrifying and the bits when he's ridiculous.

Extras

Several of the participants wanted to include extra young people in the crowd scene at the end of the play. While the story can be told without bringing more people onstage, if you have the option to do so and the correct safeguarding measures in place, it is always a lovely image seeing big ensembles onstage.

'Deborah', 'Yafa', 'Benjamin'

Frances referred to an earlier draft of the script in which she named these three as appearing at the end. She's killed off so many other characters during the play, it'd be nice to see these three surviving and storming the stage at the end.

So, what is the question?

If 'we are the answer', what is the question in the play?
  The question could be:

Why are we so screwed?

How, as human beings, do we find ourselves here?

How do we live better and live a less broken life?

Ria urged the participants to have these conversations/questionings with their groups.
  Frances noted that there's no reference to climate change in the play and yet reading the play at this moment in 2019, it resonates on that level.
  It's deliberate that the 'question' is not articulated in the play. The question is what the makers and their audience deem it to be.

Exercises for use in rehearsal

Ria took the participants through some exercises. At the end of each exercise she offered a 'director's aside' explaining when and what each is useful for.

Exercise: Circle (get to know you)

1 Form a circle.
2 Swap places so that you don't know the person next to you.
3 Split into pairs (with that person)
4 You have 2 mins (1 min. each) to discover four things about each other:
   a. Your partner's name.
   b. One thing they like.
   c. One thing they hate.
   d. One interesting fact about your partner.
5 When the time is up, share the information you've gathered with the group.
6 If you can't remember or misremember something, make it up. If this happens, your partner must endorse your make-believe discovery.

Director's aside

This exercise is best used at the beginning of a rehearsal process. It is good for team building, aims to eliminate shyness and is very gentle.

Exercise: Prison guard

1 In a circle, place enough chairs within the circle so that half the participants are standing up and half are sitting down.
2 There should be one spare chair, but with one person standing behind it.
3 The distance between the standing participant and the chair should be a little over arm's length.
4 After a quick recap of names (of the people sitting down) the person behind the spare chair should call to one of the people sitting and beckon them to come and sit on the spare chair.
5 The person standing behind them must tap them on the shoulder before they get a chance to escape to the new position.
6 Once two or three rounds of this are enjoyed, increase the difficulty by inserting a new rule: The person standing can only beckon the person sitting, by winking at them.
7 Swap sitters and standers, then repeat.

Director's aside

This exercise is good for learning and remembering names. It is also good for bringing laughter into the room.

Exercise: Circle of height

1 Organise yourself into a line according to your heights: shortest to tallest.

2 Once this is done, go down lines and say your names.

3 Now re-form the line, this time according to your house number (house names should go first and alphabetically).

4 Now organise yourselves into a circle, according to your names.

5 Going alphabetically around the circle, one person says their name and everyone has to repeat it. For example:

John: John.

Group: John!

6 Repeat the exercise one more time.

Collectively everyone repeats names with power.

Pay attention to the collective rhythm and musicality here. Of both the words, and the group.

Director's aside

This game is good for remembering names, as well as finding collective vocal strength of group. It is useful if you need to boost a room's energy. If energy drops, pick energy back up, as a group.

Exercise: Eyes up, eyes down

1 Everyone forms a circle.

2 When Ria says 'Eyes down' everyone looks down at the floor.

3 When Ria says 'Eyes up' everyone looks up, choosing one person to look at (i.e. where their eyes would be if they were looking at you).

4 If you happen to make eye contact with someone and they are likewise looking at you, then you're both 'out'. You both must step out of the circle, the circle closes up and the game carries on.

Director's aside

This game is good for after lunch and breaks. It brings laughter back into the room and is wonderfully childish.

Notes and references

1 Approaching the Play #2

A couple of participants flagged up that there is an episode of *Doctor Who* called 'Midnight' (modern series 4, episode 10) where the characters do exactly this, i.e. talk over, pre-empt each other, starting and finishing somebody's sentences.

2 Accents and Pronunciation

Frances suggests it's better not to attempt accents as it could be fraught with difficulty. It's more about the young people communicating the truth of the situation. A light symbolic touch will convey a lot more. You might need to research the pronunciation of the following words and phrases:

p. 340 – *Je t'aide à prendre ton oreille*

p. 345 – . . . Papa Ezofowicz?

p. 352 – my *umi*

p. 353 – Stresses on 'Allah', '*Rahmani*' and '*Nafsari*'

p. 353 – *Shaytani*

p. 359 – Accent on 'Jainists'?

p. 362 – Brahmi, Shankhpushpi, Ashwagandha, Jatamasi, Vacha and Sarpgandha, Matä and Pitä

p. 363 – Devi Mahatmya, Raktabija, *jugaad*

p. 365 – Mount Hermon

p. 365 – Kashi Vishwanath

p. 367 – Rakshasas

Note: Both Frances and Ria suggest that different characters can be better at pronouncing words than others. For example, Border Guard Frank can be rubbish at it!

3 Locations

See Frances's notes at the top of the script. It's okay to root it in your own location. You could almost imagine a version of this play where place names are removed. What you want to discover is the truth and universality of the situation these young people find themselves in.

4 Connections flashback

Frances read *Zero for the Young Dudes!* by Alistair McDowall after drafting her play and was struck that *Crusaders* felt almost like a prequel to it. However, that would make the ending very bleak! Frances prefers to think that they end up saving the world. Nevertheless, it's worth a read.

From a workshop led by Ria Parry
with notes by John R. Wilkinson

Witches Can't
Be Burned

by Silva Semerciyan

If you keep on doing the same thing, over and over again, you'll keep on getting the same results, time and time again. St Paul's have won the schools Playfest competition three years in a row, by selecting recognised classics from the canon and producing them at an exceptionally high level; it's a tried and trusted formula. With straight 'A's student and drama freak Anuka cast as Abigail Williams in *The Crucible* by Arthur Miller, the school seem to be well on course for another triumph, which would be a record. What could possibly go wrong?

However, as rehearsals gain momentum, Anuka has an epiphany – an experience resulting in her asking searching questions surrounding the text, the depiction and perception of female characters, the meaning of loyalty, and the values and traditions underpinning the very foundations of the school. Thus, the scene is set for a confrontation of epic proportions as Anuka seeks to break with tradition, before tradition breaks her and all young women like her, and reality begins to take on the ominous hue of Miller's fictionalised Salem.

Cast size
17–34: 14 F roles, 10 M roles, the rest any gender
Recommended for ages 14+

Silva Semerciyan is an American playwright living in the UK. Her play *I and the Village* premiered at Theatre503 in 2015 and was a finalist for the Bruntwood Prize and an Offie Award for Best New Play. Her other plays include *Another Man's Son* (winner of the William Saroyan Prize); *A Quest for Arthur* (National Theatre's Let's Play Series); *The Light Burns Blue* (Tonic Theatre's Platform Series); *Under a Cardboard Sea*, *The Window* and *The Tinderbox* (Bristol Old Vic); *Flashes* (Young Vic); and *Gather Ye Rosebuds* (winner of Best New Play, Brighton Fringe Festival). Her first radio play, *Varanasi*, was shortlisted for a BBC Audio Drama Award. She holds an MPhil in Playwriting from the University of Birmingham.

Thanks to Ola Animashawun, Tom Lyons, Audrey Sheffield, Orla O'Loughlin, Kirsten Adam and the NT Connections team; Steve Titchmarsh, Elizabeth Philps, Tom Turner, Bridget O'Donnell, Jack Maurice and students at South Gloucestershire and Stroud College; Lisa Gregan, the Bristol Old Vic and members of the Young Company; Tamsen Armstrong, Ildiko Mathe and as ever, David Caudery.

Characters

Girls of *The Crucible* cast

Sera (*plays Betty Parris*), *teaches baby ballet*
Anuka (*plays Abigail Williams*), *the leader*
Ruby (*plays Mary Warren*), *wants to be a priest*
Heloise (*plays Mercy Lewis*), *prone to taking things too far*
Maddie (*plays Susannah Walcott*), *part Transylvanian*
Layla (*plays Tituba*), *poster girl for the school*
Grace (*plays Goody Proctor*), *hockey fanatic*

Boys of *The Crucible* cast

Wolf (*plays Judge Danforth*), *the wild one*
Al (*plays Mr Hale*), *reluctant altar boy*
Skive (*plays the hangman*), *the gamer*
Bo (*plays Reverend Parris*), *the family hope*
Sam (*plays John Proctor*), *Anuka's best friend*

Teachers

Miss Alexi, *English and Drama teacher*
Mr Briggs, *English and Drama teacher*
Mr Thrower, *Headteacher*

Prefects
Lola, Tilly *and* **Evie**
Hockey girls
Parker *and* **Hill**
Other pupils of St Paul's

Setting

St Paul's, a co-educational secondary school. The play takes place in various locations in or near the school precinct.

Notes

... indicates a break in speech but continuation of internal dialogue: a character has something to say but either can't or won't

/ indicates the point of interruption in overlapping dialogue

The prefects could be either male or female, but in the tribunal sections of the interrogation sequence, the girls of *The Crucible* cast are mainly grilled by female prefects and the boys by male ones. This will allow for the kind of divisive rhetoric that can emerge in same-sex groups behind closed doors. However, not every single prefect need be female or male in these moments and elsewhere it is important that there is a mix of both sexes to prevent another kind of vilification of girls. As they are teacher-appointed leaders within the school, the prefects are the upholders of a system that they have inherited and do not question.

Because the play is challenging stereotypical representations of girls and women in theatre and literature, it's important that girls resist playing moments as bitchy even where comments may seem cutting or overly direct. The girls in *The Crucible* cast are loyal friends with a strong bond between them.

Likewise, the male banter can be punctuated with moments of sincerity to mitigate familiar representations of boys and men.

It is important that Thrower and Briggs are not depicted as consciously sexist as they do not believe they are or understand the full implications of their words and actions.

Prologue

The deep dark woods. Girls in Puritan dress are assembled around a cauldron. There is an exaggerated sense of the illicit about this gathering. A noise. **Sera** *as* **Betty** *gasps in fright.*

Anuka as Abigail   Keep your teeth, Betty Parris. T'were only the sound o' the wind in the trees. Tituba! Bring the pot. Build the fire. Boil the lot. Suzie, Betty, Mary, Mercy! Now the frogs. Drop them in. Now the hearts. Tear them up. Now the hair. Yes! From Abraham Corey.

Ruby as Mary   Thomas Faircluff.

Heloise as Mercy   Matthew Nurse.

Maddie as Susannah   Jacob Parker.

They drop them in and scurry away. **Abigail** *clutches hers.* **Tituba** *leans towards her.*

Layla as Tituba   Yessss, Miss Abby. Drop it in. Tituba know who you love. Abigail Williams gonna have John Proctor. Someday soon. His wife gonna die, and he gonna marry her. (**Abigail** *looks to the other girls with triumphant glee;* **Tituba** *hands her a vial.*) All she gotta do is drink dis blood.

Gasps. **Abigail** *hesitates briefly then drinks the blood with maximum relish. The other girls shriek in delighted disgust.* **Tituba** *starts a rhythm; she sings something exotic. The girls dance. The dancing becomes more and more feverish. They giggle and shriek hysterically. They begin to undress. Suddenly,* **Anuka** *stops shrieking hysterically. She watches the others briefly, looking perturbed. She looks to offstage. She looks at the girls again. She waves her arms to get their attention.*

Anuka   Wait, wait, wait. Stop. Stop!

The girls stop and look at her quizzically. She glances down at herself.

Why are we doing this?

Miss Alexi (*from her director's seat*)   What's the matter, Anuka? Is something wrong with your costume?

Anuka (*to the other girls*)   Why are we acting like this? It's crazy.

Ruby   Exactly. We're crazy. That's why we're all acting like this.

Heloise   Aww, is that all you stopped us for?! I was on a roll there. (*Shrieks crazily.*)

Maddie   And me! (*Dances crazily.*)

Sera (*worried*)   Miss, does this mean we'll go over time? I teach baby ballet.

Grace   Yeah, miss. I've got hockey.

Wolf (*peering in from the wings*)   Yo, can we take this stuff off now? I'm itching in places I can't get to!

Al   Are we done, miss?

Skive   Can we go, miss?

Mr Briggs   Freeze! You lot stay right where you are. What seems to be the trouble, Anuka?

Anuka   Do we have to do this play?

Reactions from cast members to her boldness.

Miss Alexi   Anuka, the competition is in three weeks. We've been rehearsing for months. Yes we have to do this play. Why?

Anuka   I don't like it.

More reactions.

Mr Briggs   Thank you, Anuka. We'll bear your eloquent critique in mind when you're holding the prize cup in the assembly hall. Now can we please begin from / Tituba's line –

Anuka   I mean it, Miss Alexi. We shouldn't have to do this.

Miss Alexi (*falteringly*)   I – I know this scene isn't actually in the play, but it's faithful to Miller's description. Listen, I know it's a challenging play. But once you've really internalised your character, I promise you'll / love it –

Mr Briggs   It's a masterpiece. Do you know how many productions of *The Crucible* there are going on at this minute? Hundreds if not thousands. St Paul's has won Playfest three years in a row because I always chose classic repertoire and rehearsed it to the highest standard. We don't want to lose now. It's Miss Alexi's directorial debut . . .

Miss Alexi   Honestly, Anuka, you're doing a fantastic job with Abigail. You're really capturing her ruthlessness and manipulation of the other girls.

Mr Briggs   Because we do want to win Playfest, don't we? Four years in a row, it'd be a record.

Anuka   . . . Yes . . .

Miss Alexi   All right, then. Can we please take it from Tituba's line, 'All she gotta do is drink dis blood'. Thank you, Layla.

Anuka (*taking off her pilgrim bonnet*)   I'm sorry. I can't.

She walks off.

Bus Stop

Optional slide: 'Two weeks and six days to the competition.' Somewhere in the near or far distance we can see a banner that reads: 'Ofsted Outstanding: Mr Thrower Headteacher.' The pupils wait for their buses. Conversations might interweave at times or happen simultaneously. The important thing is that we hear and notice the key moments below amidst an energetic, free-flowing momentum.

Anuka *alone is striking in her stillness and silence. As the others witter on, she is seated apart from the group, reading her playscript of* The Crucible. *There is a curious pile of personal items in the road, before the bus shelter. At intervals, pupils add to this pile. It is growing to be a sizeable mass.* **Maddie** *skateboards in, breathless, stops and doubles over panting.*

Maddie   Phew! Thought for sure I'd missed it. (*Of the skateboard.*) The motor's busted – I'm knackered just from the car park. (*Noticing the pile in the road.*) What's all this?

Ruby *has casually placed an umbrella on the pile.*

Heloise   It's called property pile-up. Basically, top trumps meets traffic violation. (*To* **Ruby**.) I see your umbrella and raise you a pair of prescription glasses.

Heloise *places a glasses case in the road.* **Ruby** *acknowledges the trump with a grimacing nod.* **Maddie** *flips her skateboard over to get a look at the motor.*

Heloise   I wish the bus would get here. I swear the drivers park at the top of the hill and give each other handies.

Maddie   Someday we'll go everywhere by jet pack. Do you think there'll be sky rage? I definitely get pavement rage. And road rage.

Ruby   Yeah, Mum says she feels least Christian when driving.

Maddie *growls in frustration at the skateboard's defunct motor and puts it in the road.*

Parker (*looking at* **Wolf**'*s phone*)   Oi! Wolf, you foreskin. Don't write that. That's libel, man. You can't just say whatever you want about someone.

Wolf   Oh yeah? What about the time you told the entire school I've got scabies?

Parker   You did have scabies. Or was it fleas?

Skive   Yo, Hill. Wake me up when the bus gets here. I was up 'til three playing those middle-age noobs in Arizona.

Bo   That's you someday, Skive.

Hill (*to* **Skive**)   I'm not your mother, Skive. Set your alarm.

Skive   Can't. I lost my phone.

He indicates the property pile in the road.

Heloise   That's insane, Ruby. You don't even believe in God.

Ruby   Does that matter?

Heloise   Well, it is customary for becoming a priest.

Ruby   Listen, it's a total doss, right? All you have to do is put on a costume and perform a monologue every Sunday. And best of all, if people don't do what you say, you get to condemn them to hell.

Heloise   You can't be a priest, Ruby. You've got a porn-star name.

Ruby   I'd change it to Rebecca.

Heloise   But there aren't any women priests, are there?

Ruby   Great, I'd be the first, then. Hashtag trailblazer! If you don't count Madonna at Eurovision.

Heloise   You're winding me up right?

Ruby   What? Judging from Father K's car, the pay is decent, plus you get free housing and it's *really* hard to get fired.

Heloise   So be one then, and leave us sinners in peace.

Ruby   That's just it. I can't. Father K won't even let me serve on the altar. Al falls asleep up there every week, but that's ok because he's the future of the church.

Al   That is correct, my child.

He places his Religious Studies textbook in the road.

Bo   He always gets that little chunk of white right there on his bottom lip. Why does he always get that little chunk?

Sam   I know! It's, like, wipe that away, Mr Briggs, can't you feel that?

Bo   He sits there bangin' on about the Greeks and thinks no one can see what his hands are doing under the table.

Sam   To be fair, he's only housekeeping. Nothing recreational.

Maddie (*of* **Layla**'s *green glasses*)   What's with the green glasses, Layla? You're not reading.

Layla   Green's better than grey. I'm making the world a better place.

Maddie   Aren't you supposed to use rose-tinted for that?

Layla   Naw, green overrides all other colours. It's just one big united kingdom of *Shrek*.

Wolf   And then give me your hand –

Sera   I'm *not* giving you my hand. Use your own hand.

Wolf   How else can I demonstrate?

Bo   Hey, Wolf. That there is sexy harassment, dude.

Parker   Yeah, Wolf, dismount. Since when are you into acting, anyway?

Wolf   It's better than rubbing sticks with a bunch of boys scouts.

Heloise (*fed up of waiting*)   Aw, stuff this.

She heaves her rucksack into the road and lies down beside it. The others laugh at the extremeness of this. But when she doesn't show any signs of moving . . .

Ruby   Helly. Come on. What are you doing? Get up.

Sera   Heloise, that's very irresponsible. You could get seriously injured.

Bo   Come on, Hel, drivers keep looking over. Someone might call an ambulance.

Heloise   What? I'm making the bus get here quicker. Either it will rock up to spoil the fun or else we won't notice the wait.

Grace *swiftly moves to yank* **Heloise** *out of the road and sit her down on the bench.*

Heloise *sits in a huff, arms folded, ego bruised. The others hurry to fish their property off the road.*

Hill (*with a hint of mockery*)   So. You're all doing the play? What's it about?

Bo   Americans.

Al   He means old-fashioned Americans. Like before Donald of House Trump.

Bo   Like in the olden days. Back in the pilgrim times.

Al   They sound like a bunch of cowboys trying to do Shakespeare.

Sera   It's set in this weird village where everyone's insanely religious.

Bo   Like seriously proper religious.

Sera   Worse than Mrs Gurnsey.

Al   Mrs Gurnsey who watches *Passion of the Christ* every Sunday and sobs all the way through it and eats Maltesers.

Sera   Exactly, and the people in this play are worse . . .

Wolf   Sam has to kiss Grace. He's the lead, John Proctor. (*As a dig.*) Grace plays his husband.

Grace   Shut up, Scabies. They had to fumigate the whole costume cupboard because of you.

Wolf (*to* **Parker**)   See?! (*Loudly to all.*) I'll have you know I'm completely cured. (*To* Grace.) Like you're a brilliant actor, Popeye. You're only happy when you're hitting something with a stick.

Al   Get this. Skive's the hangman so he doesn't have any lines.

Parker (*nudging* **Skive** *with his foot*)   Skive, wake up, dude. You just missed your bus.

Skive (*realises he's being teased*)   Aw, go suck a knife.

Hill   Guys! You haven't told me anything. What actually happens in the play?

Wolf   It's about witch hunts. You know, in Salem. Back in the 1600s. Basically, the girls are evil, the men are good. The end.

Anuka *slams her play script shut and rises abruptly.*

Anuka (*suddenly loud*)   It's not right.

A pause. All look at her. All look at each other.

Bo (*to the others*)   She speaks . . .

Anuka   It's not . . . fair. The girls are all dodgy . . . Doesn't anyone else think so?

She looks from disinterested face to disinterested face.

Hill   What's the matter, Anuka, have you got a rubbish part or something?

Sera   She's Abigail Williams, the female lead. Anuka, no matter how you feel, you can't just walk out on a rehearsal like you did the other day. It's less than three weeks to Playfest.

Anuka   I couldn't help it. I mean, why are the girls like that? Shrieking their heads off and acting all mental and accusing everyone of being a witch. We're not like that.

Bo   It's a play. People always do weird stuff in plays. Like that guy that pulls his own eyes out.

Heloise   Yeah, man, don't be such a mood hoover. It's kind of fun.

Anuka   I'm going to talk to Miss Alexi. I don't want to play Abigail anymore.

A strong reaction from all the girls and **Sam**.

Sam   Anuka, you can't quit the play. You're the one who convinced me to be in the stupid thing in the first place.

Anuka   Trust me, Sam. I'm not quitting. I'm just going to ask for a better part.

Drama Classroom

Optional slide: 'Two weeks and five days to the competition.' There are body-length scrolls of paper with outline drawings of individual girls from The Crucible *and a list of their key character traits. We can see words like: 'Corrupt, sexually promiscuous, mentally unstable, parents killed by Indians.'* **Miss Alexi** *sits before them, stapling large packets of paper. The aggravated sound of the stapler punctuates the scene from time to time.*

Miss Alexi   What happened? You were so excited when you got Abigail. You've never had a main part before, and here I've given you the best female part in the show and you don't seem . . . well . . . (*She doesn't say 'grateful'.*)

Anuka   Why'd you cast me if I'm rubbish?

Miss Alexi   I didn't say that. You're one of the best young actors I've worked with. And if you're really serious about drama school some day –

Anuka   Cambridge. Footlights. I want to do a degree in History as well.

Miss Alexi   That's excellent. I'm sure you'll achieve everything you set out to do and play all the great roles – Blanche DuBois, Lady Macbeth, Phèdre –

Anuka   So why can't I play John Proctor?

Miss Alexi   Anuka . . . this isn't like you. I'd expect this of one of the others, but not you. You've been one of my strongest pupils all year – articulate, creative . . . Your performance is being marked, remember. I want you to do well.

Anuka   I swear I'd give everything to the part. Girls play men all the time. Last year, Grace played Mr Peachum in *The Threepenny Opera*. She even had to stuff her pants with a sock.

Miss Alexi   Come on, Anuka. It's a distraction. It doesn't serve the play.

Anuka   Why do we have to serve the play?

Miss Alexi   Because . . . that's what you do. This isn't a panto. The play is meant to be a serious commentary about the unchecked power of government as exemplified by the / McCarthy hearings—

Anuka   I know, it's just . . . John Proctor has all the big choices and best speeches. If I'm the best actor, why can't I have the best part?

Miss Alexi *is briefly at a loss.*

Miss Alexi   Churchill Academy is doing *The Master Builder*. St Cuthbert's is doing *Hamlet*. We don't want to get pipped to the post by them, do we? This is my final word, Anuka. If you're not happy with it, there are lots of girls who'd kill to play Abigail Williams. (*She grinds down on the stapler.*)

Den

Optional slide: 'Two weeks and three days to the competition.' A wood beside the school's playing fields. **Anuka** *is building a den out of tree branches of varying lengths.*

Sam *enters. He watches* **Anuka** *for a few seconds and then starts helping her.*

Sam   So what's this make? Third one? Fourth one?

Anuka   Fifth.

Sam   Wow. That's more than in Year 1, when Miss James said you couldn't use your dinosaur as baby Jesus in the carol concert. Is this one gonna stand?

Anuka   I haven't decided yet.

Sam   That bad, huh?

Anuka   Worse. She just wouldn't listen.

Wolf *enters with* **Bo**, **Al** *and* **Skive**.

Wolf   Oi oi! What you makin', a Puritan love shack? (*To Sam.*) I thought you were coming back to mine.

Skive   Still sulking, Anuka? Here, have some monster munch. Clear out all your angst and anything else you got in there. This stuff passes through you like a food bullet.

Anuka   I don't need to calm down.

Skive   Er, I think you do. It's the dumbest thing I ever heard. And I've heard some pretty dumb things – I sit next to Wolf in psychology.

Anuka   How can you say that? This play makes out that all girls are totally irrational, hysterical, screeching demons. It's 2020 – you can't just do it straight, you have to put some sort of modern spin on it.

Skive   I dunno about the play, but sounds like Miss Alexi was pretty clear about what you could spin on.

Anuka *looks sharply to* **Skive** *and moves to square off and give him a piece of her mind.* **Sam** *intervenes to keep the peace.*

Sam   Back off, Skive.

Skive *retreats and joins* **Wolf** *and* **Al**.

Sam   He does have a point, though. She was never gonna say yes to such a radical idea.

Anuka   It's not a radical idea, that's the point. Come on, not you as well, Sam.

Sam   Nuka, I'm on your side, 100 per cent. Though I'm not sure when you were gonna tell me you'd nicked my part.

Anuka   Ah, yeah. Sorry. I didn't think you'd mind.

Sam   I don't. Just surprised you didn't ask.

Anuka (*to the group as a whole*)   So how are we going to fight this? We've got to question what they're making us do.

Al   There's no point. They'd kick you out of the school before they'd mess with Playfest. It's sacred.

Wolf   Yeah, man, if we win, I might get into Bournemouth. They want extracurriculars, and I don't think binge watching *The Walking Dead* and the ability to down a six pack of Red Bull in under four minutes counts.

Bo   Sorry, mate. Mum says one wrong move and I'll have to go live with my dad. She expects me to be a doctor and buy her a Nissan Qashqai.

Skive   My career goal is to become a *hikikomori*. That's one of those people that never leave their room and play video games all day long and possibly own a blow-up doll named Shadow.

Wolf   Oh yeah, man. You'd make a good one!

Sam (*to* **Anuka**)   You can't fight them on your own, but what if we go back to Miss Alexi, and I say I want to play Abigail Williams?

The boys react with scorn.

Bo   Pff! It'll look like the school's trying to be all experimental. Or say something. They'd hate the idea.

Skive   I'm not sure they would. I'm always lighting my farts with a Bunsen burner in chemistry and no one objects to that.

Anuka (*to* **Sam**)   Really? You'd do that?

Sam   Yeah. Of course.

Al   Come on. This school is like a million years old. A few of the older teachers actually met Jesus.

Wolf (*laughing*)   Yeah, Thrower pierced his side. (*He demonstrates a javelin-style spear throw.*)

Al   The school motto is 'Serving society through blind adherence to convention'.

Skive   It's not. Is it?

Al   Might as well be. Try this and you'll have the whole history of the school against you.

Anuka   Maybe, but I've had an idea. Round up the guys and meet me in the drama room tomorrow lunchtime, I'll bring the girls. Like you say, we've got to fight this together and I think I know exactly how to tip the odds back in our favour.

Sam   Ok, but what are you –

Anuka   Trust me?

Sam   One hundred per cent.

Costume Cupboard

Optional slide: 'Two weeks and one day to the competition.' **Anuka**, **Layla**, **Grace**, **Sera**, **Ruby**, **Heloise** *and* **Maddie** *enter the costume and props room taking in the treasure trove of theatrical objects with obvious delight.*

Heloise   Then Thrower lines us all up in a row and makes us go down on our knees to check. And I go what's the big deal, sir? And *he* goes, get this, 'You don't want to give the male teachers the wrong idea'. So now every time I put on a skirt I have to picture some male teacher getting the wrong idea. I wonder if they prefer to 'get the wrong idea' in the shower or on the drive in . . .

Layla   Guys, we shouldn't be in here. They might think we're trying to steal something.

Heloise   This old junk? Oo! (*Swipes up a sword and points it threateningly.*) Girls! Stop that dancing at once! And put your kit back on before I get a chubbie!

Maddie   Naff off, Uncle Parris, or I'll stab you – with this! (*Grabs her own weird-looking sword, looks at it in amazement.*) Oh, hello, weird sword.

She turns and lunges. They start sparring in a naff way. **Maddie** *stabs* **Heloise**. **Heloise** *dies with maximum theatricality.*

Layla   Look at all these nighties. What're they called, baby dolls?

Anuka   *Guys?*

Sera (*explaining helpfully*)   They're whore costumes from *Cabaret*. And the corsets are for the whores in *Les Mis* the year before. They're keeping the hot pants for the whores in *Miss Saigon*.

Maddie (*wearing something vampirish*)   I vant to suck your blood.

Ruby   Wait, you're Transylvanian for real, aren't you?

Maddie   I'm not Dracula! There's more to Transylvania than Vlad the Impaler, ok!

Anuka   GUYS?!

They all stop and give her their attention at last.

Sera   Anuka, please. (*School teacherish.*) Indoor voices . . .

Anuka   Will you come with me to talk to Miss Alexi? We should *all* have the male parts. Not just me. Think about it. We'd get to lead the courtroom scene. Ruby, you could play Reverend Parris. Helly, you could play Giles Corey. And Maddie, you could be Mr Hale. Miss Alexi says the girls are great parts, but that's not true. Most of them hardly speak at all.

Her enthusiasm is met with sidelong glances between the other girls.

Heloise   I never get to play a girl.

Ruby   Me neither. Not a proper girl. I'm always the mum or the gran because of my cup size.

Maddie   Yeah, if there's a princess or a maiden fair, it's always Sera.

Sera   Sorry! I can't help how I look.

Grace   I've played men since the dawn of time. I had to play Juliet's dad and wear a moustache. Sera got to wear a red velvet gown and post photos all over Instagram.

Sera (*dreamily*)   I loved that dress . . .

Anuka   This is different. We're not getting dumped in the rubbish male parts. We're claiming the best ones for ourselves.

Grace   The guys would slaughter me . . . I have a hard enough time as it is.

Heloise   Sorry, but you do have really big forearms, G.

Layla   I don't want to play some old guy. I already have a big part as Tituba.

Heloise   Yeah, great big servant part, Layla.

Layla   Whatever. I can't kick off. If I kick off, it's *this* face kicking off.

Heloise Are you kidding? You're poster child for the school. I'm borstal girl.

Ruby If Father K finds out, he'll give me a four-hour lecture and make me polish all the crucifixes.

Maddie My mum would make me quit the play. She already thinks actors are nothing but strippers.

Sera We don't want to get in trouble. The whole school and all the parents and the board of governors and some theatre big shots are going to be there watching us. They're expecting us to win.

Anuka Do this, and we'll not only win, we'll open people's eyes. Make them think.

Heloise We wouldn't actually be doing anything wrong . . .

Sam *and the boys come in.*

Wolf Oi oi! What gives? Anything good in here?

Heloise Took you guys long enough. Don't tell me you actually ate the shepherd's pie.

Skive No way, man, too much shepherd in it.

Al Whoa . . . How many dresses?

Bo It's like a dress graveyard.

Wolf (*another dig at* **Grace**) Or should we say prom night for girls' hockey? How's it going, Miss Trunchbull? Found anything that fits over them meat hooks?

Grace You like? There's some prettier ones over there.

Anuka Hey, guys. Dare you to try on some dresses.

The guys laugh.

Bo Yeah, Al, what's the hold-up? Try on a dress. You'll look positively lovely.

Al You try on a dress, Bo Peep. You can go on *RuPaul* and sing 'Like a Virgin'.

Wolf I'll try on a dress. Bring it on! Come on, Skive, tuck in your shaft and put on a bonnet.

He flings a dress at **Skive**. **Skive** *dodges it like it's a turd.*

Skive No way. You can use one to stem the flow of blood from my severed artery. That's when I'll put on a dress.

Heloise Relax, Skive. It won't make your voice go up an octave or anything. (*Direct challenge.*) We'll do it if you'll do it.

Bo No comparison. Girls in trousers doesn't lead to assault in public stairwells.

The girls start poring over the male costumes and enjoying the hats and trousers. All except **Grace**.

Heloise   Come on, Grace. Don't be so miserable. Here, try this! (*She flings something at* **Grace**.)

Maddie   Let's go, Wolf. You said you would.

Wolf *tentatively puts a dress over his head. The boys think it's funny and all start changing into costumes.*

Heloise   Let's check those skirt lengths, ladies. On your knees!

The boys go down to their knees and **Heloise** *walks along the line of them tutting and making critical comments. They carry on larking about. The boys might mimic famous female actors and then bits of* The Crucible, *e.g. 'He bited me on the breast'. Everyone is really getting into it except* **Skive** *who is mortified and shaking his head in disbelief and* **Grace** *who is going through something darker. Suddenly a* **Prefect** *enters. She stops short and gives them a disapproving frown.*

Prefect   What are you doing?

Maddie (*slowly raises a nightie*)   Just checking out the delightful whore costumes.

Prefect   I can see what you're up to. Anuka and her gang. I'll have to report you.

The **Prefect** *takes a photo with her phone. The girls exchange looks of disbelief.* **Wolf** *gets in her path; he grabs her phone and throws it to* **Al**.

Prefect   Give me my phone. (*When they don't . . .*) Doesn't matter. I can tell them what I've seen.

Bo (*looking down at the dress he's wearing*)   That's it, we're dead. They'll find our bodies floating in the duck pond by Saturday.

Skive   Smash the phone, dude.

Sera   Skive! You know violence is never the answer.

Al   You smash it, Skive. Father K would make me polish all the crucifixes.

Anuka *calmly puts out her hand.*

Anuka   Give me the phone.

Wolf *complies.* **Anuka** *deletes the photo and hands it to the* **Prefect**. *The* **Prefect** *leaves.*

Wolf   Bloody prefects. They think they're teachers or something.

Al   Miss Alexi's little spy.

Maddie   Miss Alexi's little snitch. She can't treat us like that.

Sam   Let's quit the play. That'd serve her right.

Wolf   Yeah.

Skive   Totally.

Anuka   No. Let's do our own *Crucible*.

A pause. The others exchange sceptical looks.

Why not? We can do it. We can meet in the woods by the playing fields and rehearse our own version. Girls play the boys, boys play the girls. Perform it at Playfest instead of Miss Alexi's. The judges will love it. We can toe the line in rehearsals so she never suspects and then reveal it on the big day.

Ruby   That would never work. Playfest is in, like, two weeks and we're getting marked on it.

Wolf   I'm not playing a girl, all right? Not in a million years.

Anuka   Go on. What are you so scared of?

Al   Well you see, Nuka, back in year eight, Wolf lost his trainers and his mother made him wear his sister's to PE this one time –

Wolf   Shut up, man.

Al   – and some guys from class ripped the everlasting piss out of him . . .

Wolf   Or I'll tell them about the Year 6 camping trip!

Al   – and he's never been quite the same since.

Anuka   That's not going to happen.

Skive   Yeah, cause this time you'll have Miss Trunchbull to protect you. (*To* **Grace**.) Yo, Trunchbull, when you shave your arms, does it cause the tattoos to fade?

Grace *raises her shirt to reveal terrible bruises all over her torso. A stunned silence.*

Grace   Some guys followed me home. They kept going on at me. Calling me Butch Cassidy, Hockey Arms. I got mad and took a swing with my stick. My dad and brothers would just say I had it coming . . . I change in the toilet cubicles so the girls on the team won't see and tell Mr Johnson.

She storms out.

Anuka   Nice one, guys. I'm quitting the play. Hope it goes well for you.

She starts to leave.

Sam   No, Anuka, wait. She's right. Look at the way they run this place. (*He looks to the other guys.*) Guys?

Lots of sidelong glances as they consider. **Wolf** *grabs a pilgrim bonnet and puts it on.*

Wolf   Bring it.

The Stage

Optional slide: 'Thirteen days to the competition.' The Crucible set is partly painted. **Mr Briggs** *is directing* **Sam** *and* **Anuka** *in a pivotal moment from the play.*

Sam (*to* **Anuka**)   Whore!

Mr Briggs   Hold up, Sam. Think about what you're saying. You're not just calling her a whore because she's not a virgin. This girl has accused your innocent wife of being a witch. She hopes your wife will hang for it so she can have you. You are calling her a whore because she's a vindictive, sex-struck killer who must be stopped at all costs. Do it again.

Sam (*to* **Anuka**)   WHORE!

Mr Briggs   Anuka, come here.

Anuka *approaches.*

Mr Briggs   Stand here, will you? Stand right in front of him. That's it, right up in his grill. Go on.

Anuka *stands right before* **Sam**. *They exchange knowing looks.*

Mr Briggs   All right, now. Again, Sam. Right to her face.

Sam (*backing down slightly*)   Whore!

Mr Briggs   Come on, Sam. Don't back off. Get right in there.

Sam   WHORE!

Mr Briggs   You can do better than that. Again. Go for it!

Sam   Sir, I don't really –

Mr Briggs   Like this, Sam. (*To* **Anuka**.) WHORE!

Anuka *is startled and upset in spite of herself.* **Miss Alexi** *has entered and stands looking dumfounded.*

Miss Alexi   Raef? (*Correcting herself.*) Mr Briggs? What is going on?

Mr Briggs   Oh hello. We're just going over Proctor's denunciation of Abigail. I think we're finally / starting to –

Miss Alexi   Could I speak with you a moment, please?

Mr Briggs   Er yeah, just for a moment . . . We've still got a lot to get through.

She draws him to one side.

Miss Alexi   Raef, I'd prefer to handle the more sensitive moments in the play myself. I've already staged this scene.

Mr Briggs   Yeah, I know. But they're struggling with the subtext.

Miss Alexi   We went over it last week. I gave Anuka my word that it would be shown as morally ambiguous, if not downright reprehensible on the part of Proctor.

Mr Briggs   Yeah, they get that. It's just Sam wasn't quite able to identify with Proctor. I thought it would help if he had my take on the situation.

Miss Alexi   Your take?

Mr Briggs   Yeah. See things from a man's point of view. He's only a boy.

Miss Alexi   I'm sorry, but I'm not sure it's appropriate to delve into personal viewpoints. Particularly by differentiating perspectives on what constitutes a whore. I hope you've never had occasion to shout 'whore' to a woman's face.

Mr Briggs   That's not what I'm saying. Are you trying to tell me you don't identify with the female characters more than the male ones? This is the play. We can't back down from the uncomfortable stuff or patronise them.

Miss Alexi   Thanks for your input, Raef. I'll take over from here. See you tomorrow.

Mr Briggs   Ah gosh. This is awkward . . . Clive has asked me to step up my involvement in the play. He's cleared some of my workload, so I can stay for the full sessions from now on.

He returns to **Anuka** *and* **Sam**.

Mr Briggs   Where were we?

Anuka   Whore.

Playing Fields

Optional slide: 'Twelve days to the competition.' **Anuka** *and the rest of the cast are rehearsing their own version in the woods.*

Skive (*filming with his phone, doing movie-trailer voice*)   One man . . . One sex-struck killer . . . One little town called . . . Salem.

Wolf, **Bo** *and* **Al** *are all wearing pilgrim bonnets and huddling together.*

Wolf (*as girl*)   I saw Goody Howe with the Devil!

Bo (*as girl*)   I saw Goody Bishop with the Devil!

Al (*as girl*)   I saw Goody Good with the Devil!

Anuka   Come on, guys. That's shouting, not shrieking. This isn't a football match. Pretend you're on fire.

Wolf (*hysterical*)   I saw Goody Hughes with the Devil! I saw her write in his diary. She looked like Bellatrix Lestrange wearing Fatface!

Anuka   All right . . . Let's take it again from the top.

Layla   You know you're good at this, Anuka.

Others chime their agreement. **Anuka** *tries to hide how pleased she is.*

Layla   Maybe Miss Alexi will be so blown away that she'll forgive everything and take you under her wing. That's how Ella got into that directing thing in London. She did all this extra stuff, got loads of experience. Miss A mentored her through everything.

Wolf   Yo, what gives? Are we rehearsing or what?

Skive   Stop saying 'yo', Wolf. Your dad wears tweed.

Anuka   Maybe we should break things up to save time. *(To the boys.)* Why don't you guys practise the crazy dancing –

Wolf   Aye, captain! *(He starts twerking.)*

Skive   Can I still be the hangman? Or do I suddenly have to be a hanglady?

Anuka *(to girls)*   Why don't you do the courtroom scene in gibberish like Miss Alexi taught us.

The boys start rehearsing the bonfire dance. The girls start performing the courtroom scene in gibberish. **Anuka** *draws* **Al** *aside to rehearse with him.*

Anuka   Can we skip to the Proctor and Mary Warren scene? I just want to go over the slap if it's alright? Sam said it looked fake. Sam, will you watch?

She moves into place, revs up for it.

Al   Wait. Why's he slapping her anyway?

Anuka   To stop her from going to court. So she can't keep adding fuel to the fire. Without her and the other girls, they don't have any spectral evidence.

Al   You what? What's spectral evidence?

Anuka   Like Miss Alexi said about. Like if I say I had a dream that you sent out your evil spirit to hurt me. Your evil spirit is your spectre. Me saying that in court is spectral evidence. Ok, you ready?

Al *is playing* **Mary Warren**. **Anuka** *is playing* **John Proctor**. **Sam** *watches.*

Anuka as Proctor *(to* **Al**)   Mary Warren! 'How do you go to Salem when I forbid it?! Do you mock me?!'

She stage slaps **Al**.

Sam   Fake.

Anuka *tries again.*

Sam   Fake.

Anuka *(thinks, then to* **Al**)   Can I slap you for real?

Al   What?

Anuka   It won't hurt, I promise. Here, slap me.

Al   No way. I haven't hit anyone in the face since my brother and me fought over the TV remote. That's mental.

He moves away slightly. She looks to **Sam**, *sensing something else is brewing.*

Anuka *(to* **Al**)   Is something wrong?

Al   . . . I don't know . . . It's just . . . Mr Briggs gave us this big speech in English today. About how this is meant to be a rewarding experience and stuff. How, you know, winning the competition could really help to set us up for life. Instead, we could get suspended for doing this. It's basically sabotaging the play.

Anuka   They'll never find out. Not til Playfest. And then it will be so good they won't get mad.

Al   Er yeah . . . it's just . . . Mr Briggs sort of asked me to be assistant director.

Anuka (*shocked*)   You're assistant director?

Al   *Yeah . . .*

From the other girls' rehearsal, bits of dialogue from The Crucible *come through.*

Layla as Danforth   Disrespect indeed! It is disruption. This is the highest court of the supreme government of this province, do you know it?

Al   Nuka?

Anuka   No, that's great. That's really great. Congratulations. *(Indicating the script.)* Shall we go again?

Al   Er . . . yeah, sure.

Anuka (*to Al*)   'How do you go to Salem when I forbid it?! Do you mock me?!'

She slaps him, for real and a bit too hard.

Al   Ow! Anuka!

The others all stop and look over, concerned.

Anuka (*genuine*)   Oh sorry! I'm sorry, Al, I . . .

He goes off in a strop. The others crowd round him to hear what happened.

Sam   Don't worry. He's had worse.

Anuka   He hates the play. He's been late to every rehearsal so far. He thinks great acting is the guy from *Deadpool*. But apparently, that's the job description for assistant director.

Sam   It's probably just so he won't get bored and quit.

Anuka   When did Mr Briggs take over, anyway? I thought he was only supposed to be an advisor this year.

Sam   Don't get mad. Just keep going. You're great at this. And we are going to win.

Backstage

Optional slide: 'Eleven days to the competition.' The set of The Crucible *is partly painted, partly assembled and so there is a partial view of Salem village with Salem*

*harbour in the distance. The cast are congregated together before it, speaking in
hushed tones.*

Sera   What, you mean they've hauled her in? (*To* **Layla**.) Are you . . . are you sure?

Layla   Yeah, man, I was right there. Helly and me were in the canteen. One of the
prefects comes up and goes, 'Heloise, Mr Briggs and Miss Alexi would like a word
with you'. And takes her off.

A slight pause.

Ruby   They know.

Grace   No. There's no way.

Layla   She's been in there with them for ages.

Sera   In where? Where have they taken her?

Layla   The interrogation room . . .

Ruby   Do you think she'll tell them? Do you think she'll say it's us –

Maddie   Calm down. I'm sure she hasn't said anything.

Anuka   Guys, we can't let her take the rap. This whole thing was my idea.

Wolf   Let her. She's an idiot. She's been spouting off to some of the other teachers
about how rubbish the play is when we told her to keep her big mouth shut.

Sera (*worried*)   There isn't really an interrogation room, is there?

Skive   Oh yeah. It's behind a bookcase in Thrower's office. A proper torture
chamber.

Layla   What are we going to do? We should all decide what to do.

Sam   We don't say anything. That's what we do.

Anuka   But Helly . . .

Sam   You never rat on your friends. She won't. And neither will we.

Al   I don't get it. How'd they find out? Someone must have tipped them off.

Maddie   The prefects, who else?

Wolf   Tipped them off about what? What could the prefects say? They don't know
anything about what we've been doing.

Maddie   Maybe they saw us in the woods.

Wolf   We'd have seen them. It's not like you can sneak up in a red blazer.

Wolf *gives* **Bo** *a sidelong glance, then moves to get up in his face.*

Wolf   It was you, wasn't it, Bo Peep? Too scared of breaking the rules?

Bo   What? Get out of my face, Wolf, or I will hurt you.

Wolf   You did, didn't you? You narked.

Al   Yeah, man. I bet he did. (*To* **Bo**.) You've always been a ball hog and you never share answers.

Bo   Back off, altar boy. I haven't done anything.

Sera   Guys, let's not turn on each other. It must have been a prefect.

Wolf   It was you. Admit it was you.

Bo   Back off, Scabies!

They start scrapping.

Sera   Guys, stop! If they see you fighting, they'll know it's us –

Ruby   Someone's coming!

*** *

The prefects form a tribunal. **Anuka** *and her friends stand before them.*

Prefect   All right, Ladies. Mr Thrower wants to know what the plan is and who's in charge.

Silence.

Prefect   It's the boys, right? One of the boys? All of the boys?

Silence.

Ruby   Where's Helly? Why won't you let us see her?

Prefect   Heloise used profanities in front of a member of staff and is now in detention. Listen. We know what guys are like. Boys will be boys, right? But why should you get dragged down with them?

Silence.

Prefect   They named you all, without a second thought. But we were sure they were lying to save their own necks.

Maddie   What's the big deal? It's just a play.

Prefect (*to* **Maddie**)   Yes, we understand you have a habit of getting kicked off the school play.

Maddie   That's not true. My mum was sick last year and I had to get my little sisters from school –

Sera   Did they really name us?

Anuka (*sotto to* **Sera**)   Don't.

Prefect   Oh yeah. Of course, if it *is* you guys . . . all you have to do is confess and take your punishment. Then you can put this whole thing behind you.

Ruby   What's the punishment?

Prefect   A week of detention and an apology to your fellow cast members. But if you don't own up, it will be a suspension. Think how that will look on your record. Could really impact on your life.

Prefect   What she means is, you'll all be mums by next year.

Sera *is at risk of breaking.* **Maddie** *subtly takes her by the arm.*

Prefect   Wouldn't risk it if I was you. Just tell us who's been up to what and this will all be over.

Silence.

Prefect   All right, then. Hope your babies are smarter than you.

***

A **Prefect** *grills a group of girls.*

Prefect   You sit next to Madelena Gunesch in Chemistry, don't you?

Lola   Dracula? Yeah, why?

Prefect   She's planning to throw the competition at Playfest. Do you know anything about that?

Tilly   Why would we talk about drama in science?

Prefect   You can't lie about something this big. You'll get it in the neck from Thrower. If he finds out you're banding together with the instigators –

Evie   Whoa, who are you calling a liar?

Prefect   You're protecting her, aren't you. And all the while, she and her friends laugh at you behind your backs.

Prefect   They grassed you up to Thrower for smoking behind the bike shed.

Lola   Yeah, well we do. And by the school gates.

Tilly   And in the toilets. They got that right.

Evie   You're making fools of yourselves. And take those stupid badges off. What are you, MI5?

***

Prefects *with the girls' hockey team.*

Prefect   Has Grace Comstock been absent from any practices lately?

Hockey Girl   What's it to you?

Prefect   She's planning to embarrass the school at the Playfest.

Hockey Girl   How? By announcing our hockey scores?

Prefect   Mr Johnson decides who's in and who's out on game days, right? We might have to have a word with him.

Hockey Girl   Are you threatening us?

Prefect   No, we're just reminding you that actions have consequences. And sometimes inactions have consequences, too.

Prefect   Are you in on this? Part of her little group? Because now is the time to speak up – before Thrower starts suspending people.

Hockey Girl   Why are you asking us? Just because we *know* Grace? Why don't you go stomp on some Year 7s or kill some kittens or whatever's next on your list?

***

Male **Prefects** *are with* **Sam**, **Wolf**, **Al**, **Bo** *and* **Skive**.

Prefect   It's the girls, isn't it?

The boys maintain their silence.

Prefect   You're involved, too, we know you are. But we also know it wasn't your idea and you don't care one way or the other.

Prefect   So just own up, guys. There's no dodging this one.

Prefect   Then you can take your slap on the wrists and we'll all be on our way.

Skive   Sod off.

Wolf   You can find us in the canteen – eating your loved ones.

Wolf *and* **Skive** *start to leave.*

Prefect   Wouldn't do that. You don't want to wreck your future.

The guys stop and look at the **Prefects**.

Prefect   Thrower isn't taking any prisoners. He's got half the world breathing down his neck. The board for one. The parents. Ofsted. And you're just five guys out of a school.

Prefect   The girls have nothing to lose. Think about it. Some day, they'll marry Richard Branson and start squeezing them out. You get suspended, you're done. Imagine having to ride a bike to work when you're fifty . . .

Prefect   All you have to do is name the girls and Mr Thrower will take it from there.

Wolf   No one's telling you anything so you can go tell Tosser to come get us.

Prefect   He will. He's already contacted your parents.

Bo *looks to* **Al**, *concerned.*

Skive   My dad can't read, so . . . send him a photograph of Thrower's boot up this –

He turns and bends.

Bo   It's the girls.

Al   Shut up, Bo. What's the matter with you?

Prefect   Thank you. Which ones?

Wolf   Bo, you absolute tool, shut your mouth.

Bo   What? It's obvious they already know. All the girls.

Prefect   Which girls is all the girls?

Sam   Shut up, Bo. They've got our backs.

Bo   We don't know that. They're not my friends. You guys can stick your neck on the line for a bunch of girls that would never date you, but not me.

Skive   The incel has spoken.

Bo *reacts angrily;* **Wolf** *rushes to restrain him.*

Wolf   Bo! You hit him, you'll be living with your dad by the end of the week.

Prefect   Which girls? Come on, Bo. You're not like the rest of these stem cells. You're predicted four A stars and a slap on the back from the entire board of governors. Go on. Say it. Which girls?

Sam   Bo. Don't do it.

Bo (*backing down*)   I'm sure you can figure it out for yourselves . . .

A slight pause.

Prefect   Bo, have you heard of Samson and Delilah?

Skive   From Year 10?

Prefect   No, Skive. From the Bible. Samson was this insanely strong man. He could literally wrestle a lion to death – fight off loads of guys in one go like The Mountain or Jackie Chan. But what no one knew was that the source of his strength was his magic hair.

Prefect   Like the bug-eyed girl in *Tangled*.

Prefect   And there was this girl called Delilah. And one day, he stupidly told her about his hair thing.

Prefect   Because she was well fit and it seemed a way in.

Prefect   And that same night . . . she got a knife.

Prefect   Scissors.

Prefect   This is like 300 BC. They didn't have scissors. She took a knife . . .

Prefect   And she cut his hair off.

Prefect   And when he woke up, he needed to fight someone right away. But he was all weak all of a sudden. So he got killed. And Delilah went off with the stronger guy and lived happily ever after. Do you see what I'm getting at? The girls have set you up for a fall. Don't let them. Be the Samson who gets away.

Rebuild

Optional slide: 'Eight days to the competition.' **Anuka** *and* **Sam** *are once again working together to rebuild the den in the woods.*

Sam   What'd you smash it up for?

Anuka   It wasn't me. I'm not the only one around here who's mad about what's been happening.

Sam   Yeah, man. Wolf was raging after the meeting with the prefects.

Anuka   It's like the whole school's gone insane.

Sam   Crazy. Thirty more pulled in and questioned.

Anuka   Mate, I think we should own up. It's not fair on everyone else. Thrower and Briggs are getting their pants in a massive bundle.

Sam   Forget them. Don't say anything.

Anuka   We should stop. People are scared.

Sam   Besides Sera?

Anuka   Yeah . . . Grace, Maddie, Bo. They definitely don't want to rehearse in the woods anymore. They're convinced they're being spied on.

Sam   It's not that. It's just too much work, Anuka. The competition is too soon. Don't feel bad, it was a good idea.

Anuka   . . . Yeah . . . Thanks . . .

She thinks.

What if we did just one scene? The courtroom scene. Everyone could manage that. We can't just go ahead with their version of the play. Think of all those Year 8s and 9s in the audience, my little sister, my mum, *my dad.* My dad would have to watch me strip off – (*She breaks off at the sight of a prefect approaching.*)

Sam *turns to see what she's looking at. The* **Prefect** *arrives wearing a knowing smirk.*

Prefect   Anuka. Mr Thrower wants to see you.

Anuka *and* **Sam** *look to one another.*

Sam   Why her?

Prefect   Don't play innocent.

Sam   She's not going anywhere.

Prefect   You go, then, Sam. Tell him everything.

Sam   Oh, I'll say something to him. (*To Anuka.*) Stay here.

He starts towards the **Prefect**.

Anuka   Sam, don't. You'll get detention.

Sam   I'd rather get kicked out than grovel to Thrower.

She takes him to one side so the **Prefect** *can't hear them.*

Anuka   Seriously. I'll talk to him. I'll explain everything. I'll convince him to let us do our version. Watch some *Inbetweeners*. I'll be back in ten.

Headteacher's Office

Anuka *stands before* **Mr Thrower** *who is seated magisterially in a swivel chair. There are numerous awards, placards and certificates of achievement.*

Mr Thrower   Good afternoon, Anuka. I trust you know why you're here.

Anuka   It's a competition, Mr Thrower. Aren't competitions supposed to be fun?

Mr Thrower   And when you walk out of rehearsals. Do you think you're allowing the other pupils to have fun?

Anuka   Maybe not, but. I think they should know *The Crucible* is . . . a bad play.

Mr Thrower   Bad? You're a top student. Surely you can do better than that.

Anuka   Bad for girls.

Mr Thrower   Oh yeah? How so? (*When she hesitates again.*) Come on . . .

Anuka   Well . . . like why do the girls have to move together as one group all the time – what are they a coven? And why don't we know very much about any of them? The author just calls Mercy Lewis a 'fat, sly, merciless wretch'. And . . . the whole play seems to hinge on Abigail's desire, right? She'll stop at nothing to have John Proctor. In real life, she was only like eleven and he was sixty! But that didn't stop the author from genuinely believing they had some kind of romantic thing going which makes me think he doesn't know girls very well or can't do maths –

Mr Thrower   Actually, you've just illustrated what makes the play great. It can be interpreted in so many ways. We owe it to the author to always give him the benefit of the doubt.

Anuka   Sir, I want us to win. We all want to win. Would we put so much effort into rehearsing if we didn't? Just please let me explain what we've / been doing –

Mr Thrower   I know there are more alternative schools that fancy radical interpretations of the classics. The kids who go to them become artists, actors, fine. This school produces the next generation of leaders: doctors, lawyers, businessmen. They want to be able to say they performed one of the great roles of the literary canon. Not indulge in rampant cross-dressing.

Anuka   Sir, the play is offensive and the only way to make it less offensive is to help an audience see / the things that –

Mr Thrower   Anuka, do you understand that you are veering towards defamatory behaviour? Miller's work deserves to be treated with the utmost respect. I believe someday he will be ranked with Shakespeare as one of the titans of the last millennium. I myself played John Proctor many moons ago and it was one of the highlights of my youth. Don't take that away from Sam. He's your best friend, isn't he?

She looks down; she hadn't thought of that.

I'd like the names of everyone involved.

Anuka   . . .

Mr Thrower   The other girls indicated that you pressurised them into colluding with you.

Anuka   I don't believe that. They would never –

Mr Thrower   By 'they' I take it you mean, (*reading*) Heloise Martin, Madelena Gunesch, Sera Tailor, Ruby White, Grace Comstock, Layla Mackie –

Anuka   You think we'd stab each other in the back, don't you? Without a second thought. All girls are mean girls, right? There's no loyalty. Not if some other girl has something we want or need. We scheme, don't we, and we tell lies. We gang up on each other. We steal boyfriends. We're petty and shallow and nasty. Except we're not. I trust my friends and they trust me. They don't band together in groups shrieking and pointing fingers and blaming me for how I make them feel. But you do, sir. And the other teachers. Every time you check our skirt lengths, every time you inspect our nails and make us remove our piercings and send us home to change our shoes – you're saying we're dangerous. We shouldn't have to play these rubbish parts anymore. They misrepresent the truth. The play is supposed to be an attack on some politicians from, like, a hundred years ago, so how come I'm the one who feels like dirt when I have to act in it? I thought when you aim at one thing and hit a load of others you didn't mean to, it's called a *mistake*. (*Holding up the play text.*) That's what he did. He went for one man and hit half the frickin' world. I'm not telling you anything.

Mr Thrower (*managing to keep his temper*)   All right. You've had your say. Mr Briggs will find some new girls to replace you and the rest of your little group.

Anuka (*shocked*)   What? Only the girls? We haven't done anything wrong.

Mr Thrower   I know that you were planning to perform your own version of the play, in an attempt to seriously undermine the authority of the teaching staff in this school. And the fact that you show no guilt or remorse signifies, to me, a frightening disregard for the effects of your actions.

Anuka   So why are you only punishing the girls?

Mr Thrower   Are you prepared to offer me any names?

Anuka   . . .

Mr Thrower   Your mother has been called to come and get you. You're suspended for the rest of the week. Good afternoon.

412   Silva Semerciyan

Debrief

Optional slide: 'After the suspension.' The pupils are at the bus stop. An aura of tension.

Parker (*with a slight note of mocking*)   So . . . how's the play going?

Hill   Parker, don't be a dick. (*To the others.*) He's back from an exhilarating canoe trip with the other Brownies.

Parker   Bite this, Hill.

Hill (*to* **Bo**)   You kissed or slapped anyone yet?

Bo   Naw, I play an old fart. Nothing to report.

Al   Me neither. Sam's the only one who sees any action.

Sam   Not anymore. I'm quitting.

Maddie (*to the other boys*)   You guys are quitting too, right?

The boys look at one other.

Wolf   Well . . .

Al   Errrrrrr . . .

Bo   I mean . . . what good would that do?

Skive   Yeah, won't that seem a bit suspicious?

Wolf (*to* **Sam**)   You can't quit. Come on, man. They'd never find a replacement in time, and you're . . . (*sotto*) good.

Sam   I feel like a total knob for going to rehearsals now . . .

Anuka   Sam, I told you. You have to do it. There's no point in us all screwing up our grades. I know you've always got my back.

Sam   I'll think about it.

Hill   Bus is coming.

Sam   See you later, Nuka? We can go over the final solution stuff for history.

Anuka   Yeah, sure. I could do with a final solution.

The boys all go off. The girls are all downcast.

Ruby   So for confirmation class, Father K made us all dress up as superheroes because, you know, Jesus is the ultimate superhero, and I couldn't think of anyone—

Maddie   Wonder woman.

Ruby   I didn't feel like waxing. And I didn't have a body suit for Cat Woman, but anyway she's a bit of a murderer. So I went as Cleopatra. And Father K took me aside and asked if I was really ready to confirm my faith.

Sera   That's like Miss Mandy, she said I should leave it with baby ballet for a few weeks. I can kind of see her point. Good role models and stuff.

Layla *accidentally drops her green glasses.* **Maddie** *scoops them up.*

Layla *quickly puts them back on.*

Maddie   Are you crying? You're crying. Those are tears dripping down.

Heloise (*to* **Layla**)   Mate, don't worry about it. It's just a play.

Layla   It's not that . . . it's . . . a couple of weeks ago, Mr Thrower asked me to do a photo shoot for the school brochure. I never want to be in it, but I always say yes. Today Mrs Hughes takes me aside and says they won't be needing me after all.

Grace   Forget them. When we're done with this place, we'll never look back.

Layla   That's just it. I've begun to think it's not any better out there. Mum's always saying, 'Don't live up to their low expectations. Rise above it all.' I'm sick of trying to be better than everyone. I want to be just as bad.

Grace   You could never be bad.

Heloise *looks more closely at* **Grace**. **Grace** *has a bruise on her neck and lower jaw.*

Heloise   Is that a bruise?

Grace (*evasively*)   Hockey. Got hit with a ball.

Heloise (*inspecting more closely*)   Those are finger marks. Who was it – the same guys? Who are they? I'll kill them!

Maddie   Oh my days. Did your parents freak out?

Grace   Yeah. At first. Then Mum said something along the lines of maybe it's a bit of a wake-up call.

Ruby   You have to report them, Grace.

Grace   To who? Thrower? Like he'd listen.

A pause as they silently acknowledge this.

Anuka (*who has been seething silently*)   Nobody listens to us. We have to do something. Make them listen.

Sera   Yes, we should write a letter!

Maddie   Pfff! They'd use it for a dart board.

Layla   How about passive resistance like Martin Luther King? Stage a sit-in?

Heloise   Some girls did that – just ended up getting pelted with spit wads for a few hours.

Ruby   Jesus believed in fighting back: 'I did not come to bring peace but a sword.'

Sera   The pen is mightier than the sword.

Anuka   No, it isn't. They ignore what we write. They ignore what we say. It would take a fire to get their attention.

She becomes silent, thoughtful. The others don't like this silence.

Heloise   Whoa, Anuka . . . Let's not go crazy stations here.

Anuka   The competition. Everyone will be there. All the parents. Thrower, the board of governors, the theatres, the papers. Theatre is all about surprise, right? Make your own rules and then break them. We can use the trial scene. Make them see. We're not witches and we won't be burned anymore.

Heloise   I don't get it, how's that going to make them see?

Anuka   Because we'll do it our way. I've got some ideas but I'm gonna need your input as well.

Sera   What are you on about, Anuka, what ideas, how can we help?

Anuka   Meet me in the woods in an hour. And bring pen and paper. Are you in?

All the girls nod and express agreement. They're in, apart from **Sera**. *A pause; everyone stares at* **Sera.**

Sera   Oh go on then, why not? What have we got to lose?

Anuka   Come on, the bus is here.

Playfest

It is St Paul's performance of The Crucible. *Onstage, the courtroom scene is* under way.

Wolf as Danforth   Do you know, Mr Proctor, that the entire contention of the state is that heaven is talking through these children?

Sam as Proctor   I know that, sir.

Wolf as Danforth   And you, Mary Warren, how came you to accuse people of sending their spirits against you?

St Paul's Girl as Mary   It were pretense, sir.

Wolf as Danforth   And the other girls? They were also pretending?

Suddenly, **Anuka, Layla, Heloise, Ruby, Maddie, Sera** *and* **Grace** *walk onto the* stage.

Heloise as Mercy   Yes, sir.

Maddie as Susannah   Yes, sir.

Sera as Betty   Yes, sir.

Layla as Tituba   That's right, sir. We were pretending.

An awkward pause. It's clear **Wolf** *and the others on stage had no prior knowledge of this.*

Wolf as Danforth   Girls, what . . . what are? . . . . you can't . . .

Sam   Anuka –?

Anuka as Abigail   I, Abigail Williams, have come to withdraw my accusation.

Layla as Tituba   And I, Tituba.

Heloise as Mercy   And I, Mercy Lewis.

Ruby as Mary   And I, Mary Warren.

Sera as Betty   And I, Betty Parris.

Maddie as Susannah   And I, Susannah Walcott.

A slight pause.

Bo as Parris   That's – enough. Abigail, go home. And take the rest of . . . your gang with you.

Anuka as Abigail   No, Uncle. We started this and we're the ones who can end it.

Wolf as Danforth   You can't . . . This is . . . . contempt of court. Er . . . Bailiff?

He gestures to **Skive** *who moves forward and makes a gesture of 'what do I do?'*

Ruby as Mary   We call Reverend Hale as our witness.

Al *looks to* **Wolf** *for help.* **Wolf** *gestures for him to play along.* **Al** *hesitantly steps forward.*

Heloise as Mercy   Reverend Hale, you were brought to Salem as an expert on witches. Where did you gain all this knowledge?

Al as Hale   . . . From . . . books?

Heloise as Mercy   Will you please explain the meaning of 'spectral evidence'?

Al as Hale   Er, it's, er . . . evidence . . . from a person . . . that's based on a vision they had of someone sending their spectre – their sort of evil spirit – to hurt them.

Layla as Tituba   And Reverend Hale, what's the main problem with spectral evidence? The reason it's been thrown out of courts in the past?

Al as Hale   . . . It can be made up . . .?

Sera as Betty   That's right. Like we did. The question is, why did you all believe us?

They pull out copies of old-looking books, and when **Anuka** *gives them the nod, they start up a rhythm by slapping the books and then begin a well-rehearsed and impressive routine which builds in intensity throughout the following.*

Anuka as Abigail   There is a dark force in Salem, but not the one you think.

Layla as Titbua   It's fear. Fear of the unknown.

Grace   Fear of difference.

Ruby as Mary   Fear of change.

Maddie as Susannah   We left one continent for another. We left so-called civilisation for a wilderness. So we could have a fresh start. And yet we brought all the same old beliefs with us.

Anuka as Abigail   The only thing that should be on trial today is fear.

Heloise as Mercy   And ignorance.

Layla as Tituba   Suppression of ideas.

Grace   And distrust of anyone who doesn't conform.

Layla as Tituba   We told you stories. Ones we made up. You had taken stories away from the people of Salem. We gave them back.

Heloise as Mercy   Why were you so quick to believe our lies when you'd never once listened to our truths?

Sera as Betty   This time, you must hear the truth. Goody Proctor, Goody Corey and Goody Nurse are no more witches than you, sir, (*pointing to* **Judge Danforth**) are the devil.

Layla as Tituba   Or you, sir, (*pointing to* **Parris**) are an angel.

Ruby as Mary   Or you, sir, (*pointing to* **Hale**) can ever conquer a wilderness with fear.

The girls start to make a pile of the books in the middle of the stage. They appear to be creating a bonfire – one of them exits the stage and returns with a petrol can and proceeds to pour a liquid on the pile.

Bo as Parris (*genuinely worried by this*)   Stop it. What are you doing?

Sam as Proctor   Er, Abigail . . .?

Wolf as Danforth   You can't do this. People have already died because of you.

Heloise as Mercy (*to* **Danforth**)   And you, Judge Danforth.

Layla as Tituba   And you, Reverend Parris.

Ruby as Mary   And your books, Reverend Hale.

Anuka as Abigail (*pointing to the pile of books*)   This is where the witches are. The only place they've ever been. This is where we learn what our world was . . . and is . . . and should be.

Heloise as Mercy   Where we conjure dreams.

Sera as Betty   Sometimes nightmares.

Maddie as Susannah   Give shape to ideas.

Layla as Tituba   And let ideas go.

Ruby as Mary   And from the old, make something new.

The girls gather in closer around the books. **Heloise** *pulls out a lighter. We see* **Miss Alexi** *now, hovering, ready to spring onto the stage but fearful. The lighter is passed from girl to girl until at last,* **Anuka** *holds the petrol can and lighter over the pile of books. She and* **Miss Alexi** *lock eyes. Just as* **Miss Alexi** *begins to rush towards her,* **Anuka** *turns the petrol can around, to reveal the word 'water' written in big block capitals on the side of it.* **Miss Alexi** *stops dead in her tracks. The girls remove their pilgrim bonnets and hold them over the pile of books. They look a bit like flowers blooming.*

Anuka as Abigail   Don't give in to fear. Take new ideas and give them strength and then let them fly!

All the girls   Let them fly!

They toss their bonnets into the air. They rain down. Stillness. Silence. They play is over. The actors glance at each other uncertainly. The audience is unsure. **Miss Alexi** *starts to clap. The remaining members of the cast come to the side of the stage and slowly begin clapping too. The applause grows louder and louder as the audience joins in.*

Ruins

Optional slide: 'The day after the competition.' The woods behind the playing fields. The forest school den lies in ruins. **Anuka** *and* **Sam** *are starting to build it again.*

Anuka   Can you believe it? Fourth year running! Sera must have posted a hundred photos of us with the prize cup.

Sam   Yeah. You're on top of the world.

Anuka   And you. All of us. We did it! Even Miss Alexi said well done. I was hoping she'd be in to tell us our marks today. I bet she's either in Majorca or a foetal position thanking the lord it's all over. Can you believe that supply teacher trying to get us to play hangman?! Bo must be feeling sorry he grassed us up. He offered to lend me his notes for History. Anyway, the suspension won't matter now that we won. I never believed he would nark, but he's always been a bit like that.

Sam (*slowly*)   He didn't nark. I did.

Anuka *stops, branch in hands. From his manner, she can tell he means it.*

Anuka   . . . What?

Sam   I had to, Nuka. I couldn't let a play ruin my whole life. I thought for sure you'd get sick of the extra work and give up. But you kept going and going and it all got a bit too real . . . I didn't name names or anything. I just sort of . . . dropped a hint.

Anuka   I can't believe it. You would never have done that to Wolf. Or Al or Bo or even Skive.

Sam   Nuka, I swear. I never said your name. (*Off her annoyed manner.*) You think you can stop the whole world from doing *The Crucible*? Grow up. Maybe you just don't get it. Ok, the girls look bad. The men don't exactly look brilliant. Everyone goes mental. And ok, you made up a new trial scene and the judges liked it though only because they're trying to be all PC but you can't change the past. The girls in Salem really did accuse people and get them killed. They really did scream and have fits and they probably couldn't even read and there's no way any of them would have been able to stand up in court and speak like lawyers.

Anuka   We've been friends since we were born. Doesn't that mean anything?

Sam   What do you expect it to mean?

A slight pause.

Anuka (*in disbelief*)   You sold me out. You sold me out, Sam.

She is upset by this, starts dismantling the den and scattering the branches.

Sam   What are you doing?

Anuka   If we wipe all traces of the den, do you think they'll build something completely different somewhere else?

Sam   Anuka. Anuka. Hey . . .

Anuka   No one will remember this. None of it. Couple of weeks, it won't matter at all. I'll remember, though. So will you.

He is contrite. He goes to her and puts his arms around her.

Sam   I'm sorry, Nuka. I swear I never thought they would make such a big deal about it.

Anuka   . . . It's ok . . .

She breaks the hug, fetches her rucksack and slings it on her back. She begins to walk off.

Sam   So see you at assembly? Yeah? Thrower's gonna take personal credit for us winning. I can't wait to see his face . . . both of them, can you? Heloise is going to spit. (*She keeps on walking.*) Nuka? Anuka? . . .

Assembly

The assembly hall. It is draped with vertical banners of the great men of yore including Newton, Locke, Shakespeare, etc. . . . but only one woman, Elizabeth I. **Mr Thrower, Briggs,** *other teachers and a group of prefects stand before the assembled pupils.* **Miss Alexi** *is conspicuously absent.*

Mr Thrower   Good morning. We have called this special assembly in honour of our recent win at Playfest.

Spontaneous applause. A chant of 'stand up, stand up, stand up'. **Anuka** *and the others bashfully stand up and soak in the moment. They are greeted with a wave of applause and whoops.*

Mr Thrower   The staff and students of St Paul's have been lauded across the country and they know they owe a debt of gratitude to you, their peers.

More cheers.

St Paul's Girl   Where's Miss Alexi?

St Paul's Boy   Yeah, where's Miss Alexi?! Give it up for Miss Alexi!

More cheers.

Mr Thrower   . . . Sadly, Miss Alexi has made the decision to move on. Which brings me to the issue of what happened at the end of the play. This cannot be overlooked. To be clear. I believe that although there was obviously a core group of instigators, the entire student body turned a blind eye to the things they were seeing and hearing. This is a gross dereliction of personal responsibility and loyalty to your school, your families and wider society, and as such, you should all be ashamed. And for which, appropriate disciplinary action will be administered across the board. Behaviour of this sort cannot and never will be tolerated.

Anuka *and her friends look at each other, taken aback by this turn, and slowly sit back down.*

Mr Thrower   However, we are aware that just one girl among you was the ring leader. One girl among you took it upon herself to sabotage last night's performance. Motivated, as she was, by a malicious desire to ruin the play, for warped and indefensible reasons of her own. She knows who she is. And I suspect you all do, too. So I say directly to that individual, if you don't come forward to admit your guilt, right now, before everyone gathered here, we will be forced to suspend all the girls in the cast until the end of the academic year – effectively terminating their education. This is your last chance to show some semblance of honour.

Anuka (*stands up, raising her hand, a sudden hush*)   Mr Thrower?

Sam *immediately rises.*

Sam   Sir, can I say something?

Mr Thrower (*sharply*)   Sit down, Sam. Yes, Anuka. What have you to say for yourself?

Anuka *looks to her friends, then to the rest of the assembly, then back to* **Mr Thrower**. *All her anger is gone . . . she speaks with simplicity and calm.*

Anuka   You told me I could be anything. All the teachers. Since primary school. Teachers are always telling us we can be anything. But that's not how you treat us. Sir, I was the leader. It was me.

Heloise (*jumping up*)   No, Mr Thrower. It was me!

Grace (*stands up*)   It was me.

Layla (*stands up*)   It was me.

Maddie (*stands up*)   It was me.

Ruby (*stands up*)   It was me.

Sera (*stands up*)   It was me.

Mr Thrower   All right, ladies, if that's how you / want it –

Sam (*stands up*)   It was me.

Wolf (*stands up*)   It was me.

Al (*stands up*)   It was me.

Other boys from the cast stand, then other pupils in the auditorium stand saying 'It was me'. **Anuka** *looks to either side at her fellow pupils. She looks back at* **Mr Thrower**.

End.

Witches Can't Be Burned

BY SILVA SEMERCIYAN

Notes on rehearsal and staging, drawn from a workshop with the writer, held at the National Theatre, October 2019

Introduction

After initial introductions, lead director Orla O'Loughlin invited the group to raise any questions or areas that they'd like to address during the workshop.

The group came up with the following:

- How much of the original text of *The Crucible* is necessary for the company to know in order to unlock the play?
- Sets
  - How naturalistic or minimalist can you go?
  - How could the play work on scales/budgets?
- Casting
  - Getting the gender balance right
  - Ensemble parts – across group size. Managing a lot of bodies onstage
  - Multi-roling
- What are the rules of the play and what is open to interpretation?
- Scene changes and transitions as the play has a number of different locations
- Does it encompass one performance style or are there different styles to discover?
- Character
  - How to get depth out of the students
- Bus stop scene
  - Unlocking the meaning
  - Logistics of staging it
- Overlapping dialogue and how it works
- Interested in the politics and how to empower the young participants to make decisions for themselves in the process?

How Silva came to write the play

Silva Semerciyan shared with the group that she saw a production of *The Crucible* and was struck by how the girls were depicted as hysterical and hypersexualised. The notion that this play is a 'masterpiece' and therefore untouchable and not to be questioned led her to write her own play – the girls in *Witches Can't Be Burned* have a similar awakening. When you start to make the unseen visible, it's hard to stop – from questioning why Smurfette is the only female Smurf to classical literature. Silva did further research into *The Crucible*'s playwright Arthur Miller and the Salem witch trials, and examined what other choices were available for him to make. The decision to look at McCarthyism didn't have to come at the expense of the female characters.

Rehearsing this play is also about encouraging your young people to question everything, but this can be focused on the play's big themes about gender and dehumanising the female characters. The idea of feminist critical theory can be quite daunting – what is in the current consciousness and culture that you could bring into the rehearsal room? This play feels very live and active as a social discourse. You could ask the students to bring in examples from the news, TV, social media. Ask them why this is a play for right now. We're in a time when classics are being flipped; from race to class, it's de rigueur to flip and question, to represent society. How can classic work meet the twenty-first century?

Themes

In response to the group's questions, the conversation centred around some of the play's big themes.

Gender

A play is not just a play – drama teachers and the plays they choose can have an impact.

- Elizabeth Proctor isn't a hysterical character, but equally she doesn't step outside her gender role; she reinforces the male.
- Prefects: In the interrogation scenes, there is a preference to have them match the gender of those they are interrogating to get the right dynamic, so far as you can with your group.
- The male teachers don't realise they're differentiating, so many other factors are allowing and enabling them to. The Head isn't meant to be a full villain, but the whole apparatus of society is enabling his actions. He is unable to transcend his position in the hierarchy.
- The female teacher is thrown under the bus. Her role is the most precarious in this model; she has the lowest status.
- Everything that imparts status is part of this gendered paradigm that imparts privilege.
- Age is important in terms of hierarchy in schools as well as gender. True of *The Crucible* too: it's age with gender.

Educational institutions

- Be ready to have difficult conversations that arise as a result of this work, if it reflects things in your own institution.
- Young people vs institutions and the potential for change.
- The name St Paul's might suggest a faith school, but don't be tied to this. It allows the play to echo the religion in *The Crucible*, but could easily still be an academy. Rather than setting the play at your school, let the students and your audience make connections between your school and the one in this play.
- What does this mean for your institution? What's your institution's relationship to the institution in this play?
- Miss Alexi is sympathetic – she understands Anuka but is constrained by her situation. She isn't intended to be all the negative traits of an overbearing drama teacher – she is nuanced and reasonable, she is trying her best.

Approaching the challenges of the play in rehearsal

Removing clothes

The Crucible itself contains this and is produced in schools, so it's worth discussing with your students. Take this direction in the play as little or as far as is appropriate for your group. Even the way a bonnet comes off can tell us what's coming next and can signal how uncomfortable Anuka is with it.

Race

Who is in the group? Make sure the context of the play is seeing those people and their identities.

- Headscarves and casting
  - As with removing clothes, interpret this however is appropriate for your group and do as little as you need.
  - It doesn't need to be a Christian faith school; multi-faith or state may feel more appropriate.
  - In the bus stop game, they can be low-risk items depending on the character; not everyone needs to be raising the stakes with clothing or other personal items.
- Tituba
  - An enslaved woman, the historical accuracy around her race throws open questions. She's probably a woman of colour; is she black or mixed race or Native American? Acknowledge the casting choice you make.
  - She may have a different accent, but it doesn't need to be specific if the other members of the cast aren't being asked to do accents.

Exercises

Exercise: Reading

Orla cast the group and they read the opening. Beginnings and endings are so important – the beginning for clarity and establishing the world, the end for the final image and ideas. Silva has given you stage directions, so these were read too so that the group could be mindful of the choice of every word. It's worth paying attention to these when you begin.

Exercise: Working in groups

Orla divided the group in two and asked them to work on the first scene for twenty minutes. The way to do it is to do it; Orla encouraged everyone to get up so they had something to go on. It helps to understand the logistics and have a mutual place to work from. The opening scene is an invitation to your company to imagine the 'wrong' version of this opening, what the audience might think they're sitting down to watch.

Reflections:

- The scene is high energy.
- It sets up the power play, the authorial voice of the writer to be respected.
- It contains Anuka's epiphany – how quickly does she get there? When do we see it?
- It doesn't need to be funny or sent up – play into audience expectations.
- Is this a dress rehearsal? Or more clearly an earlier rehearsal? It depends on what you want the moment of Anuka's interruption to be. What are the stakes of that moment? Whatever your answer, what are they wearing? Would bonnets be enough to convince the audience of this version at the beginning?
- How much in terms of technical elements is there? How big does this make Anuka's interruption?
- Playfest is important, whether it's actually a big competition or not.
- They have won Playfest three times, so there is thought and care in this version of *The Crucible*.
- You have one chance to surprise the audience and this is the moment. What are the expectations, how are you challenging the audience?
- Contemporary references can work, but make them earnest and commit.
- Scale of sets – in this exercise only chairs were used and the meaning of the scene was clear; it was clear they signified a cauldron for example. You can signify this whatever your budget.
- Are there scripts on stage? Where?
- Three weeks before a deadline can still be chaos. You can be true to that, or to the rules of the world of this play. What are the conditions that will serve the telling of this story?

- What is the cost for Anuka to put her hand up and say no? What is the cost to the group of her doing this? How is the group dynamic changed? Something to examine with your students.

- Does Anuka normally speak up, or is this a shift? You can show in the reactions of the other girls how big a deal this is. What does that suggest about their closeness?

- What moment prompts Anuka to speak up?

- The boys are offstage and in the wings.

Exercise: Transitions

The groups worked from the end of Scene One and into Scene Two to create options for transitions.

Ideas for transitions included:

- Pace – Anuka still and the others fast, or vice versa.

- Going from slow motion to normal speed.

- Both can help you control what your audience is looking at, where their focus is. Your main character can tell us this.

- Transitions should be quick and not take up too much time. Move the story along where possible.

- Make a definite choice to move to the next scene.

- The group working as an ensemble and then breaking into separate tasks/ business is satisfying to watch.

- You could start to put away the pile to get ready for the next scene, so it's easier to then get into the next transition.

- Where the cauldron was, the pile was. A focal point. If it is a cauldron, what is it, could things come out of it?

Bus stop scene

The bus stop scene came up in a number of questions at the beginning, so the group looked at it practically.

Meaning

They are playing a game of chicken with the bus, daring it to come because it is late. Each character's relation to risk becomes clear here, e.g. Heloise putting her body on the road. You could perhaps punctuate the dialogue with a new item each time – feel free to add more items than are named in the script. The young people in your groups may see echoes of protest, of Extinction Rebellion (for example) and the power of young people. You don't need to use a motorised skateboard; use what you have or an analogue for this, e.g. heelies or a scooter.

Reflections on approaching the scene practically

- The more unruly it is, the more natural, the better.
- Each performer should always be doing something – taking a selfie, chatting, on their phone.
- Ask your students to observe behaviour at their bus stop and bring in examples.
- The large group can be helpful in telling us where to focus – sometimes you can use the geography of the space, but also use that to guide the eye.
- There is something very satisfying for an audience to see an ensemble working at the same time.
- You could have someone go between each of the locations – giving the audience someone to lead their attention and focus.
- It almost needs to be choreographed so that cues can be picked up and an audience knows where to look.

You can empower your young people by giving them the opportunity to experiment and explore scenes in a practical way and then come back and share. What worked, what didn't? You don't have to know how to do it all – pick the best bits! The young people will feel ownership if they have created things. Let them have the conversations for themselves. Through this, you also work out what doesn't work too. In the spirit of discovery, you get the buy-in from them. And it means you are not underestimating them either; they have great ideas.

Exercise: Editing

Once each group had an established version of these two scenes, Orla and Silva suggested things to try. The group kept the general shape of their scenes, but with new suggestions and tasks they drew out some of the ideas that had been discussed. The group made the following observations as a result of this work.

Major and minor dialogue

Major dialogue: the written dialogue in the scene.

Minor dialogue: improvised/devised dialogue.

The group experimented with major and minor conversation and volume on stage. All members of the ensemble had to be active and engaged, but how much will pull focus?

- Dialogue is always major. The audience needs to know the plot, and to get to know these characters.
- Minor should be in support – making us believe in the world – but never overtake.
- Minor keeps energy in the scene.
- Keep everyone in the same space, don't split the major from the minor too much physically so you don't split the audience's attention.

- It will depend on your group and their vocal control.
- Sustain it – if it comes and goes it is distracting. It's about the confidence to commit to it.
- It could make a great improv task for your group to decide what they're talking about at the bus stop, in the classroom, etc.

Point of focus

- Putting Anuka in the centre of the bus stop scene means that she doesn't get lost in the scene. Make the ensemble interact and work around her.
- Everyone could make one entrance or exit throughout the scene except Anuka – she is still, the group creates a sense of movement.
- Could Anuka's movements be more stylised than the others onstage?
- Does it matter if you lose her for a moment, even in the centre? What is the effect when she then speaks?
- Is her silence a source of tension for the others? How does she normally behave, and is this different?
- How does Sam interact with her, or clock her behaviour, if they are best friends? What will his reaction tell the audience?
- Anuka's silence is because she's thinking. She is not necessarily someone who is inclined to think she's always right, so she is re-examining the play for more information.
- What is the geography of the scene? Mark out where the school is, the direction of the bus, so actors can play the real and present situation of waiting for a bus.
- Working this way is taste-driven – all the participants can feed in, try out ideas, decide what works. Your job as director is to pick which ideas work for your production.

Another new set of rules were introduced for this bus stop scene, which included:

- Everyone comes and goes once.
- Remove the chairs being used to stage the scene.
- Mark out the exact beginning and end of the pavement.
- Agree on the direction of travel for the bus, what is at each exit.

Observations for this run of the scene included:

- It was great to have it clear where the danger was. A precipice.
- Helping the audience know where they are is quite important. Keep the bus alive – they want the bus to come.
- There was a clearer sense of time and of geography.
- Everyone was able to make interesting and smart choices about coming and going – you can then make clear decisions about these and really choreograph them.

- Bags are important – they can indicate character, you can have every prop you need in there. How do they carry their bag that gives characterisation? A bag might mean they don't need a uniform, so you could have something simpler?

- Light and sound can assist you, but they're not the thing. Can you do it without those and create movement with purpose and clarity? You need to be resourceful and find it with your group. That version then allows the audience to find it in themselves.

- It is important to highlight and remember these reasons when it comes to working on the play with your young people – to remind yourself and them that this is why you're making this play together.

Question and answer with Silva Semerciyan

Some final questions were asked of Silva about specific moments:

The den – how far built do you imagine it being? Have they been building it for years? Is it theirs, their little posse?

There's a clearing in these woods, with branches propped up in the same place; no matter where the sticks end up, it's always the same structure. This is intended as a metaphor – rebuilding structure everywhere they go. This can be done as simply as you need. You can reject the literal reading and see what that opens up. What does being in a den do to the body? Could you mark something on the floor? What does building a den do to the speed of your transitions?

The trial scene comes near the end of their performance, but there's also a fourth act. Is this the end of their Playfest performance?

It can be – it's still a sizeable chunk of the play to be believable for such a competition. The trial scene comes near the end of their performance, but there's also a fourth act in *The Crucible*.

From a workshop led by Orla O'Loughlin
with notes by Katherine Nesbitt

Dungeness

by Chris Thompson

In a remote part of the UK, where nothing ever happens, a group of teenagers share a safe house for LGBT+ young people.

While their shared home welcomes difference, it can be tricky for self-appointed group leader Birdie to keep the peace. The group must decide how they want to commemorate an attack that happened to LGBT+ people, in a country far away. How do you take to the streets and protest if you're not ready to tell the world who you are? If you're invisible, does your voice still count? A play about love, commemoration and protest.

Cast size
9 (plus a choir)
Recommended for ages 14+

Chris Thompson is a writer for stage and screen. Theatre includes: *Of Kith and Kin* (Sheffield Theatres and Bush Theatre); *Albion* (Bush Theatre); *Carthage* (Finborough Theatre), *Trueno* (National Theatre of Peru); and *Dungeness* (NT Connections).

Chris won a Pearson Playwriting Award and was nominated for Best New Play and Most Promising New Playwright in the Offie Awards for *Carthage*. *Albion* won the Simon Gray Award. He was the Channel 4 Playwright in Residence at the Finborough Theatre in 2014 and is an alumni of the 2018 C4 Screenwriting Course. He has led several of the writers groups at the Royal Court Theatre as well as the Bush Theatre's Emerging Writers Group.

In his previous career Chris was a social worker and over the course of twelve years worked in child protection, youth offending and young people's sexual health. More info at: www.christhompsonwriter.com

Characters

Birdie
Orson
Jotham
Jen
Adira
Franny
Tana
Caia

Setting

New Romney town centre. Not far from Dungeness beach.

The communal room of a semi-independent home for young people. It's a large house that has been converted for communal living for young people. It's a strange mix between attempted homeliness and doctor's waiting room. All the doors are fire doors, and there are emergency fire exit signs and a fire blanket. It feels like there's been a risk assessment on every bit of furniture because there probably has. The TV is locked in a cupboard. There are beanbags and a sofa and arm chairs and the stained carpet looks like it's from a school staff room. The room has been painted bright and happy colours by previous residents, which makes it all the more depressing.

The window is frosted so the light comes in but you can't see in or out. The same window is cracked from where someone has thrown a stone at it from the outside.

Somewhere on the walls are the house ground rules and a wall display which are referred to later in the play. Also on the wall are the Stonewall posters, which say, 'Some people are gay/trans/bi etc. Get over it.' And next to them is a washing-up rota.

Text

/ means the following speaker overlaps.

– means a character deliberately remaining silent or struggling to find the words.

They've just started a house meeting. Everyone is there except **Caia**.

Birdie   I say BOOM.

Silence.

I say BOOM.

Silence.

I say BOOM-CHICKA.

Silence.

I say BOOM-CHICKA-ROCKA-BOOM.

I say BOOM-CHICKA-ROCKA-BOOM.

Jen?

BOOM-CHICKA-ROCKA-BOOM, Jen.

Jen? I say BOOM-CHICKA-ROCKA-BOOM, Jen?

Jen   –

Birdie   BOOM-CHICKA-ROCKA-BOOM, Adira?

Adira? BOOM-CHICKA-ROCKA-BOOM?

Adira   –

Birdie   Lots of energy, guys, yeah come on? Lots of upbeat positive energy.

Adira   –

Birdie   OK, Orson, I'm not gonna even bother.

Franny.

BOOM-CHICKA-ROCKA-BOOM, Franny.

Yeah? Like that do you, Franny? Want some of Birdie's energy?

Franny   –

Birdie   Ooo, careful, who knows where I might go next, Tana?

It could be anyone, Tana.

Where am I gonna go next, Tana?

BOOM-CHICKA-ROCKA-BOOM, Tana. Yes!

Tana   –

Birdie   No?

Lots of energy, come on let's get you all up on your feet and energised, Jotham, you love this one, I know you do. Don't leave me hanging, Jotham, I'm looking to you. Ready? Let's do it, come on Jotham. Energy, eye contact, cool, yeah?

Jotham, ready, this one's for you.

I say BOOM-CHICKA-ROCKA-BOOM.

Orson   Don't do it, Jotham.

Birdie   BOOM-CHICKA-ROCKA-BOOM.

Orson   Stay strong.

Birdie   I say BOOM-CHICKA-ROCKA-BOOM, Jotham.

Orson   Don't let her break you.

Birdie   BOOM-CHICKA-ROCKA-BOOM, Jotham.

BOOM-CHICKA-ROCKA-BOOM, Jotham.

Orson   This is what she does. She picks off a weak one.

Birdie   BOOM-CHICKA-ROCKA-BOOM, Jotham.

Orson   Jotham.

Birdie   BOOM-CHICKA-ROCKA-BOOM.

Orson   Jotham.

Birdie   BOOM-CHICKA-ROCKA-BOOM.

Orson   No, Jotham.

Birdie   I say BOOM-CHICKA-ROCKA-BOOM, Jotham.

Orson   Don't let her beat you.

Birdie   BOOM-CHICKA-ROCKA-BOOM.

BOOM-CHICKA-ROCKA-BOOM.

You want to.

Don't you? Don't you, Jotham?

Yeah?

You want it?

It's coming.

Birdie's coming.

BOOM-CHICKA-ROCKA-BOOM, Jotham.

That's what I say, Jotham.

Orson   Stay strong, Jotham,

Birdie   I say BOOM-CHICKA-ROCKA-BOOM.

Orson   This is bigger than you.

Birdie   BOOM-CHIKCA-ROCKA-BOOM, Jotham.

Orson   Eyes on me, Jotham.

Birdie   BOOM-CHICKA-ROCKA-BOOM, JOTHAM!

Orson   Look at me.

Birdie   BOOM-CHICKA-ROCKA-BOOM, JOTHAM!

Orson   Resist.

Birdie   BOOM-CHICKA-ROCKA-BOOM HE WANTS IT.

Orson   Stay strong. Eyes on me.

Birdie   BOOM-CHICKA-ROCKA-BOOM, JOTHAM!

Orson   No!

Birdie   BOOM-CHICKA-ROCKA-BOOM.

Orson   Jotham, no!

Jotham   I say boom-chicka-rocka-boom.

Birdie   YES! YES YOU DO.

YES YOU DO BLOODY SAY IT. THAT'S WHAT I'M TALKING ABOUT. COME ON!

Orson   You're weak.

Birdie   BOOM-CHICKA-ROCKA-BOOM, Jotham.

Jotham   I say BOOM-CHICKA-ROCKA-BOOM, Birdie.

Birdie   Now we're rolling.

BOOM-CHICKA-ROCKA-BOOM, Jen.

Jen   You won't break me.

Birdie   Oh yeah?

Orson   Dig deep, Jen.

Birdie   Boom-chicka-shut-your-face, Orson.

Adira   Please, make it stop.

Birdie   This is your meeting, guys.

Your space; your meeting.

This feels good doesn't it? All of us connecting and communicating, alert, full of energy.

Woo! Yeah!

OK, so what I'm hearing you say is that /

Adira   That this is shit.

Birdie   I'm hearing you say you all really enjoyed the icebreaker.

She finds her agenda.

Fun and hilarious icebreaker.

Tick.

Everyone energised and ready to participate.

Tick.

Item two.

Emus.

I can't read my writing.

Oh yes: emotions.

Does anyone have any emotions?

Adira   I'd like to kill myself.

Birdie   Right that's quite a biggie there, Adira, not sure we're all ready or qualified for that. Any alternative emotion you're feeling other than the one you just said that you could share instead?

Adira   Nope, it's mainly just that one.

Birdie   Well, maybe just park that for now, OK, Adira?

Lovely.

What about you, Jen?

Jen   –

Birdie   Jotham?

Jotham   –

Birdie   Adira?

Adira   –

Birdie   Any emotions, Franny? Any at all?

Franny   –

Birdie   Any emotions from anyone at all?

Do we need a reminder of the ground rules?

Number four: 'Make a positive contribution.'

I'm here to facilitate you making a positive a contribution.

Adira, you sure?

Adira   –

Birdie   Fine.

OK, let's do another icebreaker.

Groans.

Tana   Can someone please shoot me?

Adira   Count yourself lucky you don't actually live here.

Birdie   OK, then, fine, let's just sit in silence and you won't be heard and you won't get a say in how we do things at Spectrum, and sod you all, sod the lot of you, I mean it.

Thank you.

So let's get back to the agenda.

I have convened this meeting because of last night's incident.

Orson   Where's Sally?

Birdie   Sally is on annual leave.

Orson   So we can't have a meeting then.

Birdie   Yes we can.

Orson   You're not allowed to take meetings unsupervised.

Birdie   Not true.

Orson   Are you qualified yet?

Birdie   No.

Orson   There you go.

Birdie   Sally said it's fine.

Sally said I'm more than capable of taking this meeting on my own. And given there's a deadline, we have to have it now.

Orson   Yes, but /

Birdie   More than capable, Orson.

Sally's words not mine.

And I'm the oldest.

Orson   Only by two months.

Birdie   I'm not a teenager anymore and all you lot still are and a lot can happen in two months that makes someone more mature.

Jen   Like getting fingered by Becky Both-Ways behind Lidl?

Birdie   I don't discuss my private life with residents, it's unprofessional.

Orson   But you'll lock yourself in the bathroom and cry when Becky Both-Ways goes back to her boyfriend.

Very professional.

Birdie   It was painful.

Jotham   Her fingers aren't that big.

Birdie   Emotionally painful.

Jotham   ET phone home.

Birdie   Let's all have a good laugh at my suffering, thanks, great right let's move on.

We need to agree the agenda.

TV rota, washing-up rota, we'll do at the end. We have bigger fingers – fish, we have bigger fish to fry.

After last night's debacle, I want us to get this thing sorted once and for all.

Jotham   We all go as Disney princesses.

Orson   This is a silent protest.

Tana   How come you're talking then?

Birdie   I don't mean the theme for Bournemouth Pride, Jotham. We'll have to park that till next meeting.

You're all going to have to talk to each other again at some point.

Orson   They're not talking because they're protesting against you, Birdie.

Birdie   They're not talking because they all blame each other for there being no wifi.

And if we ever have a scene like last night again, I'll switch it off for a month.

So let's get to business.

As you've all seen fit to discuss it on social media, but can't seem to discuss it face to face, we're going to all put our phones in this box and you don't get them back till we have agreed how you will commemorate the two minutes' silence.

It's happening like literally in half an hour, and we need to agree what we're doing.

Orson   We don't have time.

Jen   I've got a test to revise for.

Birdie   All phones in the box please.

Jotham   What if we miss it?

Birdie   Set your alarm for thirty minutes' time, Jotham.

Adira I'm not sitting here with these idiots for half an hour. I'm not talking to them anyway.

Jen No one's talking to you either.

Jotham I am.

Tana Me too.

Jotham I'm only not talking to Orson cos he slagged off Bournemouth Pride and Bournemouth Pride is amazing.

Franny, who are you not talking to?

Franny –

Jotham Right.

Adira I'm not talking to anyone but I'm talking to Jotham a little bit.

Jen If she's not talking to me, I'm not talking to her.

And how come she's allowed to eat her dinner in her room and we're not?

Birdie Adira, you're our newest arrival, so I don't expect you to know, but here at Spectrum, we sort things out by talking.

Orson As our longest member I can tell you we sort absolutely nothing out by talking cos Birdie's in charge.

Birdie We do sort things by talking actually.

Jotham Yeah and not by emptying the kitchen bin in my bed.

Adira That wasn't me.

Jen Who was it then?

Birdie I'm going to interview you all separately about it and for the record, Orson, how do you think we got the washing-up rota if it wasn't by talking, or the TV rota, or the food-labelling system?

Jen We hate all those things.

Orson Yes, hence our silent protest.

Birdie But for now, we've got one agenda item and one agenda item only.

It's happening up and down the county, all over the world in fact. You want to be left out?

I know it happened a long way away. But we need to agree on how we're going to commemorate it.

So, phones please.

Groans.

Come on. They're not actually attached to you.

See, look. They detach from our bodies and everything. Oh my God it's not actually a claw, it's a hand.

Come on.

You know the rules.

She walks round with the box. With great difficulty, each parts with his/her/their phone.

Alarm set, Jotham?

Jotham   Yep.

Tana   That's my phone.

Jotham   Mum gave it to me when she confiscated it from you.

Tana   I'm taking it back with me.

Jen   It's his phone now.

Tana   Stop listening to our conversation.

Jen   You're in a communal space actually.

Tana   Yeah? Well it's a private conversation.

Adira   No such thing in this place.

Jotham   You lost it when you lied to Mum about going to that party so it's mine now.

Alarm is set.

And can we hurry up so we can talk about the Pride costumes?

Birdie   Not today, Jotham.

Jotham   It's not you who's got to make them.

Birdie   Jotham, I mean it. This is more important.

Jotham   OK, fine.

Go.

He sets his alarm and the phone goes off.

Birdie   Great, let's get this sorted once and for all.

Orson   Can't you lot remember anything? We're supposed to be doing a silent protest.

Birdie   No one gives a toss what you think, Orson.

Orson   I don't give you permission to speak to me like that.

Birdie   Like what?

Orson   I call that a very rude remark indeed.

Birdie   Oh do you?

Orson It's not appropriate for the youth empowerment mentors to speak to residents like that.

Sally wouldn't like it.

Birdie Sally's not here, are they?

Orson Do we need a reminder of the ground rules, Birdie?

Birdie Oh piss off.

Orson Number one: 'Everyone is entitled to be treated with respect.'

And can I just say, I felt very disempowered when you told me to piss off just now.

I felt shamed.

Birdie Orson, can I speak to you in my office please?

Orson You don't have an office.

Birdie Can you step into my office please?

Orson It's not an office.

Birdie Yes it is.

Orson No it's not.

Birdie Yes it is.

Orson It's a broom cupboard.

Birdie It's a multi-purpose room, can you come please?

Orson Into that room with the mop and bucket?

Birdie And a chair and a desk and a computer and wifi.

Jotham When can we have the wifi code again?

Birdie When Caia's done the washing-up. And when you lot start talking to each other again.

Jen How can she wash up when she's working all the time?

Jotham Where is she?

Jen Working, numbnuts.

Orson This room here with the dustpan and brush?

Birdie What do you want?

Orson And bin bags and bleach and the poster of /

Birdie What do you want?

Orson Aha. So you acknowledge our protest.

Birdie What protest?

Orson   This one.

Birdie   Against me?

Orson   We demand change.

Birdie   Of what?

Orson   This oppressive regime.

Birdie   Me?

But I'm nice.

I'm Birdie.

Orson   I have an announcement.

In the spirit of those who came before me: Pankhurst. Harvey Milk.

And some others.

I stand here before you and say, 'We protest'.

Enough is enough.

Birdie   Enough of what?

Orson   This is a takedown.

I'm going to dismantle you, Birdie.

Slowly, painfully, publicly.

I'm going to take you down.

Birdie   Is that a fact now?

Orson   Yes.

Birdie   You think you've got what it takes?

Orson   Oh yes.

And more.

Birdie   Got what it takes to come for me do you, Orson?

Orson   I've got what it takes to come for you, Birdie

Birdie   OK, let's go.

Orson   Let's go where?

Birdie   Let's go, figuratively, let's go as in you think you've got what it takes, so let's go.

Orson   Where do you wanna go, Birdie? Into the broom cupboard.

Birdie   Take the piss out of my multi-purpose room again, go on, do it and let's see what happens.

Tana   OK, stop.

Orson   This is a silent protest, Tana.

Birdie   Well shut your mouth then, Orson.

Tana   It's bullying.

Birdie   I'm not bullying him.

Tana   He's bullying you.

Birdie   I'm not being bullied.

Tana   Yes you are.

Birdie   No I'm not.

Tana   You are.

Orson   Tana, it's a silent protest.

Tana   Let's vote.

Hands up if you think Orson is bullying Birdie.

Orson   You don't even live here.

Tana   Hands up.

Birdie   This isn't on the agenda.

Tana   Who thinks Orson is bullying Birdie?

Everyone puts up his/her/their hands.

Birdie   He's not.

He's really not. I'm fine, guys, honestly.

What Orson is doing is a good example of 'acting out'.

Orson   Learn that in college this week did you?

Birdie   Orson is not happy with himself as a person, there are bits about himself he doesn't like and instead of saying, let me take ownership of that, he's come in and acted out.

And maybe I did learn it and you can't handle it because I'm the year above you and you don't know about it yet and you don't like that do you?

You can't handle me, can you?

You can't handle Birdie.

Orson   This is a coup, the ground rules no longer apply.

Birdie   The ground rules always apply.

And you guys wrote them yourselves, including you, Orson: your signature's on the bottom too. So sit down please and let's carry on.

Orson   REVOLUTION.

Birdie   Yes, Orson.

Orson   RAGE. REVOLUTION. REVOLT.

Shout it with me, everyone. RAGE, REVOLUTION, REVOLT.

Adira   Orson, you pressured us into not speaking and I'm not cool with that so sit down and shut up and let's get this dumb meeting over.

Orson   The ground rules, remember.

RAGE /

Adira   Do you want to eat the ground /

Orson   REVOLUTION /

Adira   – rules, Orson, cos I'll rip them off the wall and /

Orson   REVOLT.

Birdie   Right, stop!

We get it, Orson.

Thank you.

OK.

Right, can we carry on now please?

Back to the agenda.

Enter **Caia** *dressed as Ronald McDonald.*

Caia   Who took my burgers away?

Where is the hamburglar? I'm going to find them.

Orson   Who the hell are you?

Caia   I'm Ronald McDonald.

Who the hell are you?

Orson   We're in the middle of a coup here.

Caia   A coup!

How thrilling.

My, don't we all look sad.

Birdie   Can we have just one house meeting without all this, please?

Caia   You, girl.

Jen   Me?

Caia Yes, you.

Caia Why are you so sad?

Jen Why is Ronald McDonald talking to me?

Caia Ronald McDonald will not be silenced!

He comes with a message.

On this day, a day when love wins over hate, a day of coming together, a day of unity, a day of communities rising up all over the globe, in one bright voice, Ronald McDonald brings a message of hope.

Birdie Yes, babes.

Orson RAGE. REVOLUTION.

Adira Orson, do you have to do this every day?

Birdie Orson can choose *not* to do this every day if he likes.

Caia A message of hope, guys.

Birdie And if you are planning a coup, you need to put that in writing with twenty-four hours' advance warning and we need to do a risk assessment.

Caia Ronald McDonald will not be silenced!

You will hear him.

But you shall not fear him.

Birdie OK, can we all listen to Ronald McDonald's message of hope please?

Just a *quick* message of hope though please, Mr McDonald.

Jotham When are you lot gonna fix that window?

Birdie Thank you, Jotham, for using this space appropriately.

I'm happy you felt empowered and able to voice your concern safely.

Jotham Just answer the question.

Orson Yes, can you answer that please? Or is it more evidence of how you're unfit to lead this group?

Adira They'll only smash it again.

Birdie So we'll repair it.

Jotham Yeah, then they'll smash it again.

Birdie Let them.

It's not gonna ruin *my* day.

We'll repair it.

Jen   We should spend the money on something else.

Birdie   They're coming this afternoon.

Tana   Just board it up, then they can't smash it anymore.

Birdie   We're not doing that.

Tana   Why?

Birdie   If we leave it, it says this is OK, this is how we accept being treated.

We fix it because we fix it. No matter how many times they smash it.

Jen   It's a waste of money.

Birdie   There are other things we could spend it on, I agree.

Adira   Like better food.

Birdie   Like better food, or a trip to Bournemouth Pride, whatever.

Caia   Or a dishwasher.

Jen   They'll just keep on smashing it.

Tana   Why don't you put a CCTV camera up?

Birdie   We can't afford it.

Jen   Cos we spent the budget on fixing the window.

Caia   Silence, I say!

Ronald McDonald is experiencing an emotion.

Birdie   An emotion? Brilliant!

Don't panic, I'm coming.

Birdie's here, she's ready.

Tell Birdie, she's got you.

Caia   There is sadness in Ronald McDonald's heart.

Biride   Sadness. Amazing! That's great, really brilliant.

Everyone hear that? Ronald McDonald is sad, isn't that wonderful?

Anyone else?

Caia   Ronald McDonald is sad because a dear friend of his has been spurned.

Ruthlessly, callously, spurned.

Birdie   Great, Ronald, really great, tell Birdie all about it.

Caia   Isn't that right, Franny?

Jotham   What about the window?

Birdie   It will be fixed today, let's move on.

Caia   Hasn't she, Franny?

Adira   Franny, did you spurn Ronald?

Caia   No, not Ronald! No one spurns Ronald McDonald.

She has spurned one of Ronald's friends. And now she won't even speak to her.

To punish her.

Jotham   Caia, we know it's you.

Jen   She knows we know.

Birdie   Caia, can you pack it in now please?

We need to decide what we'll do for the silence.

Caia   Silence!

Birdie   No obviously silence, the question was /

Caia   No I mean: SILENCE!

Ronald must be heard.

Franny won't even speak to Ronald's friend who she callously spurned.

So, if Franny isn't talking to Caia.

Perhaps she will talk to Caia's dear and trusted friend Ronald McDonald and tell him what Caia did wrong?

Even just the tiniest clue would be helpful.

Tell Ronald McDonald all about it.

Why won't you speak to Caia?

Orson   Can I ask the group leader what her plan is to get this meeting back on track cos she seems out of her depth.

Birdie   Caia stroke Ronald McDonald and Franny. Stay behind at the end and I will facilitate a conversation between the pair of you.

Caia   I need to know now.

Franny, what did I do?

I'm dying.

Jen   Is this all you could think of?

Caia   Franny.

Beautiful, rare, gleaming pebble that you are.

I would never have said it if I thought it would upset you.

Jen   What did you say?

Birdie   This is a private conversation, you two. Maybe you should wait till you have privacy?

We need to make a decision about the silence.

Does anyone have any thoughts?

Orson   Yes.

Birdie   Anyone have any thoughts?

Orson   I do.

Birdie   Anyone at all.

Orson   Yeah, me.

Birdie   Anyone at all.

Orson   I have thoughts.

Birdie   Absolutely anyone at all.

Orson   My thought is we all go outside.

Birdie   Adira, what do you think?

Orson   She thinks we all go out together.

Adira   No I don't.

Orson   All out together.

Jen   No.

Orson   Yes.

Jen   No.

Caia   This how it's been, Birdie.

Orson   We all go out together.

Caia   Not everyone wants to do that, Orson.

Orson   Yes they do.

Adira   No we don't.

Birdie   Caia, what do you want to do?

Caia   I want to go out, hold my Franny's hand and show the world I love her and that I'm not scared and that being in love is awesome and my love is as good as theirs and I want to kiss her in the sun with the whole world watching.

That's what I want to do.

Jotham   It's raining.

Birdie Franny?

Caia She's not talking.

Birdie To you? Or to all of us?

Caia It started off me but I think she's extended the protest to society as a whole.

Birdie What are you protesting about, Franny?

Franny –

Caia She's protesting that I asked her to marry me.

Tana Oh my God that's so cute.

Caia I know, right? I got down on one knee and everything.

Jen Oh my God, that's so lame.

Caia And I know the ring was a bit naff but the man in H Samuel's said it was the best I was gonna get at my price point and one day I'll buy a nicer one, but also, who cares? Who cares about a ring?

Jotham I do.

Adira You've got to have a ring.

Jotham I know, right?

When my man proposes to me, I want a flash mob.

Adira Why should he propose to you?

Jotham Cos he's the man.

Adira But you're a man too.

Jotham Yeah, but I'm the fabulous one.

Caia Who cares about all that? I'm trying to tell you what happened.

Jen No one cares.

Tana I do.

Tell the story, Caia.

Caia It's not a story. It's a tragedy.

Jotham Stories can be tragedies.

Jen Your hair's a tragedy.

Jotham Your life's a tragedy.

Caia Listen to me.

Jotham The alarm's gonna go off.

Caia   If you all stopped interrupting me –

Adira   Can't you say it in 140 characters?

Caia   And we got the train to Dungeness and I got down on one knee on England's only desert that looks dead but it's secretly " with /

Adira   That's a no then.

Caia   Teeming with life and I said, 'Franny, I can't live without you'.

Adira   What is she? Your phone charger?

Caia   And we stood in the shadow of the power station and it was windy and I said, 'Franny, isn't love wonderful? Isn't it badass and brilliant and we've got it, so many people don't have it, we have love Franny, and Franny, will you marry me?' That's all I said.

Jen   No wonder she said no.

Caia   She didn't say no.

Tana   Did she say yes?

Caia   She didn't say anything.

She's not spoken since.

I'm dying cos I'm in Hell: it's like Primark on a Saturday; then Franny texted, didn't you my shiny pebble, she texted to say she feels marriage is – hold on, I've still got the text, and yeah that's right . . . marriage is an oppressive institution.

Tana   What does that mean?

Caia   Exactly, Tana.

What does it mean?

Jen   How come her phone doesn't have to go in the box?

Caia   But she says I should have known that because if I'd known that –

Oh God oh God oh God oh I lay myself at your feet, Franny.

FRANNY.

I will drown in the sea. I will do it. I will walk into the sea and not come back.

Birdie   OK, so why don't we just park that?

Adira   Come sit here, Caia.

Caia   Thank you, Adira.

Kind, compassionate Adira.

Adira   It's fine.

Caia   I'll just sit here and weep.

Or maybe I'll just die.

Is that what you want, Franny? Do you want me to die from the pain of loving you?

Franny   –

Caia   She doesn't deny it.

Jotham   I think she just wants you to stop talking shit.

Birdie   OK. So we're good?

Can we carry on?

Tana   What about the coup?

Jotham   TANA!

Birdie   He'd forgotten about it.

Jen   Oh no.

Orson   NEVER FORGET!

Jotham   Go hang out with your imaginary boyfriend, Orson.

Orson   RAGE, he's not imaginary actually, Jotham, REVOLUTION, just cos you haven't seen him doesn't mean he doesn't exist, REVOLT.

Jen   He's Mister 'Out and Proud', but won't show us his boyfriend.

Orson   RAAAAAAGE!

Birdie   THAT IS ENOUGH!

You want rage?

You wanna see a little bit of Birdie's rage?

I got rage. I got rage in spades and you don't want to know what your life will be like with Birdie's rage all up in your face.

So let's park the coup.

Let's park the Ross and Rachel.

Caia *puts up her hand.*

Birdie   And can we actually discuss what we're here to discuss, because time is running out and /

What, Caia? What?

Caia   I think it was very insensitive to choose such a hetero-normative example.

Birdie   Of what?

Caia   I'm not comfortable with being compared to a cis-hetero couple.

Jen   Who the hell are Ross and Rachel?

Tana   They were these dickheads in the olden days.

Caia   Proper dickheads.

Birdie   You're right. I am sorry.

Caia and Franny and anyone else, anyone else at all, including Ronald McDonald, I apologise for my insensitive choice of language. I have listened to your comments and taken the time to reflect on my own privilege and I am sorry if anyone felt devalued or shamed by my lapse of judgement.

OK?

Good.

We need to make a decision and what I am hearing is that you want to go outside.

Orson   Finally some leadership.

Jen   I'm not going out.

Jotham   Nor am I.

Adira   Nope.

Orson   What is wrong with you?

Jen   Nothing's wrong with me.

What's wrong with *you*?

Orson   We have to get out there.

Adira   I don't.

Orson   You're letting them win.

Birdie   It's not as simple as that.

Caia   It is. It so is.

Tana   Why do you all have to do the same thing?

Adira   I know, right?

Birdie   Solidarity.

Orson   Solidarity.

You're still an unfit leader though.

Birdie   We're spectrum.

We commemorate as a group.

Jen   We don't want to.

Birdie   But it matters that we do.

Jotham   No it doesn't.

Orson   I'm sorry, but it does. It absolutely does matter.

People out there want to divide us. And turn us against each other so they can have power over us. That's how they win.

But solidarity is a bond that unites us. It says I'm not scared because I've got you, and you're not scared because you've got me.

It matters because there are people very far away from us who are living in fear, more than we ever have or will, and we need to say to them, you don't need to be scared because you've got us.

We've got them and they've got us.

Jotham   Outside: no. But as a group, yes.

Tana   When is it?

Birdie   In exactly twenty-one minutes' time.

Tana   Jotham, my train leaves at quarter past.

Jotham   So?

Tana   You said you'd walk me to the station.

Jotham   Well, I can't now.

Tana   You promised.

Jotham   I want to do the silence.

Tana   I hardly see you.

Jotham   Then get a later train.

Tana   Mum bought the tickets and I have to get the train it says on my ticket.

Jotham   I'm only worth the cheapest. Thanks, Mum.

Tana   Why should we have to pay the earth just to see you?

Birdie   Tana, I think this is a private conversation.

Tana   Nothing's private in this place. I've only been here a night and I know way more about you lot than I want to.

Pack your bags and come home to Mum and Dad.

Birdie   Do you think you might be being a bit insensitive in saying that to your brother, Tana?

Tana   Stop putting ideas in his head.

Birdie   I'm not.

Tana   You're turning him against his family.

Jotham   No she's not.

Tana   You shouldn't be here, with people like him coming out with crap like that.

All that rubbish about solidarity?

What about solidarity with your family?

Jotham   This is my family.

Tana   This lot?

This lot?

Caia   What's wrong with us?

Tana   You're in the bloody funny farm.

Caia   Speak for yourself, I'm fine.

Tana   I just meant /

Jotham   I'm not going home.

Orson   Why don't you get a later train? They don't check your tickets down here.

Tana   I don't want to get another train. I want to do what my brother and I agreed and not to have bloody group therapy about it.

Jotham?

Jotham   Are we doing it inside or outside cos if /

Caia   Out and proud.

Adira   No.

Birdie   Can we at least agree we'll do it as a group?

Orson   We have to do it as a group.

Caia   Franny?

Franny   –

Caia   Cool.

Birdie   Jen?

Jen   What?

Birdie   We'll do it as a group, yeah?

Jen   –

Birdie   Jen.

Jen   –

Birdie   Jen, you /

Jen   I don't think she should be allowed to pray.

Birdie   Who?

Jen   Her.

Birdie   Jen, that's /

Jen   Adira, are you going to pray during the two minutes' silence?

Birdie   Jen, it's not OK to ask that.

Jen   I'm not being disrespectful, Adira, are you gonna pray?

Jotham   So what if she does?

Tana   Jotham, let's go.

Jen   I don't want to be in some prayer circle. If she prays I want to be separate.

Caia   Who cares what she does?

Jen   It's insensitive.

Birdie   You're the one being insensitive.

Jen   I'm not being rude, but I'm not doing it.

You lot, do what you want, but I'm not doing a prayer circle.

Tana   Are you gonna pray, Adira?

Birdie   Don't answer, babes.

Adira   Why can't I answer?

Orson   She means you don't have to answer, but she's an incompetent group leader.

Birdie   Right. No. Sorry.

Adira, we'll come back to you in a minute, but there's a really good learning opportunity here and it's important I role model appropriate levels of self-esteem, so Orson, would you come into my office please?

Orson   What office?

Birdie   Over there in the /

Orson   All I can see is a broom cupboard.

Birdie   You're just angry cos you don't have an office.

Orson   *You* don't have an office.

Birdie   It's a multi-purpose room. And come on, let's say it, we all know what this is about.

Orson   You wanna do this here.

Birdie   Let's go, Face-ache.

Orson   No one here needs you, Birdie.

Birdie   Yes they do.

Orson   You're not helping anyone.

Jotham   She's helped me.

Orson   No she's not. She's making you worse.

Jotham   Birdie was really nice to me.

Orson   If you say you want to stay inside, Birdie has failed you.

Birdie   No.

Orson   We should be taking to the streets, fight them head on, full out, but you're like, no, let's all stay in and hide.

Caia   I'm not hiding.

Orson   You're dressed as Ronald McDonald!

And look at these windows, how can you say you're not hiding?

Caia   I'm not hiding.

Orson   You're all hiding.

Tana   I'm not.

Orson   What have you got to hide from?

Tana   I'm booked on a train so let's /

Orson   What is more important? Supporting your brother or getting home on time?

Things are changing. Everything is changing, but you can't see it because you can't see out past these damn windows.

Birdie   We know things are changing. We did a wall display about it.

She points to a wall display entitled 'Things are Changing'.

Orson   'Don't be too out there.'

Birdie   Who said that?

Orson   You do. Every day.

Birdie   No I don't, and even if I did, don't you think that's sensible?

Orson   Locking yourselves away.

Birdie   When I lived here we couldn't even open the curtains.

Orson   You think this is progress?

A bit of sunlight.

Birdie   It *is* progress.

Orson   It's not.

It's not, Birdie.

You're going backwards.

Birdie   I know you resent being here.

Orson   I hate it here.

Adira   Me too.

Tana   And me.

Jotham   You don't have to live here.

Tana   Nor do you.

Adira   How can you expect him to go home?

Tana   Who, him?

Adira   How can he go home?

Tana   You just get on a train, it's not hard.

Birdie   Everyone hates it here, great.

Caia   I don't.

Birdie   You love everything, Caia.

Orson   Why do you give a crap if everyone likes you or not?

Birdie   I don't.

Orson   You need everyone to like you.

Well, newsflash, we think you're an armpit.

Birdie   You don't like it here, OK, fine, you've made that clear but don't make it personal please.

Orson   She's done one term of a youth work diploma and this is how she goes on.

Birdie   And what have you done?

Orson   You're not qualified to do this.

Birdie   Sorry, Orson, what youth work qualifications do you have?

Orson   None.

Birdie   Exactly.

And furthermore, I used to be a resident here. I painted these walls.

Orson   'Been there, done that' is not a qualification.

How do you think it makes them feel when you say you've all got to hide away?

Birdie   I'm not saying that.

Orson   You are.

Birdie   I'm not. I'm saying you've got a choice.

Orson   As long as everyone does it together.

Birdie   I would like it for us all to do it together, yes.

Orson   Inside.

Birdie   Wherever we want, I don't mind.

Orson   You should mind. If you were doing your job you'd say we've got to get out and be seen, show them we're not ashamed.

All these laws they made against us, they told us we were disgusting. We've got to say, we're not, we know we're not.

The love I feel for my boyfriend is not disgusting.

Get out, be seen, Birdie.

Get up in their faces, not run back into the closet.

Birdie   *It's a multi-purpose room.*

Orson   The 'closet' closet. This lot are the sheep and you're the dog rounding them all up.

Birdie   You can't even be seen out with your boyfriend.

Orson   I just don't bring him here, that's different.

Adira   Because he's not real.

Jotham   I don't want to go outside.

Birdie   You don't have to.

Orson   Yes you do.

Jotham, yes you do. Because if you don't, they've won.

You too, Adira, and you, Jen.

Where's the fight? Where's the pride? Where's the shoulders back, chest out, come for me pride?

Jen   I left mine at home.

Adira   My dog ate it.

Orson   This isn't funny.

I get that you're scared. But this is bigger than you.

And what is that fear?

What actually is it?

You're scared because of what they'll say? They've already said it.

You're scared of what they might do? They've already done it.

So that fear, it's based on what *might* happen, but everything that might happen already has.

So what does that tell you?

Jotham   It tells me I'm never gonna get a boyfriend.

Orson   It tells you there's nothing left to be afraid of.

Jotham   Oh, and that.

Orson   There's nothing left to be afraid of, guys.

Adira   That's so easy for you to say, Orson.

Not all of us have your life.

Jen   No one cares, Adira.

Birdie   I do.

Jen   Maybe you should say a prayer, see where that gets you.

Jotham   OK, you need to stop.

Jen   Are you going to pray, Adira?

Jotham   Leave her alone, Jen.

Adira   I can handle her.

Jotham   When are you two gonna get a room and be done with it?

Jen   I don't wanna get a room with her.

Adira   Gross.

Jotham   Adira, Jen is so into you, it's off the scale.

Jen   Are you gonna pray?

Jotham   That's it, change the subject.

Adira   Of course I'm gonna pray.

Jen   This is what I mean.

They don't give a shit about us.

Adira   I get it, Jen.

The attacker looked like me and attacked people like you.

Jen   Well, didn't they?

Adira   I'm not disagreeing.

Jen   What's your point then?

Adira   What's my point? On behalf of who? People like me? People like you? People like us?

Who gives a toss what my point is?

It's way worse for people like me after these things, I can tell you.

Jen   People like you did it.

Jotham   Shut up, Jen.

Jen   No.

Jotham   You're talking shit, Jen.

Caia   Seriously, Jen.

Aren't you gonna kick her out, Birdie?

Jen   *She* should get out.

Adira, can you leave please?

This is my safe space and you're making me feel uncomfortable.

Jotham   Shut your mouth, Jen.

Caia   Jen, you're being awful.

Jen   Get out, Adira.

You're the one that should leave.

Orson   Hey, Birdie, great job. I can't wait to tell Sally how you handled this.

Birdie   That's enough.

The ground rules clearly state that /

Orson   It's a bit late for that, don't you think, Birdie?

Jen   Every member of Spectrum has a right to be here without fear of persecution – number two /

Birdie   Every member has a right to be themselves – number eight.

Jen   Every member has a right to speak freely – number six.

Orson   We can all read.

Birdie's not got the balls, so I'll do it.

Jen, get out.

Jen   I'm not going anywhere.

Birdie   Hold on guys, we can't just /

Jen This is my safe space. You're gonna kick me out? You know how vulnerable I am.

Birdie You lose that right when you make comments like that.

Orson Better late than never, Birdie.

Birdie Leave now please, I'll make an appointment with you and we can talk about next steps.

Orson Oh, I wouldn't do it like that.

Birdie Right, you can leave too Orson.

Adira I told you I can handle it.

Honestly, you lot do my head in.

Let Jen stay.

I'm done with the lot of you anyway.

Tana Jotham, come on.

Adira What time is your train, Tana?

Tana Quarter past.

Adira Mind if I come with you?

Jen Are you leaving?

Adira Why would I want to stay here with people like you?

Jen You can't just leave.

Birdie Jen didn't mean what she said.

Tana Will you be safe?

Adira I don't care about what Jen said.

I'm sorry, but I literally can't stay here any longer.

I'll just grab a bag and send my brothers down for my stuff.

Can I come with you, Tana?

Jotham Are we allowed to just leave?

Caia This isn't prison, Jotham.

Adira Yes it bloody is.

Birdie We need to talk to your social worker, Adira.

Caia But Adira, we love you.

Birdie We do.

Jotham Jen really does.

Adira I don't want your love. No offence.

I want Mum's love. And Dad's love and my brothers'.

Birdie They need time, babes.

Adria They've had time.

More than enough time.

Jen What if they kick you out again?

Adira I'm not coming back here if they do.

Birdie You need to think this through.

Adira I have.

Birdie You can leave, but why don't we plan it?

Go home for a weekend at a time; build up it slowly.

Adira I'd rather just do it and be done.

Birdie I don't think that's a good idea.

Caia Will you add me on Facebook?

Adira I'll add you all.

Birdie Adira, I can't stop you.

But you don't need to rush off.

Adira Yeah I do.

I'm sorry but I'm done.

I'm so done.

And you can't stop me.

Birdie I'm not stopping you.

Adira You are.

Birdie Plan it. Don't rush. That's what I'm saying.

Adira I don't want to.

I want to go home now.

Don't pressure me to do something I don't want to do.

Birdie OK.

If it's your choice, I stand by you.

But I want you to know that we really do wish you well.

And whatever happens, you know we'll always be here.

Adira   Thanks yeah.

But do you have any idea how depressing that is?

This place is shit and, no offence, you're all twats.

I miss my mum. And she's not here, she's there.

And I know what she said.

She said she wished I was dead, that having a gay child was worse than death. I know she said that.

But even so –

Jotham, you know what I mean.

Tana   Why would Jotham understand that?

Adira   And Orson, you say revolution but /

Tana   No hold on.

Jotham?

Why would you get that?

Caia   There's not enough love, that's what I think.

Tana   What's my brother said to you?

Adira, what's he told you?

Adira   –

Tana   What's he told you?

Jotham   Forget it.

Tana   No.

Jotham   Leave it.

Tana   What have you said?

Jotham   I've not said nothing.

Tana   Then why did she say /

Adira   I didn't say /

Tana   Yeah you did.

Jotham   I said leave it, OK?

Tana   No.

Birdie   Tana, your brother clearly /

Tana   Stay out of my family's business.

Birdie   We have a confidentiality agreement.

Tana   You're talking about my family.

Adira   I wasn't.

Tana   You said, 'Jotham, you get it'.

Jotham   Tana, please.

Tana   I have a right to know what's been said about me.

Caia   No one said anything.

Tana   Bullshit, what has he said about us?

Jotham   I haven't said nothing.

Tana   Yeah you have.

Jotham   You're humiliating me.

Tana   What about me?

Jotham   You're gonna miss your train, let's go.

Tana   No don't worry, we're talking, it's nice.

Jotham   Please.

Tana   What has my brother said?

Can someone please answer my question?

Answer me.

Silence.

Eventually –

Adira   He said /

Birdie   Ground rules, Adira.

Adira   He said your mum and dad kicked him out.

When he came out your dad beat the crap out of him.

Which is what happened to me. So we kind of bonded over it.

Tana   He said that?

Is that what he said?

Birdie   Adira, that /

Adira   It's family, Birdie.

Tana   Jotham, get your stuff and we'll go.

If we get a taxi we'll just make it.

Jotham   –

He may be crying.

Tana   Jotham, come on.

You lot are twats.

My brother's coming with me.

Adira   Can I share your cab?

Tana   Anyone else want to get out of this dump?

Jotham   It's not a dump, Tana.

It's my home.

Tana   *It's not your home, Jotham.*

These freaks are not your family.

Orson   Hey.

Tana   You're freaks. You're mental and you're turning him away from his family.

Birdie   You need to leave now please, Tana.

Orson   Are we all leaving? There'll be no one left.

Good job, Birdie.

Jen   We're not turning him away from his mum and dad, Tana. They turned away from him.

Tana   How the hell would you know?

Jotham   Please don't.

Tana   We went to *Wicked*.

Pizza Express, then *Wicked*.

Do you know what that took for my mum and dad to do that?

Have you seen *Wicked*?

It's shit.

It's got singing monkeys, what's all that about?

But do you know what it took for my mum and dad to do that?

Absolutely nothing.

Nothing at all, Jotham.

And I've got Dad crying down the phone every night saying bring our boy back, wondering what they did wrong.

I said maybe we should have seen *Billy Elliot*, but Mum said that was too on the nose, so we went with the singing monkeys, and we were allowed a glass of Prosecco with our dough balls and we said cheers and, by the way, it was way more than I got when I passed my driving test.

We were so proud of you, Jotham.

You don't belong here.

None of you do.

Adira   Do you want me to help you pack? We'll still get the train.

Tana   I'm so sorry your mum said that to you, Adira. I'm so sorry. If you need to stay with us, you can share my bedroom anytime you like.

But for Jotham to say what he said.

When it did actually happen to you.

Jotham, that's –

I wish you could have our mum, Adira.

And our dad.

Adira   Thanks.

I don't.

My mum's amazing.

Jen   How can you say that?

Adira   If you met her.

Jen   Yeah but she told you she /

Adira   I know.

And yeah, it was the worst thing ever.

But I'm still here.

In stupid Dungeness, on the edge of the bloody country. Are we even on the map? All I can see is the sea, there's never any signal and now there's no wifi thanks to you lot and I just want to look at my Snapchat /

Jotham   No one's messaged you, babes.

Adira   And send a message on Whatsapp and no one here looks like me. I see them staring at me, you all know they do.

Caia   They stare at us too, when I hold Franny's hand.

Adira   That's different.

And social services sent me out here to keep myself safe but I don't feel safer.

You don't know what I did to try and change this. For this not to be me. I prayed, so hard, so so hard, and, yeah, all along I thought this would be easier for everyone if I was dead.

So I go back and I say to them, *you* change. This is on you. You won't pray the gay away, you won't change our family's reputation, it won't do anything.

I'm gonna do the two minutes' silence. In the taxi or on the platform, I don't care, wherever I am, I'll do it. And I will pray for the victims and their families.

And I'm gonna pray for the strength to forgive my mum.

And I want to be there to help her. Because I need her to help me.

And one day, I think she will.

I still think you're all twats, though.

Jotham   But you'll add us on Facebook?

Adira   Of course.

It was me who put the bin in Jotham's bed.

Jotham   I knew it!

Adira   There's a limit to how many times we can hear 'Let It Go', Jotham.

I prayed for patience. But you sing it a lot.

Forgive me?

Jotham   Of course I forgive you, babes.

I was gonna make you a fierce outfit for Bournemouth Pride.

Shall I send it to you?

Adira   Why don't you bring it up to me one day?

What's so good about Bournemouth Pride anyway?

Jotham   Is she on glue?

Is this girl on glue?

What is so good about Bournemouth Pride?

Do you know where that yellow brick road leads?

Bournemouth Pride, that's where, babes.

Do you know what's at the end of the rainbow, Adira?

Bournemouth Pride, that's what.

And I swear I am going to be crowned queen of Bournemouth Pride and I'm gonna lead the parade on the winner's float, I'm gonna sit on my throne with my crown and drive through the streets of Bournemouth serving fuck-you realness and I'm gonna look so sickening, you lot are gonna gag, hunties.

And all the haters, I'm gonna make them eat it.

OK?

Caia   Yes, queen!

Orson   He'll put a dress on and drive through Bournemouth pulled by a tractor but he won't stand out in the street and protest in his jeans and t-shirt.

What have you got to say to that, Jotham?

Tana   Leave my brother alone.

Orson   Your brother's a hypocrite.

Jotham   No more than you.

Tana   My brother is amazing actually.

And at least he's not a bully.

So it's none of your business what he does.

Orson   Come on, Jotham, what have you got to say?

Jotham   Obviously it's sad and everything, and I don't mean to be shallow, but can I have Adira's bedroom please?

Orson   Typical. Such a pageant queen. Being fabulous doesn't make you safe.

Jotham   It does for me.

Orson   I don't want to be fabulous.

Jotham   There's no danger there, babes.

Orson   But it's a mask. What happens when you take it off?

Caia   Stop, no stop, I can't go on no please don't look at me, don't look at me. Oh the pain.

Jen   Was it not about you for five seconds?

Birdie   Sorry, Adira, your moment's over.

Adira   Fine by me.

Caia   I have dreams.

Vast, open dreams.

Don't you?

Jotham   Who?

Caia   All of you?

Jotham   All of us what?

Caia   Have dreams?

Jotham   I'm still a virgin, so it's just the one dream at the moment.

Orson   You don't want it enough, Jotham, that's your problem.

Jotham   I do really want it.

Orson   The only person standing between you and your virginity is *you.*

Jotham   Well, no, you need another person really don't you?

Caia   Not to dream, Jotham. You don't need another person to dream.

Adira   I'm gonna get my bag.

Tana   Jotham, I'm gonna pack you a bag.

Start saying your goodbyes?

Jotham   You can't make me.

Adira   Tana, I'll help you.

Exit **Adira** *and* **Tana**.

Caia   Franny. Why?

Why are you torturing me like this?

Birdie   You're sixteen. I think you need to calm down a bit.

Caia   I can't make you love me, Franny, I know that. Oh Franny, beautiful, elegant and strange creature that you are, so out of context in this shitty house in Dungeness, England, I say to you this:

I love you. I absolutely fucking love you.

Franny   –

Caia   FRANNY!

Enter **Adira** *and* **Tana** *with their bags.*

Adira   Is Ronald McDonald dead?

Orson   No, just in love.

Come on, Franny, give her a break.

Caia   I'll take lectures in love from anyone except you.

Orson   I've never given anyone lectures, thank you very much.

Caia   What do you know anyway, you have to fake a boyfriend.

Orson   He's real.

Caia   All your talk of love in the open, where is he then?

Orson   We don't kiss in the shadows any more than you do.

It's private that's all.

Caia   You're a hypocrite.

Adria   It's time to go.

Birdie   I can't make you stay, but I need to tell your social worker where you are.

Adira   I texted him.

Birdie   I'm sorry to see you go.

We love you and you'll always be welcome.

I hope your time at Spectrum was helpful.

Adira   Not really.

But thanks for being nice.

I'll send my brothers down for the rest of my stuff.

Birdie   Here's an evaluation form.

Or you can do it online.

Or you know, don't.

Adira *hugs everyone goodbye.*

She gets to **Jen** *last.*

Adira   See you, Jen.

Jen   –

Birdie   Is there anything you want to say to Adira, Jen?

Jen   –

Adira   Well, goodbye.

We're cool. Just so you know. It's all good.

We're gonna miss the train.

Jotham   I'm not coming, Tana.

Tana   I know.

Jotham   You'll come back down though?

Tana   Maybe.

Dunno.

You could come up for the weekend?

Jotham   Yeah.

Maybe.

Tana   You're my best brother.

I'm sorry I called you all freaks. You're not.

You're my best. OK?

Bye, Jotham.

Jotham   Bye.

Adira   OK, so see you, I guess.

Tana and **Adira** *make their way to the door with their bags.*

Jotham   I really miss Mum and Dad, Tana.

And you.

Especially you.

Tana   OK.

Jotham   Will you tell them I miss them?

A moment.

Tana   No.

Come on, Adira.

Exit **Tana** *and* **Adira**.

Jen   They're dropping like flies.

Caia   You should have told her.

Jen   Told her what?

Caia   You're like a stone, I can't bear it, Jen.

Jen   Yeah? Well at least I'm not on the floor dressed as Ronald McDonald.

Caia   I don't care.

I don't care.

I'm sixteen, OK, so obviously that means I don't know shit.

But if life has taught me something, it's to be kind. And if you find someone that loves you, it's good. It's really good, Jen.

Jen   I don't love her.

Caia   Falling in love is very hard. Believe me. It's very hard.

But pretending you *haven't* fallen in love is even harder.

Birdie   OK, this is good. This is really good.

Jen, Jen, look at you, all connected and listening.

Jen   Shut up.

She's not gonna call me, is she, Birdie?

Birdie   Are you OK?

Jen   She's gone; you're kicking me out. I'm not having a very good day actually.

Birdie   Can we make a deal?

Jen   About what?

Birdie   What you said to Adira was wrong. And if you can't see that, I want to help you get to a point where you can.

And if I'm gonna do that, I'll need you to stick around. And, you know, we'd miss you.

So can we make a deal? If you want to, you can stay, but there's a condition.

You stop throwing stones at our window please.

Jen *thinks.*

Eventually she empties some pebbles from her pockets and gives them to **Birdie**.

Birdie   Thank you.

Thank you.

Did you see that, Orson? It's what, in the trade, we call a breakthrough moment.

BOOM-CHICKA-ROCKA-SUCK-ON-THAT.

Right. We've got to make up our minds.

Inside or outside?

Together or separate?

Orson   Don't give them the choice.

Jotham   I don't want to do it outside.

Orson   I think you'll regret it.

Jotham   I know what happened was awful and I want to say that. But I don't know how because doing it outside it's /

Orson   It's the only way. You want to show your anger and solidarity, it counts for nothing unless people see it.

Birdie   Don't pressurise him.

Orson   Someone's got to.

Caia   I'm going outside and I'm taking my Franny's hand /

Orson   There we go.

That's what I'm talking about.

Birdie   Orson, stop it.

You're not in charge.

Orson   Well, you certainly aren't either.

What kind of outfit do you call this?

You've got two that just left right under your nose, you've got one who thinks she's Ronald McDonald and one who's smashing the place in every time we go to bed.

Birdie   You're part of the same group.

Orson   I'm at least a year older than everyone here.

At least.

Birdie   Except me.

Jotham   So, what, that makes you better?

Orson   It makes me more mature.

Jen   It makes you a dickhead.

Orson   You're all cowards.

You make me sick the lot of you.

Birdie   Oi, that's enough.

Jotham   I'm not doing the silence with him.

Jen   Or me.

Orson   We all do it together.

Birdie   Why?

Orson   I can't believe you need that explaining.

Caia   Orson, stop being so unkind.

Orson   Oh shut up, Ronald McDonald, go get me a Big Mac.

Caia   Hey.

Birdie   That's not helpful.

Orson   Oh get back in your closet.

Birdie   It's a multi-purpose room.

Jotham   We're running out of time.

Orson   Why don't you put your dress on, princess?

Jotham   Oh you'd like that would you?

Orson   Birdie, get it together.

Caia   She's got it together . . .

Jotham   Stop bullying us, Orson.

Orson   You think you're being bullied, look how the world treats you.

Birdie   Everyone please calm down.

Orson   Go get fingered then dumped again.

Birdie   She broke my heart, Orson.

Orson   I'm going outside, who's coming?

Jotham   I want to stay here.

Orson   Nice bit of pride you got going on, princess.

Jotham   I am proud.

Orson   No you're not.

Birdie   What do you know?

Caia   Ronald McDonald says –

Jotham   Fuck off, Ronald. You look like a joke.

Caia   You fuck off.

Birdie   We haven't got time for this.

Orson   Everyone out together.

Jotham   You are not in charge.

Orson   Nor are you.

Birdie   I'm in charge.

Orson   Good one, Birdie.

Birdie   I swear to God, I'm gonna kill you.

Jotham   Get him, Birdie.

Caia   Stop it, you lot.

Jotham   I'll get you, my pretty, and your little dog too.

Orson   I don't have a dog.

Birdie   Shut up, Orson.

Orson   Who's got a dog?

Jotham   Fly, my pretties.

Orson   Not so big now are you?

Jotham   I am big. It's Bournemouth Pride that got small.

Orson He's speaking in tongues.

Jotham You're a shit gay, Orson.

Orson *You're* a shit gay.

Jotham I am a great gay.

Orson You're a great gay bellend.

And you, Birdie.

Birdie What about me?

Orson Call yourself a lesbian?

My mum's a bigger lesbian than you.

Birdie I'm not surprised. Have you seen your dad?

Orson I'm gonna kill you.

Birdie Not if I kill you first.

Jotham Stella!

Orson Who the fuck is Stella?

Birdie Come on, Orson, I swear to God you are so done.

Orson Yeah?

Etc.

The argument descends into an enormous ad lib argument.

It gets louder and louder and more vicious until everyone is stood up screaming in each other's faces. When we think it can't get any worse . . .

Franny HEY!

STOP IT

ALL OF YOU.

I SAID, STOP IT.

Silence.

Caia Franny!

You're alive.

It's a miracle.

Enter **Adira** *and* **Tana**.

Adira There's all these people in the streets, we couldn't get a taxi.

Tana We knew we were gonna miss the train so we came back.

What's going on?

Caia   Franny has come back to us, that's what's happened.

Franny   I'll tell you what's going on.

Orson. You're a real wanker sometimes.

Birdie is trying.

She is trying so hard.

And you lot. You smug, entitled idiots.

You think someone blowing you up is the biggest thing you've got to worry about?

You're doing a good enough job of that on your own.

What do you want? What do you *actually want*?

When we walk down the streets holding hands, we're making a statement. When we kiss at the bus stop or at the movies, we're making a statement.

And love starts where the movies end. It's scary, cos you have to show someone the bits of you you don't even show yourself, but lots of things in life are scary and you still do it.

I know you lot don't like Orson. I get it. I don't like him much either. But he's found someone and if that's what he wants in life then leave him alone.

And Orson, Birdie is trying. Give her a break.

Jotham doesn't have to go outside, and Jen, Adira doesn't have to love you back if she can't. You can't make her. But you fell in love, you should be happy that you can, because if you can now, you will again, and one time that person will love you back and it will be amazing and wonderful and you'll never be the same again because you were brave enough to let someone love you and that's what's at the end of the rainbow.

Jotham   No, it is actually Bournemouth Pride.

Franny   So I ask you again. All of you.

What do you actually want?

Jotham   I think I preferred her when she wasn't speaking.

Birdie   I know what I want.

I can tell you exactly what I want.

All these haters out there. They're nothing.

All you lot, saying you hate me, even though I'm trying, I'm really trying. Doesn't mean a thing.

Believe me. No can hate me more than I do sometimes.

Franny   But what do you want?

Birdie What I want is to look at myself in the mirror and maybe one day, just one out of the seven, for me to look in the mirror and like what I see. Just one day out of seven to look at myself and say, 'Today, I'm enough'.

And I can. I can do it.

I don't know where I learned to hate myself so much, but I will be damned if I'm gonna let it get in my way.

That's what I want.

Because today, I'm enough.

Caia I know what I want.

Franny, I know I've been a bit over the top, looking back I can see how this might have all come across as a bit, I don't know, desperate or something.

But I love you. And I want you as my wife. And if one day, you then become my husband, I want that too.

Franny, please.

Will you marry me?

Franny –

Jotham's *alarm goes off.*

Jotham It's time.

Caia Franny?

Birdie Everyone ready?

Caia Franny?

Birdie Caia, you'll have to wait.

Orson But we haven't decided.

Birdie We'll have to do it just as we are.

Take us as they find us, right?

Jotham It's time.

Birdie OK. Ready everyone?

Jotham I'm ready.

Adira We're all ready.

House lights up slowly through the following.

Birdie We will all now observe two minutes' silence.

Stand if you wish, or stay seated, but I ask all of us to honour this moment.

For all those living in fear, far from us, or on our doorstep, we show you our solidarity; for all those fighting for their right to love, to be themselves in all corners of the world, for all those who have fought before us. For everyone who has fought in the name of love.

We stand in solidarity and we remember them now. And we say, *Love wins.*

Two minutes' silence.

We begin now.

We observe two minutes' silence.

After the silence.

From outside we can hear a choir sing a song we know.

Through the frosted window we get the sense of a crowd congregating. We see the blurred shapes of rainbow flags drifting by. More and more people are walking by the window.

The song gets louder and louder through the following.

Birdie   Thank you, everyone.

Caia   Franny?

Jen   What's all that noise?

Jotham   It sounds like an army.

Birdie   Let's go see.

Exit **Birdie**, **Orson**, **Tana** *and* **Jotham**.

Now the whole crowd is singing along.

Franny   Caia.

I love you too.

But of course I'm not gonna marry you.

I'm sixteen.

Enter **Jotham**.

Jotham   Guys, you've got to come see this.

Guys, come on.

Caia, Franny, Adira, come on.

Jen.

They're all headed to the beach, Jen.

There's flags and banners and candles and lanterns and the sun is shining and /

Caia.

Franny.

Hurry up, you'll miss it.

Jen.

Adira.

Come on!

Come with me!

Come outside.

It's beautiful.

Adira, **Jen**, **Caia** *and* **Franny** *follow* **Jotham** *onto the street.*

We're outside now.

They join a huge throng of people with flags and banners who have taken to the streets singing the song we all know.

The rousing song builds and builds. They stand downstage taking it all in.

They sing.

We sing.

The powerful, uplifting climax of the song and a triumph of rainbow flags.

Blackout.

Dungeness

BY CHRIS THOMPSON

Notes on rehearsal and staging, drawn from a workshop with the writer, held at the National Theatre, October 2019.

Introductions and icebreakers

Lead director Rob Hastie and playwright Chris Thompson introduced themselves to the group and began with a couple of exercises to allow the group to get to know each other.

Exercise: Getting to know you

Standing in a circle, the group were asked to cross the room and shake the hands of everyone in 15 seconds.

The task was to share their names and where they are from, describing both their group and geographical location.

Exercise: Checking in – fist to five

This is a highly effective visual indicator of accessing scale in a group.

The group were asked to place their hands in the air like a fist. They were asked: 'How confident do you feel about directing this play with your young people? 0 being not confident at all and 5 being super-ready?' 0, 1, 2, 3, 4, 5 – the group held up the number of fingers they felt answered the question.

You could then repeat this exercise at the end of the day to see if anyone's response has changed.

How Chris came to write the play

'I wanted to write a play that I wished I'd had at school when I was growing up. I wanted to reflect on the fact that growing up would have been easier if I had seen a play like this. It can be an isolating experience not seeing people like you and I was interested in the idea of shame and how that happens. I have had first-hand experience of teachers being unsure about how to deal with homophobic bullying, and I don't think that schools are safe places yet. So I wanted to grasp the nettle and talk about faith, culture and have a variety of views on stage. I didn't want to be scared of discomfort or making an audience think, but I still wanted to find universal themes – love and connection. My background is in social care and as teenagers we are bound by what is right and wrong. I was keen to put the plurality of LGBTQ+ experiences in places where it was still unsafe or frowned upon.

'I am interested in what protest means. This play is an act of commemoration. I wanted to think about a major event that had happened before the play starts; it could perhaps be the Orlando shootings in 2016. In reaction to something like that, there is a tension between a feeling that you should be open about who you are, to protest and say "this isn't ok", but also your right to privacy about how you live your life. I still have to check is it safe to hold my boyfriend's hand in public and so it felt really important to me to write the play I wish I'd had when I was younger. It's a remarkable thing to put it in the space and it is political.'

Approaching the play

Exercise: What is scary and what is exciting?

Rob asked the group to write down:

1 The thing that scared them the most about directing this play.
2 The thing that excited them the most about directing this play.

A few responses from the group were as follows.

1 What scares you?

I'm scared of a parent audience's response. The school is very open but I am scared that they may stifle the play and the process.

I'm afraid that the kids might feel vulnerable, especially if they are on the cusp of coming out.

It's a fast paced play and I'm worried about getting carried away with it, also about getting the tone right between weight and humour.

I want to avoid stereotypes.

2 What excites you?

I'm excited about having the conversation with parents . . . this play will allow us to open up the dialogue about these themes. It's an opportunity.

I'm excited about discovering the relationships and characters.

I'm excited about the learning curve for me . . . it's new material and I'm excited to learn more about dialogues that happen within these communities . . . it's going to be mind opening.

Chris said:

'In response to the fear about stereotypes, so much about representation is about one character, i.e. all gay people are like that. When we see other straight people we don't think that. There is the luxury of more than one gay person! If it comes from a real place for the actor, don't shy away from that. Working with someone straight who is playing a gay character, it can take time for them to allow themselves to let go. Give yourself and your cast permission to go there, celebrate it, shouting from the rooftops, etc.! So much of this play is about masks – why is someone dressed as Ronald McDonald, for example?! You can lean into the camp-ness and go for it.'

Exercise: So what is it about?

In groups of four, Rob asked each group to describe the play in the following ways:

Group 1: As if telling a stranger in a lift.

Group 2: As if telling concerned head teacher.

Group 3: As if telling a pre-teen child.

Group 4: As if it was a blurb on the back of a published book.

Group 5: As if it was a Hollywood movie, what would the tagline be?

This can be a brilliant, entertaining way of getting to know the play and getting to the heart of what it is about.

Exercise: Evidence gathering

This is an evidence-gathering exercise, focusing on what is said and written in the play. It can help you to start making choices which will inform your work and it can be helpful to do with your actors depending on their level of experience.

Divide a piece of paper into four columns. Look through the play and note down the following in the relevant column:

Column 1: Everything that anyone says to your character that tells them about you. It should be relevant to your character.

Column 2: Everything your character says about them themselves to other people.

Column 3: Things you say directly to other people that is about them/how you feel about them.

Column 4: Things that you say to the group about other characters.

The group was split into eight smaller groups and each one was assigned a character. Some observations the groups noted were:

Birdie

She's got good intentions but the execution may not be how she wants it to be. With her 'boom chicka boom' game, it starts off positive then she shifts. She clings to rules like a life preserver at sea. She realises that there is chaos in their lives and the rules give her a place of sanity in a world of chaos.

Chris said: 'Birdie focuses on other people's problems to avoid dealing with her own . . . her arc is about her ability to be honest and she comes to terms with that at the end of the play.'

Orson

He tells people he does not get acknowledged. You can tell he is competitive, e.g. 'Only two months between our ages'. He keeps reminding people that they should be together. Franny says to him, 'You're a real wanker sometimes . . .'

Adira

A powerful character. There are a lot of things that she is opposed to, being a girl, her race, etc. She is harsh with Orson and she is kind of jealous of him. At the start she is harsh with the group – she addresses them like idiots, 'We don't all have your life . . .' and recognises that people have come here for different reasons. She has baggage but wears it really well. She is quiet for a long time but when she does speak it is fully charged and she is able to be the joker as well as a peacemaker.

Jen

Jen doesn't speak about herself a lot. She deflects and turns things back on everyone else. There is a lot about Jen that you can assume, but don't know. She is bitter but has been hurt: 'You are sad.' The group are openly cruel to her. Why is she like this? What are the reasons this happens? She goes hard on Adira. She is often looking for opportunities for outrage. She is acutely aware of the injustice of the world.

Tana

Tana could be a party girl, naughty at home. She sticks up for Birdie. She is an outsider. She needs to get a train. She is an outsider to the group. Her brother is here. She has a driver's licence. She is the older sister coming to visit her brother. She has come down to pick him up. She wants to be accepting but she will also turn on other people. 'None of you should be here.' It is interesting that she wants to be open but there is a lack of understanding. She is supportive.

Chris said: 'It is interesting to be the voice that perhaps echoes thoughts from the audience. There are opportunities with Tana for that discussion. We live in such binaries, we have lost the ability for nuance and people are complicated . . . she speaks without a filter.'

Jotham

He could be easily manipulated by others. Perhaps a follower. He is perhaps more focused on the material things in life. Someone calls him 'numbnuts'. He likes to play the joker and work out how he can be the centre of attention. He is dismissive of Birdie's emotions. He has a pre-established idea of the rich gay, the perfect gay; it feels like he has a cemented idea of what it is to be gay. He does not accept masks. He says, 'Caia we know it's you'. He does not respect Birdie and there is a tension between them. It backs up the idea that he is not focused on what is going on; he focuses on the window. He is not really taking it all in. He does not seem to be as in the moment as the rest of them. He also seems well liked by the others. None of the other characters seem threatened by him. He does not know who he is. Jotham is the theatre kid.

Rob said: 'We can all assume stereotypes. If we adopt some of them off the peg, that is going to help us build a personality that we feel comfortable with.'

Chris said: 'Jotham is in fact really vulnerable and is scared of being known. He finds it really challenging with Orson and he questions all the things that are wrong. He has the least self-awareness.'

Caia

She seems independent. She enters as Ronald McDonald. The counterpoint is that she might seem professional and then dresses as a clown. What is the function of the Ronald McDonald? Why is she dressed like this today?

Chris said: 'She has just come from a children's party dressed as Ronald. I wanted to see a visual mask as a way of kind of being someone else . . . it gives her the freedom to be different and unique. We have such a limited vocabulary to be ourselves, we want to be but it's so difficult. And it is FUNNY!'

Franny

She doesn't say much throughout the whole play. She is like the conscience of the other characters. She is direct with people. She tells it like it is. She is described as 'beautiful', 'aware' and 'gleaming'. She could be otherworldly to the members of the group. Her silence is active.

Chris said: 'To withhold your voice is also powerful . . . she is silenced as that marriage proposal illuminates that Caia does not know her at all. The protest is about society as a whole. She could possibly identify as male but has not yet transitioned . . . no matter who you are, getting married at sixteen is preposterous!'

Rob articulated that the next step of this exercise would be to filter through what are objective and what are subjective facts. Be clear on opinions and personal feelings that are not actually facts. It can be interesting to consider where those opinions come from, what is making you have a particular opinion.

Rob said: 'It is worth highlighting the subjective and objective facts. The real driver of this play are the characters and their interactions. They know each other quite well and bring a lot of baggage to the room. If I was directing it I would make the clear invitation to base everything on the play. There is a lot of room for back story and what happens outside of the play, but you want to make sure that you are referencing this with evidence in the play. An exercise like this [evidence gathering] can help us spot all the gaps that need filling before you start your collective imagining.'

Exercise: Character constellations

Start by drawing a circle in the centre of a piece of paper. Write your character's name. In circles orbiting this central circle, draw other circles and fill in the other characters' names in the play. Make a line joining the inner and outer circles. Write your feelings towards them at the beginning of the play, using the evidence gathered in the previous exercise to inform the relationships.

Approaching rehearsals

Rob said that one challenge of this piece is to work out a basic rehearsal structure. He would find it helpful to go through and break it into rehearsal chunks which might let us understand the ebb and flow, the events, the funnier parts or the more moving parts. A great exercise is to look at the time limit in the scene. There is a clock written into the structure of it, which can help keep the pace up.

Rob suggested that the group begin this process, looking at ten-page sections and finding out where the natural shifts are. He assured the group there were no right or wrong answers.

Some of the suggested possible breaks were as follows. Your group might find something different.

Section 1:

p. 438: When Birdie collects the phones in.

Section 2:

p. 444: When Ronald enters.

p. 449: When Franny does not answer.

Section 3:

p. 453: When Tana puts Jotham on the spot.

p. 455: When Birdie askes Orson to go back to the office.

Section 4:

p. 461: Birdie: 'Leave now please, I'll make an appointment . . .'

p. 464: *Silence.*

Rob noted that sometimes the silences would need to be embedded in a run so you know how long they feel.

Section 5:

p. 469: When Adira and Tana exit.

p. 472: When Jen gives the pebbles back or perhaps just after that.

Section 6:

p. 478: After the two-minute silence.

Starting a safe and open rehearsal process

Rob said: 'This play has the potential to change lives. It can be useful to ask what is the contract you want to set up with your group of young people in order to create a safe rehearsal space? You will all have your methods and habits for the people you are working with. Think specifically about what you are going to have to say about this play.'

Options that were offered by the group

An agreement with them to learn from it and be in it, in terms of the text and ownership.

Commitment to the project.

Respect for the themes and be open to explore what will be required of them.

You could get them to write and perform a monologue from the character's perspective as a way of auditioning actors.

Everyone in this play is celebrated and there will be those who will seize this opportunity to express something, so there needs to be a way of setting up the safe space during your process.

Chris said: 'There is a pastoral duty of care with this production. You should try to keep the actors safe, not so much with the audience but with themselves. This play gives the opportunity to expose young people to some important conversations and experiences.'

What questions do you think you will be asked by your young people?

The group responded with the following:

Do I have to be there if I am playing Franny?

You can make it clear to them that it is required of the text that Franny is there throughout and is an important presence even though she doesn't speak until later. She can react to what is going on around her. The moment she speaks is significant. Whoever plays Franny needs to be a strong performer.

[Rob] You could consider what kind of work you could do with Franny when she is not speaking. You could help find her responses that she does not share. How can you ensure that you keep her inner thoughts going and encourage your actors to think about what they are not saying? How tuned in are they with the argument? You could vocalise their reactions.

I'm not gay or trans, so how do I play someone who is?

[Chris] Encourage them to remember that they are actors and it is their job to act. They don't need to get too bogged down in it. It is a play and there will be an audience who share this play and enjoy it.

The challenge professionally is to open the conversation about oppressed homophobia. This play is about love and people. It is a real conversation opener and there are opportunities to ask questions about identity and language.

[Rob] This play might present some real challenges to the group and it's important to share those moments and use them as opportunities to learn more about each other and the play.

If I'm not part of the LGBTQ+ community, so do I have a right to tell this story?

[Chris] Theatre is a collaborative process and I am a Big Old Gay! The fact I have written it means I am collaborating with you and we are making this play together and the play exists. To not do it feels a sad thing. Trust yourself to be nuanced and to not make judgements . . . we all know people.

The end of the play

The group discussed the final section of the play and how to achieve it. The play is quite naturalistic and then becomes more expressionistic at the end.

Rob suggested it could be interesting to recruit the audience, giving them things to hold, etc. to enable the moment to expand.

Chris said: 'I would definitely make the final moments last as long as you can and then edit to make it shorter. Be bright, be brief and then get out! When we hand it to the audience, there has to be total control of that moment . . . it has to be a ballet in your mind! When you nail this moment, it will be extraordinary. It is a moment of upbeat joy, the fist in the air! It is all about celebration.'

How you transition from inside to outside is a theatrical moment to consider. The moment is so explosive that you can abandon logic in the last five minutes of the play and focus on what is going to have the biggest impact.

If you have the resources, there could be a place for live musicians in the final song moments.

The audience

Rob asked: 'What are the tools that you have to make an audience feel helped and empowered during these final moments?'

Suggestions from the group were as follows:

Infiltrate the audience with other youth theatre members.

Flood it with other actors; it is a delightful moment when you see a huge crowd in a play that is small.

You could use the well-known *Les Misérables* image of the barricade and the use of flags as a tool to engage and unify.

You could pre-record 'get your flags out', as a rallying cry.

There could be pre-recorded applause.

You could create a sound design that played recorded audience 'chatter'. With sound, you can explore the idea of dropping a sound out as well as adding it in.

There is a design solution perhaps with bunting/confetti cannons/flooding the auditorium with props, flags, etc.

You could accompany the song with movement/dance, and/or explore the power of a flash mob! The audience needs to be told what to do. They need to know what the cue is.

Another solution is volume: crank up the volume and people will often feel safer.

Rob said: 'Birdie could drive the moment and take on the role of leading the audience, but be careful that you are not overly exposing your cast – they should feel supported and empowered so that they can encourage the audience to feel this way too!'

Chris said: 'Whatever you decide, story and character should still take priority. The actors should still be heard. It should build from "Come outside it's beautiful". Be wary of the house lights as they can feel exposing for an audience.

'I think it is necessary to have the song and the moment of participation to give a clear ending to the production. For me it's about using the grammar of theatre to provoke thought. It's about not forcing the audience into anything. Let the thinking happen afterwards. It is a joyful moment. The ending is a triumph of togetherness. Your production will not fail even if the audience do not join in.'

Exercise: Song time

Chris mentioned some examples of songs that had been used effectively in previous versions, for example 'This Is Me', 'The Greatest Showman', 'All You Need Is Love' and 'We Found Love in a Hopeless Place'. The group listed some options of potential songs for the ending and shared them:

'Born This Way'

'Hounds of Love'

'I'm Coming Out'

'Believe'

'Everything Is Gonna Be Alright'

'Young Hearts'

'Somewhere over the Rainbow' (Blanks version)

'Freedom'

'We Found Love'

'Power' (Little Mix)

'We Are Family'

'Titanium'

'You Got the Love'

'This Is Me' (*The Greatest Showman*)

'Stop' (The Spice Girls)

'Champion' (RuPaul)

'Love Today' (Mika)

Performance style

Rob said: 'Most UK actor training is based on a Stanislavski process of action and intention. Everything is about changing another person. Actors ask 'What am I trying to achieve, what do I want?' In each unit in the play, what is the intention, what is the action, what is each character doing to take them towards the thing that they want?'

This play is about a group of characters who are sharing the same space for a length of time. It is a group discussion. There is an acting tool that can be helpful to use in this performance style:

Exercise: Targeting

The group read the scene from p. 440 to the end of p. 444 between Birdie and Orson. The group worked in pairs to identify some of the *targets* within the scenes.

Targets

Rob said: 'Think about the target, who are characters talking to? Who are they trying to reach even if the text is addressed to a group? Make it specific. If figuring out each person's intention, the most obvious thing would be for them to change each other. But when there is an audience it might be helpful to consider other people who might be a target of the interaction.'

The group considered the following line on p. 441 as an example:

Orson   Do we need a reminder of the ground rules, Birdie?

Rob said: 'Who is the obvious target of the line? (Birdie) Can you imagine a target might be someone else? (Could it be that he is trying to get everyone else to back him in that moment?)'

Orson   Everyone is entitled to be treated with respect. (p. 441)

Rob said: 'The target could be someone outside the room. It could be his drama teacher, twenty years ago, who said he would never make it, or it could be himself. Sometimes the target could be the audience. It could be the gods or the universe. It could be a target in their family or their past. All of these things become possible when you break out of just who the person is talking to.

'There is no right or wrong but there are options that give the most dramatic juice that will help your actors in the scene. Where is the grit in the play? It is helpful to ask the questions: "Are we being true to the complexity of people in this play? Are we unpacking all the options?"'

Below is the section of text on p. 441 with the group's offers of potential targets in bold capitals:

Orson   Do we need a reminder of the ground rules, Birdie? **BIRDIE**

Birdie   Oh piss off. **ORSON**

Orson   Number one: 'Everyone is entitled to be treated with respect.' **SALLY**
And can I just say, I felt very disempowered when you told me to piss off just now.
BIRDIE
I felt shamed. **EVERYONE**

Birdie   Orson, can I speak to you in my office please? **EVERYONE**

Orson   You don't have an office. **BIRDIE/TANA**

Birdie   Can you step into my office please? **EVERYONE**

Orson   It's not an office. **BIRDIE**

Birdie   Yes it is. **ORSON**

Orson   No it's not. **BIRDIE**

Birdie   Yes it is. **ORSON**

Orson   It's a broom cupboard. **EVERYONE**

Birdie   It's a multi-purpose room, can you come please? **ORSON**

Exercise: Who is offstage?

Rob said: 'It is really important for your cast to have a collective sense of any offstage characters. Who is Sally for example? Invite your cast to write down everything that comes into their heads when they think of that person. You could do this after they have done some work on getting to know the play already. Collate them all and stick them up into the shape of the person in the room.'

Staging and design options

What are the challenges of directing this piece in different spaces?

End on?

In the round?

Thrust?

Traverse?

Rob said: 'The play is mainly eight people sitting around talking. People love watching people and if you get the characters right the stage business will come from that. The fascination we have of watching each other is about the lens; what we would see if we went in close on each of you. I might not know the answers but I would have lots of questions. What is the lens through which these characters are watched? There might also be reasons to highlight a particular person's story. If your arrangement of the people in the space is in a circle or semicircle, what are the dramatic possibilities of such a configuration? You could keep the naturalistic truth or you could make it very stylised.

'How can you keep changing the stage picture to keep the space alive and animated? Could you explore certain props that characters interact with? Could you find variation in the type of furniture and explore power games in the room? Where does each character end up in the space?

'You could do a run where actors get closer to the person you want to affect or get far away from someone they feel animosity towards?'

Chris said: 'You could have two extra seats to give you more options of where the focus is? It doesn't have to be musical chairs.'

Exercise: Design

When thinking about the design, it could be helpful to consider what story it tells for an audience, what it gives for the actors to do and what opportunity does it have to shift the stage picture. In teams of five, participants were assigned a specific material to make a version of their set. The materials were:

Cardboard

Sheets/cloth

Blu Tack

Bricks

Wooden sticks

Tables

The groups then shared their design presentations. After each presentation Rob asked the group to highlight something that they had not thought of before that was now potentially worth exploring.

1   Tables. You could upend them/cut them up and weld them back together. The tables could be used to set up office space. The top of the table could be the office notice board.

This idea threw up the potential of being able to see the physical space of the office and of the space being claustrophobic and potentially relating to their inner world.

2   Wood. There could be a conceptual space within the design. A treehouse, a picket fence painted pride colours, rocking chair, pallet, tree stump, a bamboo door and a bookshelf, a bonsai tree that they could care for . . . perhaps there could be an isolated suspended space.

This idea introduced the possibility of having items onstage that are symbolic of the characters. You could invite the actors to do an exercise where they 'move in' to the space and make it their own, which might throw up some interesting design possibilities.

3 Bricks. You could create an end on configuration that has a row of bricks at the front that they step out of, like giant LEGO bricks.

This idea opened the possibility of a physical fourth wall that the cast could physically break down.

4 Blu Tack. The sofa and chairs could all made out of Blu Tack. Blu Tack bean bags. The noticeboard could be dangled from it. All the letters could be made out of Blu Tack.

This introduced the idea of the set being mouldable. Touch it and it leaves an impression.

5 Sheets. You could have a curtain in the background with rules written onto the back. The colours could be faded with the odd splash of colour. You could have bean bags/comfort blankets. The people behind could perhaps in shadow for the parade at the end.

This material threw up the possibility of exploring shadows, colour and a moment where the cloth could be torn down.

6 Cardboard. You could have three cubes to create a filing cabinet. A cardboard box as a table, chairs that are reinforced. You could de-flap a box and make it into a rug made out of cardboard. The kitchen could be represented by boxes on their sides and there could be cardboard boxes for the phones.

This material introduced the idea of the box as a metaphor of being without a home and moving. There is potential to create and institutional space as well as having a sense of it being homely.

With the design, Rob and Chris both agreed that as the play is set in a particular place, it may not flourish if it is pushed through the lens of a directorial concept, so the challenge is how to create a design that tells the story of that particular place and frame the characters, amplify the themes and delight the audience with how they interact with the space.

Question and answer with Chris and Rob

What have we learned in the two years since the play was last performed as part of Connections?

[Chris] The identities of trans/gay people are debated by other people, their very existence. People still have to come out, then they are going to hear their lives debated. I didn't expect the need and hunger for a play like this.

Can you talk a bit about Jotham's character?

[Chris] I wanted to show that the coming-out process can be okay . . . it doesn't mean that the legacy is not still there . . . it's very hard to isolate a child from that. You absorb the disgust that is put into people. It's an internalised homophobia. I am interested in the historical sense, the gay collective memories, past selves and present. I think it's important to say that everyone's coming out story is different.

Why Dungeness?

[Chris] It's my favourite place in the country. There is a power station. It looks barren but has incredible resilience. It is teeming with life, resilience, joy and love. I wanted them to feel very isolated in a place that is barren but so beautiful.

What language are we allowed to use? Since the play was last performed, there has been an advance in the language associated with the LGBTQ+ experience.

[Chris] It's okay to not be up to speed with the lingo. There is no shame in not knowing. It would be good to have confidence about the themes and have the freedom to discover and use the language that is okay.

I was interested in how much they were drawn together as social class?

[Chris] I think there is a range of people in there. Your identity is yours. I am known as a 'gay working-class writer', but there is of course more to any of us. Sexuality cuts across ethnicity, class and religion.

What kind of housing is it?

[Chris] They all have their own room, shared bathroom, kitchen. Day-to-day living in close proximity to each other. They wouldn't necessarily choose to live with each other. Birdie is a key worker. Siblings would be allowed to stay. Sometimes it would be sanctioned.

Could you clarify the characters and their gender breakdown?

[Chris]

Birdie: Gay woman, trans
Orson: Cis gay man
Adira: Cis gay female
Jen: Female, could be trans, gay or bi
Tana: Cis straight female (if you're desperate it could be played by a male actor)
Jotham: Cis, gay, not trans
Caia: Cis gay female
Franny: Attracted to women but non-binary, on a journey but not cis.

Can you tell us about the characters' names?

[Chris] The names are non-specific. They are heightened, slightly otherworldly and this gives permission for the play to feel other worldly too. The names don't root it in a particular place which opens it up to being more inclusive, rather than shutting it down. With Adira, she wears a headscarf that indicates faith. There are other names that could speak to the Islamic faith. It would be fine to change the name. There are certain roles that are locked and others that are totally open to ethnicity.

Does Adira have to be of Muslim faith? Would another religion work as well?

[Chris] I would like it kept. I feel there is a lack of representation on stage.

Could Orson arrive at being male, as opposed to how they are born?

[Chris] Orson is a gay man and identifies as such. To offset against Jotham.

Could any of the characters be cast gender blind?

[Chris] It's difficult as the play is about gender. I think Tana could be gender-blind, but I think that is the only one really.

[Rob] Changing the gender of the character and ignoring the gender of the actors is problematic in this play. Instead, you could retain all the gender identities of the character, but it so happens that it is played by an actor of a different gender. Everything is possible in the imaginative world.

Are any of the characters non-binary?

[Chris] Franny could be, yes. It's important for this play that you have that conversation with the actors. Find out what is important for them and give them the opportunity to be brilliant.

Do the accents have to be British?

[Chris] I am happy for them to be from anywhere in the UK. Focus on the truth and emotion.

Why Boom Chicka Boom as the game that Birdie plays with the group?

[Chris] We have all sat through some very cringey ice-breakers! It's a way of getting us to know who the characters are very quickly. It sets the quick dynamic of the place, keeps the pace up and feels like a prologue.

With the characters, they are very relatable, especially Adira – were there any difficult characters to write?

[Chris] They were all difficult but Birdie was the easiest. I did lots of work in the research period to ensure they are truthful. I was a social care worker for twelve years so adolescence is in my blood.

Who is Stella?

[Chris] It's a reference to the play *A Streetcar Named Desire*.

[Rob] It is Tennessee Williams' most gothic play, there are lots of underlying tensions . . . there is real aggression between Blanche and Stella as opposites, and there is a big climactic scene where Stanley is drunk and he stands at the end of the apartment and yells 'Stella'. In the movie of it, Marlon Brando is at his most primal!

[Chris] There are lots of queer overtones and references in there.

What do you think is the most effective beginning?

[Chris] It is a real-time play that jumps into a particular moment. A pre-show could distract us down another route. I would suggest a short burst of music and just start!

How respectful should we be to the text?

[Rob] There are plays where there is flexibility for devising, but this is a play that does not lend itself to that. The play as written is the play that your young people should perform.

[Chis] When it was performed last time, I saw a couple of things from the writer's perspective. The play is what the play is – the number of characters is set. One group shared the lines amongst other people, but that is not the play. I have to be strict on that. The most successful versions were the ones where the director took some time discovering the nuances of the characters and their world and really told the story. It can be really dynamic when you focus on the simple storytelling ingredients: how the characters bring the space alive, the detail of each character and their stories. Remember that the heart of the play is the people in it.

From a workshop led by Rob Hastie
with notes by Shane Dempsey

The Changing Room

by Chris Bush

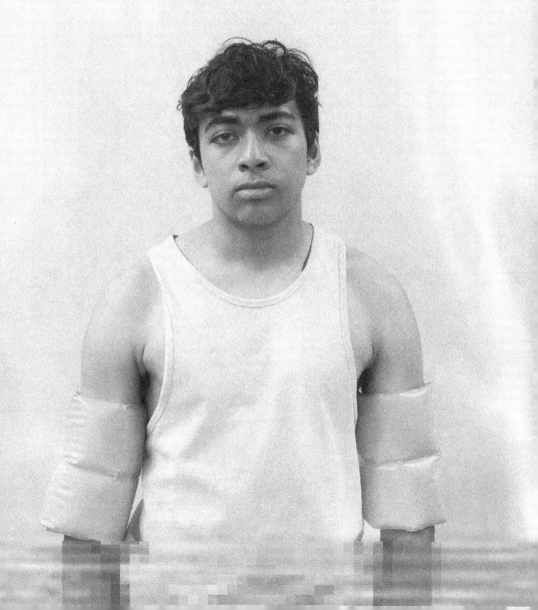

A lyrical piece about existing on the cusp of growing up. Are we teenagers? Are we children? What are we? It's about bodies in flux and perspectives shifting; knowing change is coming but not what that change will look like.

Set in and around a swimming pool, *The Changing Room* follows a group of teens full of excitement, impatience and uncertainty, each with their own secret worries and desires for what comes next.

The Changing Room was previously published by Methuen Drama in the *National Theatre Connections 2019* anthology.

Cast size
10–50
Suitable for all ages

Chris Bush is an award-winning playwright, lyricist and theatre-maker. Her recent productions include *The Assassination of Katie Hopkins* (Theatr Clwyd, UK Theatre Award winner 2018); *Pericles* (National Theatre – Olivier); *Standing at the Sky's Edge, Steel, What We Wished For, A Dream, The Sheffield Mysteries* (all Sheffield Theatres); *The Changing Room* (NT Connections); *Scenes from the End of the World* (Yard/Royal Central School of Speech and Drama); *A Declaration from the People* (National Theatre – Dorfman); *Larksong* (New Vic, Newcastle-under-Lyme); *Cards on the Table* (Royal Exchange, Manchester); *Tony! The Blair Musical* (York Theatre Royal); *Sleight & Hand* (Edinburgh Fringe/BBC Arts and live screened into cinemas); *Poking the Bear* (Theatre503); *The Bureau of Lost Things* (Theatre503/Rose Bruford); *Odd* (Perfect Pitch/Royal & Derngate Northampton); and *Wolf* (NT Studio). Chris has won awards at the UK Theatre Awards, National Young Playwrights' Festival, Perfect Pitch, Sunday Times Edinburgh Competition and a Brit Writers' Award.

The Changing Room

BY CHRIS BUSH

Notes on rehearsal and staging, drawn from a workshop with the writer, held at the National Theatre, October 2019

Director exercises

Lead director Ned Bennett introduced the workshop by laying out some of the techniques and exercises from his methods and ways of working:

'My through line is going to be: how do we run rooms that are exercise based, and allow those exercises to work into the staging. This play gives us so much theatricality that it inevitably then means so much staging and movement, and [these exercises] help the process to feel more organic and allow it to not just become an exercise in remembering all that.'

Ned ran a series of high-energy and collaborative warm-ups designed to get the group working together, which are documented here.

Exercise: Secret handshake

Section one

- Split the room into four groups.
- In each of the four groups, learn the names of other people, making sure to go around the circle multiple times to cement the names.
- Change places in the circle and see if you still know the names in the new order.
- In your groups, you now need to come up with a three-part secret handshake.
- Learn it in your group and make sure everyone knows it.
- Now move around the room.
- As you move around the room, make eye contact with people. If they are not in your group, give them a high ten (a high five with two hands). If they are in your group, you are going to do your secret handshake.
- Experiment with tempo and volume: triumphant high tens, covert secret handshakes.

Section two

- Combine from four separate groups into two larger groups.
- In your newly formed combined groups, teach the secret handshake to each other to make one combined secret handshake of six moves.
- Now move back around the room.
- You have three options: 1) your three-part handshake; b) your combined six-part handshake; c) a high ten with people in neither group.

- Push further the levels of super triumphant joy in the hight ten, and then make the secrecy in the handshake even more covert.

Exercise: Partner sharing

- In pairs label yourselves A and B.
- As move to the edge of the room on either side looking in.
- Bs create a circle in the middle looking out.
- Re-join pairs.
- As now tell Bs about their journey in that morning in the *most boring, pedantic detail.*
- Swap over.
- As move along one step to the left and this time share your journey, *but the action adventure version of their journey.* Add a cliffhanger.
- Swap. Hear back multiple versions.
- As move along once more and share your initial impressions of the play.
- Share back.
- Bs share initial difficulties of staging the play.
- Share back.

Exercise: Crazy hands

- In pairs, stand opposite each other and with both hands slap your thighs.
- Then you send your hands either both to the left, above, then to the right.
- You are doing it randomly opposite your partner; however, if you both accidentally go in the same direction (i.e. you both to go the left), you add a high ten in before the next movement.
- You always return to slapping your thighs after a direction or a high ten.

Exercise: Speed dating

- In groups or pairs.
- Meet someone. You are going to present them to the group in the following structure:
  - This is [*their name*].
  - One line of information about them.
  - This is [*their name*].
  - However, when sharing the information about them, you replace all key bits of information with their name.

    E.g. *This is Sarah. Sarah teaches at Sarah Academy and loves to play Sarah at the weekends.*

Approaching the play

Exercise: What are the challenges of the play?

In small groups, participants looked at what they found were the difficulties and challenges of staging this play, in the specific environments in which the practitioners will be working, and with each different group of students. The group shared the following:

- How do you interpret the themes of the play as the language is often so choral?
- How do you establish the aesthetic rules of the different locations like the changing rooms or the swimming pool?
- How do you stage a swimming pool? Do you need one?
- What is the best way of working with the ensemble?
- How do you break the text into sections?
- How do you create the various worlds, and are they necessary?
- How do you approach the songs and musicality? Do you need/want a band? Is it possible? Is it possible with a solo musician, and what are the ramifications of that?
- How best to teach and approach the songs to the young people?
- How do you deal with the balance between humour and the light material in the foreground whilst still maintaining a sense of the darker material and themes?
- Can you balance the mix of naturalism and abstraction?
- How do you make the performers feel comfortable delivering lines that are maybe deemed to be risqué in a school environment, and where they might not normally be allowed to say such things?
- How do you manage to avoid imposing your experience as teenagers and allow them to communicate their own ideas?
- What are the conversations that you may or may not want to have with your group surrounding specific themes?

Themes

The group created an 'exhaustive and pedantic' list of themes from the play (in no specific order):

- Adolescence
- Body image
- Identity
- Inadequacy
- Belonging
- Fitting in
- Parenthood
- Embarrassment
- Exposure
- Puberty
- Authority
- Anxiety

- Nostalgia
- Relationships
- Fantasy vs reality
- Growing up
- Sex
- Sexuality
- Complex new emotions

- Expectations
- Acceptance
- Loss of innocence
- Nudity
- Perception of adulthood
- Bullying
- Crushes and first love

Ned posed the group the following questions in relation to staging the play: What are the guts and soul of the play? What is the gesture of the play to the audience? How do you express that? What is the experience for the audience?

The final question was: Are there particular themes that you think are vital in the production of the play, but may raise complex questions about how to bring them up in a rehearsal process with young people?

Next, the groups wrote 'action points' in relation to how they were going to discuss those points within their smaller groups. The different groups came up with the following:

- Balance between text and life experiences
- Keeping it anchored in the text
- Making it for them
- Togetherness
- Keeping the discussion rooted to the themes
- Discussing comfort levels
- Anonymous post-it notes to set boundaries

- Resource packs that pupils can access in relation to specific themes or topics
- Understanding your cast
- Sensitivity
- Breaking down barriers
- Time to create through play and make as a whole
- A sense of ownership
- A cast agreement or contract

Exercise: Flow, based on Anne Bogart's *Viewpoints*

Ned said: 'This is a tool for the rehearsal room which is much more about collaboration as opposed to prescribed director movement . . . it is predominantly non-verbal, and I've found it very useful for devising with young people.'

- Walk around the room. Keep your eyes up.
- Try to have a soft focus. Try to take the group in, instead of individuals.

    Now drop in six different parameters and add them in as and when you feel ready.

The parameters are:

1 Stop and start.
2 Radical shifts in tempo.

3   Following – up close or at a distance.

4   Orbiting – up close or at a distance.

5   Finding negative spaces – seeing a gap between people and moving into them.

6   Changing direction.

- Recognise how much you are reacting with your immediate vicinity vs people across the space.
- Take your focus off yourself and put it into the group. Notice what the people across the room or beside you are doing.
- Notice if you are disappearing into your own zone. Keep looking up and seeing the opportunities across the room.
- Wherever possible, take the noise of your feet out of the equation.
- Notice which of the six you have a bias against. Try to include more the ones that you avoid.
- Treat it as a game. Go with the flow and avoid planning your movement.

Ned said: 'The jargon that Bogart uses for the *Viewpoints* work is really useful when trying to analyse what notes to give. She talks about the actor in terms of what they are doing, both *reading* and *writing* the space. When she refers to reading, she is talking about observing, receiving, listening, and when she is talking about writing, she literally means: what is the action that they are creating? This is very useful if you have a very confident actor who is blasting the audience with their text, but not actually receiving back whatever the other person is giving.'

- Develop the exercise: *only writing*. Try as much as possible to ignore the rest of the group. Orbiting, following, finding negative space is now not possible.

  Now swap: *only reading*. Exploit the group for what happens. It is about being overly aware of what is going on around you. See everything that happens in the room as information to be dictated by.

Questions for rehearsal: What do you notice are the differences between only reading and only writing? What is a good balance to achieve as an actor?

Exercise: Viewpoints

Developing on from the flow exercise, start to add the following viewpoints into the movement:

1   Tempo. (*As a marker of 1–10, experiment with continuing with the flows and move the speeds. How does it feel to blink 1 speed out of 10?*) Alter the speeds so now there is only 2 – as slow as you can move, and as fast as you can move. How do you move so slowly that you almost don't notice? How can you find propulsion to move you faster than you imagined? Alter the numbers of the group, to allow some members of the group to watch, and some to experiment in a more open space.

- Add in audience members to allow them to cross the space, using either one of the two speed options, as and when desired.
- Experiment with everyone at the slowest speed: how far can you push the idea that you are still moving, but as slow as humanly possible?
- One at a time, drop the speed back to a normal speed, and move to the edges of the room.

2 Duration. Experiment with how long or how short a look, or an exploration can feel.

3 Repetition.

4 Kinaesthetic response (*a spontaneous reaction to a motion that occurs outside of oneself*).

Exercise: The frog game

Exercise objective: to explore the viewpoint of kinaesthetic response.

- Four participants.
- Squatting as frogs, you move around the space.
- At any one point, only x number of people are allowed to stand up (x to be decided by facilitator – e.g. 'One frog!' Only one person is then allowed to be a frog, the others must be tall. However as soon as one goes back down, the other goes up, etc.).
- Play around with the dynamic – swapping who is allowed to stand, and who must remain as frogs.
- If one frog stands up, another must go down.
- Play around with forcing other people to become frogs whilst maintaining the objective (only x number at any time, as decided by the facilitator)

Exercise: The lane exercise

- Create five lanes on the floor with masking tape or similar.
- You can move on the following ways: up and down the lanes, laying down, stillness, jumping on the spot.
- Experiment moving in the following ways as a development of kinaesthetic response – in response to what other people are doing in the other lanes.
- Development: push the extremities of duration and tempo.
- Development: build in the balance of reading and writing. How are you triggered by people in the other lanes vs how much are you creating your own movement?
- Development: you can only look forwards, you cannot look left or right.
- Build in the idea of running away from impending adulthood.

Ned said: 'The aim of this exercise in the long run is to make action which is much more expressive – how long are you doing something for? Is it absolutely ages? Or a single glimpse? What effect does that have?'

Devising around a theme from the play

- Choose a potent theme from the play that resonates with your group.
- Choose a theme that viscerally interests you, as opposed to just cerebrally.
- Now create a non-literal, expressive, abstract response to the theme you have chosen that works within the lanes of a swimming pool.

Ned said: 'My advice would be to create a very rough framework that is set, but which would allow for variation if you were to present it.'

Exercise: Points of concentration

Ned said: 'I thought it would be useful to look at some rehearsal techniques which will also help with line learning. "Points of Concentration" is a Mike Alfred exercise to feed in the given and imagined circumstances.

'It's about giving the actor a preoccupation with one given or imagined circumstance at a time, and it's about them thinking around that thing laterally.

'So, rather than having a one-track mind about what the circumstance might be, it's about having an imaginative daydream around it; e.g. if you're preoccupied with the floor, your mind wanders to seeing the bit of dirt on the floor, your mind wanders to thinking about where it came from, the ladder that was used to move the lights, what was being lit, etc.

'It's a way of running it and shifting the parameters. I've found particularly with young people that suddenly they learn the lines faster, because it mixes up the thought process and gives them a greater dexterity of text.

'It is about encouraging an imaginative response rather than how to do the scene.'

- In groups, grab some paper, scripts and marker pens.
- With your page in landscape, draw three columns with the following headings:
  - *Technical* (as it sounds – maybe literally sightlines, floor patterns, etc.)
  - *Immediate and previous* (it could be someone has just stolen your phone, or as simple as, 'It is 1 p.m.')
  - *The human condition* (anything massive that makes us human and is relative to the play)
- Think of it as a tree: the actors' imagination goes up one branch, and then goes along the next branch, and so on. It allows you to reverse engineer the subconscious thought process.
- Choosing a scene from the play, go through and fill the columns in, using the information that is in the script and also making up what you think is useful for the actor to know.
- Try to avoid things that are too prescriptive or tell the actors how to act the play.
- Encourage the actor to pursue what they want in the scene whilst being consumed by something else.

Exercise: Physical exploration of points of concentration

- Give actors a small section of text and a point of concentration from the list.
- Encourage them to surrender everything other than the one thing they are preoccupied with and allow them to think literally, and think it through in images.
- One image comes to you, and the next, and so on.

Ned said: 'It allows them to layer in a thought process instead of just telling them. I find that the younger the students, the more easily they get it. If you say, "Dream about the idea of seeing *The Avengers*", they can totally imagine it – you have to try to not censor the images that they are coming with.'

The group then fed back and discussed the following:

- It is useful to have limitations by simplifying the exercise to get far more out of it.
- Ned: 'By giving the actors the space to run whole units, it allows them to get further quicker. You have to hold your nerve to give preoccupations which will do what you want each individual note to do.'
- The goal is to allow it to feel free and organic, and not to discuss everything they have done, which may make it feel cemented.
- Each action has its own integrity.
- Ned: 'I would do this exercise before then running the text.'

Exercise: Articulating the perspective

This is an exercise to make actors feel less self-conscious.

Ned introduced the following lines based on an exercise from Declan Donnellan's *The Actor and the Target*.

Repeat the following lines:

No

There's you

There's me

And there's the space

- Say a line each going around the circle.
- Swap places.
- Say a line targeting someone in the circle.
- See the person opposite you as a teenager.
- Re-form into two smaller circles.
- Picking someone in the space and seeing them as a teenager, now choose a version of that teenager – someone found with a knife, someone who had no hope and got all Bs, etc.

Ned said: 'Donnellan's approach is very much the other side of the coin to Stanislavski. If you have the action, or transitive verb, your perspective of the target is what causes you to choose that action.'

Let's look at this in practice:

- Get into pairs.
- Label yourselves A and B
- A says all lines together. Then B says all the lines.
- Open it out to move around the space, and to use each other more.
- A is now a teenager. B is an adult. Instead of trying to act *your* role, see the person opposite you for what they are.
- Choose two extreme versions or perspectives of how you see your opposite: a teenager with no hope, or a future Nobel Prize winner, a down-and-out adult or your absolute idol. Change your perspective of the other person as you speak, and as you listen.
- Allow your perspective to shift between the phrases. For 'No', you might see them as one thing, then for 'There's you', they become another.

The group then took this exercise and looked at it in relation to the script. In groups of six, they looked at short sections of text and applied the exercise and the techniques. Ned provided examples of the following perspectives:

1 How they're perfect.
2 How they're flawed.
3 The compassion.
4 Something they are capable of.
5 Metaphorical, e.g. animal/mythical creature.
6 Defining them by something they've done.
7 Sharpening of the given circumstances.
8 What they are doing (Meisner).

Ned said: 'This exercise is about externalising what they are targeting and forcing actors to not think about themselves. Your character work is not on your character, but on your imaginative response to how you view the character opposite.'

Question and answer with Chris Bush and Ned Bennett

What is it about a swimming pool [and] a changing room that made you write this?
[Chris] I think the first version of this play was a little fifteen-minute thing in Sheffield where I'm from and it existed solely in the abstract. It was about young people on the verge of not feeling like children any more but not feeling like adults either. I fleshed it out for Connections and the location became more crucial. For me it is about it being in a communal space – certainly it's somewhere that I would hang out when I was a teenager. It isn't an educational space, you're not sitting in the dark like in a cinema,

but it is also a place that is inevitably exposing, you are aware of change, and you are aware of bodies around you.

It's interesting that Ned's exercises focus not just on your acting, but instead on seeing what the actor opposite you is doing is interesting – I know it's not an exclusively teenage thing, but there is a thing about that age where you are really aware of everyone around you.

What is the play about?
[Chris] I think it's about change, and change which is both sometimes absolutely welcome and sometimes undesired and terrifying, still inevitable, and uncertain.

I think if there is one simplified key idea it is that you know change is coming, but you don't know what the other side of it looks like. It is totally universal and is always going to be a struggle.

Where did the music come from?
[Chris] The initial version was a mixture of very short scenes, naturalistic dialogue and choral dialogue. Using music felt like a natural evolution. It's such an accessible medium, and music gives such an emotional shorthand. You can convey more emotion in four bars of music than you can in four pages of dialogue. It gives it a different texture in a play that isn't rooted in naturalism.

Is there a sense of any characters that continue throughout?
[Chris] I think I can say with some certainty that the letters that are assigned are totally arbitrary. There is a little shadowing with Alex where we meet them later on, but beyond that it feels like everyone is quite separate and existing in their own moment. I don't know what would be the smallest number of characters, but they can either be totally different people, or not – you can definitely find dozens of different versions.

How would you feel if we assign names?
[Chris] I don't have an issue with that if it helps your actors.

My school is quite strict. At my home performance, is it okay if I remove some of the language?
[Chris] I'm totally relaxed about those kind of small changes. I feel it is very PG-13 but I get that it might be more problematic in some places than others. I trust you all to deal with it. Equally, if you felt like, 'It's ridiculous that my kids aren't saying fuck at all,' feel free to add those in, as long as you still keep it feeling authentic.

When you were writing the play, was there a vision you had with the company lines?
[Chris] I don't know. I think that maybe it is a slight red herring to think of the stuff marked as company as choral, i.e. we all speak in unison. My instinct is that you should use that relatively sparingly, so a section that has twenty lines might only have a dozen unison words to make it hit. It partially depends on things like how big your space is and can they be heard, but often the more voices you try to do at once makes it mushier, and it might make the intensity less specific, which would be a shame.

It's also sometimes a little difficult to land the pace – one of the main notes at the top of the script is that you can go faster than you think, but that is much easier for a single voice. It's about finding that happy medium when you are using a larger company but whilst still being tight on cues and audible.

If it is not marked as song, could they still sing parts of the words?
[Chris] I hadn't thought about that but if you are keen to try it, I would say try it. My instinct is that with some of the very fast sections that are almost rapped, singing it would slow the pace when lots of it has a natural drive – but it sounds fun and I'd encourage you to try it.

How much did you write it as a comedy?
[Chris] I think it is a comedy. I can't imagine writing something that doesn't have jokes in it. It's easier for a character to make you cry if they've made you laugh first. I think and hope that allowing yourself those moments of laugh-out-loud humour buy you the moments of earnestness and sincerity, but if the humour wasn't there it might become a bit schmaltzy.

We were thinking about having a band onstage, with the students playing the music. Can we then arrange the music for drums and guitar?
[Chris] 100 per cent. You basically get a vocal line and chord charts. We encourage you to take that and do with it as you will.

We have very little resources in regards to staging. Some of the direction refers to cubicles – are you bothered about the staging?
[Chris] Of the productions I saw last time, some had substantial budgets, but I also saw black-box performances with basically no set, and it worked absolutely fine. I think there are stage directions about cubicles but you could absolutely find a million ways to not represent those. The section that most specifically might require staging is the presto/chango magic sequence, but there are lots of lo-fi ways of doing that and still achieving the same thing.

[Ned] It feels to me that the play is asking for a lo-fi expressive approach. I'd rather see the play with 400 empty loo rolls than something where someone has naturalistically built a swimming pool.

How would you stage the swimming pool? Or how have you seen it done?
[Chris] I've seen it done in various different ways. My instinct is you probably need a relatively flexible playing space. Bear in mind I'm not a designer, I wouldn't want to build a swimming pool and set it in the pool, even with all the budget, because sometimes we're meant to be in the pool, or sometimes we are meant to be in the changing rooms. It would feel like that was a waste of the space.

For those of you that might have the resources, I'm always a big fan of a textured space in some way – trying to find the textured space of the tiles, or the hard materials, or the pool noodles, rather than going, here is a geographic laying-out of a swimming pool, because the show is more lyrical than that and not rooted in one place. How else do you suggest a space beyond the physical space? Can you make the whole place smell of chlorine and chips? Is there something else that you can make to trigger the memory of a gym bag on the shoulder?

[Ned] It feels like it's more about expressing the energy of the play rather than getting hung up on creating one space. What can be a container that makes what the actors can do the most expressive, rather than something that is naturalistic in any way?

Can I ask about sound? In part three it talks about mouthed conversations/muffled/ distortions – is there anything else I should be discussing sound wise?
[Chris] I think the only point you might want a soundscape are the bold sections that feel like they exist in a slightly different world – perhaps they exist under water, or sections that should feel different to the company sections. It could be done with pre-recorded sound, or music, but off the top of my head, it's quite non-prescriptive.

When you were writing it, did you listen to any specific songs?
[Chris] Most of it was written on the guitar because that's my first instrument. I could say they are all simple songs because I wanted to do something childish and naïve, or I could say that's because that's how I play the guitar, which is probably more accurate.

I hear it as guitar and band because that's my musical background, but I think it's totally up for grabs.

I would be totally up for a young company telling me that they do not listen to this, and want to re-work it into a different style, and I hope that the songs are simple and robust enough that they could take being moved into a different genre.

How much of it is to do with your own personal experience and how much of it is to do with hypothetical teenage situations?
[Chris] It certainly isn't autobiographical. It was a mixture of trying to remember what was going on back in the day, and also improvising and devising with some young people in Sheffield for the original short version. It is all a bit of a jumble. I feel I'm probably quite threaded all the way through it, but not in any specific moments.

What is your favourite bit?
[Chris] Actually I was going to read a section and the end line to that I think is my favourite line, to show how fast I think it can be done.
   [Chris then read the following section very quickly:]

And it's okay
It is okay
More than okay
But here's one part that grates –
That somehow I should be grateful
To learn from your mistakes
I should appreciate –
And yes, I do appreciate
All that you do, and blah-de-blah-de-blah –
But *I* should live based on the way *you* are,
And the choices you would make
Treating me like a baby
While saying the kids grow up too fast these days
Can't be dating –
Debating the pros and cons of each new acquaintance –
Equating my life to hers
And I should defer, should show respect
Accept that she knows best
Count myself blessed

Because this is the shit she wished she'd got from her mum
And it's all 'there's no rush'
And 'walk before you run'
Because the kids grow up too fast these days
So what? You're saying I should be juvenile?
You can't have it both ways –
Can't praise maturity and maintain I'm still a child,
Or is what you're asking of me
To somehow embody both, simultaneously?
So I'm sorry – honestly I am, and yes,
I'm well aware you only want the best
All in my best interest to protect me
And who am I to complain?
Because the kids grow up too fast these days
And I say, 'Mum – Juliet got married when she was fourteen!'
She says, 'And that ended well, did it?'

Suggested references

Anne Bogart's *Viewpoints*
Mike Alfreds' *Different Every Night*
Declan Donnellan's *The Actor and the Target*

From a workshop led by Ned Bennett
with notes by Joseph Hancock

Participating Companies

1812 Youth Theatre
20Twenty Academy
A Will and A Way Acting School
Aberconwy
Aberdeen College of Performing Arts
Aberystwyth Arts Centre Youth Theatre
Acorn Young People's Theatre
Actors Workshop
Allstars Theatre Company
Alperton Community School
Alumni
Anglo European School
Ardclough Youth Theatre
Ark Alexandra Academy
Artemis College
Artemis Studios
Arts Academy
artsdepot Performance Company
ARTY
Barbara Priestman Academy
Barton Peveril
BDC Company
Bedford College
Belfast School of Performing Arts
Berzerk Productions
BHASVIC Theatre Company
Bilborough 6th Form College
Birkenhead High School Academy
Bishop Ramsey
Bishops High School
Bloxham School
Blue Bee Productions
Bluecoat Wollaton School
Boomsatsuma
Brackley Youth Theatre
Brampton Manor
Brewery Arts Centre
Bristol Old Vic
Brookfields SEN School
Bury Grammar School
Caithness Young Company
CAPA College
CAPA College Dance Company
Carney Academy Sheffield
Cast Youth Theatre
CASTEnsemble
Cavendish School

CAYT Crescent Arts Youth Theatre
Cheltenham Everyman Youth Theatre
Cheltenham Youth Theatre
Churchill Theatre Young Company
City of Oxford College
Cockburn School
Connect4
Connected Youth Theatre
Coppice Performing Arts School
Cramlington Youth Dramatic Society
C-SaW Theatre Company
Curious Connections
Dalkeith High School
Darrick Wood Secondary School
Delanté Détras Theatre Company
Drama Lab Jersey
Drama with Laura Classes
Dudley College Performing Arts
Easy Street Theatre Company
Eden Court Youth Theatre
Elms Ensemble
Everyman Youth Theatre
Evolve Theatre Company
Fabula Arts Youth Theatre
Falkirk Youth Theatre
FBS
Felpham Community College
Fire & Steel Theatre Company
Fleet Street Studios
Flying High Young Company
Fortrose Academy Youth Theatre
Freddie's Connect
Further Stages Theatre Company
    Wimbledon
Garage Theatre Company
George Dixon Academy
Glasgow Acting Academy SCIO
Globe Youth Theatre
Go East
Great Torrington School
Group 64 Theatre for Young People
Gulbenkian
Hackney Shed Collective
Halesowen College
Hamilton Grammar School
Harrow Youth Theatre
Hayesfield School

Hayworth Players
Headington School Oxford
High Definition Drama
Huntingdon Youth Theatre
Imaginarium Young Actors
Intangible Inc
InterACT Youth Theatre
Jcoss Theatre Company
John Lyon
Kesteven and Grantham Girls' School
Kildare Youth Theatre
Kilgraston School
Kindred Drama
King Edward VI Five Ways School
Kings Youth Theatre
Kirkgate Youth Theatre
Knightswood Secondary School
Knox Academy
Kola Nuts
Lady Manners School
Lakeside Youth Theatre
Lambeth College
Launch Theatre & Performance Training at
    Cornwall College
Lincoln Young Company
Lister
Liverpool Empire Youth Musical Theatre
    Company
Lumos Theatre
Lymm High School
MAAD: Matthew Arnold School
Malton School
Mark Rutherford School
Merchant Taylors' Girls School
METYouth1306
Mill Hill County High School
Millburn Academy Drama Club
Mishmak Youth Theatre
Monoux College
Mossbourne Vicotoria Park Academy
Mount Temple
Mr. Sands Youth Theatre
Multiplicity Theatre Company
Netherwood Academy
New College, Swindon
New Vic Youth Theatre
Newcastle and South Tyneside Youth Theatre
Newcastle High School for Girls
NMPAT Young Actors Company
NormaL

North Hertfordshire College
Nottingham College Actors
Nottingham Playhouse Young Company
Nu.Dynamic Theatre Company
Nuffield Southampton Community Youth
    Theatre
Nuffield Southampton Youth Theatre
Oaklands
Oldham College
Orbit Productions
Ormiston Rivers Academy
Oslo International School
Outwood Academy Hemsworth
Oxford Playhouse
PACE Youth Theatre
PACT Theatre Company
Page2Stage Youth Theatre
Paulet High School & Sixth Form
Peake Productions
Peanuts Rep
Perfect Circle Youth Theatre
Phenix Youth Theatre
PlayActing Youth Theatre
Port Glasgow High School
Professional Theatre Programme
Pukka Productions
Pump House CYT
Queen's Young Company
RATzcool
Ravens Wood School
Raynes Park High School
Redbridge Youth Theatre Workshop
Reepham High School Drama Club
Ricards Lodge High School
Ringwood School
Riverside Theatre
Roundwood Park School
Royal & Derngate: Connect
Royal & Derngate: Create
Rushden Academy Performing Arts
Sandwell College Young Directors
Scarborough Sixth Form College
Shadow Syndicate
Shakespearia
Shazam Theatre company SCIO
Sheffield People's Theatre
Shenfield High School
Sherman Youth Theatre
SHS Acting Company
Silhouette Youth Theatre

Sir Henry Floyd Grammar School
Slow Theatre Company
Smithills School
South Hunsley School
Spotlight Drama Youth Theatre
SRWA Theatre Company
St Anselm's College
St Gregory's Bath
St John Plessington Catholic College
St Mary's Catholic College
St Peter's School, Dorset
St Peter's School, York
St Richard's Drama Stars
St Saviour's and St Olave's School
St Thomas More Catholic High School
St Ives School Youth Theatre
Stag Youth Theatre
Stagecoach Cambridge and Cambourne
Stagecoach Chorleywood
Stagecoach East Kilbride
Stagedoor Learning
Steel Valley Beacon
Sterts Youth Theatre Company
Stockport Academy
Story Makers
Stratford Youth Theatre CIC
Suffolk New College Performing Arts
Sunbury Manor School
TADAA
Thame Youth Theatre
The Actors Centre Theatre Company
The Basement
The Boaty Theatre Company
The Bourne Academy
The Chantry School
The City Academy Hackney
The College Merthyr Tydfil
The Commonweal School
The Company of Teens
The Customs House Youth Theatre
The Drama Studio
The Forest School
The Fulham Boys School
The Heathland Players
The Lowry Young Company
The McMillan Youth Theatre Company
The Oaks Academy

The Petchey Academy
The Plough Youth Theatre Seniors
The Regent Academy
The Swanage School
Theatre by the Lake
Theatre Peckham Youth Company
Theatre Royal Youth
Theatre Unboxed
TheatreEast
Totnes Progressive School
TQ1 Theatre Company
Trinity Youth Theatre
Turing House Drama
Twyford High School Drama Company
UAK
Union Youth Theatre
UROCK Theatre Company
Urswick Youth Theatre
Valley Park
Vandyke Upper School
Warwick Arts Centre Connections Company
Weavers Academy
Wellington College
West Yorkshire Drama Academy
Westfield Arts College
Weymouth Drama Club Curtain Raisers
White City Youth Theatre
Wildcats Theatre School
Wildern School
Wiltshire College Performing Arts
Winstanley College
Wirral Grammar School for Girls
Wisbech Grammar School
Wolf Voice
Wollaston School Theatre Company
Woodchurch High School
Worlds End Productions London
Worthing College
WV Company
Yew Tree Youth Theatre
York Theatre Royal Youth Theatre
Young and Unique @ Callington Community
   College
Young Dramatic Arts
Young People's Theatre
Youth Arts Centre, Isle of Man
Youth Theatre Plus

Partner Theatres

Aberystwyth Arts Centre
The Albany
artsdepot
Bristol Old Vic
Cast, Doncaster
Chichester Festival Theatre
Derby Theatre
Eden Court
The Garage, Norwich
HOME Manchester
Leeds Playhouse
The Lowry
Lyric Hammersmith
Lyric Theatre, Belfast
Marlowe Theatre
The North Wall, Oxford
Northern Stage
Norwich Playhouse
Nottingham Playhouse
Nuffield Southampton Theatres
Queens Theatre, Hornchurch
Royal & Derngate
Sheffield Theatres
Sherman Theatre
Soho Theatre
Theatre by the Lake
Theatre Royal Plymouth
Theatre Royal Stratford East
Traverse Theatre
Warwick Arts Centre
York Theatre Royal

Performing Rights

Application for permission to perform, etc. should be made before rehearsals begin to the following representatives:

For *Wind / Rush Generation(s), Tuesday* and *Witches Can't Be Burned*
Permissions Department
Bloomsbury Publishing Plc
50 Bedford Square
London WC1B 3DP
performance.permissions@bloomsbury.com

For *A series of public apologies (in response to an unfortunate incident in the school lavatories)*
Dalzell & Beresford
The Paddock Suite
The Courtyard
55 Charterhouse St
Farringdon
London EC1M 6HA

For *The IT* and *Dungeness*
Independent Talent
40 Whitfield St
Bloomsbury
London W1T 2RH

For *The Marxist in Heaven* and *Crusaders*
United Agents
12–26 Lexington Street
London W1F 0LE

For *The Changing Room* and *Look Up*
Berlin Associates
7 Tyers Gate
London SE1 3HX

Copyrights

National Theatre Connections Team 2020

Kirsten Adam	*Connections Producer*
Arianne Welsh	*Connections 2020 Co-Producer*
Carmel Macaree	*Connections Assistant Producer*
Georgia Choudhuri	*Connections Assistant*
Ola Animashawun	*Connections Dramaturg*
Alice King-Farlow	*Director of Learning*
Paula Hamilton	*Deputy Director of Learning*
Virginia Leaver	*General Manager*

Workshop notes edited by Kate Budgen

The National Theatre

National Theatre
Upper Ground
London SE1 9PX
Registered charity no: 224223

Director of the National Theatre
Rufus Norris
Executive Director
Lisa Burger

CPSIA information can be obtained
at www.ICGtesting.com
Printed in the USA
LVHW080813030321
680385LV00009B/64